Business Leaders and New Varieties of Capitalism in Post-Communist Europe

Business leaders exert extraordinary influence on institution building in market economies but they think and act within institutional settings. This book combines both an elite approach with a varieties-of-capitalism approach. Comparing Poland, Hungary and East and West Germany, we perceive the transformations in East Central Europe and in Germany after 1989 as being intertwined.

Based on a joint survey, this book seeks to measure the level of the convergence of ideas among European business leaders, assuming it to be more extensive than the institutional convergence expected under the dominance of neoliberal discourse. Analysing the institutional framework, organizational features like size, ownership and labour relations, and subjective characteristics like age, social origin, career patterns and attitudes of the recent business elites, we found significant differences between countries and the types of organization. The growing importance of economic degrees and internationalization shows astonishingly little explanatory power on the views of business leaders. The idea of a coordinated market economy is still relatively widespread among Germans, while their Hungarian and Polish counterparts are more likely to display a minimalist view of corporate responsibility to society and adverse attitudes towards employee representation. However, their attitudes frequently tend to be inconsistent, which mirrors the mixed type of capitalism in East Central Europe.

Katharina Bluhm is a Professor of Sociology at the Free University Berlin, Germany.

Bernd Martens is a Senior Researcher in the Friedrich-Schiller University, Jena, Germany.

Vera Trappmann is a Junior Professor of Macro Sociology at the Otto-von-Guericke University Magdeburg, Germany.

Routledge Contemporary Russia and Eastern Europe Series

Business Leaders and New Varieties of Capitalism in Post-Communist Europe

Edited by
Katharina Bluhm, Bernd Martens
and Vera Trappmann

Routledge
Taylor & Francis Group

LONDON AND NEW YORK

First published 2014
by Routledge
2 Park Square, Milton Park, Abingdon, Oxfordshire OX14 4RN

Simultaneously published in the USA and Canada
by Routledge
711 Third Avenue, New York, NY 10017

First issued in paperback 2016

*Routledge is an imprint of the Taylor & Francis Group, an informa
business*

British Library Cataloguing in Publication Data
A catalogue record for this book is available from the British Library

Library of Congress Cataloguing in Publication Data
Business leaders and new varieties of capitalism in post-communist
Europe / edited by Katharina Bluhm, Bernd Martens, and Vera
Trappmann.
    pages cm. – (Routledge contemporary Russia and Eastern Europe
series; 48)
    Includes bibliographical references and index.
    1. Elite (Social sciences) — Europe, Eastern. 2. Leaders) — Europe,
Eastern. 3. Capitalism) — Europe, Eastern. 4. Post-communism)
— Europe, Eastern. I. Bluhm, Katharina. II. Martens, Bernd,
1955- III. Trappmann, Vera.
    HN380.7.Z9E415 2014
    306.3'420943–dc23
                                                            2013006151

ISBN 13: 978-1-138-65208-8 (pbk)
ISBN 13: 978-0-415-80963-4 (hbk)

Typeset in Times New Roman
by RefineCatch Limited, Bungay, Suffolk

Cover design Marina Dafova

Contents

Figures

Tables

Contributors

Dénes Bank is CEO of GKI Economic Research Co. He studied economics at the Corvinus University of Budapest and is currently working on his PhD thesis on corporate social responsibility and structural changes in Hungary. He has published articles on social responsibility, labour care and the macroeconomic and sectoral changes in Hungary.

Katharina Bluhm is professor of sociology at the Free University Berlin and holds a double affiliation with the Institute for East European Studies and the Institute of Sociology. Her main research areas include economic sociology, work and labour relations and comparative political economy. She has widely published on institutional transformation in East Germany and varieties of capitalism in Central and Eastern Europe. Among her recent research interests are economic elites and corporate social responsibility.

Nikolett Geszler is a PhD student at the Doctoral School of Sociology at Corvinus University of Budapest. She has worked on occupational prestige, the international career potential of economic and political elites, and business leaders' income. Her main research interest is gender and work-life balance.

Béla Janky is associate professor of sociology at the Budapest University of Technology and Economics. He has published a book and several articles on the roots and consequences of the norms of solidarity in modern welfare states. He has empirically investigated and modelled the collective action problems of industrial workers using game theory; moreover he has analysed the changes in corporate strategies in post-communist Hungary. His research interests also include the integration of the Roma population in Hungary, ethnic stereotypes and rational choice models of non-selfish behaviour.

Krzysztof Jasiecki is professor of sociology at the Institute of Philosophy and Sociology at the Polish Academy of Sciences in Warsaw. He has published books and articles on the new generations of young Polish political leaders; origin, strategies and social profile of political and economic elites; and on Poland's accession to the EU. He empirically investigated the emergence of the new Polish business elite; economic interest groups and lobbying; and methods of promoting Polish exports to EU markets. His research interests also include wealth in contemporary Poland and studies on 'Polish capitalism' in the VoC perspective.

György Lengyel is professor of sociology at the Institute of Sociology and Social Policy at Corvinus University of Budapest. He has published several books and articles on elites, entrepreneurs, economic sociology and related topics. He has organized international workshops and conferences and has participated in several international research projects. He is the editor-in-chief of *Corvinus Journal of Sociology and Social Policy* and academic director of the Doctoral School of Sociology.

Bernd Martens is a senior researcher at the Friedrich-Schiller-University Jena. He is an expert in quantitative research, with huge expertise in CATI-methods, on both a methodological and theoretical level. He has authored several books and articles in the field, such as the sociology of technology, professions, and environment. His current research interests focus on the sociology of management and the transformation process of East German companies.

Zita Ördög is a PhD student at the Doctoral School of Sociology at Corvinus University of Budapest. She has worked on occupational prestige and managerial incomes of Hungarian state-owned companies, which is her primary research topic.

Dariusz Przybysz is assistant professor of sociology at the Institute of Philosophy and Sociology at the Polish Academy of Sciences. He studied sociology at Warsaw University, completing his PhD on log-linear models for mobility tables and panel data. His primary research interests focus on the application of mathematical methods in social sciences. He has authored and co-authored several articles on methodology, analyses of marital and friendship homogamy, social mobility and rationale choice theory.

Vera Trappmann is Junior Professor of macro-sociology and European Societies at the Institute of Sociology at Otto-von-Guericke University Magdeburg. Her main research areas are comparative political economy, economic sociology, and work and labour relations with a particular interest in restructuring. She has published widely on Europeanization, industrial relations and trade unions in Central and Eastern Europe. Her current research interests include sustainability and corporate social responsibility.

Acknowledgements

This book is the result of a collaboration between sociologists from various Central European universities over the past four years. The research project, entitled 'Economic Elites in Enlarged Europe', was part of the Collaborative Research Center 580 (SFB 580) at the Universities of Halle and Jena, running from 2001 to 2012. Funding by the German Research Foundation (DFG) allowed us to develop a joint research design and an integrated data set on which most of the book chapters are based. The coordination of the collaboration and the German part of the project were conducted by Katharina Bluhm, Bernd Martens and Vera Trappmann who at the beginning of this project worked together in Jena. The survey in Hungary was supervised by György Lengyel from the Corvinus University and Béla Janky from the Budapest University of Technology and Economics; the Polish survey was in the hands of Krzysztof Jasiecki and Dariusz Przybysz from the Polish Academy of Sciences. We express deep thanks to the SFB 580 and the DFG for giving us the opportunity for this research. We are also grateful to Barty Begley, Franz K. Zurbrugg and Kyle Simmons for supporting us in the production of this book.

1 Introduction

Business leaders and the new varieties of capitalism in post-communist Europe

Katharina Bluhm, Bernd Martens and Vera Trappmann

Introduction

The research on economic actors in Central and Eastern Europe (CEE) can be divided into two periods. In the early stages of the transition from planned to market economy, elite research played an important role, for several reasons. As the implementation of the market economy and electoral democracy was not the result of an evolutionary process but started with top-down decisions, the role of elites, and elite conflicts and collaborations, was crucial; the transition of the 'cadre elite' to a pluralist, sectorally differentiated elite was in the making and the question was who would gain control over these sectors, especially to what extent would the old 'cadre elites' manage to become the new 'propertied class' by converting their political power into economic capital. In the early studies, this issue of 'class formation' was raised within the classic elite categories of elite reproduction vs circulation (cf. for example Dogan and Higley 1998; Eyal *et al.* 1998; Higley and Lengyel 2000; Walder 2003; King and Szelényi 2005; for a critique of the elite approach, see Burawoy 2001).

With the growing literature on the emerging varieties of capitalism, that has focused particularly on the new EU member states since the beginning of the new century, the institutionalist approach has come more to the forefront, shifting the focus from personalized elites to corporations and organizations. The privatization of key sectors to foreign investors and the additional inflow of foreign capital has hindered the emergence of the envisioned 'grand bourgeoisie' in most of the East Central European countries. Now the emergence of a Polanyian 'comprador service sector' has been observed, consisting of top managers in western subsidiaries and their domestic subcontractors, who work in the interests of foreign investors instead of representing an autonomous national economic elite (Drahokoupil 2008a, 2008b). From that perspective, it seems less important who the elite actually are and what their views on the market economy might be.

In this book, we bring the two perspectives closer together. Apart from historically rare breakdowns, elites act in certain institutional settings. Institutions shape what they perceive as their rational interests and influence their ideas about the surrounding world. Institutionalists explore these settings but often view actors only as institutionally constructed entities who perform like Marxian 'character masks', following only institutionalized rational interests. Blending out individual actors, the institutionalists also tend to underestimate the role of ideas in creating, stabilizing and changing institutions.

In the literature, there are several theoretical suggestions on how to grasp this interaction. One influential attempt was provided by Arthur Denzau and Douglass North (1994), who expand the rational choice framework using the concept of 'shared mental models', as internal representations which individuals create in order to interpret the environment in a situation of uncertainty (ibid.: 4). 'Mental models' are permanently under revision through experience-based learning processes and are framed by 'ideologies' which the authors define as 'action-outcome mappings'. Ideology in this sense relates the utility-relevant outcomes to possible actions' (ibid.: 15), that is, a chosen action is assumed to lead to a certain outcome.

Sociological new institutionalism perceives 'cognitive schemata' or 'common beliefs' as an element or 'pillar' of institutions with a view to Max Weber's premise that 'action is social only to the extent that the actor attaches meaning to the behaviour' (Scott 2008: 56–8; DiMaggio and Powell 1991). In this view, different levels of institutionalization of cognitive schemata and beliefs exist until they are taken for granted. In the German institutionalist tradition, ideas take on an even more crucial role as complex institutions are regarded as guided by *leitideen* – ideas on which institutions are built (Lepsius 1990a, 1990b; Rehberg 2002).

Although it is acknowledged that people not only follow their interests but also have ideas that if they are collectively shared may become crucial for institutional stability and change, this cognitive dimension is widely unexplored in the recent literature on the varieties of capitalism. Considering Denzau and North's definition of ideology, we can formulate, however, one basic assumption. As different institutional frameworks shape corporate strategies in different ways, making some strategic choices precisely therefore more effective than others, people also adopt specific 'action-outcome' mappings about what serves a purpose best and how business should be conducted in general. This underlying assumption is most obvious when it comes to the understanding of company's goals. While the Anglo-Saxon corporate governance system is usually associated with a narrow shareholder-value-oriented understanding of company goals, business leaders in Continental (western) Europe in general and Germany in particular are supposed to share an understanding of company goals that does consider a wider set of organized stakeholders and which is institutionalized in participation practices (see e.g., Albert 1993; Streeck 1997; Höpner 2003). Although the definitions of company goals are institutionally constructed by laws and rules, it should also find wide agreement among economic actors in order to be stable. Thus the institutionalist view suggests a *correspondence* between 'ideologies' and institutional structures. However, ideas are not determined by institutions: the way business leaders perceive their environment may also be influenced by the *zeitgeist* in public discourse, individual experience and by the immediate organizational setting in which they operate. This is precisely why ideas also represent a source of institutional erosion and change.

The goal of our research project has been to examine business leaders within changing institutional settings. Therefore we study key aspects of these institutional changes, a defined set of socio-political attitudes on the part of business leaders, and what shapes these attitudes. For the institutional dimension, we chose a comparison of three countries: Poland, Hungary and Germany. With this collection of countries, we take a unique position in the literature of transition or post-transition. The inclusion of Germany means that on the one hand we can expand the post-socialist comparisons of business leaders to a forgotten case, East Germany. On the other hand, it also allows us an East–West comparison that parallels the transition in East Central Europe with the changes in Germany after the end of the European and German divide, that is with the economic and institutional transformation of the biggest market economy in the European Union. It is only in this context that we use the term post-communism, rejecting the widespread equation of communism and state socialism; we reserve the term post-communist Europe for a Europe after the fall of the Berlin wall that marked the end of the Cold War. For the regime change from planned to market economy we speak of 'post-socialist' transition or transformation as this fits better with the self-characterization of the Soviet-type regimes as socialism, while the term 'communism' only refers to the ruling Communist Party system.

From the neoliberal public discourse that dominated the last two decades, the transformations in both East Central Europe and Germany are supposed to have gone in the same direction of deregulation and liberalization. The two transformations are intertwined, first because the German reunification not only led to an encompassing transfer of institutions to East Germany but also accelerated the institutional change in West Germany. In addition, (West-)German industrial companies play a major role as investors in East Germany, Hungary and Poland; and finally, Hungary and Poland have in part a pre-Soviet institutional history with Germany or Austria, which was important in the institutional re-building after the collapse (cf. Bohle and Greskovits 2012). Hence, we take on a kind of *Central European* perspective in this book that includes Poland, Hungary and Germany, looking for tendencies of convergence and the role of historic legacies.

The *hypothesis* we started this project with has been that the convergence of ideas went further than the institutional convergence since institutions create path dependency and inertia, and because in both transformational settings neoliberalism has become a *leitidee* for institutional change in the 1990s.

In Poland and Hungary not only the initial 'shock therapy' but the whole transition period was shaped by this *leitidee* or 'action-outcome mapping'. A rapid withdrawal of state from market regulation and equally quick establishment of hard-budget 'real' ownership (cf. Kornai 1990) represented the key actions to be taken for establishing efficient resource allocation and an increase of general welfare at least in the longer run. Gil Eyal, Iván Szelényi and Eleanor Townsley in their famous study on CEE elites ('Making capitalism without capitalists', 1998: 87) suggested for the entire 'post-communist power block' a stark affinity with anti-collectivist, individualistic ideologies, as well as with monetarism, and an aversion to state intervention that is usually identified with a Friedmanian kind of neoliberalism (cf. also Machonin *et al.* 2006). Scholars of the post-socialist transition overwhelmingly agreed on the discourse hegemony of neoliberalism in East Central Europe at least until the financial crisis – even though the elites in the individual countries varied in their rigour in following its market liberal recipe (see Chapter 2 and 3 of this volume; cf. Orenstein 2001; Rae 2008; Shield 2012).[1]

At the same time, the neoliberal discourse also gained ground in the western part of Continental Europe, nurtured by the collapse of the planned economy – a development that reached its peak in Germany under the coalition between the Social Democratic Party (SPD) and the Green Party under Chancellor Gerhard Schröder at the beginning of the twenty-first-century, whose tax, labour market and pension reforms represented a massive blow against key institutions of the 'German model' (cf. Chapter 4). This agenda stands at the end of a decade-long public discourse about the encrusted structures of the corporatist German system, the overburdening costs of the welfare system and the persistently high rates of long-term unemployment in the West but particularly in the radically deindustrialized East Germany following the abrupt integration of the East German economy into the West German currency and markets. The tool-kit of neoliberalism promised, here too, to be the best solution, as it promised to guide CEE safely through the 'valley of tears' of 'shock therapy'. And for most of the observers of this development it was common sense that business leaders shared in the belief system of hegemonic neoliberal discourse (cf. Imbusch and Rucht 2007; Hartmann 2006). Hence there were good reasons to argue that the perception of key market-economy institutions on the part of the economic decision-makers might converge into a similar set of ideas or 'mental model': the German transformation of institutions was moving more slowly but in the same direction of abandoning coordination, along which Hungary, Poland and even East Germany were already travelling.

The financial crisis and the subsequent European crisis have partly changed the public discourses – in Hungary under Victor Orbàn even very drastically. The neoliberal tool-kit has lost some of its attractiveness in all three countries. Although the austerity measures enforced by the European Union and Conservative–Liberal coalition under Chancellor Angela Merkel in order to solve the debt crisis in several European countries looks very much the same, this is rather driven in Germany by the institutionalized lesson of the 'Great Inflation' of 1929 and by concrete politics rather than by Milton Friedman's monetarism. Our empirical study was conducted in 2009/10, at the peak of the financial crisis but before the outbreak of the European currency crisis. However, our mixed findings are more than a single snapshot. Belief systems do not change that quickly and the attitudes of managers have to be separated from public discourses. In addition, we can test some of our results alongside a panel analysis which we conducted in Germany in three waves beginning in 2002, encompassing the heyday of the neoliberal discourse in Germany, and indicating a striking continuity in the views of business leaders.

In the following sections, we explain in more detail the country selection of Poland, Hungary and East and West Germany for the comparison. We do this with reference to the two strands of literature we refer to: the early elite research and the debate on the emerging varieties of capitalism in CEE, which provide frameworks by which to locate East Germany, Hungary and Poland in the wider set of post-socialist countries. After this review we summarize the central research questions, the sampling and the method. We conclude with a short overview of major findings and the structure of the book.

Poland, Hungary and East Germany in the typology of elite configurations

The research on the transition from planned to market economy (here meant as a narrow reform-driven period) is linked to elites in two related ways. On the one hand, elite configurations in the turbulent time of the dissolution of the Soviet bloc are regarded as crucial for path, speed and extensiveness of regime change (cf. Dogan and Higley 1998; King and Szelényi 2005). On the other hand, path, speed and extensiveness of this change offer different opportunities for elites in terms of political influence, careers and asset appropriation. One of the most encompassing typologies for grasping these elite opportunities during the transition process was formed by Andrew G. Walder (2003). Walder identifies four types along two dimensions: a) extensiveness or, perhaps better, speed of regime change and b) regulatory/policy constraints on asset appropriation. With slight changes, the typology still provides a good tool by which to situate the East Central European countries in the wider set of post-socialist elite configurations that shaped the first generation of post-socialist business leaders. The typology also has the advantage of integrating East Germany.

Crucial for Walder is the continuity or collapse of the ruling Communist Party. Where the Party stayed in power, it resisted privatization of large state assets, like in Belarus, or was capable of governing a gradual transition in the economy, as in China or Vietnam (Table 1.1, type 2). In this situation, the privatization is slow but also institutionally restricted; 'cadres' retain their posts (and may use them to enhance their income). Yet, if the Communist Party is in favour of market-reforms, a new corporate elite may emerge 'from below' (cf. King and Szelényi 2005). The Slovenian case of gradualism and elite continuity is also seen as belonging to this category (cf. Frane and Tomšič 2002, 2012).

When the regime collapses but the Communist Party survives largely intact under a new name after abandoning its commitment to public property and central planning, then the constraints on asset appropriation are weak. There are no influential counter-elites or civil society who might take control over the initial period of asset transfer (Table 1.1, type 4). The situation permits the widespread transfer of state assets into the hands of officials and their families and associates, as happened in many of the newly independent republics after their rapid withdrawal from the Soviet Union saw very little in the way of internal regime change (Walder 2003: 903). It provides political and state officials with the opportunity to stay in office or to move into business – a version of 'elite circulation' that the classics of the elite theory did not have in mind.

Table 1.1 Elite opportunity in four types of transition economy

		Speed of regime and elite change	
		High	**Low**
High		**Type 1**	**Type 2**
		Pattern of regime change: Communist hierarchies collapse, ruling party shrinks into electoral party and loses early election. Systematic privatization of public assets is orderly and relatively well regulated and with participation of western foreign investors. *Pattern of elite change:* High rates of elite turnover in both political and economic organizations replaced by lower ranking members and former outsiders. Limited mobility of political and state officials into propertied and corporate elites. Crucial source of survival in elite positions: cultural capital (education/skills).	*Pattern of regime change:* No collapse, communist hierarchies continue to exercise power but under a reform-oriented fraction or this fraction dominates the economic and institutional change as new party in a competitive party system; retains control over appointments and public assets. Privatization gradual and orderly, gradual opening for foreign investors. *Pattern of elite change:* Low rates of elite turnover. Political and state officials retain posts (use them to enhance incomes for themselves and family members), but limited movement into new properties or corporate elite.
Low		**Type 3**	**Type 4**
		Pattern of regime change: Communist hierarchies collapse, ruling party shrinks into electoral party and loses early election. Systematic privatization chaotic and poorly regulated and monitored; permitted extensive asset appropriation by political and state officials, managers and new 'business men' with privileged state access or mafia-like use of violence, while foreign investors are systematically kept out. *Pattern of elite change:* High rates of turnover in political elites, but extensive opportunities for movement into propertied and corporate elites. Advantages for the skilled and highly educated managers to replace the old guard are smaller.	*Pattern of regime change:* No collapse, communist hierarchies survive and transform themselves into a new form of authoritarian power bloc. The Party retains control over appointments but privatizes assets with little transparency and external participation. *Pattern of elite change:* Low rate of elite turnover. Political and state officials have option of extracting incomes from their posts or leaving their posts as assets are privatized. Formation of new propertied and corporate elite out of the old elite.

Policy and institutional constraints on asset appropriation

Source: Walder (2003: 905 and 907). Integrated and slightly adapted in one table.

Constraints on asset appropriation are equally weak when 'in the midst of extensive regime change the state rapidly privatizes public assets without establishing barriers to prevent insiders from seizing control' (Walder 2003: 903). In type 3 (see again Table 1.1), managers of state enterprises and heads of industrial bureaus and ministries retain their posts as they privatize the industries and emerge as 'modern corporate executives' (ibid.). But one has to add that also young entrepreneurs with privileged access to state power used the opportunities of regime change to become not only 'grand bourgeois' but 'oligarchs' who control entire branches of the economy (cf. Krishtanovskaia and White 1999; Åslund 2005, 2007). Russia and Ukraine are typical examples here, but also Romania, Bulgaria, Albania and Serbia under Slobodan Milošević fit into this category.

According to this typology, Hungary, Poland and East Germany belong in one and the same type, type 1, combining a high-speed and extensive transition in which the communist hierarchies collapse near the outset of the reform coupled with a 'privatization that transfers assets under transparent rules' (Walder 2003: 903). The former German Democratic Republic appears to most closely approximate this 'pure type of transitional economy' (ibid.: 906) but also the Czech Republic, Estonia and the other Baltic states can be counted in this group. Slovakia moved from type 2 to type 1 after a lost decade of standstill under President Vladimír Mečiar, which seems to be easier than a movement from type 4 to type 1, that is when the redistribution of public assets is well underway, as is observed in the cases of Bulgaria and Romania.

Worth noting is that the type-1 countries applied various mixtures of privatization methods, from early direct sales to foreign investors in East Germany, Hungary and Estonia, to a mix of early mass privatization and direct strategic sales in the Czech Republic, and early insider privatization on behalf of employees and managers combined with a later mass privatization and gradual direct sales to strategic investors in Poland. And also the constraints on asset appropriation varied significantly. In East Germany the constraints for insiders was very strict, as the privatization agency (*Treuhandanstalt*) preferred western investors to state-enterprise managers or employees (cf. Chapter 5), not to mention the strong restrictions of any attempts to appropriate assets by the East German nomenklatura elite or on their behalf by those within the West German state. Yet, the outcomes of the *Treuhand*-privatization were quite often at odds with what was intended since many investors – worried about the rise of potential East German competitors to their West German companies – only took over production sites in order to close them down and to sell the remaining assets. In Hungary, the early start of reforms allowed an insider privatization at the onset that was neither under the control of regulators nor transparent (cf. Stark and Bruszt 1998), while the Polish insider privatization was much more closely scrutinized, especially by the reform-socialist 'employee councils' (Hanley 1999). The model for all mass privatizations in the post-soviet sphere, Vaclav Klaus' voucher privatization, led to a general asset stripping by managers of industrial enterprises and financial institutes, which alerted the World Bank and the European Union and forced the government to develop corporate governance rules and was not so different to what happened in countries not belonging to this type (Orenstein 2001; Myant 2003; Bluhm 2007).[2]

What unifies the East Central European countries, however, is the relatively early influence of foreign players – foreign investors and the European Union. In all these countries, including East Germany, large proportions of state enterprises were directly sold to foreign companies, which has meant that national elites were not able to maintain control over assets (Walder 2003: 903; King and Szelényi 2005). The early promise of accession to the European Union ensured that the Czech Republic, Hungary and Poland remained on this track (cf. Grabbe 2006; Kutter and Trappmann 2006; Bluhm 2007).

Varying approaches to capitalism

The debate on the emerging versions of capitalism began with the adaptation of Max Weber's term 'political capitalism', which was used with partly different meanings: as appropriation of public assets by the nomenklatura – the new 'grand bourgeoisie' (Staniszkis 1991); as 'rational acquisition of profits', which 'happens under the tutelage of the state' as Szelényi and his colleagues put it (Eyal *et al.* 1998: 172); as a specific mode of accumulation driven by political rather than economic logic (King 2002); or even close to Joe S. Hellman's term of a 'state captured' by economic actors and clientelistic networks (cf. Hellman 1998; Ganev 2009). From the end of the twentieth century, it became clear that the concept of 'political capitalism' was not sufficient to grasp the whole post-socialist world and that the different transition paths have starkly deepened the dissimilarities between regions and countries. Particularly after access to the European Union, the various concepts provided little explanatory power for East Central European countries.

Since then, research has shifted increasingly to theories which are suited to identifying the increasing variation within the former Soviet bloc. Again there are two major sets of theories that are applied here. The first approach to capitalisms in Central *and* Eastern Europe can be situated within political economy focusing on the interaction of key actors and institutions. The second approach has stemmed from the renewed interest in Karl Polanyi's work *The Great Transformation*, published in 1944.

The most prominent institutionalist framework applied to the East is the Varieties-of-Capitalism (VoC) approach by Peter A. Hall and David Soskice (2001), differentiating mainly between two versions of modern capitalism, according to the mode of coordination among economic actors: the *'liberal market economy'* (LME), where coordination occurs predominantly via markets and hierarchies; and the *'coordinated market economy'* (CME), where networks and/or associations allow close cooperation beyond markets and hierarchical control.[3]

In a first round of concept transfer, scholars tried to use the VoC approach directly for categorizing the newly emerged market economies. Magnus Feldmann (2006) and Clemens Buchen (2007) contrast Estonia, as the closest to an LME, with Slovenia, which they determined as the only CME among the post-socialist countries, by analysing the key institutional spheres of the political economy according to Hall and Soskice (2001): company financing and corporate governance; the institutions of labour representation; skill formation; and inter-firm coordination (for innovation and standard setting). East Central Europe lies here somewhere in between the two poles, indicating that a sequential institutional comparison allows no clear classification of the countries into one of the existing types of modern capitalism, that is most of the post-socialist countries fit in neither of the existing categories.[4]

Mark Knell and Martin Srholec (2007) try to fix this by developing an index for the degree of 'strategic coordination', which includes the regulation of the labour market and business as well as social cohesion (Gini, highest marginal personal income tax rate and government final consumption expenditures). For statistical reasons, they included almost *all* post-socialist states. It was not surprising that Belarus, with a persistently low level of marketization, turned out to have the highest degree of extra-market 'strategic coordination', followed by Ukraine, Slovenia, Croatia, Romania, the Czech Republic and Uzbekistan, while coordination between economic actors via markets is supposed to be dominant in Bulgaria, Moldova, Poland, Slovakia, Hungary, Estonia and Russia (ibid.) – countries which are very different in their transition paths and levels of success. David Lane (2007) differentiates between a 'continental European type of capitalism' that comes close to CME (by Hall and Soskice) but with a greater state influence on economic coordination, since corporatist self-regulation is weak in the post-socialist market economies. According to Lane, not only Slovenia but also the Czech Republic, Hungary, Poland and even Estonia belong in this category, while Russia is seen as a 'hybrid state-market uncoordinated capitalism', which moves more and more towards a specific version of 'state-led capitalism' (Lane 2011).

The simple extension of the VoC approaches to all post-socialist economies ignores, however, its fundamental assumptions (Hall and Soskice 2001: 21). The whole argument of the VoC approach is designed for the most advanced market economies only. Hall and Soskice argue that the LME and CME represent different complementary sets of institutions that foster (but do not determine) different successful strategies in global competition. In sociological terms, the approach takes for granted the 'functional differentiation' of state and economy and the existence of a Weberian rational bureaucracy; they are not issues in their theory of modern capitalism. Strategic coordination serves as a means to solve collective action problems in an open global economy beyond 'market and hierarchy' and not for rent seeking. Rephrasing a criticism once made of Robert Putnam's social capital theory, the dark side of network coordination remains out of sight in the VoC literature (Bluhm 2010). The positive view of networks and of the rule of associations for coordinating the economy is the result of a long western debate against neoclassic preferences for arm's length market coordination (see e.g., Powell 1990; Williamson 1996). Yet, under conditions in which this state is described as patrimonial rather than rational and in which corruption and clientelism are still endemic, negative forms of 'strategic coordination' can hardly be ignored (on the reception of Weber, cf. Volkov 2000; King and Szelényi 2005; King 2007; Ganev 2009). Even in the countries with the best record in this respect, a substantial lack of institutional and contractual trust, ineffective law enforcement and institutional inconsistency are still an issue (see Chapter 2, 3 and 6).

The restriction of the VoC approach to the most advanced market economies produces yet another limitation for its application to the post-socialist economies, precisely for the institutionally relatively mature market economies in East Central Europe, which accelerated their regime change through western integration and transnationalization of their key sectors in manufacturing and the banking sector (see more in Chapter 2 and 3). Hall and Soskice were often criticized for their focus on the national level of institution building and change as decisive for the political economy of a country even in the time of globalization and 'Europeanization' (cf. Crouch and Farrell 2004; for a response, see Hancké *et al.* 2007). Since the VoC typology refers to countries that host companies at the leading edge of transnational value-chains, global competition is conceptualized as rivalry among relatively autonomous 'equals' (i.e., large multinational corporations, MNCs); asymmetry and dependency within the global value-chains are, therefore, blended out. The VoC approach also fails to grasp the variety of new capitalisms in East Central Europe because of the region's high degree of dependency on transnational actors and its consequences for institution building. Lawrence P. King (2007) and King and Szelényi (2005) therefore speak of a 'dependent liberal capitalism'; others coined the term 'foreign-led capitalism' (cf. Myant and Drahokoupil 2011). The concept closest to the Hall and Soskice CME–LME typology was developed by Andreas Nölke and Arjan Vliegenthart (2009), who introduced the *'dependent market economy'* (DME) as a third type of capitalism alongside LME and CME. In terms of company financing and corporate governance, it stresses the dependence on intra-firm hierarchies within transnational companies controlled by headquarters outside the region, producing relatively complex industrial goods, which pursue an appeasement of skilled labour and company-level collective agreements, while their expenditures on training is limited, as they restrict their 'embedding' to regional or national intra-firm networks. DMEs did not develop the full set of institutions present in CMEs nor LMEs (for more details, see Chapter 2).

The strength of the 'DME' concept lies in the inclusion of a value-chain perspective, which was previously absent in the VoC approach, and therefore its ability to grasp a crucial feature of the newly established market economies in East Central Europe. Therefore Krzysztof Jasiecki for Poland (Chapter 2) and György Lengyel and Dénes Bank for Hungary (Chapter 3) use this approach, although they refer to it with various levels of deference. East Germany, too, shares features of a 'DME'. We would even argue that German unification led to an extreme case of economic dependency on western value-chains, even though they are no longer 'foreign' (see Chapter 4 and 5).

However, Nölke and Vliegenthart only suggested this DME type for the Visegrád Four (Poland, Hungary, the Czech Republic and Slovakia). The production of durable, complex, capital-intensive commodities in these countries – quite similar to the branch structure in Western Europe – separates them from the Baltic states and the Commonwealth of Independent States (CIS) (Nölke and

Vliegenthart 2009).[5] Yet, with the break-up of the Soviet bloc, not only did varying market economies emerge but also varying dependencies, both in terms of integration into and specialization within transnational value-chains and in terms of on whom the economies are dependent (in addition to the already existing forms of dependency). The Baltic states, too, embraced a 'western-led' modernization strategy and belong to the most advanced market economies in CEE. Yet they did not achieve an industrial reorganization to the same degree as East Central Europe did, and they produce more labour-intensive products rather than complex industrial goods with relatively high demands in terms of capital, technology and skills. Thus, the 'dependent market capitalism' characterizes only a very specific version of dependence, embracing countries 'that due to their peculiar history managed to escape one peril usually attributed to dependency: lasting scarcity of human capital' (Bohle and Greskovits 2012: 12).

The shift of analysis from national institutions to a transnational influence has brought to the fore the issue of the kind of institution building and support needed by MNCs. Yet, institution building in the various countries is fuelled by different influences. In East Germany we have to consider, of course, the institution transfer from West Germany and the reaction of the new East German entrepreneurs to the misfit between the transferred institutions and the economic development in the former German Democratic Republic (GDR) (see Chapter 4 and 8). Even when MNCs control key sectors and the national institutional system is still in the making, their influence follows different, often contradictory logics, as Krzysztof Jasiecki shows for Poland in this volume (see Chapter 2). The impact of MNCs on education is a good example. Nölke and Vliegenthart (2009: 678) argue that in a DME there is no need for an 'LME-type system of general-skill education combined with massive research and development (R & D) expenditures', or 'for a CME-type system of comprehensive vocational training'. Yet this tells us little about the actual direction in which the educational system develops. The Polish education system since 1989 has rapidly abandoned the socialist heritage of extensive vocational training and dramatically extended tertiary education but at the cost of quality. A similar development, though less radical, occurred in Hungary, in East Germany and the Czech Republic (cf. Bluhm 2007; Kogan 2008), a variation that can hardly be explained within the DME framework. And even in the Czech Republic, where the vocational training system could rely on a strong manufacturing tradition, German industrial MNCs failed to prevail with their ideas of a German-style dual vocational training system in the reform period of the 1990s (cf. Bluhm 2007).

In our book, we apply the notion of 'foreign-led' or 'DME', in order to grasp the specific position of Poland, Hungary and East Germany compared to the European core economies. Nonetheless, we reject the idea that dependency sufficiently determines the institutional features of these market economies because it tends to overstress the role of foreign investors in the institution building of a specific country and underestimates the influence of domestic actors and legacies. The approach can also hardly explain why Hungary became so much more vulnerable to financial and European debt crisis than other DMEs.

A different approach to capitalism in CEE starts with Karl Polanyi's *The Great Transformation* ([1944] 1957), an approach thereafter best elaborated by Dorothee Bohle and Béla Greskovits, who share many of the general criticisms of the VoC approach, a criticism that in part also finds it source in Polanyi (Bohle and Greskovits 2007a; 2009; and 2012; cf. Streeck 2009 and 2012).[6] Polanyi's analysis of the 'disembedding' of markets out of society is very instructive for post-socialist development, as the establishment of an autonomous private economic sector and the re-establishment of money, land and labour as 'fictitious commodities' represent the economic core of the transition project. The metaphor of 'disembedding' and 're-embedding' also provides a crucial insight for the post-socialist transformation, as it points to the need in liberalized markets for re-regulation and compensation policies in order to function in a stable and socially cohesive manner.

On the basis of Polanyi's cycles of pro-market 'movement' and protective 'counter movements', Bohle and Greskovits (2012) developed a set of analytical tools to identify 'post-socialist regimes' which bring state policy (industrial and welfare policy) back in. While in the firm-centred VoC approach the state is perceived as one element among others of coordination, represented in each of the above-mentioned institutional dimensions (cf. Hancké *et al.* 2007: 15), in the Polanyian conceptualization the state takes centre-stage. Bohle and Greskovits distinguish regimes according to the integration in the 'neoliberal global and European order', the rigour of marketization and the attempts to compensate for its social costs and how the conflicts on social objectives are governed. They draw a 'diamond' with six 'corners' reaching from government accountability, corporatism/interest mediation, welfare state, macroeconomic coordination to market efficiency/commodification and democratic interest representation.

Three regime types are identified: firstly, a *'pure neoliberal regime'* in the Baltic states with a weak welfare state. Secondly, Slovenia with its *'democratic corporatism'* is on the opposite side. And thirdly, the Visegrád countries are here again in the same family, constituting the *'embedded neoliberal regime'* (later followed by Croatia) that consists of a neoliberal strategy of economic transition (liberalization, deregulation, fast privatization, macroeconomic stabilization) with a 'foreign-led reindustrialization' and a more socially inclusive strategy but also relatively weak collective regulation and corporatist interest mediation (Bohle and Greskovits 2012: 22–3, and in more detail 182–222). Bulgaria and Romania are sometimes characterized as 'non-regimes' (ibid.: 17–24). Both countries made early concessions to labour that Bohle and Greskovits explain by the early combination of initially strong and militant labour and the hegemony of unreformed post-communist parties that impeded 'market radicalism' (ibid.: 190). Yet, due to their strong legacies of 'patrimonial communism', the two Southeast European countries failed to build states capable of avoiding 'state capture'. In recent times, they have taken a neoliberal direction but their weak states and low level of political participation still set them apart from the Baltic states. Bulgaria and Romania are also described by Bohle and Greskovits as 'uncoordinated capitalism' (interestingly this is a VoC category).

East Germany is not included here because it hard to say that the *New Länder* developed their own post-socialist regime, although one could argue that the abrupt liberalization and privatization combined with extensive compensation of social costs fits remarkably well with the 'embedded neoliberal' type. With the West German welfare state behind them, the compensation of the social costs of this transition policy was historically uniquely high.

The shift towards a policy-centred approach in the VoC analysis has many advantages over a firm- and coordination-centred approach, as Bohle and Greskovits show. We therefore partly share this view. Krzysztof Jasiecki (Chapter 2) points to an integration of state policies into the concept of capitalism and includes the role of civil society in his analysis. György Lengyel and Dénes Bank also refer to Polanyi's famous title in heading their chapter on Hungary 'the small transformation' (Chapter 3). They argue that the institutional solutions and social setting of the handling of fictitious commodities are influenced by both the historic legacies and the specific paths of the transition towards capitalism, which are not only shaped by 'dependency'. The Corporate Social Responsibility (CSR) movement that has reached East Central Europe in recent years can also be interpreted as an attempt at 're-embedding' companies in the wider society after they gave up most of the social functions they had carried out under state socialism (see more Chapter 7).

However, we have decided against giving up the VoC approach completely, because the Polanyian approach also has its limits. The Polanyian perspective on capitalism is even more market centred than the VoC approach, which systematically includes economic coordination beyond markets. It is the market that has to be re-embedded in society by regulation, and compensation of social costs mainly refers to labour market institutions and the welfare state.[7] The crucial question for capitalist theory, of how the capitalist process of value-adding and innovation is organized and to what extent this organization varies, can only be answered with reference to additional theories that have no systematic link to the embeddedness metaphor. Moreover, while Hall and Soskice in their original contribution to the VoC debate (2001) had too few reflections on the constitution of the state and the correspondence between the varieties of capitalism and the varieties of welfare regimes (cf. Streeck and Yamuara 2001; Ebbinghaus and Manow 2001), the Polanyians tend to view institutions mainly as *external* constraints of self-regulating markets, which is precisely why the approach is suitable for conceptualizing counter movements of market re-regulation in the interest of the wider society (cf. Streeck 2012; Bohle and Greskovits 2012). The institution building as a solution to transaction problems *within* the economic sector, that is *between* economic actors, however, is hard to grasp in this sense[8] – at least again not without additional assumptions that significantly complicate the argument.[9] The reforms under the German Chancellor Schröder which we refer to in Chapter 4 can be interpreted as a decisive step back, towards 'disembedding' markets. Yet, the specific mode of institutional change can only partly be understood as fight for market de-regulation and re-regulation. Hence, we do not regard the macro and policy-oriented Polanyian approach as a substitute for the more micro-oriented VoC approach on institutions and economic actors operating in different institutional spheres. Both conceptualizations of varieties of capitalism provide, in our understanding, different sets of *heuristic tools* that have complementary strengths (and also their respective weaknesses) and are therefore not really to be understood as substitutes one for the other.

Why compare most-similar cases?

Despite the differences explored above, all approaches see East Central European countries in one and the same category of 'foreign-led' or 'dependent' market economies that included a high elite turnover at the onset. For our focus, this closeness is decisive as it allows us to take a Central European perspective. West Germany has heavily contributed to the emergence of the specific type of DME in East Central Europe and in so doing transformed its own institutions, which had represented a model for the 'CME' (Hall and Soskice 2001). The similarity in terms of industrial specialization and skills in this region presented a huge opportunity to German core industries such as automotive and mechanical engineering to shift abroad parts of the high-and-medium-priced flexible quality production. While several factors came together in the process of the erosion of the 'German model', the changes within its industrial core can hardly be explained without the shifting power relationships between management and labour due to the new exit option for companies to East Central Europe. Hence it is worth bringing both developments, that of East Central Europe and that of West Germany, together in a perspective of intertwined transformations that was ideologically framed – at least at level of public discourse – with a similar neoliberal *zeitgeist* (see Chapter 4).

We agree with the dependency literature that MNCs have a greater impact on the institutions of the political economy in DMEs than in the mature western market economies, but they are far from determining institutional outcomes, partly because they stem from different institutional settings themselves, partly because they are far from being the only player in the game and because institution building does not start from scratch. And dependency may shape interests but does not represent an ideological frame for business leaders to view their environment. Therefore it remains an important research question to understand the 'mental models' of the individual actors – in our study, the business leaders.

It is still fascinating that for East Central Europe the 'CME' has not been a serious option for the new political leaders, in spite of the strong wish for a 'return to Europe'; only for the East Germans has the (West-) 'German model' and the welfare promises linked to it been a first choice. This apparent lack of appeal may have to do with the strong influence of 'Anglo-Saxon' government advisors and the widespread view that the 'CME' is still too close to socialism. Yet it may be also explained by the fact that the collaboration in CMEs, which is not primarily rent seeking, relies on complex institutional support which is hard to build. When politicians in East Central Europe favoured this path, they referred rather to Japan's or South Korea's company networks than to the 'German model,' which relies relatively strongly on intermediary organizations (see for Poland, Bohle 2002).

While the introduction of a LME seems to be easier at first glance, in reality the institutions found within the emerging market economies in East Central Europe were taken from different models in different institutional spheres. Jon Elster *et al.* (1998) coined this 'regime shopping', which is a factor contributing to the difficulties in grasping their institutional characteristics, as discussed above. And here we see the first significant differences in the collection of countries studied here.

At the beginning of transition, East Germany, transformed into a collection of five *New Länder*, had no other institutional choice but to adopt the complete institutional system of West Germany, which was adapted and changed afterwards. So, the new East German regions are, in their institution building, the closest to the CME type of any of the countries studied here. In contrast to East Germany and Hungary, Poland has seen the most pronounced orientation towards neoliberalism. The high legitimacy of the *Solidarity* movement could not only be used to push through the 'shock therapy' agenda strongly advised by external actors, which altered *Solidarity's* political identity (Ost 2005; Trappmann 2013), but also made it easier to abandon state-socialist institutional legacies – on which a more CME-type structure might have been built (see Chapters 2 and 8). The early introduction of the works-council model in Hungary (although mainly reduced to information and consultation with weak co-determination rights) displays a greater tendency toward Continental European CMEs in the original institutional choices. East Germany, Hungary and Poland also vary in the degree of social compensation. We thus concluded that the respective distances of East Germany, Hungary and Poland from the CME structure vary in spite of their similarities mentioned above. Hence we contrasted our initial convergence thesis with the assumption that 'mental models' of business leaders still vary from West Germany to Poland – if institutions matter.

Research questions, sampling and method

In the book, we combine an institutional approach with an elite survey. The survey was conducted in 2009/10, via telephone interviews in Poland and Germany, and face-to-face interviews in Hungary by each country team. Each survey was carried out in the national language, having been translated from a common English questionnaire. In a first step, we want to find out who the business leaders are, how they made their careers and how they perceive their role in society, in employee relationships and the relationship between state and business.[10] In a second step, we explore what best explains variations: *socio-demographic characteristics of the respondents*; the *(country-specific) institutional environment*; or *organizational features*. Regarding socio-demographic characteristics, we expected two features to be crucial, the age of the respondents and their career paths.[11] Twenty years after the Berlin wall came down, we expect a new generation of business leaders to be taking over the top positions in business, who have spent their entire professional life under the hegemonic neoliberal discourse. For East Central Europeans, these business leaders will have made decisive steps of their career under market conditions after the turbulent time of privatization. A starting hypothesis, therefore, has been that the new generation differs from the first post-socialist cohort in both their careers and views.

Careers paths, including education, are important subjective variables in the western debate on varying capitalisms and ideas. Scholars widely assume that types of careers especially in large companies are fostered by types of capitalism, and also markedly shape the attitudes of the managers. On the one hand, many scholars perceive LMEs as related to the existence of a volatile market for executives, with short-term appointments and a focus on economic and general (economic) management skills. CMEs on the other hand are assumed to correspond with long-lasting in-house careers that are supposed to establish strong loyalty to a single company and its employees, and a rather specialist-oriented management style often relying on engineering, scientific and technical qualifications.[12] The on-going internationalization of management careers supposedly transmits new global, that is Anglo-Saxon, business ideas. Our study will explore whether this kind of interplay holds in empirical research on the influence of careers on attitudes.

Our approach differs in another way from classic elite studies, as we apply a broad understanding of business elites, defining them as persons who hold top positions in very large companies and banks but also in medium-sized companies. With that, we stress a positional elite in decision-making processes and in terms of control over crucial societal resources, rather than the relationship to other elite sections at national level. Only this decision allows us to include East Germans and a variety of ownership types. But we also argue that this broader view is more suitable to a VoC perspective that should not focus only on the biggest companies in a society (Bluhm and Schmidt 2008).

With a relatively extensive section on organizational features, our survey differs yet further from other quantitative elite studies. This allows us to refer careers and attitudes to company size, ownership, the presence of works councils and unions, etc. In terms of sectors, we focus on manufacturing and the financial sector, that is the core branches of the 'German model' and precisely those sectors on which the dependency argument mainly relies. The basic distinction we apply in each chapter comprises four company types: *medium-sized companies* (45 to 249 employees), *large companies* (250 to 999 employees), *very large companies* (1,000 employees and more), *banks* and *insurance companies* (see in more detail Table 1.2).

For the very large companies, we followed a well-established method in elite research, taking the most reliable top-500 lists in each country and scrolling from the top down to contact the very largest firms first. We were quite successful in establishing contacts with very large firms and banks, even taking into consideration the different national compositions of the economy (Table A1.1, means and medians of employees). The large and medium-sized companies were selected from country-specific pools of companies' addresses, the manufacturing sector being mainly represented by mechanical engineering, metalworking, and

Table 1.2 Composition of the sample

Sample characteristics	Company types of the sample			
	Medium-sized companies (45–249)	Large companies (250–999)	Very large companies (≥ 1,000)	Banks
Poland	81	39	26	19
Hungary	105	20	24	20
Germany	314	86	79	44
Mean number of employees	115	482	8,807	2,345
Median of employees	100	428	3,500	516
Companies in West Germany	114	48	74	43
First-level West Germans	156	60	56	28
Companies in East Germany	200	38	5	1
First-level East Germans	129	14	1	1
% of respondents working at the first hierarchical level	91.1	87.1	79.8	82.9
% of respondents holding shares of the current company (all respondents)	45.3	19.7	9.5	3.7
% of respondents holding shares of the current company (top level only)	49.1	22.1	11.9	4.7

the electrical, chemical, and food industries, with some national peculiarities. The target persons of data collection were members of the first hierarchical level (CEOs, managing directors, other members of the board of managers, and entrepreneurs) (see Table 1.2). In two cases, Hungary and Germany, the survey of large and medium-sized companies was part of a panel study, the third wave in Germany, and the seventh wave in Hungary.

We only approached Poles, Hungarians and Germans in their respective countries (no German in Hungary for example). For Germany, we created two sub-samples. We first distinguished between East and West German companies according to the location of the company. Since around one-third of the East German companies are run by West Germans, we created a second sample according to the respondents' geographic origin, that is whether they come from East or West Germany.[13] This second sample is particularly used when we analyse the subjective characteristics and attitudes of business leaders, that is in combination with the variable of 'first-level' respondent (see Table 1.2).

Structure of the book and major results

The book is divided into two parts. In the first part, country-case studies explore the peculiarities of each country's transformation and of the change in business leaders in the context of the VoC debate (Chapter 2–4). Each case study has its particular appeal, as the Polish, Hungarian and German authors take their own view on the transformation since the end of state socialism. *Krzysztof Jasiecki* for Poland and *György Lengyel* and *Dénes Bank* for Hungary show the ambivalent outcomes of the transition of these countries towards DME. While *Katharina Bluhm, Bernd Martens* and *Vera Trappmann* analyse the institutional change of the German version of CME (in this respect, they speak of the 'German model') and observe 'the long shadow' of the *leitideen* of these institutional settings.

In the second part, we do cross-country analysis of data from our survey, exploring links between institutional features of the countries, organizational and socio-demographic characteristics on the one side and attitudes on the other. In the first cross-country analysis *Bluhm* and *Martens* investigate the social origin of the recent generation of business leaders, their educational background and career patterns (Chapter 5). In Chapter 6, *Janky* and *Lengyel* explore business leaders' trust in formal rules, norms and contracts and to what extent this trust can be explained by country-specific institutional legacies, organizational features and the individual characteristics of business leaders. *Bluhm* and *Trappmann* investigate the cognitive concepts of corporate responsibility that business leaders share, and again they test the effects of country, organizational and socio-demographic variables (Chapter 7), while *Trappmann, Jasiecki* and *Przybysz* (Chapter 8) focus on the practice and perception of collective interest representation and employee relations. Finally, *Lengyel, Geszler* and *Ördög* explore how business leaders' income and social influence are related to country-specific, organizational and individual features. They show that income is a crucial variable here (Chapter 9).

To summarize the major survey results, we show that generational change is in fact well underway, but with important differences between the Poland, Hungary, and East and West Germany. For the post-socialist transition cases, these differences reflect the variations in the respective transition paths towards DME. Contrary to our expectations, however, the assumed difference in the socialization between the older and younger generation of business leaders contributed little to explaining variation in attitudes within our sample. The same is true for career paths, although changes in the careers from the first post-socialist age cohort to the new generation could be observed. A striking variation is found, however, for Poland and Hungary when we explore the impact of foreign ownership. Subsidiaries of foreign companies have younger top managers with higher cultural capital than their domestic counterparts – an impact that was not manifest in West Germany.

A primary result of this study is that the socio-political attitudes of post-socialist business leaders differ from those of the West Germans in our sample when we control for the four company types (see Table 1.2). West Germans on the one side still significantly more often believe in the efficiency of neocorporatist self-regulation and the performance of a 'social market economy'. Business leaders in the more liberal, post-socialist environments are, on the other hand, more shareholder-oriented, more often believers in maximizing profits as the only company goal and inclined to reject collaboration with organized labour.

But, East Germans, Hungarians and Polish business leaders also vary significantly. We argue, therefore, for a high correspondence between *institutional framework* and *learning experience* on the one side and the *beliefs* of business leaders on the other.

East Germans are both distinct from their post-socialist neighbours and from their West German cousins. Towards unions they share a particularly adverse view with Polish business leaders. In the literature, the East German hostility towards unions is partly seen as the result of labour weakness in the context of deindustrialization in the 1990s, partly as a size effect (smaller businesses), and as a reaction to the union policy during the transition that dramatically increased labour costs. In other aspects however, East Germans are closer to the West Germans than to Hungarians or Poles. We did not find that East German business leaders entirely reject the 'German model'. They also share a relatively high level of institutional trust and faith in the social balance of the market economy, which we ascribe to the quality of the transferred West German institutions.

Polish business leaders are clearly the most market 'radicals' and the most adverse to collective self-binding. Importantly, the hostility towards employee representation is here also more often shared by business leaders in large companies. They perceive corporate responsibility toward society in a Friedmanite narrow sense more often than do their German counterparts. At the same time, they are more likely to agree with state intervention, in terms both of regulation of the market economy and redistribution, than their German counterparts. This etatist view, however, goes along with lower institutional and contractual trust and with scepticism about the social performance of the market economy. Poland has also the largest share of managers with a patriarchal leadership style that seems partly to serve to replace the weakly institutionalized formal labour representation.

Hungarian business leaders come close to their Polish counterparts in many respects. Among them, the Friedmanite view on corporate responsibility and a pro-state intervention are more widespread than in Germany. They are also less adverse to organized labour and works councils than are the Poles, which corresponds with its better institutionalization compared to Poland, and they are the most inclined in our sample to agree to state regulation and redistribution (what we call, without normative bias, 'etatism'). At the same time, the lack of firmly institutionalized norms, and institutions governing business relationships, leads to a low level of contractual trust in Poland, though this level is even slightly lower again in Hungary. This Hungarian result is particularly intriguing in the light of the country's long tradition of entrepreneurship under reform communism and its western integration after 1989. It will be shown that it is precisely the ambivalence of the reform-communist heritage that has contributed much to this result.

Next to country differences, *organizational features* play a major role in variation. For experienced-based learning, size of a company and private ownership seems to play a bigger role than socio-demographic characteristics. This is especially important regarding labour relations. Despite the neocorporatist tradition in Germany, managers of medium-sized companies and entrepreneurs in all three countries show more distance from collective self-binding in negotiations with unions than do large companies and employed managers, and perceive them as more adverse.

Moreover, our data also reveals that the presence of labour representation significantly correlates with the positive evaluation of unions and of social partnership, controlling for size effect and country variation. This means that even in the more hostile post-socialist environments and in medium-sized companies, top managers have a more positive view of collective regulation when formal employee representation exists at company level. Institutions matter markedly in this regard, across countries.

We have also found that the careers of business leaders differ according to company type. Business leaders of smaller organizations have more often changed from a top position elsewhere into the current company, indicating that an external market for executives is more relevant for companies with flatter hierarchies. It is not surprising that entrepreneurs (in smaller business) perceive themselves as less influential in important decisions in society compared with managers in other types of companies. Bankers, in contrast, are the group that evaluate quite highly their own influence, across the three countries. But this is also true of managers in companies in foreign ownership. This would seem to correlate with the high level of interest on the part of national policymakers in attracting and keeping financial and foreign investments in the countries.

Apart from these general findings, organizational features play a varying role in the three countries. Regarding careers, foreign ownership makes a difference in Poland and Hungary but not in West Germany. In Germany, the differences between medium-sized companies and very large companies are more decisive for explaining career differences and attitudes. We interpret the varying effect of foreign ownership on careers as an indicator of the stronger segmentation between transnational and domestic sectors in post-socialist Hungary and Poland, which is typical for a dependent capitalism. Polish top managers of foreign-owned companies also differ from domestic companies in some of their views, as they are less etatist-oriented and more optimistic about social cohesion and justice in the results of the market economy, as are Polish bankers. In contrast, however, to the assumptions of the concept of 'DME', foreign ownership, when controlling for company size, is not significantly distinct from domestic ownership in terms of both the presence of labour-relations institutions and their appreciation. The assumption that, in the medium-skilled capital-intensive production of complex industrial goods typical for DME, foreign ownership as such leads to a more cooperative attitude to formal employee representation and unions is not proved.

Least influential has been the *socio-demographic characteristic* of business leaders. In all three countries, we observe an on-going social closure of the highest ranks in business, while, interestingly, Poland has the strongest elitist tradition in this respect, because not only the fathers but also the mothers of recent business leaders stem from the highest social ranks. However, neither age, nor education and career paths contributed much to explaining variation in most of the analysis of attitudes. Thus our research could not confirm that the trend towards economics degrees and the emergence of a market for executives 'cause' a change in mind-set in the way often suggested in the literature. This finding is particularly puzzling, as in the VoC debate as well as in neoinstitutionalist studies, stress is placed on the great normative power of education and of career-types (including their internationalization). Our finding can be interpreted in two ways: First our items might be too imprecise to grasp this influence. Second, the influence of the societal environment and organizational features, which shape the strategies and attitudes of business leaders, outweigh the very broad social-demographic features. We tend to the latter interpretation.

In spite of the limitations of our study, it may be safe to argue, however, that the neoliberal *leitidee* that ideologically guided the institutional change in the 1990s is not per se also the 'mental model' which business leaders in post-communist Europe share. The institutional and social environment in which managers and entrepreneurs conduct their company seems to matter much more than do hegemonic discourses in media, politics and associations for the way top managers and entrepreneurs perceive the role of the company in society, the place of labour relations and the role of the state. Against the claim of a strong anti-etatist view, we found that in post-socialist Hungary and Poland a significant percentage of business leaders welcome state intervention. Given the weak level of collective regulation not only with social partners but also in business, one can interpret this also as a call for 'strategic coordination'. Formulating the results this way, the business leaders across the countries seem closer to each other than was to be expected or than the in-depth analysis of differences suggests.

Notes

1 For an overview see Ganev (2005).
2 See, as an example, Ganev (2007) for Bulgaria and Cernat (2006) for Romania.
3 In the following debate, the typology was differentiated and expanded to western European countries which were originally subsumed under the CME type (France; Northern Europe) or not subsumed (Southern Europe) (see e.g., Schmidt 2003; Amable 2003).
4 It is worth noting, and often ignored, that Hall and Soskice (2001) never claimed that every developed market economy gains a complementarity of institutional subsystems with comparative advantages in global competition and can therefore be subsumed under a certain type of market economy.
5 For this argument, they refer to the work of Dorothee Bohle and Béla Greskovits (2007b).
6 For an overview, see Bluhm and Trappmann (2010).
7 On this point, the Polanyian conceptualization does not provide a sufficient answer to its critics against the VoC approach, as rather a theory of 'market economy' and not of capitalism (cf. Streeck 2009).
8 In this respect, the policy approach differs also from new economic sociology of the Polanyi reception, which applies the concept of embeddedness at micro-level (cf. Granovetter 1985).
9 Apart from this, the hexagonal scheme for capitalist diversity after socialism includes for each corner opposition terms which are not always convincing, as they pair dimensions which present different kinds of oppositions. See for example 'market: efficiency vs commodification', 'democracy: representation vs ungovernability, 'macroeconomic

coordination: stability vs straightjacket on development' (Bohle and Greskovits 2012: 21).

10 If we speak of attitudes in this context, we have the cognitive component of attitudes in mind (cf. Bohner 2001: 241). Therefore, we also speak of perceptions, views, concepts or beliefs.

11 The number of female business leaders in the chosen ranks and sectors was too low for conducting statistical analysis. Hence, gender is not a variation that we could explore in detail.

12 For the debate on national specific career paths, see Sorge and Warner (1980), Lane (1989), Stewart *et al.* (1994), Byrkjeflot (2001), Schmidt and Gergs (2002), Faust (2002), Höpner (2004), Beyer (2007).

13 The East or West German origin was operationalized by the question: 'Where did you live on the 30th of June 1990?' That is the day of the introduction of the German mark in the GDR.

2 Institutional transformation and business leaders of the new foreign-led capitalism in Poland

Krzysztof Jasiecki

Introduction

The development and characteristics of capitalism in Central and Eastern Europe (CEE) after 1989 show some of the limitations of the varieties of capitalism (VoC) theoretical framework which mainly distinguishes between liberal market economies (LME) and coordinated market economies (CME). The context varies strikingly from that of western market economies, not only by the relative immaturity of the market systems in each country but also by the way they were established. The post-socialist transformation consists of three simultaneous developments that continue to shape the new market economies up to today: the creation of democracies after a period of one-party communist power monopoly; the radical shift to a market-based economic and ownership model without a capitalist class; and the demarcation of state borders and consolidation of states in the countries of the former Yugoslavia, Czechoslovakia and Soviet Union (Offe 1996).

In applying the VoC approach to CEE one should therefore take into account aspects of transformation that were never part of the VoC perspective. Some scholars argue that the list of aspects necessary for understanding the new market economies should include geographic location, political traditions, efficiency of the state, rule of law, ownership relations and relation patterns between politics and business (Drahokoupil and Myant 2010). Others stress the role of the state, its macroeconomic and microeconomic policies in particular, and the development of civil society (Federowicz 2004). This chapter takes an extended VoC perspective based on this new line of research and may provide a suitable theoretical framework for a comparison of the new post-socialist capitalism with the realities of the most economically advanced countries. My interpretation combines the VoC approach of Peter A. Hall and David Soskice (2001) with the modifications proposed by Michał Federowicz (2004).

This chapter consists of three parts. Part one shows the need to cover subjects outside the mainstream of VoC literature as well as to consider the *development* of the economic model in Poland by taking into account selected aspects of its historical heritage and the political, structural and institutional contexts. Part two is an attempt to analyse the new 'Polish capitalism' in terms of its financial system, corporate governance, labour relations, inter-firm relations, educational and training system. Part three describes the background and social orientations of Polish business leaders and their attitudes toward selected institutional issues such as corporate purpose, the role of government in the economy, cooperation with social partners and the self-identification of executives. A brief conclusion follows.

Determinates of the Polish 'new capitalism'

The different nature of the object of study makes it impossible to mechanically apply the VoC approach to CEE and Poland. Although the approach does offer a useful tool for analysing different institutional spheres and the relationships between them, historic particularities of the region compared to those of countries with advanced capitalist systems, in particular older member states of the European Union, has to be taken into account. Table 2.1 outlines some of these particularities in the case of Poland. It contains key institutional and political features, defining the specific framework of economic activity consisting of public institutions, internationalization of the economy, macroeconomic policy, microeconomic perspective and the development of civil society.

Neoliberal, 'soft state' syndrome: fragmentation of reforms

From the various contemporary concepts of the role of the state, Polish elites after 1989 opted for the 'minimal state' based on the Anglo-Saxon New Right,

Table 2.1 Conditions for economic development in Poland since 1989

Variable	Characteristic
The state	• 'soft state' syndrome • weak public administration • low level of coordination between government agencies
Internationalization of economy	• dependent liberal economy • large share of foreign investors among the biggest companies • dominant role of foreign capital in the financial sector
Macroeconomic policy	• unclear vision of an economic order • unstable, inconsistent policy • limited accountability of government economic policy • weak democratic control
Microeconomic perspective	• inconsistency of the institutional environment • weakness of market and non-market mechanisms coordinating economic activities • low transparency in the transfer of public funds
Civil society	• weakness of social dialogue and civic activity • mixed, paternalistic, neocorporatist and neopluralist representation of interest • lack of civic pressure towards a more consistent institutional framework for the economy

close to the liberal market economy model in the Hall and Soskice classification. Leszek Balcerowicz, the chief architect of the neoliberal 'shock therapy' in Poland, explains this preference by pointing to the high efficiency and dynamism of the US economy at the time, calling it appropriate for a country building a new institutional system after communism.[1] The pattern, strongly supported by western governments and international economic institutions (Wedel 2001; Zielonka 2006), legitimized the interests of the new ruling elites, foreign investors and the new middle classes for whom commercialization, privatization and the creation of democracy opened up new career and financial advancement opportunities (Domański 2002; Gardawski 2001; Jasiecki 2002; Osborn and Slomczynski 2005).[2] An indication of the extent these opportunities were taken advantage of, as measured by the Gini coefficient, are the growing income and wealth inequalities: Poland belongs to the country group with the highest inequalities and apparently above the level of the other Visegrád countries (UNDP 2009).

A distinguishing feature of the political philosophy of the neoliberal elites in Poland was the adoption of a strict dichotomy between state and market. State institutions were considered contradictory to market needs. A consequence of this approach was to define the 'market revolution' in terms of individual ownership rights. The complexity of markets, their segmentation, power asymmetries and social embeddedness were widely ignored (cf. Smelser and Swedberg 1994). This dominant transformation paradigm reduced the concept of the market to competition, not noticing that it is also created by *agreements* between companies, alliances and networks. Commercialization and privatization were the major concerns. The market was considered the best coordinating mechanism of the economy, even though in mature market economies it is not the only mechanism (Stark and Bruszt 1998: 103–5).

With the domestic private sector weak after communism, the state remains the main driver of systemic changes in the creation and strengthening of capitalist market institutions. In contrast to other East Central European countries the state still holds significant shares in many large companies and is an important employer, manufacturer and purchaser of many goods and services. It has also been the leading organizer of adjustments to EU requirements, including legal changes and the management of structural funds. In spite of the clear preference of the political elites and the crucial role of state agencies in institution building, public institutions have not been reformed in accordance with a consciously selected paradigm.[3] Constant political and personnel changes have made reforms fragmentary, that is concerned with only parts of the economic order, which has led to their incongruity with the direction of transformation of other institutional spheres (Federowicz 2004). Solutions that often originated in different, frequently opposing institutional paradigms were implemented in a chaotic, parallel and uncoordinated manner.[4] From the VoC perspective, the neoclassical market system put in place in the 1990s in Poland faced the major problem of fragmentation, as it was based on a vision of capitalism that did not combine different institutions into a cohesive whole (ibid.). An early symbolic example of the lack of complementarity is the divergence between the constitutional provision stating that the basis of the Polish economic system is a 'social market economy' (Article 20 of the new constitution of 1997) and the practice of neoliberal economic policy by successive governments.

The most significant manifestation of the problem is the 'soft state' syndrome, as defined by Gunnar Myrdal (1970). Components of the Polish version of the syndrome include low efficacy of reforms, low effectiveness of public funds usage, arbitrariness of civil service decisions, power used to achieve private goals, corruption, gaps in the law as well as ineffective law enforcement, and low social discipline.[5] In certain spheres there is 'too much state' (regulations, bureaucratic control) and in others too little (law enforcement, public policies). This was confirmed by World Bank studies in 2009. The comparison of indicators such as 'perceptions of the quality of public services, the quality of the civil service and the degree of its independence from political pressures, the quality of policy formulation and implementation, and the credibility of the government's commitment to such policies' placed Poland only ahead of Romania and Bulgaria among EU countries (Kaufman *et al.* 2009). These can be interpreted as a confirmation of the persistence of 'soft state' syndrome despite the process of 'Europeanization', on-going since the mid-1990s, to raise the formal standards of democracy and governance in the public sphere.[6] Accession to the EU has had an ambivalent impact. On the one hand, harmonization with EU rules has strengthened the capacity of the Polish state to deal with the economy in line with the preferences of foreign investors for secure property rights and law enforcement. In the late 1990s EU negotiators also emphasized the need to strengthen public administration in order to properly manage EU structural funds. On the other hand, the accession has created extremely favourable conditions for foreign investors, especially for foreign direct investment (FDI) that drove the country toward a new economic dependency.

Foreign-led capitalism: multinational corporations as new key actors in the Polish economy

The low level of reliability of public institutions is linked to Poland's position in the international division of labour in comparison with developed capitalist states since this position translates into limited possibilities for action on the part of the government ('soft state' syndrome) and also shapes the further institutional development. Already, after a few years of transformation, scholars characterized the new economic system as the coexistence of a weak domestic capitalism, considerable state sector and dominant multinational corporations (MNCs) (Amsden *et al.* 1994; Berend 1996). Like other East Central European countries that joined the EU, Poland's development is based mainly on foreign capital and recently also on EU budget transfers.

Openness to international trade and foreign capital has become the crucial means to modernization for Poland's economy. With foreign-owned companies swiftly becoming the most competitive sector of the economy, their inclusion in international business networks, the benefits of scale and influx of investment capital they bring kick-starts growth and modernization. Currently, the share of companies with foreign capital, out of all companies in Poland, is nearly 40 per cent. Foreign capital controls 65 per cent of total exports from Poland and employs 28.6 per cent of all employees.[7] Foreign companies are also characterized by the highest wages and employee-training investments. Investors from the EU predominate, providing almost 87 per cent of the foreign capital invested in Poland. The biggest investors are the Netherlands, Germany and France, whose combined capital is 58 per cent of total foreign capital: the Netherlands furnishes 24 per cent of the total value of foreign capital, Germany 18 per cent, and France nearly 16 per cent.[8]

The strong position of foreign capital also permeates into other spheres of social life, for example, in the subordination of national elites to the culture and evaluation criteria of western centres, and the indiscriminate implementation of western political and economic ideas in an imitative way (Zarycki 2009). Another manifestation of such relations is the spatial management policy in big cities dominated by foreign investors who have an enormous impact on the transformation of urban areas, as in de-industrialization, office expansion, consumption patterns, construction of shopping centres and hypermarket chains, the organization of leisure, and changes to residential areas (Jałowiecki 2010; Jasiecki 2007).[9] The structural dominance of companies with foreign shareholders is reflected in the ranking of the 500 largest companies operating in Poland, published by the *Rzeczpospolita* newspaper. One-half of the most highly valued firms in the ranking are companies with majority foreign capital (49.8 per cent). A smaller group is comprised of state-owned enterprises (36.6 per cent) and private domestic companies. There is a group of relatively small domestic firms whose value constitutes only 13.6 per cent of the total value of companies, even though these private companies make up 161 of the total 500.[10] In other words, Polish private firms are much less valuable than foreign companies and domestic state companies. Foreign investors' share is even greater in the Polish banking sector: here they control about 70 per cent of capital, as compared with a 30 per cent average in 'old' EU member states.

The foreign-led strategy of modernization has thus had its price. Already in the early 1990s scholars observed that from a global perspective, the chosen road of development and growth based on the liberalization of trade with the West and free movement of foreign capital was defining the role of East Central Europe as a source of a relatively low-paid and medium-skilled work force and subcontracting companies in the interest of multinational business which produces specific risks and limits (Drahokoupil 2008; Lane 2010; Lane and Myant 2007; Bohle and Greskovits 2012).[11] A problematic consequence is the diminished control of the state over the domestic economic development as the realm of autonomous economic policy is limited. Hungarian studies have shown that the dominance of foreign investors pushes local companies into less profitable, slower-growing market niches, and that foreign banks usually give better financing conditions to MNCs (with which they have business relations in other markets as well) than to Hungarian firms (Laki 2007: 205–208). This also happens in Poland. When a foreign investor invests in a manufacturing company, the firm's bank account is transferred to the strategic investor's bank. In this way the foreign capital takes over strategic clients and takes away the best opportunities to generate profit from Polish banks (Miklaszewska 1998; Pieronkiewicz 1998). The dominance of foreign capital in the banks presented a new type of risk associated with fears that the owners might transfer financial assets to their headquarters. During the latest economic crises this led to a substantial reduction in lending by banks with foreign shareholders. And as an expert from the Polish Bank Association put it, 'as a country we do not have and in a foreseeable perspective we will not have a significant impact on the institutional and business structure of commercial banking' (ZBP 2010).

Inconsistent macroeconomic policy: development without strategy?

One of the key elements creating conditions for the development of the Polish economy is macroeconomic policy. Several factors have weakened any strategic macroeconomic approach in Polish politics until today: (1) the on-going ineffectiveness of state administration; (2) a fragmented political class; (3) the inconsistency of political reflection; (4) the low level of competence of centres of power in analysis and strategic planning (Kuzniar 2005). These factors also impede the implementation of modernization projects and their coordination.

One of the main problems of system transformation in Poland has been the lack of consistency and transparency of reforms after 1989. The 'target vision' for an economic order was gradually compromised. Even though all governments in power continued—with certain modifications—within the neoliberal economic policy started by the 'Balcerowicz plan', the rapid succession of governing coalitions resulted in significant variations being made in state priorities. Also, governments rarely prepared coherent long-term programmes of economic policy, such as for the restructuring of sectors such as mining, steel or shipbuilding. This was partly due to the ideological reluctance of new political elites to create growth strategies with the government's economic policy instruments, as these were associated with the central planning typical of state-driven socialism. Even when strategic, pro-development plans were adopted (such as the construction of highways or modernization of railway transport), they were not well translated into implementation systems. It is unfortunately the norm in Poland that public policy strategies and action programmes created by one government administration are usually stopped when a new government is formed.[12]

In 2009 a report compiled by advisors to Prime Minister Donald Tusk was published, entitled *Poland 2030*, which might be taken as the starting point for a 'new civilization project' aiming to modernize the country. Business associations have emphasized that the development of Poland requires a clear and coherent strategy of economic development that should be comprehensible to domestic and foreign investors. Implementation of the above strategy paper could have had a significant impact on choices made by entrepreneurs. But the lack of a plan for its financing, and later also the crisis in public finances, made it seem rather to be a diagnostic report than a practical tool for government policy (Boni 2009).

Poland has nevertheless developed some important institutions and systemic mechanisms for macroeconomic stabilization. Elements of continuity in the macro-economic policies of successive governments have been the exchange rate regime (floating or managed), an independent monetary policy, and a focus on attracting transnational corporations, typical for a 'dependent market economy' (Kuokstis 2011). An important element of macroeconomic stability are the provisions of the new Polish Constitution of 1997 which adopted a clause limiting the country's budget deficit and public debt levels to 60 per cent of annual gross domestic product (GDP). This policy may have contributed to Poland performing quite well during the European financial crisis in comparison to other EU countries.[13]

Yet, until 2011, no Polish government had been elected for a second term, which weakened the continuity and consistency of reforms and created a major barrier to the coherence of economic policy and institutional reforms. An example of the lack of systemic cohesion is the poor link between economic and social policies. The economic policy of Poland is usually regarded as close to neoliberal standards. However, comparison of different social policy models in the EU demonstrates that characteristics of this policy in Poland are similar to those of the South European capitalism. This model is ineffective from the point of view of employment and unfair in terms of the high poverty risk it brings. A big issue here is low labour-market participation both among the over-50s and young people under 24.[14]

A symptomatic manifestation of the weakness of the various governments' strategies and coordination was the closing down of nurseries and kindergartens (which had been transferred to local government authority during a demographic crisis caused by decreasing fertility rates). At the same time the government was searching for ways to mobilize women to join the labour market. Similarly, periods of significant economic growth were not used to carry out public finance reforms; health-service reforms were continually modified, and there were months of dispute over the direction of the pension reform first implemented ten years ago. Major policy decisions are still needed for improving the competitive environment for companies, guiding energy policy (including the diversification of oil and natural gas sources) and for supporting Polish brands, which are in crisis internally and on export markets (Jasiecki 2004). There has long been no consensus among the major parties on economic policy. In accordance with the new constitution of 1997, the executive power in Poland is divided between two centres: the government in power (usually a coalition) appointed by the Parliament, and a President, elected in a general election, who has negative legislative (veto) power.[15] In the years 2005–10 these two centres were in severe conflict, which also carried over into economic institutions, including the creation of relevant laws; the conflict also resulted in tensions between the government, the central bank and the financial supervision authority. The formation of a professional civil service has been slow and hindered by political parties and individual politicians who, as in Italy, tend to 'divide the loot' and exploit the state (Grzymała-Busse

2007). The reliability and consistency of economic policy is weakened by internal divisions in the government which are often aggravated by differences between coalition partners, as well as by the influence of various 'redistribution coalitions' and interest groups.

In these interest groups a major role is played by trade unions in large state companies and traditional sectors (energy, mining, railways etc.), by professional organizations (lawyers, doctors, teachers) and, from the mid-1990s, by foreign investors and leading domestic 'new capitalists' (Jasiecki *et al.* 2006). Many scholars also point out the weakness of democratic control over the state's economic policy (Federowicz 2004; Kowalik 2000; Ost 2005). The structural manifestation of this phenomenon is low trust in the political class and government, aversion to political parties and election turnouts lower than in other 'new democracies' in CEE. In Poland the average parliamentary election turnout after 1989 was the lowest among all post-socialist states that joined the EU: 45–50 per cent (while the average turnout for the majority of states in this group is 60–70 per cent).[16]

The microeconomic perspective: structural barriers to entrepreneurship

Limitations and incongruities in macroeconomic policy have microeconomic consequences. Inept governance has weakened the position of Polish companies, and the inconsistent institutional environment causes difficult operating conditions for firms. The *Doing Business* report, comparing such conditions, placed Poland at a distant sixty-second position among 183 countries (World Bank 2012). This illustrates only indirectly the weakness of market and non-market economic coordination mechanisms at breaking down the old structural growth barriers to the effectiveness of Polish companies. New studies of relations between companies and state administration give direct insight into this subject. Despite favourable institutional changes related to, among other things, adaptation to EU standards, interviewed entrepreneurs and managers point to continued barriers to doing business: over-volatility of legislation, difficulties in raising capital (high costs, conditions of loan guarantees) and government failure to meet deadlines in administrative decisions (Górniak 2010). Managers in all types of firms have highlighted the low efficiency of the economic court system which increases tolerance of illegal activities, manifesting itself in the lengthiness of court proceedings and significant delays in the payment of settlements after court decisions. Among firms studied which obtained such decisions, 49 per cent waited over one year for payments and 16 per cent over two years.

The latest symptom of the ineffectiveness of state economic policy on the micro-level is the failure of the government package to deal with the economic crisis. The above-mentioned study also shows that only one per cent of Polish companies have used solutions offered in the package. The following reasons were given: bureaucracy (47 per cent); lack of need due to good financial situation of company (37 per cent); lack of knowledge about instruments in the package

(37 per cent); and mismatch between proposed instruments and companies' needs (31 per cent) (ibid.).

Another frequently discussed problem is the insufficient transparency of transfers of public money to the private sector, a legacy of post-socialist standards and 'political capitalism' of the early stage of transformation and the subsequent 'soft state' situation. A symptom of this phenomenon is the controversy around the public procurement system generally associated with abuse of power and corruption that still hampers the development of public-private partnership, and decreases the number and scale of economic projects. Foreign investors including well-known IT and pharmaceutical companies are also involved in these controversies.[17] Consequently, studies of companies' competitiveness underscore a long-term pessimism expressed in conclusions such as: 'to demonstrate one's entrepreneurship in Poland is still much more difficult, labour-intensive and exhausting than in other countries'; and, 'the institutional infrastructure of the Polish economy fails to create a friendly environment for entrepreneurship and competitiveness' (Radomski 2010: 241).[18]

Civil society: a new kind of apathy

The last element of the institutional environment to be discussed here is the development of civil society, which determines citizens' ability to influence the creation of a rational economic framework. The condition of civil society is important to understanding labour relations as well as preferences and behaviour of social actors in the whole system of representation of interests. Poland has a strong tradition of civic activity, including dissidents, democratic opposition and the *Solidarity* movement in the state-socialism era. However, today only relatively few Poles get involved in societal initiatives. It is hard to disagree with those scholars who maintain that the predominant features of the public sphere in the entire CEE region are the activity of elites and apathy of the wider societies (Borragan and de Waele 2006). After an increase in independent social initiatives at the beginning of the 1990s, for the last few years an unwillingness to participate in public life has prevailed. Even though Poland is at the top of the 'Freedom House NGO Sustainability Index' rankings on the strength and overall viability of civil society organizations among CEE countries, in comparison with Western Europe the weaknesses of Polish civil society are noticeable in several dimensions such as 1) structures characterized by limited involvement and small numbers of non-governmental organization (NGO) members, weak financial condition, rather low levels of participation of volunteers and small amounts of time they devote to NGO work; 2) their weak impact on decisions taken by authorities, and 3) the little support they get from political and institutional environments, as seen in the reluctance of elites and unfavourable legal solutions.

An important barrier to the development of civil society in Poland lies in the aggressive and conflictual style of party leaders who tend towards populism in the still post-authoritarian political culture.[19] The opportunities for realizing a civil society are also weakened by the small size of the middle class and significant level of social exclusion (marginalization of the unemployed, the rural population and the elderly), as well as massive foreign employment migration (the highest in the EU).

The main features of the Polish variant of capitalism

Having drawn a general outline of the political, institutional and structural background of the new system that defined growth conditions of the Polish economy after 1989, I will now analyse the standard dimensions of the VoC approach: the financial system and corporate governance in companies, labour relations, inter-firm relations, education and occupational training. These dimensions, together with selected significant indicators, are presented in Table 2.2.

Table 2.2 The Polish variant of capitalism

Institutional dimensions in VoC	Characteristic institutional features	Indicators
Financial system and corporate governance	• underdeveloped capital market • corporate governance at an early stage of development • asymmetric protection of ownership rights	• limited access to capital • poor or medium quality work of many supervisory boards • weak position of minority shareholders
Labour relations	• poor institutionalization of employer-employee bargaining • low participation of employees in decision-making • weak trade unions • weak employers' associations • decentralization of collective bargaining • weak position of employees on the labour market ('employer's market')	• lack of, or weak collective agreements • limited representation of employee interests • very low rate of trade union membership • weakness of business associations • workplace-level negotiations play predominant role • mass structural unemployment
Inter-firm relations	• collapse of the centrally coordinated economy • fragmentation, poor cooperation and weak strategic alliances • strongly varying innovativeness of companies operating in Poland	• mass emergence of new private firms, new forms of cooperation • few joint projects • low level of innovation in domestic companies
Education and training systems	• predominant role of general education liberalization and commercialization of education	• disparity between educational structure and labour market • weak occupational training

Poland, even after accession to the EU, is still ranked among the 'emerging markets' or 'advanced emerging markets'.[20] Applying the VoC analytical tools to Poland at a relatively early stage of institutionalization and in the light of the previous analysis, it is difficult to describe its key institutions simply as clearly liberal, however the liberal components predominate in industrial relations or education and training systems. In another institutional dimension rather as a hybrid that includes strong elements of foreign-led capitalism and partly features closer to the continental structure of the Austrian or the South European (role of state enterprises, corporate governance) or cultural and organizational patterns inherit from the state-socialism era (lack of transparency, elements of corporatism, management standard). It is still an open question in which direction Poland political economy will develop further, and whether the dependency described above can be translated into a more balanced economy.

The financial system and corporate governance: the consolidation of new practices

The liberal market economy model is based on a developed financial services sector, public information about companies, high mobility and availability of capital, and regulators tolerant of acquisitions and takeovers (Hall and Soskice 2001). The financial sector in such a model is characterized by high sophistication of the financial market, high level of importance of institutional investors, high protection of minority shareholders, low ownership concentration, and an active market in corporate control, that is takeovers, mergers and acquisitions, and the development of venture capital (Amable 2003). Most of these features have not been developed in Poland. Financial experts also emphasize the weaknesses of the Polish banking system, such as the infrastructural deficit (the need for technological advances), the capital gap (relatively few resources, state fiscalism), the product gap (low quantity and quality of services) and the cost gap (high fees) (Miklaszewska 1998).

Even though over the last few years there has been significant progress in filling in the infrastructure gap, and the financial sector is one of the most modern sectors of the economy through its transnationalization, the cost gap, the capital gap and the product gap are still features of the banking sector in Poland. Similarly, if only for the lengthy administrative and court procedures, it is difficult to talk about an active market for corporate control, and there is still insufficient protection of minority shareholders due to weak law enforcement. Also the venture capital market is at an early stage of development.[21] Because private companies and the business culture associated with them are relatively new, the notion of corporate governance in Poland is itself a new issue.[22] Market reform initiators regarded the Anglo-Saxon model of corporate governance as the ideal and built the state market regulation system to resemble it. However, in the environment of recent ownership transformation, a weak capital market, ownership concentration among strategic investors, and a low level of financing of companies by banks, it turned out that the Anglo-Saxon model based on external company control could not be implemented.[23]

Where corporate governance does operate well, it is mainly in companies or sectors controlled by headquarters of transnational companies, such as the banking or automotive industry. Otherwise, control mechanisms are underdeveloped in the availability of information, capital controls, product controls (e.g., financial products) and competitive manager markets. Also, cultural and organizational patterns inherited from the state-socialism era and the first years of transformation and which define the social interpretations of management standards are not what they are in the UK or US. The two-tier governance system, predominance of internal controls as well as state ownership contributed to a lack of transparency of the Polish corporate governance system. In practice, the model (especially in domestic firms) is close to the Latin variant and, partly, the Continental European legal system. At the same time management styles of Polish business leaders are generally similar to the Anglo-American pattern of individualism and strong personal leadership positions in companies. However, in contrast, Polish managers often exhibit the 'lone wolf' syndrome, that is poor ability to establish alliances, loyalty and cooperation with different institutions (Koźmiński 2011). As a result, the organizational culture of Polish domestic companies has a paternalistic character. The same situation obtains in foreign companies, only modified and combined with the standards of the corporate owners. Generally, a Polish model of corporate governance is only emerging. There is the possibility of its further evolution in the direction of the German-Japanese model of internal supervision, or Anglo-American model with dominant external supervision (Lis and Sterniczuk 2005).

Labour relations: the erosion of employee representation

The principal feature of current labour relations in Poland is the lack of organized labour. The erosion of collective structures for workers' interest representation is part of the process discussed above. Gardawski (2009) referred to this process as the 'establishment of an ineffective model of the trade union movement'.

The weakening of organized labour had both internal and external causes. External reasons include the decline of the industrial base due to the new level of global competition after the opening of the market, the subsequent deindustrialization, commercialization and privatization which have changed the labour market and employment structures radically. In the Polish context, the factor of key significance is the creation of new jobs primarily in the small and medium-sized enterprise sector (in which there are hardly any trade unions). Yet, the fundamental problem of trade unions in Poland was the constant very high unemployment rate, reaching 20 per cent of the total number of employees at the turn of the twenty-first century in spite of economic recovery after the economic shock.

To the internal causes of the decline belong the organizational plurality, especially in the new private sector, and the escalation of political divisions among the unions that contributed to the lack of confidence of employees in collective interest representations. Another characteristic specific to Poland was the direct involvement of trade unions in politics. As Polish civil society was weak, *Solidarity* represented a major source of new political parties. As an effect of this trend, trade union cadres moved over to politics, administration and business, which led to a flagrant decline of *Solidarity* as a union and accelerated the erosion of worker representation in general.[24] *Solidarity* leaders established or supported mainly liberal and conservative parties that also contributed to the decline of the movement. They embraced the neoliberal reforms and abandoned the idea of workers' participation in the name of modernization, and facilitated the withdrawal of companies from social functions funded out of union administration funds, including vocational training. As a result, the percentage of union members among the total population of adult Poles now amounts to 6 per cent, and their percentage among hired workers decreased from 33 per cent to 17 per cent in the period 1995–2004. The highest rate of trade union membership (over 20 per cent) is observed in the public sector (EC 2006: 24–5).

Another indicator of the weakness of trade unions is the decentralization of collective labour agreements and their scarcity at the firm level. In Poland company negotiations with a low level of coordination is the predominant form of bargaining (Boni 2009: 107). Only a minority of employees in Poland are covered by collective bargaining, which takes place largely at company level. The coverage rate does not exceed 25 per cent and is diminishing. In general, equivalent agreements are not concluded in domestic private firms. In this respect, Poland belongs to the group of EU member states with a decentralized wage bargaining system, like the UK and Baltic states, where industry-wide bargaining has yielded its place to payroll decisions at the firm level (EIRO 2010: 9). The elimination of the various forms of worker representation and coordination is related to the situation on the labour market that turned into an employer's market. Besides the high unemployment rates, Poland, like Spain and Portugal, has one of the highest European percentages of persons declaring themselves employed on termed employment and has the highest number of persons who have remained out of work for 12 months or longer (36 per cent).[25]

A low level of coordination of activities is also a characteristic of trade and employer associations, in which membership is not obligatory. They have relatively few members and are quite weak organizationally, which reduces their negotiation position with regard to both the state and trade unions. Their members are mainly large and medium-sized companies, while the majority of small companies do not belong to them. There are five main associations with an employer function who are members of the Tripartite Commission: Employers of Poland, Polish Confederation of Private Employers 'Leviathan', Business Centre Club, and Polish Crafts Association. However, employers' interests are internally divided according to various criteria, including size (large/small), ownership (state-owned/private), origin of capital (domestic/foreign), and political preferences (liberal/neocorporative). Despite these limitations they are particularly influential participants in the interest-representation system, which is due to the logic of market changes but also the type of rhetoric used by their leaders, as well as the material resources of the companies. Compared to other social actors they have the best financial and professional membership basis—renowned leaders and experts (including numerous former government members), legal services,

PR agencies and lobbyists, and good relations with political decision-makers to whom they frequently offer their financial, media and organizational backing (Jasiecki 2002; 2008a).

Inter-firm relations: weak institutional support for business collaboration

The depth and scope of systemic changes in the economy have also radically transformed the structure and manner of the operation of business entities. Still, despite the political aim of an economy corresponding closely to LME, the practice of Polish capitalism has significantly diverged. In the liberal model, market relations are structured by enforceable formal contracts over which rules are specified by regulatory bodies working to stabilize business activities and lower transaction costs. The economic, institutional, and cultural environment immediately after 1989, however, has been weak in enforcing formal contracts between economic actors. To this situation contributed the 'soft state' syndrome, the fragmentariness and inconsistency of reforms, and the immature system of corporate governance, including blurred property rights and barely predictable business operation conditions, often referred to as 'wild capitalism'.

The situation began to change rapidly from the mid-nineties with the influx of foreign capital. Most foreign-owned companies worked (or still work) with local businesses at arm's length, initially reinforced by political decisions (especially in terms of participation in the privatization of state-owned banks and enterprises or companies operating in special economic zones). The foreign companies introduced new forms of coordination through the integration of subsidiaries and subcontractors in their transnational networks. Foreign investment started to foster new kinds of competition and cooperation between domestic firms by encouraging mergers and acquisitions and the creation of larger capital groups. The coexistence of large state-owned enterprises, mostly new small domestic businesses, and foreign companies produced a mosaic of diverse strategies and organizational cultures. Previous corporate bonds were cut and the new ones of very distinct character were introduced and are still being developed. The EU structural funds are important here because they demand regional collaboration. In the context of the international economic crisis the government also began more actively to promote public–private partnerships in the financial sector (increasing the share of domestic capital in banks), the chemical industry and energy. In recent years an additional stimulus to the coordination of major infrastructure projects was the organization of the European Football Championships 'Euro 2012', organized by Poland and the Ukraine.

At the same time, delays in the construction of highways and bankruptcy of large construction companies during the biggest building boom since 1989 illustrate the limitations of the current model of private–public partnership, especially the dysfunctionality of public procurement procedures, and shows the weakness of business relationships between companies (e.g., when companies do not pay each other for work done by smaller companies). Employer and business associations rarely contribute to organize sectoral cooperation of companies as they are weak. They have limited competence by law. This weak institutional support does nothing to encourage cooperation between companies which constrains mainly smaller domestic business, while foreign-owned companies with their greater economic resources are less dependent on institutional support and have developed effective patterns of business cooperation on their own.

The weakness of the current relationship between economic actors is manifested especially in the low innovativeness of domestic companies. According to Scoreboard there is a much lower rate of patents and registered brands in Poland than on average in the EU. On the EU scale average research and development outlays are 1.9 per cent of GDP. In Poland in 2008 this kind of outlay was 0.61 per cent of GDP in comparison to that of the Czech Republic at 1.47 per cent and Slovenia at 1.66 per cent. The links between science, academic centres and business are weak, and the share of innovative companies is smaller than Western Europe's (Zerka 2010: 14). The Polish system is comparable to those of the poorly performing Southern European countries (Amable 2003: 92). The main mechanism of transfer of innovations is intra-firm transfer within transnational companies.

The educational and training systems: poor adjustment to the labour market

The lack of institutional complementarity and generation of a synergy effect by cooperation between various social actors is also present in the sphere of education and vocational training. Analyses of intellectual capital lead to the conclusion that 'Poland is not well prepared to compete in the world as a knowledge-based society' (Boni 2009: 232).[26] In Poland, following the LME logic, the emphasis has been put on general skills. Facing the constant high level of unemployment following the 'shock therapy' at the beginning of the 1990s, the assumption was made that the optimal way to solve the problem was to abandon narrow professional specialization and to increase the level of general higher education, since it was judged easier for employees with such an education to adapt to the needs of employers. Vocational schools have been disappearing and the state budget has continually reduced.[27] Consequently, attractiveness and quality of professional education decreased. Liberalization and commercialization of education created room for new, mainly private, tertiary-education schools specializing in management and economics. Despite the very low government expenditures for tertiary education in comparison to the Organisation for Economic Co-operation and Development (OECD) average (*c.* 0.6 per cent of GDP in Poland as against an OECD average of *c.* one per cent), the number of students has increased dramatically with the emergence of a dynamic market for private education. The current number of tertiary students is close to two million and the enrolment rate in the 19–24 age group has reached one of the highest levels in Europe (48 per cent) and the sixth highest in the world. The education boom was fostered by the (until recently) high return on investment in higher education (salary accrual for each year of education), as the percentage of people with higher education was quite low under state-socialist conditions.

However, this success has a negative flipside. According to the World Bank (2004: 36), for many years Poland lacked a clear strategy or a coherent vision of tertiary education which would allow higher education establishments to meet the expectations of the labour market. The fast and uncontrolled increase of private tertiary education has deteriorated its quality. In the opinion of employers, the Polish system of education is poorly adjusted to the needs of the economy (Sztanderska 2010). The professional structure and skills of graduates are inadequate, which is confirmed by, among other indicators, the unemployment rate among graduates with various qualifications. In fact, the unemployment rate is rising rapidly among young people, especially among those with university degrees. At the same time, vocational and technical schools produce the weakest students, educational standards are low, and their technical equipment is outdated, while the best-skilled workers continue to emigrate to Western Europe for better paid jobs.[28] As a result, employers have difficulty finding people with proper qualifications. Also levels of adult learners are dramatically low.

In this situation, the business approach to vocational education began to change. In particular, larger companies are more and more active in building their own internal training systems. Also, the government recently launched a new plan to change the educational system, and vocational training gained new support from business associations and unions. The reforms aimed to introduce new teacher training, carry out labour-market research, develop new programmes and a new list of professions and new rules for examinations. The current government is also working on implementing a new system for monitoring the labour market and the careers of graduates, and has proposed regulatory solutions in the sphere of science and higher education.

Business leaders: background, social orientations and attitudes towards economic institutions

Rainer M. Lepsius (2007) notes that during the formation of the Federal Republic of Germany, the creation of new political institutions took place before the formation of a new political culture. A similar phenomenon, although in other circumstances, also occurred in Poland a half-century later, after the dissolution of the communist regime. New market institutions were also created – before the emergence of individual and collective actors in the market economy such as private entrepreneurs, a middle class, financial elite, employer organizations and political parties articulating the interests of the business class. After two decades there have arisen in different spheres of social life a new business elite and middle class who have influence through employer associations, private media, social and cultural associations, and ensure the representation of their interests by political parties and professional lobbying. In terms of institutional analysis, business leaders (especially from foreign companies and big domestic private companies) are not only 'rule-takers', but also have become 'rule-makers', clearly representing their own interests, views, and preferences at all levels and in all dimensions of social life (Osborn and Slomczynski 2005; Domański 2002; Jasiecki 2002; Gardawski 2001).

Our survey questioned members of managerial staff of industrial firms and financial institutions (CEOs, members of the management board, directors). Some of them were drawn from a random sample of industrial companies employing 50–999 employees prepared by the Central Statistical Office: 104 interviews were conducted with representatives of this category; 44 other interviews were carried out with respondents from industrial companies on the ranking list of the 500 largest Polish companies published by the *Rzeczpospolita* newspaper in 2009. The same ranking was used to select financial institutions (banks and insurance companies) for the 19 interviews conducted in cooperation with the Polish Banks Association. The survey was carried out between July 2009 and March 2010 using the method of computer-assisted telephone interviewing (CATI), but the majority of interviews were conducted by September 2009. Some interviews were carried out directly by pollsters. The response rate was in each category of companies relatively low, which is, however, frequent in business surveys, as respondents in top positions are usually difficult to reach. It was about 20 per cent for industrial companies selected at random, and we achieved a similar figure for financial institutions and industrial companies of more than 1,000 employees.

The interviews were conducted beginning with companies from the top of the ranking list; however, refusals and scheduling difficulties caused many of these interviewees to be replaced with respondents from lower-ranking companies. The interviews were conducted solely with Poles: 92 executive managers (CEOs), 61 executive committee members (deputy CEOs, board directors), eight plant managers and four others. In our analyses the focus of interest was the diversity of company attributes, the characteristics and opinions of respondents related to the size and type of companies, and to the form of ownership. In accordance with the other chapters of this book, three categories of industrial firms were differentiated: medium-size (50–249 employees); large (250–999 employees); and the largest (≥1000 employees). With regard to ownership, companies owned by predominantly foreign investors, state-owned companies and domestic private companies (divided into medium-size and large companies) were analysed. Answers of respondents from the finance sector were analysed separately.

Human and cultural capital: the advantages of foreign investors and financial institutions

Table 2.3 presents the basic distinguishing social features of Polish business leaders in the survey in four categories: age, education level, type of education and professional mobility. On average, in the range of 46–9 years old. The average ages of managers of companies from individual categories do not show any fundamental variance. In almost all categories of companies, with the exception of foreign companies, the largest group of executives are aged 50–9 years. Polish business leaders are getting older, which can be interpreted as an indicator that in the coming years there will be personnel and generational changes in top positions in many companies. The next group consists of managers aged 40–9 years. They dominate in foreign companies, financial institutions and state-owned enterprises. Managers in their sixties, and older, predominate in the medium-sized industrial companies and state-owned enterprises.

More variable correlations are visible if we focus on the characteristics of the age of business leaders guided by the criterion of ownership. They show an interesting effect of the influence of foreign companies on the managerial market in terms of age of respondents. Most young managers under 39 years (28 per cent) and in the interval of 40–9 years (38.5 per cent) are employed in companies with predominantly foreign investors. They also have the lowest age average and

Table 2.3 Selected characteristics of Polish business leaders: age, education and professional mobility

	Foreign companies (partly or completely)	Financial institutions	State-owned companies	Industrial companies 50–249	Industrial companies ≥ 250
Sample size[a]	N=40	N=19	N=23	N=56	N=29
Age (% per category):					
39 years and under	28.2	15.8	4.8	16.7	27.6
40–49	38.5	31.6	28.6	22.2	17.2
50–59	25.6	47.4	42.9	33.3	44.8
60 years and over	7.7	5.3	23.8	27.8	10.3
Age – average	44.2	47.4	52.5	50.2	47.5
Age – median	41	49	53	51	50
Higher education	92.5	100.0	90.5	76.8	96.6
in technology[b]	45.0	15.8	42.9	37.5	48.3
in business[b]	32.5	57.9	38.1	23.2	24.1
Doctoral degree[b]	10.0	21.1	9.5	3.6	6.9
Number of positions in professional career					
Average	3.4	4.9	4.2	3.8	4.6
Median	3	5	4	3	4
Percentage of respondents in managerial position before 1989	25.6	36.8	50.0	55.6	51.7

Notes

a In the table are given the number of responses from different sectors of companies. Calculations for some variables, however, are based in some cases on slightly smaller numbers. For example, we have information about the age of 39 (not 40) respondents from foreign companies. We do not give this information every time because it could impede the readers' comprehension of the tables. But we do mention it in the analysis, if the analysis concerns a significantly smaller number of companies.

b The basis for the calculation of percentages is all respondents from a given sector of companies.

median (see Table 2.3). The highest average age of business leaders is among the state-owned enterprises (52.5 years) and medium-sized industrial companies (50.2 years). For the sake of comparison, in foreign companies and in financial institutions the average age is much lower (respectively 44.2 and 47.4 years). Generally, business leaders from foreign companies and financial institutions are younger than their counterparts in state-owned enterprises and domestic private industrial companies which have the most executives over sixty.

Nearly 80 per cent of those polled in smaller firms, and almost all respondents from larger firms, have higher education degrees. In industrial companies, especially the large ones, there is a relatively large share of persons with degrees in technology and engineering. The high percentage reflects the pattern of managerial careers under state socialism when manufacturing was of key importance (Lane *et al.* 2007).[29] Managers of financial institutions stand out here: they all have a tertiary education (100 per cent) and the highest percentage of respondents with business degrees (almost 58 per cent), but also the most with doctorates (21 per cent). If the holding of a doctoral degree is a measure of a high cultural capital, managers of financial institutions clearly have the highest level of such capital. The number of managerial positions in which they were employed since embarking on their careers partly illustrates the dynamics of professional mobility. It is hard to say whether it reflects a stable career pattern or is predominantly result of the turbulent transition period of the last 20 years. The financial sector has been subjected to profound transformations in the last 20 years as a result of the high influx of foreign capital, this may account for the high frequency of managers switching jobs/companies that we observed among managers of financial institutions (4.9).Those transformations created demand for new personnel holding degrees in fields other than technology and applied sciences, degrees which were often obtained abroad.[30]

When we focus on the characteristics of business leaders according to the criteria of ownership and sector, is evident that management in foreign companies and financial institutions have a much smaller share of respondents who occupied managerial positions under the communist regime. This is of course linked to age and indicates that both kinds of companies have promoted managers who developed their personal competencies and qualifications under the new market conditions. Just 25.6 per cent of respondents from companies with predominantly foreign capital and 36.8 per cent of executives of financial institutions had occupied managerial positions before 1989 (see Table 2.3). In state-owned enterprises and industrial companies in the hands of domestic owners, more than half of the executives (50 per cent and nearly 56 per cent respectively) occupied managerial positions under the *ancien régime*.

Our results suggest a segmentation of the managerial market which illustrates the structural implications of foreign-led capitalism in Poland. Companies and financial institutions mostly controlled by foreign capital have advantages in human and cultural capital compared to domestic firms, both state and private. In terms of human capital the advantage is younger executives, especially in foreign companies. In terms of cultural capital the advantages are the universality of higher education and the significant share of managers with doctorates, which also distinguishes the managers of financial institutions (employing also the largest number of people with a diploma in business studies). Senior management in the financial sector also stand out by their high rate of occupational mobility. Domestic companies, both state-owned and private, tend to employ older executives who often occupied managerial positions before 1989 and rarely hold doctorates. There is a relatively large share of engineers among them but, interestingly, not as many as in the foreign-owned companies.

The internationalization of management: foreign investors and trips abroad

As argued before, the Polish transition to a market economy and the accession to the EU led to an internationalization of management measured by (among other things) foreign participation as shareholders, by the internationalization of careers (studying and working abroad), and the emergence of new kinds of social and professional identification of executives that go beyond national categories. Table 2.4 shows that, in accordance with the foreign-led modernization-thesis, foreign investors own the largest share of financial institutions and large industrial companies in our sample. They do not have any part-ownership in smaller private companies, and only very small shares of state-owned enterprises. The percentage of persons who have studied abroad for any length of time also is highest for financial institutions and large industrial companies. A similar picture is obtained by comparing the average number of months spent at foreign universities. Interestingly, far more respondents worked abroad than studied, and in this respect industrial firms and financial institutions do not differ significantly.[31] This finding indicates that the transnational networks of foreign companies are also open for Polish managers to gain experience abroad. The lowest percentage of respondents with international working experience we found was in state companies, where the percentages were even lower than for medium-sized companies (see Table 2.4). Studying and working abroad are, therefore, important indicators of the fragmentation and diversity of cultural capital in various types of companies, and of the unequal distribution of such opportunities.

Another important aspect of the internationalization of management is the self-identification of executives. Modernization, economic development, and globalization have led people to rethink their identities and to redefine them. The question of identity has become a very important issue in Poland since the 1990s, particularly in the context of the resurgence of national sovereignty and EU accession. However, identity is a multidimensional, complex phenomenon. Research into identity distinguishes different types: subjective and objective, individual and collective, affective, cognitive, etc. (Shabad and Słomczyński 2010).

In our survey, we focused on the cognitive aspect of the identity of respondents. The executives were asked 'How important is the following item for your self-characterization on a scale of 1 to 5?' The items were 'my religion', 'my nationality', 'my company', 'my profession', 'my family', 'my local community',

Table 2.4 Internationalization of management: study and work abroad, share of foreign ownership in companies, and self-characterization of executives

	Foreign companies	Financial institutions	State companies	Industrial companies 50–249	Industrial companies ≥ 250
Percentage of companies with partial or full foreign ownership	100.0	84.2	9.5	0.0	0.0
Percentage share of foreign ownership – average[a]	90.0	65.4	2.7	0.0	0.0
Percentage of respondents who studied abroad	17.5	42.1	14.3	10.7	6.9
Average number of months spent at universities abroad[b]	5.1	11.2	2.3	2.0	3.3
Percentage of respondents who worked abroad after completing education	70.0	47.4	19.0	37.5	41.4
Average number of months spent in employment abroad[c]	16.5	16,2	2.7	7.4	8.1
Percentage of respondents whose self-characterization stresses:					
Family	92.5	94.7	90.5	96.4	96.6
Company	87.5	84.2	81.0	94.6	93.1
Profession	85.0	84.2	66.7	87.5	79.3
Nationality	75.0	63.2	76.2	89.3	75.9
Local community	67.5	63.2	66.7	78.6	65.5
Europe	65.0	63.2	42.9	71.4	58.6
Global business class	55.0	52.6	42.9	50.0	37.9
Religion	50.0	31.6	61.9	55.4	48.3

Notes
a For the purpose of calculating the average, 0 value was assumed for companies with full Polish ownership.
b For the purpose of calculating the average, 0 value was assumed for persons who never studied abroad.
c For the purpose of calculating the average, 0 value was assumed for persons who never worked abroad.

'Europe' and 'the global business class'. Answers ranged from 'very important' to 'unimportant'. The bottom rows of Table 2.4 show the significance of the various terms in the respondents' self-identification. The hierarchy of self-description of Polish business leaders is rather traditional and conservative. Most respondents give categories such as family, company and profession a high priority. The lowest level of self-characterization stressing 'profession' is in state-owned companies

(66.7 per cent). This may reflect the frequent informal practice in these companies that the nomination of executives is anti-meritocratic, political in nature, linked to electoral cycles or governments in power.

In general, the percentage of respondents perceiving themselves as Europeans or part of a 'global business class' is strikingly high, even if we take the statements only as superfluous declarations. The percentage for both items is much higher in Poland than in Hungary, and regarding Europe also higher compared to East and West Germans. This corresponds to the positive image of Europe in the wider Polish society. It is highest for managers in foreign-owned companies and financial institutions. Yet it is also curiously high in industrial companies of fewer than 250 employees – these show the highest percentage of 'Europeans', but also of respondents identifying themselves with their nation (Table 2.4). As expected, self-identification with 'the global business class' was most frequent among respondents from foreign companies (55 per cent) and from financial institutions (52.6 per cent). The least frequent was among domestic industrial companies employing over 250 persons (37.9 per cent) and executives from state-owned enterprises (42.9 per cent), who are also behind the others when it comes to Europe.

How consistent are self-characterizations of Polish business leaders as Europeans and as part of the 'global business class' with the overall high level of national identification? They can be seen as an expression of the new identity of Poles which consists in both the feeling of national identity and a strong sense of belonging to a transnational community. At the same time, cosmopolitan identifications with the global business class are more frequent in foreign companies and in financial institutions—the most globalized sectors (Huntington 2005; Castells 2004).

The term 'nationality' was rarely chosen as important by (in comparison to other respondents) executives from financial institutions (63 per cent), coherent with the nature of their sector, that is the most transnational and with the largest scale of operations (the sample consisted of mainly local branches of MNCs).

The greatest diversity of views among respondents from other groups of companies concerned – besides responses to 'nationality' and 'global business class' – community and religion. Community was most often chosen as important by managers from industrial companies of medium size, which are relatively the most oriented to local markets. For state companies, medium-size and large industrial companies this identification was less strong than religion. Executives in state enterprises are not only the group with the least commitment to 'Europe' and the 'global business class' but with the strongest identification with religion. Only respondents from financial institutions and foreign companies classified religion as the least important category for a self-characterization. However, among the other groups of the respondents religion was more rarely chosen than all other categories except 'global business class'. Thus, religious identity is not a strong factor of self-identification for business leaders, especially in financial institutions. This result is interesting given that Poland is generally considered a very religious country. As we expected, concepts seen as typical for conservatives such as family, company, nationality, profession, local community and religion are particularly important to executives of medium-sized industrial companies.

Corporate purposes: profit and the common good

Corporate purposes may be defined in many ways. Companies may focus mainly on increasing profit, or, on the achievement of broader objectives, which is illustrated by the discussions surrounding 'corporate social responsibility' (CSR). In this context, Polish business leaders' definitions of the purposes of companies provide important information also on their interpretation of the social role of entrepreneurs and managers. In the sociology of Weber's tradition, subjects of this kind are examined by looking at the influence of value systems, norms and attitudes predominant in company management, in employer–employee relations and in state–business relations (Hofstede and Hofstede 2005; Hampden-Turner and Trompenaars 1993). Contemporary institutional analysis emphasizes the idea that actors and institutions are constitutive of one another, and that both are socially constructed and interdependent. Economic actors are constrained by institutions. However, when – as in CEE – the institutional form of capitalism is weak, the views of company executives as new 'rule-makers', not only on the micro-level, take on a particular importance. Their attitudes and behaviour are relevant to other economic actors, as the 'subjective expectations about the behaviour of other actors coordinate the strategic choices of individual agents' (Jackson 2010: 66).

In our research we focused on selected aspects of this question such as the perceptions of executives of the definition of companies' objectives and social functions, their perception of the role of government in the economy, and of cooperation with social partners. Table 2.5 presents respondents' attitudes towards the first of the above-mentioned dimensions. The majority of respondents agree that the objective of a firm is to maximize profit, which is the microeconomic standard of neoclassical economy. The most influential version of this approach in

Table 2.5 Defining purposes and social functions of enterprises

Percentage of respondents who agree[a] with the opinion:	Foreign companies	Financial institutions	State companies	Industrial companies 50–249	Industrial companies ≥ 250
The goal of a company has to be maximizing profit	67.5	68.4	57.1	57.1	65.5
Social responsibility of companies consists only of increasing profits	32.5	42.1	9.5	34.5	26.8
Companies should do more for the local community than what is required by law	47.5	42.1	52.4	58.9	44.8
In principle, companies are also responsible for the public weal	65.0	47.4	61.9	71.0	65.5

Note
a Respondents answered 'I fully agree' or 'I agree'.

recent decades is 'shareholder value' (SV) as the new global norm for the rules governing economic activity. 'The increased orientation to SV is itself driven by pressures from financial investors. With greater financialization, both shareholders and managers begin to view the firm as collection of assets, with the primary criterion for managing each of those assets being maximum profit extraction' (Deeg 2010: 328). This attitude is particularly evident in the responses from executives of largest industrial companies and financial institutions, which seem to confirm the view of those critics of contemporary capitalism who claim that large corporations, in their legal setup and objectives, are by definition directed towards multiplying their market value and profits and maximizing the externalization of costs (Galbraith 2004). Executives from large industrial companies (69.2 per cent), financial institutions (68.4 per cent) and foreign companies (67.5 per cent) agree the most with the profit-maximizing statement. These are companies substantially involved in transnational economic relations and which are also characterized by a significant or decisive ownership share on the part of foreign investors.

The agreement with maximization of profit as the only goal of a company is less often expressed by respondents from medium-sized industrial companies and from state-owned enterprises (both around 57 per cent), which generally are more oriented to the Polish market and have a smaller share of foreign capital. While also the idea that the social responsibility of companies is limited only to increasing profit was most strongly supported by managers from financial institutions (42.1 per cent), the lowest level of agreement with this claim was among respondents from state-owned companies (9.5 per cent).

At the same time a significant proportion of Polish business leaders' attitudes are in accordance with the broader concept of CSR, that is that companies should do more for the community than what is required by law. Thus it is difficult to say that Polish business leaders are against including social aspects in company activities (see for more Chapter 7). Interestingly, only persons who studied abroad agree relatively frequently that firms are responsible for the community and should do more than the law requires. Other variables were not relevant in this matter. They are presented in Table 2.6.

The first column contains R^2 in Table 2.6 measures for all variables.[32] The second column contains individual variables controlling firm variables. The third column contains firm variables controlling individual variables. It turns out that in general it is the individual features that play a more significant role, and that this is the case in all questions. In general, however, the observed relational strength is not great.

The role of government in the economy: divergent expectations

It may be assumed that definitions of the purpose and social functions of companies also influence management's perception of the government's role in the economy. The two issues seem to be 'two sides of the same coin'. Defining a company's purpose mainly in terms of profit maximization should, one might think, be linked

Table 2.6 Business-purpose perception correlates

	Overall R^2	partial R^2 'individual'[a] variables controlling 'firm'[b] variables	partial R^2 'firm'[b] variables controlling 'individual' variables
The goal of a company has to be maximizing profit	0.117	0.072	0.040
Social responsibility of companies consists only of increasing profits	0.206	0.123	0.061
Companies should do more for the community than what is required by law	0.080	0.060	0.016
In principle, companies are also responsible for the public weal	0.094	0.061	0.051

Notes
a Age, education, studies abroad, educational background (technical, business), time spent supervising other people's work (in years), higher education of mother and father.
b Company type (medium-size, large and the largest industrial companies, financial institutions), information whether the firm is a state-owned company, stock company, limited liability company, or in any part owned by foreign investors.

with respondents' unwillingness to accept an active role of government in the economy, which would be coherent with the neoliberal theory, that 'the best government is the least government'. After the fall of communism in Poland, public discourse was dominated by the view that the state should minimize its role in the economy. Following the tradition of neoclassical economic theory and neoliberal argumentation, new power elites often considered state institutions to be incompetent and corrupt, and government interventions ineffective.

The 'soft state' syndrome of the 1990s confirmed this assessment (though this is also a kind of self-fulfilling prophecy – elites do not reform state institutions because they believe that the best solution is the maximum expansion of market transactions in all areas of social life, which should marginalize interventions by the state).[33] Does this attitude persist after two decades of political and economic reforms? Table 2.7 shows the distribution of Polish business leaders' opinions on selected statements concerning the role of government in the economy. To get a more precise picture of their attitudes we asked them about the monitoring and regulation of the economy, the redistribution of wealth, vocational training and their attitude towards the putative nationalization of companies.

Even though the majority of executives are generally critical of state regulation of the economy, their answers show that their views are more complex and multidimensional. Their critical attitudes are expressed in different statements about government monitoring and regulation of the economy. Surprisingly, the opinion confirming the need for government intervention is expressed by

Table 2.7 Perception of the role of government in the economy

Percentage of respondents who agree[a] with the opinion:	Foreign companies	Financial institutions	State companies	Industrial companies 50–249	Industrial companies ≥ 250
The government should monitor and regulate the economy	50.0	26.3	38.1	32.1	41.4
The socio-political responsibilities of the state can only be achieved through redistribution of wealth	27.5	26.3	47.6	46.4	55.2
Vocational training is a task of government but not of business	35.0	26.3	23.8	35.7	34.5
Nationalization, even in times of crisis, is always the false path	52.5	52.6	38.1	64.3	75.9

Note
a   Respondents answered 'I fully agree' or 'I agree'.

50 per cent of respondents who are business leaders of foreign companies. It is debatable whether this is a symptom of a statist orientation in big industrial companies, or rather, especially in the case of foreign companies, of a greater knowledge of how governments in western countries have supported large companies in the financial crisis 2009/2012 (in contrast to the Polish government).[34]

The percentage of executives agreeing that the government should monitor and regulate the economy is lowest among business people in financial institutions (26.3 per cent). This result is consistent with Stiglitz' thesis (2003) that the financial sector supports market deregulation the most, and prefers self-regulation with a limited role for the state. But it is worth noting that the financial institutions in Poland, compared to their western counterparts, got through the financial crisis quite well. No banks or insurance companies have been threatened by bankruptcy. The financial sector in Poland, even in these times of crisis, is achieving very high profits and might be therefore even less interested in monitoring and regulation of the economy by the state. They see it as contrary to their interests (especially the interests of foreign investors).[35]

The relative preference for state monitoring and regulation of Polish business leaders operating medium-sized companies might also be interpreted as a call for a more efficient state. The negative aspects of unstable and inconsistent economic policy usually have more impact on smaller firms with a weaker market position and greater difficulties in getting access to loans and state aid. Interesting, though, is that agreement with redistribution among domestic companies is also quite high (and in fact even higher than agreement with state regulation), which might be interpreted as a response to the high inequality in the economy and society, while foreign companies and financial institutions regard this as less relevant, with the percentage of respondents from foreign-owned industrial companies as low as those from financial institutions, though half of them prefer state monitoring and regulation of the economy (see Table 2.7).

However, there is a clear positive correlation between the SV orientation prevailing in financial institutions and foreign companies, and their dislike of wealth redistribution by the state. In the financial sector, this is also connected with antipathy to monitoring and regulation of the economy by the government, while the 'shareholder approach' is much weaker in the large industrial companies and state-owned enterprises. The views on vocational training and the nationalization of companies follow a different trend. The vast majority of respondents in all types of companies do not agree with the thesis (which can be regarded as a manifestation of an 'etatist' view) that vocational training is a task of government but not of business. But respondents from medium-sized industrial companies (35.7 per cent) and large industrial companies (34.5 per cent) and foreign companies (35 per cent) express the view that vocational training is a problem that should be dealt with by the government. This may be a sign of dissatisfaction with graduates' and school-leavers' inadequate skill levels, or the lack of cooperation between companies, government and educational institutions (in Poland the state still plays the crucial role in education).

Analysis of respondents' answers to the above questions shows that the majority of the answers were positively correlated, that is in general, persons who agree that the government should regulate and monitor the economy more often accept similar interventions in wealth redistribution (rank correlation coefficient,[36] Kendall's tau-b = 0.19), and they also agree that occupational training should be organized by the government (tau-b = 0.31). There is a similar positive correlation between the postulate to redistribute wealth and opinions on vocational training (tau-b = 0.27), but the correlations are not high.[37] On the other hand, the nationalization coefficient shows a poor correlation with the previous ones. The majority of respondents from all sectors do not support nationalization. Probably it is perceived as a systemic 'step backwards' from the point of view of company management and market-economy rules.

It is hard to indicate definite factors determining attitudes towards government's role in the economy. Executives from stock exchange companies (usually market-oriented), are less frequently inclined to preference redistribution of wealth by the state. Simultaneously there is less reluctance towards nationalization among respondents from state-owned enterprises who know how to find their way through public ownership rules and for whom this kind of ownership change could open up new career opportunities in management of larger 'national champions'.

To sum up, even though the majority of leaders in general object to government's role in the economy, there are also clear differences in details. Most respondents oppose the opinion that the government should monitor and regulate the economy – with the interesting exception of managers from foreign companies, who are divided on this issue. Executives from domestic companies are contrastingly much more in favour of redistribution than state regulation. The vast majority of respondents in all groups do not agree with opinion that the organization of vocational training is only a governmental matter. Only managers from state companies prefer nationalization in times of crisis.

Ambivalent cooperation with social partners

In contemporary market economies, the ability to cooperate with social partners is an important source of competitive advantage. This ability, however, has various interpretations and implementations in different variants of modern market economies, such as liberalism, corporatism and etatism (Schmidt 2002). We showed earlier that in Poland, weak civil society and an ineffective model of mixed paternalistic, neocorporatist and neopluralist representation of interest has produced very limited cooperation between political, economic and social actors. This phenomenon also applies to industrial relations. For this we asked executives about their views on the importance of collective regulation, the importance of compromise in conflict over company goals, and the superfluity of trade unions and works councils in companies.

As shown in Table 2.8, most respondents declare that they appreciate the importance of collective regulation between social partners for the functioning of the economy. In the case of conflicts over company goals, compromise is important (in the latter question the exact nature of the divergence was not specified). The percentages of business people recognizing the importance of collective regulation are high in industrial companies, and also in state-owned enterprises. Executives from foreign companies agree the least often with the importance of collective regulation, given that it is these companies that in Poland are often associated with a 'Europeanization' of industrial relations, including good practice in social dialogue (Table 2.8). In response to another question about the value of achieving a compromise in conflicts over company goals, an even higher percentage of respondents agree from both categories of industrial companies, foreign companies and stated-owned enterprises. The only exception were the executives from financial institutions (47.4 per cent); as in many other issues, they were critical or sceptical of activities that go beyond the standards of the 'shareholder approach'. However, a large portion of respondents agrees with a radical statement that trade unions are superfluous. Even though this is the opinion of a minority, the numbers are quite high among respondents from medium-sized industrial companies and foreign companies (Table 2.8). Managers from state-owned enterprises and financial institutions much less frequently believe that trade unions are superfluous.

The results seem incoherent and ambivalent. For a large part of respondents, declarations in favour of compromise and agreement with social partners are accompanied by the negation of the need for trade unions. Correlation between answers to both questions is negative; however it is very weak (rank correlation coefficient,[38] Kendall's tau-b = −0.11). In fact, the answers to both questions may be treated as statistically independent of each other. The explanation may be that in Poland many entrepreneurs and managers regard trade unions as a destructive

Table 2.8 Characteristics of cooperation with social partners

Percentage of respondents who agree with the opinion:	Foreign companies	Financial institutions	State companies	Industrial companies 50–249	Industrial companies ≥ 250
Collective regulation between social partners is important for the functioning of the economy[a]	42.5	57.9	71.4	67.9	72.4
In conflicts over company goals, one should first and foremost attempt to reach a compromise[a]	80.0	47.4	71.4	89.3	75.9
Trade unions are superfluous[a]	42.5	26.3	23.8	48.2	37.9
Trade unions are superfluous[b]	14.3	0.0	26.7	38.9	11.1
Works councils are superfluous[c]	14.3	0.0	27.3	33.3	20.0

Notes
a Respondents answered 'I fully agree' or 'I agree'.
b Respondents answered 'yes'. Answered only by respondents from companies where unions operate.
c Respondents answered 'yes'. Answered only by respondents from companies where works councils operate.

force; their activity is seen by employers in categories of political aims and is associated with striving for particular interests in conflict with companies' needs. Especially those executives who manage companies in low-cost markets may perceive trade unions as a serious threat to further development.

Support declared by respondents for finding compromises with the social partners can also be interpreted as a willingness to create conditions favourable to voluntary actions that could reduce the likelihood of conflicts in companies. A question must be asked, however: What would be the nature of the joint efforts if a large group of respondents believed trade unions to be superfluous? (see the Polish case in comparison and in more detail Chapter 8).

Conclusion

The Polish model of capitalism was shaped primarily in the initial phase of system reforms during the domination of an Anglo-Saxon version of capitalism, the normative assumptions of which prevailed in international political and academic discourse. The main distinguishing feature of 'Polish capitalism' was neoliberal 'shock therapy' and the concept adopted in the early 1990s of a minimal state role in the economy. The institutional transformation towards a liberal market economy was supported by the erosion of employee representation which occurred despite the key role of the *Solidarity* union movement in the fall of communism. Poland, like the UK and Baltic states, has a decentralized compensation system where wage bargaining takes place at the level of firms. Both trade unions and employers' associations are weak. As in LMEs, general education, liberalization and commercialization have become a priority in education and training systems.

However, analysis of the determinants of 'Polish capitalism' and its major institutions show that the new variant of post-communist foreign-led capitalism is not clearly liberal. Capitalism in Poland is rather a hybrid of liberalism, etatism, and corporatism in different proportion in various institutional segments. After more than two decades of systemic changes, key institutions of 'Polish capitalism' are liberal but often incoherent, fragmented and inconsistent. An example of this inconsistency is ineffective state support of economic development, dualism of the development of domestic and foreign companies (especially in innovation), or the neoliberal economic institutions which co-exist with old institutions of distribution derived from state socialism (such as healthcare and public education). For various reasons (historical, political, structural and cultural) the neoliberal strategy of economic development does not adequately reflect the overall institutional environment. This lack of complementarity in particular illustrates aspects of the 'soft state' syndrome: relatively low effectiveness and coordination of public and private institutions; inconsistent macro- and microeconomic policy; and continuing long-term structural barriers to entrepreneurship which delay the development of modern capitalism in Poland. As a result, important institutions differs significantly from the pure model of capitalism discussed in the VoC literature, including the model of LME to which 'Polish capitalism' is often considered to belong, especially in terms of labour relations, education and training systems, representations of interest or interfirm relations. An indicative example of such differences is the underdeveloped capital market, key role of transnational companies characterized as 'foreign-led capitalism' or 'dependent market economy', and relative weakness of market and non-market mechanisms coordinating economic activities. 'Polish capitalism' is rather a hybrid that includes elements closer to cultural and organizational patterns inherit from the state-socialism era (lack of transparency, significance share of the state ownership, elements of corporatism), the continental structure of corporate governance (European legal system, predominance of internal controls, two-tier governance system). Social policy and the weakness of innovation in domestic companies are comparable to those observed in 'Mediterranean capitalism'.

Our analysis of the social background and opinions of business people reflects the findings we have discussed about Poland's variant of capitalism in three aspects. First, the institutions created in the 1990s in Poland still define the normative framework of the views of business leaders according to the standards of neoliberal economics. All categories of executives mostly agree that the goal of a company must be maximizing profit; they reject nationalization as a political solution and a large portion of them agrees that trade unions are superfluous.

Second, the segmentation in the economic sector into domestic and foreign-owned is also reflected in a different distribution of human and cultural capital. Companies with foreign ownership and financial institutions, which in Poland are also mostly controlled by foreign capital, have younger executives, more cadres who studied and worked abroad, and management with a more transnational identity. The cultural and professional capital of executives from financial institutions is the greatest, as measured by education level and type, and job mobility. They have clear advantages over executives in domestic companies, both state and private.

Third, the analysis of careers and views of Polish business leaders also reveals significant differences in their preferences in the surveyed areas. The clearest, most coherent and most distinct set of views are those of executives from foreign companies and financial institutions. Their distinctiveness is also reflected in their age, human and cultural capital, which demonstrates its structural nature. Business leaders from both types of companies strongly prefer SV (in terms of the goal of a company) and they highly dislike redistribution of wealth by the state – in the financial sector, this is also connected with antipathy toward government regulation of the economy, as well as with the lowest level among any managers of self-identification with nationality and religion. In the case of managers from the financial sector, their very pro-market orientation is determined by the organizational specificity of the sector, which in Poland is dominated by the 'financialization' introduced in the 1990s by international capital, as well as by particular professional qualifications held by managers in this category (such as business studies or stays abroad).

At the opposite pole are executives from domestic companies, especially state-owned companies and medium-size industrial companies. Managers from both show less preference for SV. Among them there is relatively strong support for the redistribution of wealth organized by the state and cooperation with the local community. Executives from state-owned enterprises are least likely to agree that 'nationalization is always the false path'. At the same time, among the managers from state-owned enterprises and medium-sized industrial companies, there is a strong identification with categories of thinking common among conservatives (including nationality and religion).

Finally, contradictions are visible in some of the issues examined, for example in the etatist orientation of the Polish business leaders in terms of regulation and state intervention. This orientation can be explained in different ways, partly as a reflection of the financial crisis that showed the limits of the neoliberal project, partly as the strong legacy of state socialism in state-owned enterprises and industrial companies (with a high proportion of managers starting their careers before 1989). Another explanation suggests that the etatist orientation may be a consequence of dissatisfaction with the 'soft state' still dominating in Poland.

Another important contradiction is associated with cooperation and social partnership in industrial relations. The majority of business leaders declare their support for collective regulation and compromise. However, a relatively large part of them also believe that trade unions are superfluous (especially executives from medium-sized and foreign companies). This seems incoherent, for it is difficult to cooperate and achieve compromise without social partners like employee representations. Our research shows that in the companies with active unions and works councils the opinion that they are superfluous is rather rare. This may indicate that there is potential for the development of employee representation and social partnership in Polish companies.

The contradictions in thinking of business leaders we have encountered in this study reflect institutional limitations and problems of the Polish variant of capitalism. The market economy in Poland has reached a new level of development, but coherent institutional changes need to be carried out, especially in the role of the state, strengthening social dialogue and so on. The current crisis of capitalism is driving such changes, and will open up new possibilities.

Notes

1 Balcerowicz held a scholarship at St. John University in New York in 1972–3, where he completed an MBA. Like most neoclassical economists at the turn of the 1980s and 1990s he criticized the Swedish and German model of capitalism, declaring them 'over-socialization' and not suitable for Poland. He also rejected the developmental patterns of Japan, the 'Asian tigers' and Latin America (Balcerowicz 1995).

2 A reconstruction of key arguments that supporters of the Anglo-Saxon model typically use in post-communist contexts provides Greskovits (2000). The views of the Polish political elite on democracy at the beginning of the 1990s, based on interviews with members of parliament, are described by Mach and Wesołowski (2000).

3 For instance, in the public administration there are institutions based on different models – modified ministries inherited from the previous system, and new agencies and institutions modelled after EU agencies, such as the Ministry of Regional Development and the former Office of the Committee for European Integration (1996–2004). New public service elites are educated in the National Public Administration School modelled on the French ENA, while at the same time local authority bodies inspired by Polish traditions before 1939 have been created, influenced by local political cultures shaped under Prussian, Austrian and Russian occupiers in the partition era.

4 In this context, some scholars have referred to the 'institutional nomadism' of the new political elites in Poland, often coming from opposition intellectuals and academics without experience in state administration. This phenomenon was manifested by the lack of a long-term strategy for institutional changes and the instrumentalization of reforms carried out in the name of ideologies or the interests of ruling groups (Kamiński and Kurczewska 1994).

5 The application of the notion of 'soft state' syndrome to Poland after 1989 was proposed by the former vice-premier for economy and labour 2001–5, Jerzy Hausner (2007: 19).

6 On the impact of EU regulatory changes, redistribution of resources, socialization of new norms and institutional adaptation, see Jasiecki (2008b). The assymmetrical relations between the Poland and the EU are characterized by Zielonka (2006), Sedelmeier (2005) and Mayhew (1998).

7 Data of the Central Statistical Office as of December 2008 prepared on the basis of annual reports submitted by companies with ten or more employees; a subgroup in this category are companies declaring involvement of foreign capital independently of the size of the share (Chojna 2010).

8 German investments in Poland go primarily into manufacturing and construction, transport, storage and communication, trade and repairs, real estate and financial intermediation (Zagoździńska 2010).

9 Foreign investors control 42 per cent of the Polish trade and repair market. However they dominate the most important forms of wholesale trade (distribution and logistics centres) and retail trade, such as large chain stores. Foreign capital, in practice, has subjugated indigenous suppliers (Kłosiewicz-Górecka 2010).

10 500 List, *Rzeczpospolita*, 29 October 2010: 28.

11 Until today this has been reflected in the structure of exports, where over a half of exported products are labour- and capital-intensive products; products with the highest technical content have a 4 per cent share in industrial exports (Misala 2010).

12 For instance, during the presentation of the National Development Strategy 2007–15 at the Ministry of Regional Development on 7 March 2007 it was pointed out that, out of over 400 strategic documents adopted after 1989, only *c.* 40 were regarded as suitable for further use.

13 Cumulative growth of Polish GDP in 2007–11 was 24 per cent. The ratings of S & P country Poland in 2006 was placed in the category of BBB+, and in May 2012 in the category of A− (Komisja 2012: 10).

14 According to an analysis based on Andre Sapir's model (2003), Hungary and Slovakia have similar unemployment rates. However, unlike Poland, the two countries are more just, i.e., the risk of poverty is lower (Hausner *et al.* 2007).

15 In Poland, the position of the Prime Minister is linked to the principle of 'constructive vote of no confidence.' The Sejm (lower house of parliament) can dismiss the prime minister only with the simultaneous arrangement of his successor. This is a procedure modelled on the position of Chancellor in Germany.

16 On voter participation in elections in Poland in a comparative perspective, see Cześnik (2009); about trust according to the European Social Survey see Domański (2009).

17 For example, recently the Central Anticorruption Bureau arrested high-level government officials who were being bribed by IT companies, including MNCs like HP and IBM. As a result of the corruption, a planned program of digitalization (e.g., electronic ID cards) was not put into place (Zieliński 2012).

18 Similar concerns were expressed by Polish entrepreneurs in the 1990s (Barlik 1998).

19 Piotr Gliński, former Chairman of the Polish Sociology Society, uses the term the 'elite's betrayal' to denote the negative attitudes of the majority of Polish politicians to NGOs and civic initiatives. The irony is that a large number of politicians began their political careers in social movements and NGOs.

20 There are many lists of countries classified as emerging markets. According to ranking of The Index Company (FTSE) Poland is located in the category of the advanced emerging markets.

21 In Poland access to credit for companies is limited by high interest, and margins which are among the highest in Europe (Jaworski 2009: 73), and the difficulty of access to loans has been exacerbated by the crisis of 2007–9. The Polish financial system does not favour the growth of savings. The large banks block the reconstruction of municipal and regional savings banks and thereby eliminate the competition that would provide cheaper credit. As a result, more than half the population has no savings in the banking system (Bratkowski and Bratkowski 2011: 148–50).

22 The Corporate Governance Forum, held since 1998, represents the beginning of the discussion on the Polish model of control of companies. In 2005, the Polish Institute of Directors (PID) was established which publishes the quarterly 'Overview of Corporate Governance' and organizes annual conferences on this issue. In 2002 it adopted a code of good practice in public companies operating on the Warsaw Stock Exchange. See http://www.pid.org.pl.

23 According to standard indicators of capital markets, such as stock-market capitalization, domestic credit to the private sector, or inward FDI stock, Poland has a lower level of performance than other countries of the Visegrád Group (Nölke and Vliegenthart 2009).

24 The paradox of the negative impact of this situation on trade unions is discussed by Gardawski (2009) and Ost (2005). According to Jan Kułakowski, former Secretary General of the World Confederation of Labour and Polish chief negotiator during the EU accession, the trade unions in Poland are unrepresentative, very few employees pay membership dues, and the unions are structurally weak and overly politicized. These remarks apply especially to *Solidarity*, which showed too little trade union activity, a result in part of its anti-system roots in the period of struggle against communism (Kułakowski and Jesień 2004).

25 According Eurostat, the number of limited-term contracts concluded in Poland in last three years was the highest in the EU. In 2010, the average number of such agreements in the EU-27 was 14.4 per cent, but in Poland it was 28.2 per cent, in Spain 25.6 per cent and in Portugal 23.3 per cent.

26 The author of this thesis, Michal Boni, was at the time the head of the team of advisors to Polish Prime Minister Donald Tusk.

27 According to the report *Qualifications for Employers'Needs* the level of computerization in schools, especially in vocational schools, is low. Schools do not satisfactorily improve students' attitudes towards work in areas such as self-discipline, responsibility and willingness to learn new skills (Sztanderska 2010: 62).

28 According to the Polish Central Statistical Office, the number of Polish migrants in 2004–7 increased from 1 million to over 2 million people in total. Only in 2008 and 2009 the office reported a slowdown in Polish migration due to the crisis in Western Europe.

29 In Poland, people with degrees in technology and engineering also enjoyed high prestige before World War II. The transition to the market economy in the 1990s popularized education in managerial and finance-related fields typical of the Anglo-Saxon business culture. Yet, another study conducted in 335 large Polish companies indicates that persons with degrees in technology still dominate among their CEOs (51.3 per cent); only 17.9 per cent of respondents had degrees in economics (Błaszczak 2010).

30 Additional analyses of managers still in their positions show that the average number of changes of employment over the career to date was only slightly related to whether a respondent started to work before 1989 or after. This result suggests that, in general, increased employment-changing is largely related to the period after the transition to the market economy.

31 The results of our research indicate a positive correlation between the size of a company and the internationalization of its management. The same positive correlation is between internationalization of management careers and ownership of foreign investors.

32 Variables are measured on the ordinal scale, thus do not meet criteria assumed for multiple linear regression. Therefore statistics and interpretations based on them must be treated with caution. Moreover, we realize that analysis results were also influenced by the type of information about firms and respondents that we managed to get.

33 In Poland the expressions 'neophytes', and 'new converts to capitalism' were used to characterize behaviours of former state enterprise managers (often also former party members), who were creating private firms invoking a neoliberal ideology which legitimized, for example, the limitation of employee rights and the marginalization of collective representation of their interests. In East Germany such definite neoliberal attitudes on the part of managers and owners in the 1990s used to be referred as the 'orthodoxy of proselytes' (Martens 2008).

34 See discussion of research on the failure of governmental anti-crisis packages in Poland earlier in this article, in the section *The microeconomic perspective: structural barriers to entrepreneurship*.

35 The re-nationalization of pension funds by the Orbán government in Hungary is an example of the effects of increasing state involvement in the economy which has raised critical objections from foreign investors, especially financial institutions.

36 Respondents answered using a five-point scale from 'I strongly disagree' to 'I strongly agree'. We used this scale for calculating rank correlation coefficients, i.e., we did not group the categories as in Table 2.8.

37 We were unable to create a one-dimensional scale demonstrating the perception of government's role in the economy based on the indicators.

38 Respondents answered using a five-point scale from 'I strongly disagree' to 'I strongly agree'; we used this scale for calculating rank correlation coefficients, i.e., we did not group the categories as in Table 2.8.

3 The 'small transformation' in Hungary

Institutional changes and economic actors

György Lengyel and Dénes Bank

Introduction

If Karl Polanyi ([1944] 1957) was right to describe the formation of capitalism – the double movement of economy and society – with the term 'great transformation', the transformation of state-socialist societies after 1989 could, in a similar vein, be described as the 'small transformation' (Lengyel 1992; Róna-Tas 1997; Lengyel and Rostoványi 2001). The reasons for this categorization are two-fold. First, most of these countries had already started a capitalist-style modernization before the state-socialist experiment; therefore their post-1989 development could be described as a 'return' to the market economy. Second, labour was – as Polanyi called it – a 'fictitious commodity' not only before, but also during state socialism, even if in a distorted form. Polanyi demonstrates how policies paved the way for the historic emergence of the capitalist market economy – a perspective which is still crucial for neoinstitutionalists and economic sociologists who emphasize that institutions and actors, norms and micromotives are interlinked (Brinton and Nee 1998; Portes 2010). Comparative 'business systems' (Whitley 1992) and 'varieties of capitalism' approaches (Hall and Soskice 2001), both based on the institutionalist tradition, have proved especially useful in understanding the specificities of the East Central European transformation (Whitley *et al.* 1996; King and Szelényi 2005; King and Sznajder 2006; McMenamin 2004; Lane 2006; Nölke and Vliegenhart 2009; Nölke 2011; for a critique see Bohle and Greskovits 2009). In this literature, Hungary is usually placed in one category with Poland, Slovakia and the Czech Republic (see Chapter 1). Hungary had, however, some unique preconditions in its return to the market economy, that are still relevant today. In the early years of transition, the country-specific legacy of state socialism seemed advantageous in giving Hungary an advanced position in terms of economic reform compared to other East Central European countries (Hankiss 1989). After access to the European Union, Hungary lost this role, and in the global financial crisis and the subsequent European debt crisis, Hungary was one of the new EU member states which were hardest hit.

In this chapter we argue that in spite of systematic similarities with other East Central European transitions, the Hungarian case – like single cases in general – can only be sufficiently explained when one takes the country-specific state-socialist legacies into account. The question posed by this chapter is, how these state-socialist legacies influenced Hungary's transition path. We show that the early elite replacement and the quasi-entrepreneurial experiences of Hungarians contributed to market liberalization and direct sales of assets to western investors. However, the low quality of government, the limits of the foreign-led growth strategy and the high welfare expectations of the population merged into a mixture of problems that accelerated during the global financial crisis.

To understand the roots and implications of this process, we first outline Hungarian reform-socialist legacies; we then discuss the interplay between elite and institutional change. We show that the early decline of cadres gave way to the quick rise of entrepreneurs, managers and bankers during and after the systemic changes. The following sections explore how it is that the Hungarian case of 'small transformation' has led to a dependent market economy (DME) and show its limits. Finally, we explore how peculiarities of the Hungarian reform socialism contributed to ambivalent and problematic social outcomes in the Hungarian transition to capitalism.[1]

The legacy of state socialism

State socialism in general can best be described as the dominance of collective property, compulsory employment, centralized planning, party hegemony and shortages (Kornai 1990, 1992). For East Central European countries, state socialism also created a new dependence on the Soviet empire. Hungary, after the 1956 revolution and the subsequent sanctions, for two decades presented a moderate version of this regime type. Concerning the Hungarian specificities of the state-socialist model, four interlinking characteristics are decisive here: the market-oriented *economic reform* at the end of the 1960s; the spread of the *second economy* from the early 1970s onward; in line with these two developments, the growing international *indebtedness of the country* due to the efforts to keep social welfare services unchanged under worsening economic conditions (Kornai 1996, Berend 2003); and the *early elite replacement* before the systemic change.

Economic reforms were introduced in 1968, then interrupted and resumed several times over the 1970s and 1980s. In spite of their stop-and-go nature, a side-effect of the economic reforms was that the policymakers became more open toward local markets and toward supranational economic organizations and foreign capital. These advantages, in turn, helped to lessen the social effects of the international oil crisis of the 1970s.

The reforms did not erode the dominance of either state ownership or compulsory employment – in other words, they did not fundamentally change the basic relations of property and labour. However, they did open the country up to market processes due to the inflow of foreign capital and a strengthening of the position of the state enterprises within the system (Jánossy 1970; Rezler 1973). State enterprises gained relative autonomy, that is, compulsory plan directives were replaced by a kind of bargaining. Research literature at the time described the emerging institutional mechanism with the term 'plan bargaining' (Bauer 1978). One of the most important effects was that the public discourse shifted towards the acceptance of market-economy institutions. Public discourse now ran along different channels, with a major dividing line separating pro-market reformists and hard-liner party bureaucrats who envisioned the dangers of excessive inequality and liberalism. The memory of the 1956 revolution, which had taught the party to behave cautiously in the face of mass emotion, also motivated the party leaders to offer not only a social safety net, as in other state-socialist countries but also opportunities for moderate personal welfare accumulation.

Though all this brought no fundamental change in state ownership and employment relations, it contributed to strengthening the *second economy*, exemplified first of all by the household plots given by agricultural cooperatives to their members, and the auxiliary activities of the co-ops, which functioned on market terms often free of state control. In the 1980s, in an attempt to level off the conspicuous differences in living standards between cities and rural areas, the formation was allowed of so-called VGMKs (enterprise work partnerships, that is, teams of industrial workers, working on outsourced tasks during their leisure time, using the equipment of the firm) and GMKs (economic work partnerships, that is, teams of part-time entrepreneurs), so that industrial workers could get extra income similar to that of farmers in the cooperatives.

The overwhelming majority of rural households (some four-fifths of the members of agricultural cooperatives) had plots provided by the cooperatives, together with certain services such as transport or purchasing of the products. In a sense, the household plots were a latent compensation for the forced collectivization of land and work in the 1940s and in the second wave after 1956. This loose system of household plots also compensated for low agricultural wages in the first economy. It served as the basis of consent to the regime in villages, where households developed successful strategies for material prosperity from the 1970s onward. The agricultural cooperatives also had industrial and service subdivisions, or subsidiary branches. In practice, the subsidiary branches were established by entrepreneurs for whom it was more convenient and legally less risky to use the umbrella organization of the cooperative. The subsidiary branches produced 60 per cent of value added to the cooperatives while the co-ops provided legal status for them (Rupp 1983).

In the early 1970s, the produce of the majority (almost two-thirds) of household plots were still mainly for the holders' own consumption. They grew vegetables and potatoes for the needs of the extended family, including sons and daughters who had already moved to nearby cities and were employed in industry or services (Juhász 2006; Szelényi 1988). When freezers became widespread during the 1980s, they provided a new solution for food preservation compared to the traditional means. Although the amount of goods devoted to family consumption grew, the proportion of production for self-support decreased as compared to the proportion produced for sale. By the late 1970s about three-quarters of the production of household plots was marketed (Gábor and Galasi 1985: 146; Kuczi 2000; Juhász 2006). In the first half of the 1980s, incomes from the second economy amounted to one-third of the wages paid in the first economy, while in terms of time budgeting, the time spent working in the second economy was equal to one-quarter that of the first economy (Gábor and Galasi 1985). This estimate includes small-scale agricultural production, self-built construction, private and semi-private activities in trade, etc. The total second-economy income around this time was estimated to be as high as one-fifth of the Hungarian gross national product (GNP). The share of small-scale agricultural production was in some cases surprisingly high. For example, more than half of all the fruit, potatoes, eggs, grapes and pigs produced in Hungary were from the second-economy sector.

This latent manufacturing of social consensus relied on maintaining state welfare provisions and the tolerance of second-economy business practices by the authorities. The ideology of market reform and the expansion of the second economy led to the reinforcement of consumer aspirations, while economic growth due to inefficiency, slowed continuously. Maintaining a social safety net and satisfying consumer aspirations led, therefore, to a growing state indebtedness to foreign banks and international organizations, which jeopardized macroeconomic stability. Hungary's foreign debts rose from US$1 billion in 1973 to over US$20 billion in 1990 because of the broad social welfare system, consumer subsidies and unprofitable state enterprises (Kornai 1996). State expenditure was as high as 64 per cent of gross domestic product (GDP) in 1989, which exceeded the comparable German and Austrian data by some 17–20 per cent at that time. The country ran up considerable debt and the signs of crisis became obvious. In 1988, Hungary, with 68 per cent debt/GDP ratio, belonged to the group of highly indebted middle-income countries which included Poland (61 per cent), Argentina (63 per cent) and Venezuela (58 per cent). The debt exceeded three times the value of Hungarian exports of goods and services (Dervis and Condon 1994).

Social tension depends, however, not only on real processes but also on how people perceive and experience the processes, the nature of which often remains hidden to them. A growing awareness that there was an economic crisis can already be observed in the second half of the 1980s. While at the beginning of the decade, only one-third of the population thought they were facing a lasting economic crisis, by the end of it three-quarters thought so, and an even greater share (four-fifths) thought that the crisis was severe (Lengyel 2012).

The acceptance of the role of the market in Hungarian public discourse however was somewhat lopsided: Hungarians did not reflect much on the social implications of a capitalist market economy. Even in the late 1980s, the majority of people still thought that unemployment was an unacceptable social phenomenon and also believed that inequalities needed to be lessened. The latter was demonstrated by survey evidence. When people were asked to estimate the income of typical occupations, and then in a separate battery of questions asked what they would consider a fair income for these occupations, two tendencies were revealed: first, for most of the occupations people's ideas of fair incomes were higher than their estimates of the actual pay. Second, it turned out that the fair wage growth suggested by the respondents was relatively higher in lower status occupations than in high-status ones. As a consequence, the spontaneously imagined 'fair income gap' was smaller than the estimated wage differences between low and high status occupations (Lengyel 2012).

Elite change and the new class of entrepreneurs

The Hungarian case is not only peculiar due to the early introduction of quasi-market elements and the role of the second economy, but also because of the sequence of elite and regime change. In contrast to most of the other transition countries (see Chapter 1), in Hungary the change of the economic elite *preceded* the political and institutional transition (Gazsó 1990, 1993; Lengyel 2007). The reason for this was a new wave of the reform process in the second half of the 1980s, triggered by the economic crisis. The proportion of newcomers in the economic elite at the end of the 1980s was significantly higher than at the beginning of the decade. According to cadre statistics for 1984, roughly two in every five members of the economic elite had got their position within the last three years; less than one in four had done it within one year (Table 3.1). A survey carried out before the new elections in 1990 revealed that the proportions of business leaders in these categories were already three in five and two in five respectively.

The turnover of cadres was particularly high in economic ministries and banks, where, in early 1990, over three-quarters of senior officials had been in their positions for no longer than three years. The reason for the accelerated elite change in ministries was that reforms needed new expertise in policy-making. The banking sector started to expand rapidly from the end of 1987, when a law on banks came into force which created several top-banker jobs (Lengyel 2007). Since they shared a reform ideology, the early turnover helped the new technocratic elite to find a common ground with the democratic opposition in 1990. The findings of a representative survey of business and political elites (Szelényi and Glass 2003) show that about three-quarters of the managers of large companies in 1993 had been in some managerial position in 1988. The corresponding share of

Table 3.1 Proportion of leaders who attained their elite position within one year, 1984–1998 (%)

	1984	*1990*	*1993*	*1998*
Ministry	26.9	53.9	15.2	16.7
Parliament	—	—	2.6	3.4
Bank	22.9	46.2	19.4	16.7
State enterprise	20.0	27.3	16.8	16.0
Private company	—	—	19.4	14.5
Economic elite	22.7	38.1	15.9	12.9
Economic elite w/o parliament	22.7	38.1	17.7	15.9
N	4,890	360	339	240

Source: Lengyel (2007: 72).

the new political elite was below 60 per cent. Another survey in the mid-1990s (Kolosi 2000) reveals that over two-fifths of the leaders of newly established private companies had been recruited from the former political and economic elite. In terms of career ladders, step-by-step continuous careers prevailed even in the first years of the transformation. In spite of the higher rate of elite circulation, at the end of the 1990s roughly half of the economic elites consisted of ex-socialist party members. All this means that the high speed of change did not lead to social ruptures in terms of elite recruitment. Over the 1990s the rate of turnover of the economic elite gradually settled back to the earlier rate or even below it, and the economic elite began to display signs of social closure (Lengyel 2007; Higley and Lengyel 2000; Kovách 2011). The rate of recruitment of persons from the upper-middle class with several diplomas and in-house careers rose significantly (on recent managerial careers, see Chapter 5).

Early elite change and elite settlement between the democratic opposition and pragmatic reform socialists (including top managers of large state-owned companies) helped to ease the road to pro-market reforms and privatization at first but did not improve the quality of government. For tactical reasons, and out of partisan interests, the political elites did not take seriously the agreements reached in the roundtable talks and frequently broke the rules of elite settlement. As a result, from the mid-1990s onward, the Hungarian population trusted the national government and parliament less than was the European average. A similar estrangement from politics could be observed among the business leaders (Lengyel and Ilonszki 2012). These processes did hamper democratic consolidation and negatively influenced business sentiments.

One of the most important aspects of the social transformation was the emergence of an entrepreneurial class in the 1990s (Czakó *et al.*1994; Kuczi 2000; Laki 2002; Róna-Tas 2002; Lengyel and Róbert 2003; Laki and Szalai 2004). At the end of the 1980s, a relatively high proportion, one-quarter of the adult population, indicated that they would enter into business in the future (Lengyel 2012). The majority did not want to be entrepreneurs, though the discounting of this option did not rest on ideological grounds or objective economic conditions, but on personal endowments, age, family ties, lack of skills. In the early 1990s the rate of would-be entrepreneurs jumped to over two-fifths, but then declined considerably, fluctuating between one-fifth and a quarter, and a decade later plummeted to below the starting level, due to the influence of the lasting crisis.

Several factors contributed to the changes in potential entrepreneurship. Most important is that the set of potential entrepreneurs was reduced by the expansion of the real entrepreneurial class: those who wanted to test their skills had got the possibility to do so over the past decades. Yet, the declining interest in setting up one's own business, shown in Table 3.2, can also be traced back to weak institutional support and a changing view on entrepreneurship in the Hungarian mass media from the mid-1990s on. At the turn of the millennium, the number of registered businesses in Hungary exceeded one million. However, only three-quarters of them were active, and the overwhelming majority were individual micro-businesses, mostly in trade and services. The entrepreneurial class was

Table 3.2 Changes in entrepreneurial inclination, 1988–2011 (%)

	1988	*1990*	*1992*	*1994*	*1996*	*2002*	*2008*	*2009*	*2011*
Would become an entrepreneur	25	44	27	23	16	12	14	16	13
It depends	4	—	10	11	11	12	19	13	16
Would not become one	71	56	63	66	73	76	67	71	71
N	2,941	986[a]	4,073	3,902	3,564	763[b]	1,441[c]	940	911

Source: Lengyel (2012).

Notes
a Dichotomous variable (yes/no).
b Regional sample, Kaposvár district.
c Regional sample, Kaposvár district, recoded 11-point scale: 7–10 = Would become entrepreneur; 4–6 = It depends; 0–3 = Would not become entrepreneur.

stratified by career patterns and possibilities. Former professionals were overrepresented among the leaders of joint ventures, while the self-employed were mainly skilled workers by origin. More than half of the entrepreneurs had no offices, with household and business not being separated. The majority could only partially exploit their potential and they relied more on start-up loans from friends and relatives than on bank loans. Many of them were 'forced' entrepreneurs, who escaped from unemployment and whose aim was just to make a living or supplement the family income, with little opportunities and ambition to expand the business. These micro-businesses are highly unstable. According to a panel survey in 1993 and 1996, one-third of the micro-businesses were closed down again. Firms run by former unemployed people were considerably overrepresented among the businesses ceasing operations, while entrepreneurs with former experience in the second economy were significantly less often among the respondents whose operations closed (Lengyel 2002).

Mode of regime change and large privatization

Some of the above-mentioned characteristics of state socialism made the early steps of the Hungarian transition peaceful and easy: both elites and masses had become accustomed to market behaviour, and the reform discourse paved the way towards entrepreneurship and privatization. At the same time the solution of the debt crisis was postponed in order to meet the welfare aspirations of the population, for which the price had to be paid later. At the beginning of the 1990s in Hungary, two very different strategies for regime change were discussed. One strategy prioritized a rapid and far-reaching privatization, while institution building played a second role. The proponents of this strategy assumed that institutions evolve over time once private ownership has become the norm in the economy. The second strategy suggested that the method of privatization was irrelevant, as long as the appropriate institutional and political environment was created that would necessarily result in an optimal property structure. Hungary chose basically the first strategy and prioritized direct sales to western investors right from the beginning. The scarcity of capital was the major reason that Hungary opened the doors to international investors, though the majority of Hungarian society was against foreign capital. As the government budget deficit started to rise dangerously, early privatization gained support from all parliamentary parties. The scarcity of capital and the government's huge budget problems contributed to the dominance of a privatization policy based on cash sales to direct investors, that is, foreign investors. The managers of state-owned enterprises had to acknowledge the political priorities concerning foreign capital although originally they hoped to increase their own autonomy.

This development was also facilitated by another aspect of Hungarian reform socialism. Since 1972 foreign investors could enter a joint venture with state enterprises and about 100 such joint ventures were established in this way up to 1988. During privatization, some of these foreign partners simply bought the rest of the enterprise (Soós 2010). Hungary was also the first in the state-socialist camp to establish institutional connections with the West through joining the International Monetary Fund (IMF) and the World Bank in 1982. However, this advantage was not fully exploited as, due to the prioritization of privatization over institutional regulation, the 'Act on the Sale of State-Owned Enterprise Assets', which guaranteed safety to foreign investments, came into force only in 1995, long after the political transition. This delay narrowed the lead in the competition for foreign investors with other fast-changing East Central European countries right from the beginning.

The first significant privatization to a foreign investor took place in 1993, followed by a large increase in the number of such deals from 1995 to 1998. In the first big privatization deal (between General Electric and Tungsram), the state's shares were sold with the stipulation that the investor would carry out a number of later investments (Holusha 1989). This kind of exchange between shares for investment promises lacked parliamentary control and became typical for the privatization deals with western investors (Tardos 1998). In the first phase, of the 2,250 state-owned enterprises and conglomerates, 1,857 were directly put into the hands of the State Privatization Agency in 1990. Many of these firms were liquidated, whereas the larger ones were broken up into ten, twenty or sometimes much more smaller units in retail food chains, pharmacies, petrol stations, etc. (Hanley *et al.* 2002; Stark and Vedres 2006; Mihályi 2010). About 1,300 enterprises were sold up to the end of 2000, at which point only 175 companies remained in state hands (Kovács 2000). Revenue flow from privatization peaked in 1995 with over €2.6 billion after the launch of comprehensive regulations on privatization. More than 60 per cent of revenue from privatization was realized in just five years, between 1993 and 1997.

In the second phase of privatization, after 2000, about half of the remaining state enterprises were also privatized; these were mainly banks and very big infrastructural companies like energy and gas suppliers, transportation companies, etc. The biggest transaction in the history of Hungarian privatization occurred in

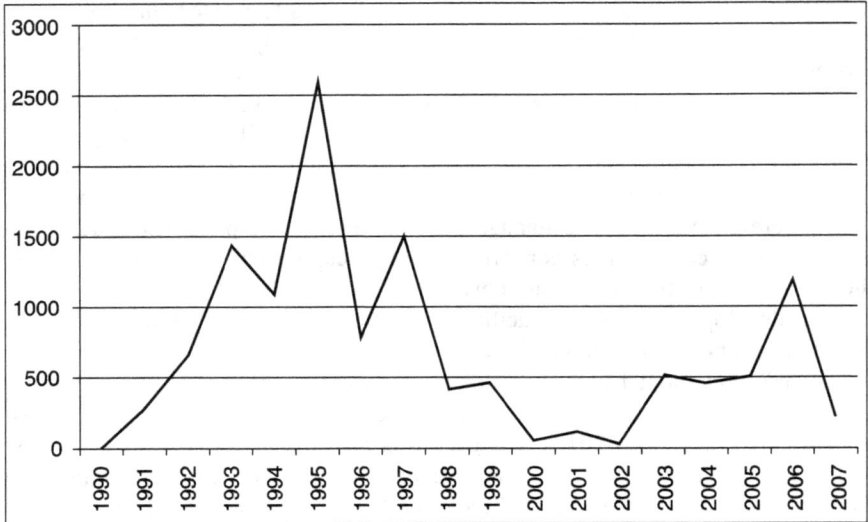

Figure 3.1 Revenue from privatization in Hungary, 1990–2007, in million €s
Source: ÁPV Zrt.

2005 with the privatization of Budapest Airport for more than €1.8 billion. According to the Hungarian Privatization and State Holding Company, the total revenue from privatization was €12.5 billion (about US$16 billion) in the period 1990–2007 (Figure 3.1). Hungary's total revenue from privatization was the highest in East Central Europe until the turn of the millennium, when Slovakia took the lead (EBRD 2005). However, the privatization revenue did less to relieve the Hungarian state from the burden of foreign debt services than had been hoped. The proportion of the debt servicing, at 12–17 per cent of GDP, remained the highest in the region (Drahokoupil 2009: 94).

   Another ratio for evaluating the speed and extensiveness of privatization is the increase in the share of the private sector. At the beginning of the transition, Poland had the highest private-sector ratio due to its agriculture sector, but soon after Hungary took the lead, according to European Bank for Reconstruction and Development (EBRD) annual reports, for reasons we have discussed in the previous section. In 1999 Hungary had the largest private sector. This ratio in Hungary has remained basically unchanged, though first the Czech Republic, then Slovakia and Estonia closed the gap on Hungary and reached the same level. In the comparative perspective of the EBRD transition-indicators, both large- and small-scale Hungarian privatization received high values, and there were only two areas out of nine for which Hungary's EBRD rating was not high, namely in competition policy and the banking sector (EBRD 2011).

   Although the remaining enterprises which might be candidates for privatization after the second privatization wave number well under 100, they include very large companies such as the Hungarian State Railways, and companies in the energy sector. These companies continue to provide services at a rather low level of quality. Some of these big, state-owned companies also cost a lot to run since no real structural reform had been carried out, and because they contribute to the financing of political parties or party-related businesses through different tenders and supports, no real intention formed to change this situation (Voszka 2005).

There were three basic aims in the Hungarian privatization. First, privatization was viewed as one of the *constituting elements of the regime change* from socialism to capitalism (an effect of the dominant neoliberal reform ideology). Second, many economists argued that a small and open economy must have an *export-oriented growth strategy*, which presupposed the *integration of Hungarian companies into the globalized network of multinational companies (MNCs)*. Third, because Hungary started its post-socialist transition with a large debt legacy, experts argued that the only way to *reduce excessive state debts and to prevent new indebtedness* was to sell the country's assets to foreign investors and attract foreign direct investment (FDI) (Mihályi 2010). While the strategy succeeded in the first and second aim, the foreign-led growth strategy did not solve the debt crisis as hoped. Moreover, the Hungarian story shows that the quickest and seemingly most suitable method of privatization, given prevailing economic conditions and necessities, may produce at best only temporary comparative advantages (Báger and Kovács 2004). The strategy failed even to impose constraints on the remaining state-owned companies' budgets, or to separate business and politics (Voszka 2005).

Early liberalization and its results

As a result of the early decisions in favour of market liberalization and privatization, Hungary became a preferred destination for foreign investment during the 1990s, which made the country almost a prototype of the DME (cf. Drahokoupil 2009; Mihályi 2010 and Chapter 1). In the beginning, the specific legacies and the early move to privatization to foreign investors seemed to pay off. However, Hungary is also a country which exemplifies the contradictions and limits of a foreign-led growth strategy.

In the 1990s, foreign proprietorship increased massively: in 1990, the number of foreign-owned companies already exceeded five thousand, but a decade later there were four times as many. Actual foreign investment in these foreign-owned businesses increased thirty-fold. Among medium-size and large companies (with an annual turnover of over HUF200 million) the share of foreign-owned companies was one-quarter in 1997 and nearly one-third by 2001. The increasing FDI inflow often followed the privatization of a large state enterprise. Already, after only a few successful privatization deals early in the privatization process, the volume of greenfield investments started to surpass annual privatization revenues. Between 1990 and 2008, four-fifths of foreign capital inflow was new greenfield investment, and according to experts most of the profits from these investments remained within Hungary (Mihályi 2010; Figure 3.2). Big foreign companies

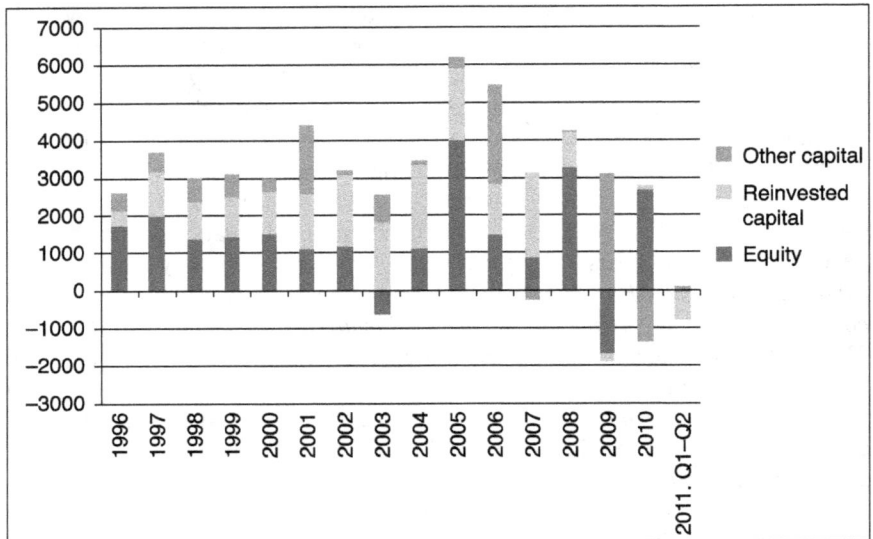

Figure 3.2 FDI inflow to Hungary, 1996–2011, in million €s
Source: National Bank of Hungary (MNB).

typically started with a smaller investment to which new – bigger – ones were later added. In addition, each investment resulted in a hundred more as the first small but successful privatizations opened terrain for greenfield investments (Soós 2009). As a result, in the first five years of transition five times more foreign capital flowed into Hungary than into the other East Central European countries altogether.

However, *annual* inward FDI was relatively low (about €1 billion on average) in the first five years of transition in Hungary, according to UNCTAD (2011). In 1995 – when revenue from privatization was highest – it jumped to nearly €4 billion, and in the next ten years fluctuated around €3 billion yearly. Outward FDI also increased significantly from the end of the 1990s in Hungary, but it remained under US$2 billion. According to a survey (Antalóczy and Éltető 2002) the most popular form of capital outflow was acquisition in order to gain market share and increase exports. In 2007 Hungarian per capita FDI inflow and outflow were among the biggest in Central and Eastern Europe (Figure 3.3).

Capital inflow to Hungary was mainly in two sectors: services (51 per cent of all inward FDI) and manufacturing industry (41 per cent of all inward FDI), but other sectors like construction and agriculture were neglected, where increases lagged behind the GDP growth rate. Within industry, most of the foreign direct investments were in the vehicle and electronics sectors, which contributed to the better performance of these sectors (HCSO 2007). In industry, the annual average increase in gross production was 3.5 per cent from 1968 to 1989, whereas it

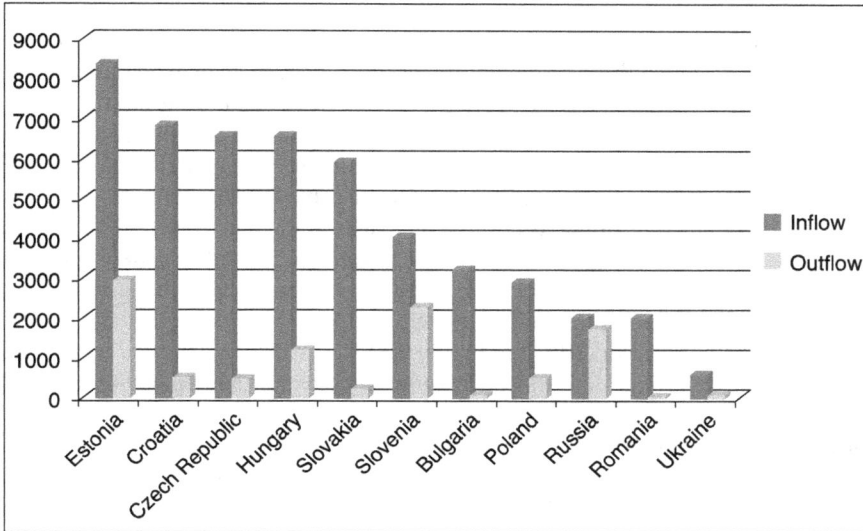

Figure 3.3 FDI per capita in some post-socialist countries in 2007, €s
Source: Hunya (2008) and Mihályi (2010).

was 4.8 per cent in the period 1989–2007 (NBH 2007). This means that it was not just higher than the GDP growth rate, but the pace of the increase also rose.

According to the Hungarian Central Statistical Office (HCSO), Hungary's foreign trade with its main trading partner, Germany, was six times higher in 2007 than in 1990. Germany's share within Hungary's foreign trade was nearly 30 per cent, higher than the other 14 countries of the EU-15 together in 2007. Thirty per cent of Hungary's FDI came from Germany as well, which reflects a strong economic dependency. Hungary, according to the transnationality index (TNI)[2] – together with Belgium, Estonia, Ireland, Slovakia, Czech Republic and the Netherlands (UNCTAD 2008) – belongs to the group of highly transnationalized EU countries. Two-thirds of the largest companies and banks were partially or totally in foreign ownership by the turn of the millennium. The TNI of Hungary was significantly higher than that of Poland or Germany already in the early 1990s, since it opened its markets to foreign investors during transition (UNCTAD 2002). A decade later the situation had not changed. The TNI of Hungary was 33.5 per cent in 2005, while that of Poland and Germany were around 20 and 10 respectively (UNCTAD 2008: 12). Meanwhile foreign trade with Eastern European countries did drop to less than one-tenth of previous levels during the two decades.

From 2005, FDI in Hungary started to decrease and in 2009 became negative. In 2010 FDI inflow was again about 40 per cent higher compared to the previous year after some direct investment by big companies (e.g., the new Mercedes-Benz facility) – which may have indicated some recuperation. However, the increasing fluctuation in FDI after the end of privatization became a major source of uncertainty for labour-market policies. Moreover, from 2006 the main reason for the significant increase was the inflow of loans and investments in government securities with which the government financed its welfare-state expenditures.

As a sign of the lasting crisis, Hungary's GDP dropped during the first years of transition and it was ten years before it rose again above the level of the late-1980s. GDP then increased until 2006, almost in parallel with Poland, Slovakia and Slovenia. In 2006, FDI was 68 per cent of GDP – close to the ratio in the Netherlands and Ireland (Hunya and Schwarzhappel 2008). GDP turned into slow growth and stagnation in Hungary from 2007.[3] And in spite of privatization, transnationalization and high debt-service payments, the government debt/GDP ratio did not improve in the long run. After significant ups and downs it is still at 81 per cent in 2012 (see Figure 3.4).

The focus on foreign-led growth in some sectors and the neglecting of other sectors in the transformation process, agriculture in particular, led to highly uneven regional development that again widened the gap between centre and rural periphery within Hungary. Most of the foreign direct investments went to only three of the seven regions of the country (Antalóczy and Sass 2005). The role of Budapest was the most significant – its economy had a 57 per cent share of the total FDI coming into Hungary – although, compared to the capitals of Portugal or Spain, where this rate is over 70 per cent, it cannot be considered very high. The regional distribution of FDI hardly changed in Hungary after 1994. There is a strong statistical correlation between FDI and per capita GDP volume and growth at both regional and county level. The same relation can be identified between FDI, industrial exports and employment. In contrast to the benefits reaped by those regions which did receive FDI, for many rural areas, market liberalization and privatization led to impoverishment, concentration of wealth and rural depopulation (ibid.).

Within the manufacturing sector, a gap has emerged and widened in terms of working conditions, payment and corporate culture. As foreign-owned companies work more effectively and produce for western markets, they also pay their managers more than do companies fully owned by Hungarians. They also transfer part of their corporate culture to subsidiaries. One increasingly important element of the corporate culture of large MNCs in particular is 'corporate social responsibility' (CSR). After the disappearance of the 'social' and 'caring' big state-socialist companies (see also Chapter 7), it is mainly these MNCs that are active in the social sphere in Hungary. Most of the Hungarian subsidiaries of large MNCs consider CSR a priority issue and dedicate financial resources to it (UNDP 2007), whereas even years after transition it is not yet an integral part of the corporate culture in domestic companies (Bank *et al.* 2009). This may show that MNCs promote the transfer of their corporate culture to local branches in order to have stronger ties with them, resulting in a more solid dependence. Furthermore, MNCs prefer to focus on internal CSR (ibid.) – a strategic appeasement of workers that is of crucial importance in keeping wages low, avoiding costly strikes and retaining skilled labour in order to protect large investments and maintain the comparative advantage of local branches. These labour relations contribute to a gap in business culture between MNCs and local companies.

Transformation of the banking sector

From the late eighties on, numerous foreign banks entered the Hungarian market and from 1997 – when the Hungarian state-owned banks were privatized – foreign banks became influential owners of this sector. According to experts, banks that entered the Hungarian market early with a wide range of activities became the most successful. An important feature of these banks was that the new owners hired managers who had proper information about the Hungarian banking market, that is, Hungarian insiders from this sector (Várhegyi 2001). Over the 1990s, the Hungarian banking sector exhibited a paradoxical phenomenon: although foreign investors entered the Hungarian banking market the earliest and in the greatest volumes compared to other transforming East Central European countries, their market share in Hungary remained lower for quite a long time. One reason is that in spite of the rapid privatization program, the Hungarian government hesitated to privatize the two big national financial institutions, OTP and Takarékbank, and did so only under pressure from the European Union, that is, at the beginning of the accession process (cf. Grabbe 2006). The biggest Hungarian bank, OTP – with one-quarter of the Hungarian banking market – was privatized only in 1999 and is now over 70 per cent foreign-investor owned (Table 3.3). Yet even if Hungarian banks remained longer under Hungarian state control, their ownership structure gradually changed because of the increasing involvement of foreign financial investors, who step by step gained majority shares.

Due to the arrival of foreign investors, the level of concentration in the banking market decreased and quality of service rose. The stronger competition resulted in lower operation costs and average interest-rate margins (Várhegyi 2001). Greenfield investments and an increase in capital stock contributed to a greater stability of the sector. Only some ten years after transition did foreign banking

Table 3.3 Market share and ownership of the biggest banks in Hungary, 2010

	Balance Sheet Total ('000 billion HUF)	Market share (%)	Share of foreign ownership (%)	Main owners
OTP Group	8.1	25	71	Foreign investors (71%) Domestic investors (25%) Management (2%)
K&H	3.2	10	100	KBC (Belgium)
Erste	3.0	9	100	Erste (Austria)
MKB	2.9	9	100	Bayern LB (Germany)
CIB	2.5	8	100	Intesa Sanpaolo (Italy)

Source: Hungarian Banking Association (2011).

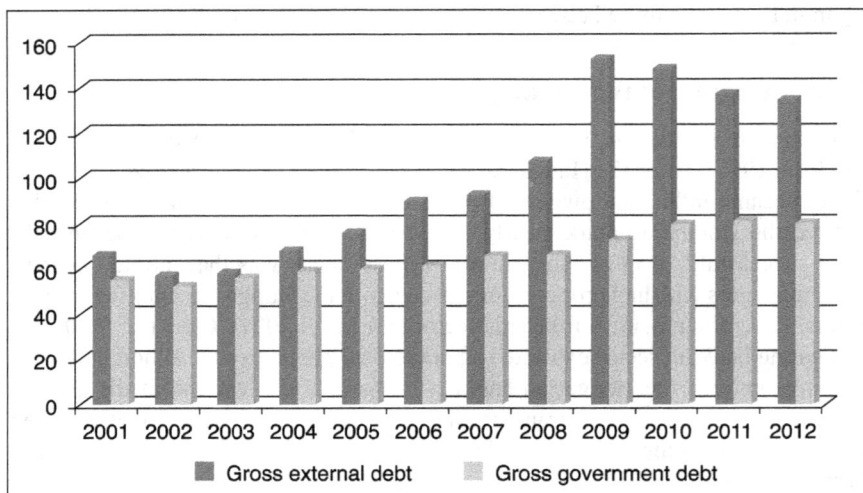

Figure 3.4 Hungarian gross external debt and gross government debt in % of GDP, between 2001–2012

Source: Eurostat and ECB online database.

investors begin to invest heavily in sectors other than business banking, as that market was now rather full. And the arrival of foreign banks also helped increase FDI for other sectors, as western investors prefer to maintain already well-established bank relationships.

However, the highly transnational banking sector contributed to the further increase of gross external debts (including household debts) as well. While the gross external debt (including household debts) was not significantly higher than the government debt until the early 2000s, the excessive marketing activity of the banks towards households from 2004 caused it to grow very strongly. It exceeded 150 per cent of GDP in 2009.

The percentage is not exceptionally high for Europe: the rate is higher in three-quarters of the eurozone countries and in some of them (for example in the Netherlands, Ireland, Luxemburg, Malta, Cyprus) the ratio is much higher. But in Hungary, a growing number of perhaps naïve and over-ambitious Hungarian households, who had sought to satisfy their consumer aspirations in spite of low wage increases, were unable to service their debts when the interest rates increased. (As we shall see in the next section, growing consumer aspirations on the one hand, and the rejection of inequality on the other, simultaneously characterize the attitude of the population.) According to the Hungarian Financial Supervisory Authority, out of 1.2 million Hungarian mortgage-loan contracts, one-quarter had some difficulties in paying in June 2011. Over 10 per cent of all mortgage loans had delays in payments of over 90 days; 87 per cent of these were foreign-currency loans. The marked weakening of the Hungarian forint thus affected severely about

100,000 households. In order to avoid further social tensions and a deeper financial crisis, the government introduced several packages, beginning in mid-2011, to lessen the burdens of households with foreign-currency loans that were mainly financed by the extra tax levied on the banks, totalling HUF120 billion in 2012. In political rhetoric, bankers and especially foreign banks became the scapegoats for the crisis and the mismanaged transformation process.

Employment, business sentiments and the new grey economy

While most of the political parties agreed to the high-speed privatization in the 1990s, a major part of society had and still has mixed feelings about privatization and the outcome of the transition to market economy. Formerly vague concepts of market and entrepreneurship on the one hand, and an inclination towards more equal distribution on the other, were in conflict in people's minds. Above all, the acceptance of unemployment as an unavoidable consequence of market economy, which was already low before the transition, further declined with practical experience of mass unemployment. In contrast, a majority of managers and entrepreneurs considered unemployment an unavoidable social phenomenon (Lengyel 2007). Many people entering the new job markets had expected safe and easy jobs, and expressed their severe disappointment in surveys (Lengyel and Neumann 2002).

With privatization, the employment structure changed drastically. While in 1992 about 60 per cent of the active population worked in state enterprises or administration, in 1996 this proportion was only 40 per cent, which dropped to under one-quarter by 2011. With the increasing speed of privatization from 1993 onward, the official unemployment rate sharply increased, as the new private sector only partly managed to compensate for the job losses in the state sector. After EU accession, the unemployment rate increased again and accelerated with the economic crisis after 2008 that led to an increase in bankruptcies and cost-cutting measures by employers. In 2011, the official unemployment rate in Hungary was slightly higher than the EU-27 average (10.9 vs. 9.4 per cent).

The greater lasting problem is the *low employment rate* (Köllő 2009). In the 1990s not even half of the active population was officially employed (see Figure 3.5). Roughly every fourth person lost his or her job after the rapid privatization and subsequent rationalization. A similar effect can also be observed for other post-socialist EU member states but on a less drastic scale. The second lowest employment rate is in Romania, with 58.3 per cent, which is still 2.5 percentage points higher than that of Hungary. Even 20 years after the end of state socialism, employment rate in Hungary is among the lowest in the European Union and has only slightly improved since the mid-1990s.

The differences between these countries are often explained by variations in privatization method and speed but also by the varying degrees of compensation of the social costs by the welfare states (cf. Bohle and Greskovits 2012). In Hungary, the pacification of the population in the face of their uncertainty and

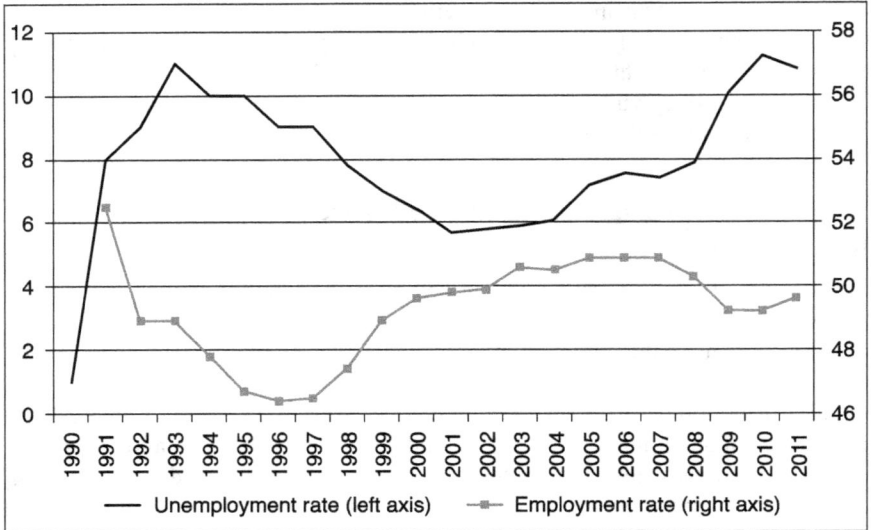

Figure 3.5 Employment and unemployment rate in Hungary, 1990–2011
Source: HCSO (KSH).

scepticism was secured by early retirement and disability pension schemes which were applied in the 1990s in order to relieve the shock to the labour markets. These measures contributed to the phenomenon of the exceptionally low employment rate in Hungary.

The 1990s in Hungary witnessed low employment on the one hand, and increasing consumer aspirations on the other, in spite of the fact that the real value of wages hardly changed on average during the 20 years after transition, according to HCSO. The economic sentiment index shown in Figure 3.6 reflects this phenomenon. The competing political elites made the population believe that consumers' aspirations were realistic and that a virulent debt crisis could be avoided.

The index measures both consumer and business confidence. The consumer confidence index is calculated from responses to questions concerning the actual and the expected financial position of households, the actual and the expected economic situation of the country, and the purchase of higher-value consumer durables. The business confidence index is calculated from the responses of enterprises in industry, trade, construction and services to questions concerning the state of business and expectations.[4] The country's economic sentiments were influenced by several social processes, among others by changing preferences, the signs of crisis, and policy measures to mitigate them, as well as by the effects of electoral cycles. Both parts of the index increased until 1998 and then entered into a slightly decreasing trend with strong consumer confidence fluctuations and moderate business confidence fluctuations until the economic financial crisis in

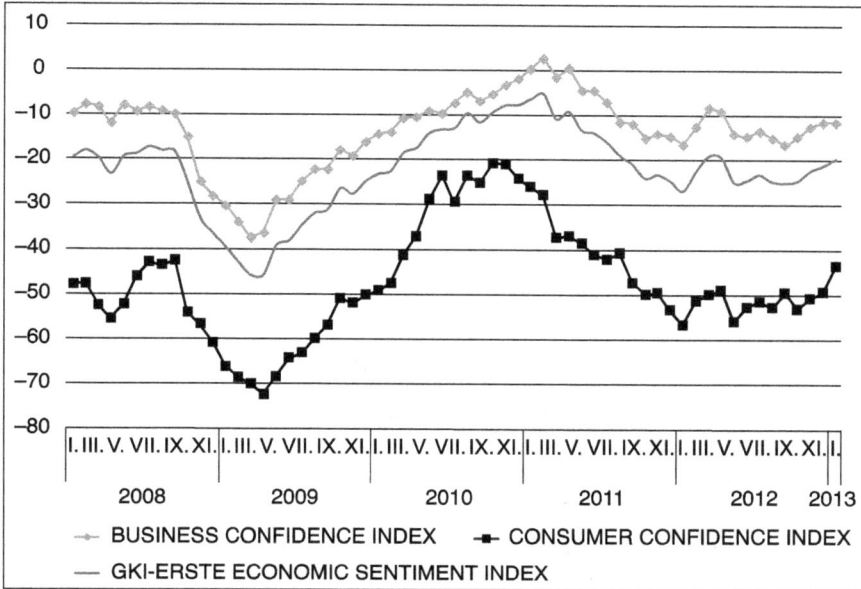

Figure 3.6 Consumer and business confidence, 2008–2013
Source: GKI (2013).

2008, when it fell very sharply. Hungarian expectations were higher than the EU average between 2002 and 2005, and lower between 2006 and 2009. Expectations hit bottom in Hungary in May 2009, while in the beginning of 2011 they returned to a similar level as in the middle of the previous decade. The crisis had a more significant negative effect on the value of the Hungarian indicator compared to Poland and Germany. After the global economic crisis, of these three countries only Germany maintained its former level of optimism.

The simultaneity of high unemployment and growing consumer aspirations can only partly be explained by developments in the new official private sector, where wages remained low. Many of the early retired and demobilized employees moved into the grey zone of unregistered work. In 2011, the grey economy represented about one-fifth of the European economy, for Hungary this ratio was slightly higher (one-quarter). The grey economy in Hungary showed the same patterns as in other parts of the European Union: the most-involved sectors were construction, trade, tourism, personal services and agriculture, because non-registered work is easiest to find in these areas. According to a survey by Visa Europe (2011), the main stimulating factors behind the grey economy in Hungary were the lack of trust in the government and the complicated tax system.

The lack of confidence in business prospects is interlinked with a low level of institutional trust. Hungary is still in the bottom quintile in Europe in terms of

Table 3.4 Gini index[a], 2000–2010

	2000	2005	2010
Hungary	26.0	27.6	24.1
Germany	25.0	26.1	29.3
Poland	30.0	35.6	31.1
EU-27	—	30.6	30.5
CEE countries[b]	26.8	28.4	27.2

Source: Eurostat, SILC.

Notes
a Gini index measures the extent to which the distribution of income (or, in some cases, consumption expenditure) among individuals or households within an economy deviates from a perfectly equal distribution. Thus a Gini index of 0 represents perfect equality, while an index of 100 implies perfect inequality.
b Hungary, Poland, Slovakia, Slovenia, Czech Republic, Romania.

institutional trust and below the average concerning generalized trust (Tóth 2009; Giczi and Sik 2009; Szántó *et al.* 2011). In our 2009/10 survey in Poland, Hungary and Germany, a significantly smaller proportion of Hungarian business leaders accept rule-breaking behaviour than of Polish and German leaders. On the other hand, a much higher proportion of Hungarian business leaders agree that undocumented payments and bribes are frequent (for more, see Chapter 6).

The compensation of the social costs of transition by the state and the development of a new grey sector may have contributed to the fact that Hungary has a similarly low level of inequality as countries who had a slower increase of unemployment in the 1990s, such as Slovakia, the Czech Republic and Slovenia (amongst East Central European countries traditionally, Slovenia has had the lowest Gini index) (Table 3.4).

Although Hungarian inequality has grown significantly compared to state-socialist times, it is still less than in Germany and in Poland; it is below the EU-27 average and even below the East Central European average. At the same time, the perceived social differences increased notably, resulting in more social tension.

Conclusion

During state socialism, Hungary was largely dependent on the Soviet Union in political and economic terms. Its political orientation – above all in foreign affairs – was closely determined by the Soviet regime. With the breakdown of the Soviet Union and the turn towards fast privatization and an FDI-driven growth strategy, Hungary like other East Central European countries turned *from a dependent planned economy to a DME*. In Polanyian terms, the double movement of economy and society during this 'small transformation' led to a double dependence: DME here and now means structural inclusion into the periphery of the western markets on the one hand, and dependence on surviving habits after state socialism on the other.

One may argue that the final reasons for dependence or independence – the determinants of the type of business system – are not national peculiarities, but international structural positions. Distances and relationships to markets and great powers are certainly important determining factors for the scope and nature of dependence. Nonetheless, the space of manoeuvre as well as the quality of elites and institutional settings are not exclusively determined by structural positions, but are also shaped by country-specific factors.

Hungarian country-specific legacies seemed to provide the country with a unique advantage compared to their post-socialist neighbours but also contributed to a peculiar mix of problems that Hungary accumulated for more than two decades after its politicians opened the border that had divided Europe. The accelerated elite circulation as a consequence of reforms triggered by the economic and debt crisis in the 1980s resulted in a younger, better-educated elite who were more open to markets and privatization. The early elite circulation and elite consensus on the transition path paved the road to an open market society, as did the experiences of the population with quasi-entrepreneurship and markets in the second economy.

With the catching up of Hungary's post-socialist neighbours in the race for western FDI, the advantages of an early start quickly disappeared. Moreover, the foreign-led growth model turned out to be not sufficient to match the compensation costs and the expectations of the population regarding how personal welfare would improve in the market economy.

The Hungarian population, unlike the Polish, was not socialized on material hardship, oppression and opposition during the last decades of state socialism. It did not have to suffer ideological rigidity for as long as the East Germans nor did it develop corporatist arrangements as widely as in West Germany. A widespread belief in pro-market reforms, relative social safety and a slow accumulation of private wealth based on double employment in the first and second economies were the characteristics of the Hungarian version of state socialism after 1956. The second economy meant extensive extra work, but it was interwoven with soft forms of rule-breaking, such as tax avoidance and loose work discipline in one's primary job. Labour market safety combined with widespread activities in the second economy increased consumer aspirations.

Maintaining social security while the first economy stagnated led eventually to the collapse of the peculiar reform-socialist deal between the population and the party elites. The 'small transformation' from a dependent planned economy to a DME re-established high levels of uncertainty and insecurity in the labour market, and labour became a 'fictitious commodity' again in its full form, without the distortion of obligatory employment.

Income-maximizing, work-oriented behaviour of the potential workforce is a necessary component of capitalism (Lane 2006). Looked at in light of the institutional legacy, we may say that this precondition is not met in the Hungarian case. The rate of employment is among the lowest in the EU and can be attributed to state-socialist legacies in two respects. First, obligatory work under state socialism encouraged people's dependence on the state and weakened self-responsibility. Second, the involvement in the second economy increased the proportion of those who were interested only in keeping their job in the first economy while concentrating their efforts in the second economy. No wonder that during the systemic changes large parts of the former labour force exploited the possibilities of early retirement schemes.

At the same time, the consumer aspirations of the population that developed under state socialism combined a low level of acceptance of social inequality also forced the varying governments and competing parties to maintain social compensation for the hardships of the transition. In addition, the elite settlement has evaporated, and political actors and institutions have become untrustworthy in the eyes of the public. Governing elites fell into the cycle of irresponsible promises and budget cuts, which was mirrored in the population by successive waves of gullibility and frustration, as illustrated by trends in consumer confidence and entrepreneurial inclination, as well as electoral extremism. Rapid privatization and wide-ranging transnationalization contributed to the improvement of material conditions in the short run. However, accumulated indebtedness and 'double dependence' have made Hungary's social actors especially vulnerable in times of crisis.

Notes

1 We would like to thank the editors of this volume and Tibor Kuczi (Corvinus University of Budapest) for their comments.
2 TNI is an average of the relative weight of FDI inflow in investment, FDI stock as per cent of GDP, employment in foreign affiliates as per cent of total employment, and the value added of foreign affiliates as per cent of GDP.
3 In terms of the gross domestic product measured in PPS per inhabitant, Poland and Hungary are almost on the same level (according to 2010 data). By 2011 Hungary reached 55 per cent of the level of Germany, and 66 per cent of the EU average; in 1995 these figures were 40 and 51 per cent respectively.
4 The economic confidence index is the weighted average of the consumer confidence index and the business confidence index. The axis of the graph shows the change in the assessment of the topics involved in the confidence index, where value 0 reflects stagnation, −100 extreme deterioration and +100 extreme improvement since the last survey.

4 The long shadow of the 'German model'

Business leaders in social and institutional change

Katharina Bluhm, Bernd Martens and Vera Trappmann

Introduction

Capitalism in Germany evolved in a distinct mode, with the persistence of pre-capitalist forms of social organization and the inclusion of organized social groups in economic and political decision-making, which made it particularly responsive to labour interest at the macro and micro level (Streeck 2011; Allen 2010). In its search for alternative ways of organizing the economy compared to American-style capitalism, post-war Germany was long held up as a best-practice case; the 'German model' promised the reconciliation of capitalism with social interests. This model has come under immense pressure for a number of reasons, most of them economic but some also rooted in ideological conflict. With the demise of state socialism in Central and Eastern Europe, the liberal expression of capitalism seemed to have outplayed all other economic systems. Across Europe, welfare states were cut back and took on activating policies (Gilbert 2004). The German welfare state was also weakened by the costly unification, and the collective bargaining system came under threat with the emerging market economy in East Germany even though, ironically, most of the formal institutions of the 'German model' were transferred to the East.[1]

While the gradual transformation of the German model in its core institutions has been widely documented,[2] it is unknown how this institutional change is linked to the actors' perception of the 'German model'. There is little research about to what extent '[. . .] changes in underlying expectations, attitudes and values in business, policy-making, and in the wider society are the fundamental forces driving the country away from its traditional model' (Hassel 2010: 103). How do business leaders perceive the core institutions of the 'German model'? Do they still believe in its comparative advantages and the desirability of social reconciliation? Or have they embraced the neoliberal shareholder view, as widely discussed in the literature before the financial crisis, suggesting a fundamental reassessment of the 'German model' by the economic actors? Is the perception of the 'German model' still split along the former intra-German border or do we rather observe a divide between large and medium-sized companies, the so-called German *Mittelstand*, which is traditionally far removed from the pressures of the capital market but is also reluctant with regard to unions?

Our research answers those questions in combining an institutional and actor-related perspective. In a first step, we sketch the dynamics and reasons for the accelerating transformation of the 'German model' after unification. Before the financial crisis most of the scholars in the field described these dynamics as 'erosion', but since then it seems to have had a glorious renaissance. We argue that both positions are too short-sighted: while the erosion thesis overestimates the institutional break, the renaissance viewpoint underestimates the level of change. Proponents of the erosion of the 'German model' see not only external forces at work but have also argued with an *internal* cultural turn to which changes in the recruitment of the economic elite have heavily contributed. In a second step, we therefore reconstruct how scholars have discussed the interplay between changing recruitment, beliefs and institutions. Turning to our empirical data in a third step, we analyse the social origins, education and career patterns of our respondents and their attitudes towards the 'German model'. The advantage of our research is that we can actually test the impacts of these subjective features on the beliefs of business leaders and refer this to other subjective and objective variables such as geographic origin (East/West), age, company ownership or company size.

Our research shows a strong agreement with key ideas of the 'German model' despite its transformation. Yet, at the same time it shows also a high degree of indecisiveness when we analyse the attitudes in more detail. We learn that social origin, education and career patterns contribute little to any explanation of the variations in attitudes, and that the most striking line of differentiation runs between East and West, suggesting that the different experiences before and after the unification still matter. Yet company size is also relevant. Top managers of very large companies are not only more decided in their beliefs; they are also more often in favour of the 'German model' than respondents of smaller companies. In the conclusion we suggest an interpretation of this finding that fits the pattern of institutional change.

Erosions or renewal of the 'German model'?

The 'German model' was renowned for its long-term perspectives in all areas – financial markets, employment relations, product innovations, and altogether for high economic and social stability. Industrial output was marked by high export rates and 'diversified quality production' (Sorge and Streeck 1988) embedded in cooperative networks of firms in the same sector. This success relied in particular on the industrial relations and training system: social partnership between labour and capital; consensus orientation manifested in co-determination and wage bargaining; patterns of long-term employment; and employers offering vocational training within a dual system of responsibilities shared between state and business that produced a skilled workforce attuned to the needs of industry. This type of coordinated market economy seemed to enjoy high comparative institutional advantages for economic development (cf. Hall and Soskice 2001). However, from the mid-1970s, increasing structural unemployment, a decline in traditional industries, and the first endeavours to flexibilize the labour regime started to exert strong pressure for change.

Regarding the 1990s, critics argued that stability had become stagnation, causing Germany to be stuck in a 'high equilibrium trap': 'The same institutions that once provided for economic prosperity and social cohesion today impede adjustment and stand in the way of a sustainable response to new problems' (Kitschelt and Streeck 2004: 1). Critics called for a fundamental break with and a cutting back on the institutional web that was hindering prosperity. The limitations of the – nationally-based – diversified quality production, under conditions of growing global cost and innovation pressure, is one explanation often offered (Streeck 1997). Scholars usually name a mix of different causes for the accelerated institutional erosion of the 'German model' in this decade: an attractive 'exit option' close by, that is, in the emerging market economies in East Central Europe; the growing influence of the globalized financial market; the ongoing market integration of the European Union that favours the liberal model; and German reunification.

The mode of reunification particularly exacerbated the situation in several respects. First, the rapid de-industrialization of East Germany led to an almost 50 per cent decline in employment, through redundancy, early retirement, withdrawal from the labour market and public retraining programmes (Wiesenthal 2003: 42), all of which resulted in high numbers of beneficiaries of public transfers.[3] Second, the reunification was, to a great extent, paid for with West German social security funds, that is, by employers and employees, emptying public coffers, and by an increase in payroll taxes for health and unemployment insurance systems, which again raised labour costs and provoked further layoffs. Public financial transfers came to €800 billion – between 1990 and 2002 – (by comparison, gross domestic product – GDP – was €1,156 billion in 1990). While many West German companies gained short-term profits from the sudden surge in domestic demand, they preferred to relocate production to East Central Europe rather than to East Germany. Third, the reunification of Germany entailed a complete transfer of Western institutions to the East, which accelerated the weakening of the 'German model'. The overstretching of the welfare state was accompanied by the rapid erosion of the transferred industrial-relations system, as East German companies were not able to pay the wages negotiated by the transferred West German employers' associations and unions, contributing to a rapid estrangement from the institution of sector-wide collective bargaining (ibid.: 37). 'With the benefit of hindsight, we can see that this pattern of unification has contributed to the weakening of the German political economy' (ibid.: 56).

Fundamental responses were rolled out in the second half of the 1990s by the 'social partners' and in the early 2000s with the 'Agenda 2010' reforms of the SPD–Green Party coalition, which in particular made the regulation of employment more flexible, representing a withdrawal from some of the old social compromises. Two sets of institutional changes were introduced in relation to collective bargaining and re-commodification of labour. The pronounced aim of both was to reduce labour costs, as employment was deemed too expensive in Germany.

The first set of institutional changes, justified by the need to reduce wage costs, aimed to decentralize collective bargaining and dismantle regional industry-wide wage agreements in various ways. First, through 'organized decentralization' as a shift from multi-employer bargaining at the sectoral and central level to single-employer bargaining through the signing of company-based wage agreements with unions (Crouch 1995: 316). This shift was especially explicit in East Germany (Behrens *et al.* 2001).

Second, decentralization occurred through the unions' accepting 'opening clauses', under economic pressure, which empowered works councils and management to flexibilize standards at company level, especially so-called production-site agreements (*Standortvereinbarungen*). They contained workforce concessions in exchange for fixed-term employment guarantees to stop redundancies due to production shifts towards East Central Europe (Streeck and Hassel 2003; Seifert and Massa-Wirth 2005). The modified collective bargaining system weakened trade unions and enhanced works councils' bargaining power, and was a major factor in a wage development below productivity growth and the drastic decline of unit labour costs in Germany relative to the eurozone, of almost 10 per cent between 1999 and 2006 (ECB 2007: 64). It also contributed to far greater diversity of working conditions at company level.

In addition to the flexibilization, the ongoing decline in membership in both trade unions and employers' associations led to a sharp decline in the general bargaining coverage which lies at the European average, with approximately 65 per cent in 2009, that is, 65 per cent in West and 51 per cent in East Germany. If we only refer to sectoral agreements, the percentage is even lower with 56 per cent in West Germany and 38 per cent in the East (Bispinck *et al.* 2010: 3).

The demonstrated flexibility in wage-setting and an increase in working hours was accompanied with an increase in the share of employees on low wages, – particularly among women (31.3 per cent), unqualified workers (29.3 per cent), workers under 25 years of age (39.2 per cent) and foreign workers (25.9 per cent) – in agriculture, household-related as well as care-related services – that goes beyond the European average, while at the same time the wage differences between the lowest (D1) and middle tenth has dramatically increased and is only surpassed by Poland, Estonia, Latvia and Slovenia (Bosch and Kalina 2005: 37–40; Bispinck 2007: 20). The working poor have become a reality in Germany, with approximately 2 million people earning an income under the state social aid threshold (Becker 2006).

The second set of institutional changes, the so-called Hartz reforms or Agenda 2010,[4] exchanged the principle of ensuring people's standard of living during periods of unemployment for that of 'activating' the unemployed to bring them back into work more quickly and effectively. Measures for doing this included limiting the right to refuse low-pay or long-commute work offers, as well as a forced cooperation between city councils (responsible for distributing social aid) and local agencies of the federal labour agency (responsible for distributing unemployment benefits).[5] While this kind of 'activating' labour-market policy had been carried out before in Denmark, the Netherlands and the UK, it led to widespread public protest in Germany and, as a consequence, the loss of the early elections in 2005 for the Social Democrats and a historic low in the 2009 election. Thus, the renunciation by the Social Democrats of the inherent consensus of the 'German model' did not find popularity with the electorate.

In contrast to labour relations, the traditional German dual system of vocational training partly financed by companies remained institutionally untouched. However, here too changes have occurred over the last two decades, most of them not part of any formal reform project. Between 1976 and 1985 the dual system experienced the greatest period of expansion often called a 'triumph of German corporatism' (Baethge *et al.* 2007: 25). Employers' associations, Chambers of Commerce, unions and politicians as well as managers and works councils in the companies pulled together in order to increase the number of new contracts within the dual system beyond the economic needs of the companies, in order to meet the demands of school leavers. This additional training was understood as a social commitment to society (ibid.). Especially since the early 1990s a major decline has been observed in new training offers from companies within the dual system, as well as a failure of new corporatist initiatives. Martin Baethge and others (ibid.) name two major reasons for the weakened commitment of companies. First, the structural change within the economy – increase in employment in the service sector, which is traditionally much less involved in the dual training system, and the increase in tertiary education; second the implementation of a strictly cost- and profit-driven management that meant a decentralization of the costs for vocational training, transforming them from a company-wide overhead to expenditure by departments or by newly formed cost centres and profit centres. With this shift, training became tightly linked to financial calculations, binding training expenditures to more short-term economic interests (ibid.: 27–30). Also, the abundance of skilled workers in East Germany and in East Central Europe may have contributed to the drop of apprenticeship offers in the early 1990s, while in East Germany the creation of similar vocational training programmes as in the West could only occur with heavy public investment.[6] As a result, and due also to demographic change, Germany began to suffer from a so-called 'skilled-worker gap' from the end of the first decade of the new century, which could not be filled by the training endeavours of the companies, even in the manufacturing sector, the traditional core of the dual system (ibid.).

Concerning the corporate governance system, the SPD–Green Party coalition under Chancellor Gerhard Schröder was also a crucial actor in its historic reform. The new tax law of 2000/2001, in particular, totally and immediately abolished the taxation of profits from the sale of large share-blocks held by shareholders in German companies. This reform was intended to unravel inter-locking ownerships, and eased the withdrawal of the large German for-profit banks and insurance companies from their traditional central positions within the 'Deutschland AG' (Höpner and Krempel 2004; Höpner and Streeck 2003).[7] Large German private banks transformed themselves 'from credit providers for national firms into competitive players in the international financial industry' to meet the profit expectation of the globalized capital market (Streeck 2009: 79; for more, see Beyer 2003).[8]

The consequences for the German corporate-governance system are disputed. Wolfgang Streeck, Martin Höpner, Jürgen Beyer and others stress that with the dissolution of 'Deutschland AG', a fundamental break occurred with the traditional German corporate governance system and a shift from network to market. The dramatic increase in the earnings of top managers in very large companies compared to the pre-1989 period, even though it may be 'moderate' by US standards, is often named as an indicator of the increasing marketization (cf. Höpner 2004).[9]

Sigurt Vitols (2005: 358), in contrast, argues that the change of the system is 'less dramatic than many have claimed'. He lists four reasons. First, the system of bank monitoring and control was mainly concentrated on the very large, publicly-listed companies. For other listed companies, the concentration of ownership typical for the coordinated market economy remains quite high. In addition, even among large companies, only a few are publicly listed at all and therefore attached to the capital market. Second, the withdrawal of the big German for-profit banks did lead to a decline in cross-company shareholdings but not to a complete dissolution. Vitols points to the distribution of shareholdings in general (and not only to the network position of big banks, i.e. the number of shares and positions held in other companies). According to his analyses, non-financial companies have been the most important shareholders throughout the post-war period and kept one-third of the holdings despite a significant reduction. Third, there is no tradition of 'independent' directors as in the Anglo-Saxon governance system. In response to the withdrawal of the German banks, former management-board members of the companies moved to the supervisory boards of the very large listed companies when they retired, thus keeping the control internal instead of causing an increase in independent external control (cf. Rang 2004). Fourth, Vitols (ibid.) observes that 'neither the dual board structure nor the board level co-determination' by works councils and unions 'have been seriously called into question in the political debate'. He interprets the maintenance of these institutions as 'a supporting factor for the consensus approach in decision making between stakeholders, including employee representatives, which is a hallmark of the German corporate governance system' (ibid.: 366). This still implies that the chairperson of the management board is understood more as coordinator of the collective work of the board rather than as a 'strong CEO'. All of its members remain jointly accountable for management decisions.[10]

Furthermore, there has been no run towards the alternative institutional solution offered by the EU regulation of European companies (*Societas Europaea, SE*) since the end of 2004 – which allows the option of the Anglo-Saxon single-body system and could even be used to abandon or reduce co-determination in supervisory boards. In 2010 out of the 58 largest listed companies in Germany from the Forbes 'Global 2000' list, only eight adopted the SE and only one has no employees on the advisory board. Hence, there are good reasons to reject the 'thesis of convergence' with the Anglo-American model; and Vitols is right in pointing to the corporate governance system as a whole.

On the other hand, the gradual transformation has not stopped. In reaction to the financial crisis and unsatisfied with the outcomes of institutional change, the ruling 'Great Coalition' (SPD–CDU) under Chancellor Angela Merkel (2005–9) sought tighter restrictions in order to foster an Anglo-Saxon 'culture of independent directors' – first in the context of the German Corporate Governance Code[11] and then, in 2009, directly with a law that sets a 'cooling-off-period' of two years before a member of management or the executive board can be appointed to the supervisory board.[12] At the level of business, we can also observe underlying shifts. In spite of the formal stability of the German dual-board system, there is an ongoing reinterpretation, especially with regard to the position of the chairperson within the collective management board. The changing meanings are visible in the reduction of the number of board members over the last years as well as in the usage of terms. Of the 58 companies on the Forbes Global list mentioned above, we find that 29 call their *Vorstandsvorsitzende* (chairperson) not 'chair' on their English websites but 'CEO'; ten of them use both terms ('chairperson' and 'CEO'), eight companies call their chairmen (there was apparently no chairwoman) of the management board 'CEOs' even on their websites in German, evidently indicating how they understand his (usual) role. Among them are both SE companies and German joint-stock companies (AGs) as well as highly internationalized and less internationalized companies.

Finally, although the dissolution of 'Deutschland AG' has affected only the largest German companies listed on the stock markets, the bank-company relationship has changed significantly. Long before the Second Capital Accord (Basel II) came into effect in 2007 in the EU, German private and, somewhat later, savings banks began to introduce new reporting and lending standards that tied loans to detailed information, business plans and formalized rating procedures. This development contributed to the increasing importance of managerial accounting systems also in medium-sized companies and to growing profit sensitivity here as well (cf. Bluhm and Martens 2009).

In summary, the institutional transformation in German capitalism has been widespread but has occurred, to a large extent, within and alongside the traditional coordinating institutions (cf. also Hassel 2010). Employment flexibility has increased by consensus, with labour agreeing to concessions regarding pay and working time in exchange for job security for core workers, with an increasing share of workers occupied at the periphery through short-term contracts or agency work. The dual vocational training system is still in place but takes on fewer students. The big for-profit banks have forfeited their key positions within the traditional company network, and the corporate governance system is undergoing a transformation. In spite of this, many of the core institutions of the corporate governance system are still in place, while their meanings and functions are changing. Clearly, the mode of German unification has contributed to this but can hardly be perceived as the only or even major source or impetus for change.

It is open to discussion how to interpret this systematic transformation and where it will lead in the long run, even more so since the financial and the consequent euro crisis (cf. also Allen 2010). The positions taken by scholars range from continuing erosion and a movement towards neoliberalism (Streeck 2009; Dörre 2010), to a kind of institutional recombination beyond a path-dependent adaptation (as proposed by Thelen 2004) but not abandoning core institutions completely. Palier and Thelen (2010) describe this mode of change as the institutionalization of a new 'dualism' between sectors and labour markets that saves complementary advantages at the cost of the 'excluded', while Lane (2000) points to a more encompassing hybridization. The dualism thesis seems to fit best to the apparent renewal of the German export model in the European crisis. However, the suggestion that the 'German model' has remained at least partly intact is misleading as it underestimates the institutional changes within the core industrial sectors and does not see that the preservation of the comparative advantages of the 'German model' was paid for with an uncoupling of wages from productivity and a dramatic increase in social inequality.

Business leaders in the driver's seat?

The debate on business leaders as drivers of institutional change is nurtured by the observation that the adoption of shareholder-value concepts, especially by big German companies in the second half of the 1990s, is not simply the result of the growing external pressure of the capital market, but has been motivated 'from within'. In other words, top managers have readily embraced the new 'shareholder-value' concept (cf. Dörre and Brinkmann 2005; Höpner 2004; Kädtler and Faust 2008; Faust *et al.* 2011; Kädtler 2010). There are two lines of argument here, in which it is assumed that: (1) the change in *career patterns* has caused a great deal of detachment from the 'German model'; or, alternatively, (2) the *opportunity structure* has changed in favour of management and was grasped by them. The two positions are sometimes overlapping but should be systematically separated.

In the first line of argumentation, scholars perceive a relatively strong connection between change in the career paths of top managers in large companies and changing attitudes, perceptions and values (cf. Höpner 2003; 2004; Beyer 2007), or at least the changing career patterns indicate a weakening of the cultural influence of the traditional, cooperative 'German model' (Freye 2009a). Martin Höpner (2004) posits that a decrease in the relevance of 'in-house careers' and a significant shortening of tenure in the highest positions leads to a growing 'marketizing' of manager careers (Höpner 2003 and 2004),[13] which he links to the adoption of 'Anglo-American' management concepts. Others also stress the declining loyalty to companies and employees (cf. Dörre 2002; Kotthoff and Wagner 2008 for middle management; Freye 2009a for board members).

The observation of changing career patterns is frequently combined with two other findings: for one, the dwindling importance of vocational training as a first step in the careers of board members, which training was once seen as responsible for 'less professional and social distance between management and non-management personnel' in international comparisons (Maurice *et al.* 1979: 315), and for another, the decline of engineers among the top managers of large companies, a profile once seen as typical for German managers. This was supposed to tie them more closely to their occupation (instead of being 'generalists') and thereby moderate financial considerations (Lane 1989; Byrkjeflot 2001; Jackson *et al.* 2005). Martin Höpner (2003 and 2004) for the 40 biggest *manufacturing* companies (base-year 1996) and Jürgen Beyer (2007) for the 100 largest German companies in 2003 posit that an increase in chairpersons with business and economics degrees contributes to the financialization of the companies and the devaluation of the 'German model'.[14]

The thesis of a turning away from the traditional career patterns and educational background is contradicted by other scholars, partly by different findings and samples, partly by different interpretations of similar findings (Hartmann 2006; Freye 2009a; Pohlmann 2009: 523). They see no retreat of engineers from boardrooms and question the assumption of a waning importance of 'in-house careers' in the last two decades. For example, in Freye's sample of 48 chairpersons, also in the *manufacturing* sector in 2005, 58 per cent of top managers still had a technical degree, which comes close to the findings of studies in the 1960s and 1970s (cf. Kruk 1972; Pross and Boetticher 1971; Zapf 1965); while 47.9 per cent had a degree in economics/business, which is even more than in 1960, after a decline in the 1970s and 1980s according to Freye (2009a: 95; cf. Kruk 1972). Hartmann (2006) confirms the growing importance of economics degrees based on a sample of the economic elite from the 100 biggest German companies *independent of sector*. According to him, slightly more than one-third of chairpersons have an academic background as engineers or natural scientists (36.4 per cent engineers/natural scientists to 41 per cent economists), which comes close to the findings of Höpner. However, the rise of economics degrees is not thought to occur at the expense of the engineers, but of lawyers.

With respect to career patterns, Hartmann disputes a decline of the traditional pattern since the mid-1990s, and therefore speaks of its astonishing *stability* (2006: 440–3, 2009; cf. Pohlmann 2009), while Freye observes rather a shift from 'company-careers' to 'holding-careers' over recent decades. Therefore Freye does not completely reject the idea of an emerging market for executives, but argues for a growing *'internal'* labour market for executives, while external recruiting is increasing as well (2009a and b). Freye explains the growing detachment of top managers from the 'German model' by three phenomena: a) the increasing international experience of managers with other institutional versions of capitalism, as it becomes more and more important to have studied and/or worked abroad; b) the decline in inter-sectoral careers, for example, shifts between business and politics; and c) the waning presence of lawyers in top positions. She claims that this retreat of lawyers is responsible for a growing estrangement of top managers from non-economic societal expectations and from the state (Freye 2009a: 178).

Michael Hartmann most clearly speaks along the second line of argumentation, which points to the opportunity structure and how it has been used by executives. He perceives the importance of career changes as overstated and rejects the thesis of a direct connection between change in career paths and change in attitudes (cf. critique on Höpner, Hartmann 2006). For him, it is not so much the 'marketization' and the resulting uncoupling of the different functional elites that has contributed to the deep crisis of 'Deutschland AG', but the shift in the total societal power relation – to the serious disadvantage of employees – that has led the economic elites to a fundamental reassessment of this model (Hartmann 2006: 452–5). The 'class-compromise' of the post-war Federal Republic, with the multiple levels of mediation characteristic of the 'German model', has lost its former esteem among the economic elites. The room for manoeuvre opened by the fall of the Eastern bloc and the much-touted globalization is now used by players simply to strengthen their own position. That means that the change in attitudes is not due to the changed characteristics of the actors, but grounded primarily in a new opportunity structure and legitimated by a new hegemonic discourse.

However, Hartmann also argues that there is a growing egotism and social irresponsibility in the economic elites based on social exclusiveness, which means, in effect, that the educational expansion of the 1970s did not lead to a social opening of elite positions in the German economy, but rather to further social closure, in spite of the country's non-elite educational institutions (Hartmann and Kopp 2001; Hartmann 2000, 2007). Thus, he too establishes links between actor characteristics and changing attitudes in a certain way.

Both lines of argumentation share a similar problem. The studies from which the authors draw their conclusions have their strength in an almost perfect sampling, as they gained most of the information by document analysis of Curricula vitae, annual reports, firm data banks, etc. Only the research conducted by the Cologne Max-Planck-Institute (see Beyer, Höpner, Streeck, and others) included a written questionnaire for board members, but they did not try to explore attitudes. Hence all the conclusions about the linkage between career patterns and attitudes rely on theoretical assumptions only. The same holds true for Hartmann's argument on top manager social irresponsibility, since he concludes from a general discourse level to the micro level of individual perceptions. In short, both lines of argumentation ascribe central importance to the shift in attitudes, which is not examined, but presupposed.

Background, career patterns and attitudes of German business leaders

In the following sections we offer an empirical account of business leaders' perception of the 'German model' and we use descriptive variables to explain variations in attitudes. After a short description of our sample, we explore the social origins, education and career patterns of our respondents, trying to figure out whether and to what extent changes can be observed here, controlled by three other variables: East-West origin; company size; and age of the respondents. Based on these findings, we analyse patterns of orientations linked to the 'German model' and investigate correlations between attitudes and these descriptive variables, in order to test the proposed linkages between actor characteristics and a reassessment of the 'German model'. As our use of the sample varies from that of the other chapters of the book, we start with a short description of the German sample.

Description of the sample

The German sample consists of medium-sized (45–249 employees), large (250–999 employees), and very large (with 1,000 and more employees) companies, from the manufacturing sector and banks (Table 4.1). The addresses of the companies of the manufacturing industry and banks came from data bases of Chambers of Commerce and commercial sources. We used the list of the largest banks and companies in Germany collected by the *Frankfurter Allgemeine Zeitung* and the Hoppenstedt database. The survey was conducted by telephone (computer-assisted telephone interviewing) in 2009/10. The target persons were members of the highest hierarchical level of the companies. In detail, these persons were chairpersons, managing directors, their deputies or other members of the management boards. We spoke to 53 chairpersons (*Vorstandsvorsitzende*), 361 members of the management boards, and 32 plant managers of medium-sized to very large companies.[15]

The success we had in interviewing the business leaders varied with the size of the company. Predictably, top managers of very large companies and banks were more reluctant to participate (Table 4.1). The relatively high response rate on the part of the medium-sized companies can also be partly explained by the fact that they had already agreed to participate in a panel investigation of changes in German management a couple of years ago, a study now running the third wave.

As we restrict our attention to only the '*first-level*' respondents in this chapter, our sample of 'very large companies' comprises 14 companies with more than 10,000 employees, 31 companies have more than 5,000, and 63 companies have 1,000 employees or more. Five of those very large companies are banks. We use the size of company staff as the basic measurement for characterizing the companies, since alternatives (for example volume of sales) cause more problems (large numbers of missing values and lesser certainty of validity). The German sample includes 145 East German and 300 West German business leaders measured by their place of living before the currency union of 1990.[16] The East

Table 4.1 Features of the German sample, all cases

Characteristics of the respondents	Number of employees, industrial companies		Banks
	45–999 (m, l)	≥ 1,000 (xl)	
Number of cases	400	79	44
Response rate (% of cases relates to all solicited companies of the category in question)	45.1	14.1	15.1
% of women	8.3	6.3	4.5
% of respondents at the top hierarchical level	89.8	73.4	67.4
% of companies in East Germany	59.5	6.3	2.3

Germans usually run medium-sized companies in East Germany, often as owners with minor shareholdings, while about one-third of the East German companies are managed by West Germans. This proportion was relatively stable during the three panel waves. The presence of East Germans at the top of the largest companies and banks is negligible.

We are well aware that our sample implies a broader understanding of business leadership than those used by the studies discussed above. But there are good reasons that not only justify such an approach but even make it essential. One characteristic feature of the German industry and corporate governance system is the existence of a large proportion of medium-sized and relatively large but unlisted companies (*Mittelstand*), especially in the manufacturing sector, which make up the largest share of German GDP and control significant societal resources (Bluhm and Martens 2011). We argue that a restriction in studies to the biggest public-listed companies and their leaders might lead to a misperception of the dynamic of change in the German business community.

In the following sections, we do not differentiate between industrial and financial sectors. This is the usual procedure in elite research where the size of the company, as an operationalization of power, is a common analytic dimension, but where branch does not play a role. Nonetheless, a strong bias toward manufacturing remains, which has been the core sector of the 'German model'.

Social origin, qualification and careers

We operationalize *social origin* by social stratum of the respondents' fathers according to the Goldthorpe class scheme (Erikson and Goldthorpe 1992).[17] It is noticeable that service class positions I and II (e.g. higher-grade professionals and officials, top managers of large *and* small companies (with ten employees and more), and lower-grade managers of large companies, large proprietors) in East and West Germany dominate, with a relative frequency of around 50 per cent. If one uses, as benchmark, the weighted distributions of the current German General Population Survey of the Social Sciences (Allbus 2008), the share of the service classes I and II in our random sample of business leaders is approximately two to three times greater than in the population. Thus in the observed group of business leaders we find generally a recruitment from comparatively higher social strata. In our sample, the percentages of business leaders having fathers with an occupation in service classes I and II are slightly lower than those from the Potsdamer Elite Study of the 1990s (Bürklin *et al.* 1997: 82), in which two-thirds of the economic elite members come from these social strata. The reason for this difference may be that the Potsdam study only included the biggest German companies, where the percentage of board members from lower classes is presumably still lower (Hartmann 2006). A somewhat larger proportion of children of skilled workers can be found only in the respondents of East German origin of our sample. For the remaining occupational classes, the percentages are only about half as great as in the General Population Survey of 2008. By what mechanisms children from higher social classes are promoted towards managerial careers, we have to leave open here. There are, contrary to what one might expect in a sample that includes many medium-sized companies run by managing owners, no significant correlations between social origin and ownership of company stock. Hence, the finding that higher social strata clearly favour one's becoming a business leader holds true for the whole German sample from medium-sized to very large companies. This positive correlation between higher social origins and top positions in management exists for western as well as eastern Germans.

In the debate on the role of engineering *qualifications*, our sample provides us with three findings. First, if we look at all West Germans, 49 per cent have an engineering/technical degree, which is even a bit higher than in Hartmann, as mentioned above. Yet, if we take the board members of the *very large manufacturing* companies in our sample, which have been the focus of the 'decline thesis', the engineers drop to 39 per cent, while 52 per cent of top managers have economics degrees – a finding quite close to Höpner and indicating in fact a clear change compared with earlier studies focusing on manufacturing (cf. Pross and Boetticher 1971). The percentage of engineers is higher in medium-sized companies (see Table 4.2) and, here again, it is higher in East Germany than in the West. Among East Germans the corresponding percentage with technical qualifications is highest, at 86 per cent. This 'continuation' of the German engineering tradition is essentially related to the period of political transformation after 1990, when technical qualifications were systematically preferred because engineers and technicians were considered to have been politically less corrupted. Yet this holds true only for top management, because on lower hierarchical levels of management a reverse trend towards economics qualifications is detectable in our panel analyses from the last ten years.

With regard to vocational training, our analysis produces a mixed outcome: The relevance of this first step in a managerial career is highly dependent on company size. Business leaders of very large companies have less often done vocational training (48.3 per cent) than business leaders of medium-sized companies (75.9 per cent, Table 4.2). Yet, the percentage is higher in the East than in the West, and declines in both parts of the country with age. During the years of our panel study (2002–10), there is a successive decline of the relevance of vocational training for managerial careers, which was traditionally high in Germany.

On the basis of our sample, we can distinguish three *different career paths*. By the term 'in-house career' we refer to a working life that takes place entirely – with the exception of an early 'search period' of five years – in the very same company where the respondent now works.[18] The opposite of the 'in-house career' is what we call the 'parachute career', where managers take over executive positions without ever having worked in that company before. Usually they will have held a high position in the previous company. The third type is an 'external-internal path' career, in which the person begins in one company, then changes to the current company and eventually advances to his or her present position.

A result is that the 'parachute career' represents the predominant path to the top of all types of companies (45 per cent of the respondents are 'parachutists'),

Table 4.2 Characteristics of the German sample of business leaders, only top hierarchical level

Characteristics of the business leaders	Number of employees, industrial firms				Banks
	sm[a]	lm[b]	l[c]	xl[d]	b[e]
Mean year of birth	1956	1957	1957	1959	1957
% of women	9.6	6.7	4.1	5.2	3.4
% with vocational training	79.3	72.7	61.6	48.3	89.7
% with higher education degree	83.0	90.7	91.9	96.6	75.9
% of engineers	67.9	57.4	54.4	39.3	0.0
% studying business	29.5	40.4	45.6	51.8	90.9
% who studied abroad	9.8	14.0	20.6	35.7	18.2
% working more than 5 months abroad since starting to work	31.8	45.1	63.8	81.1	25.0
Mean year of start of work	1978	1979	1981	1985	1979
Mean year of the first managerial position	1985	1985	1986	1990	1986
Starting year in the current company	1990	1991	1992	1997	1995
Mean number of companies worked in	3.0	2.8	3.3	3.3	3.3
% in same economic sector as previously	51.5	39.4	50.9	50.0	90.9
% previous company in Germany	94.9	93.6	85.5	87.0	95.5
Median term of work abroad (in months)	5	15	25	35	6

Notes
a sm means 45–99 employees.
b lm means 100–249 employees.
c l means 250–999 employees.
d xl means 1,000 or more employees.
e b = banks.

while the 'in-house career' appears to be much less prevalent at 30 per cent. One-quarter follows the 'external-internal path'. Remarkably, there are no significant differences according to company size or between East and West. In this respect we confirm the findings of earlier studies of declining 'in-house careers' (Kruk 1972; Bleicher 1983: 141–3; Hartmann 1995: 464; Walgenbach and Kieser 1995: 279–80). Only a minority of business leaders follow 'in-house careers'. If we separate the chairpersons from other members of management boards, we find an even higher percentage for the 'parachute' group: 52.8 per cent versus 46.0 per cent (others), respectively, that is, the very highest positions, especially in large and very large companies, are mainly filled from outside, while still a slight majority of business leaders has to take at least one prior career step within the company before they became a board member, executive or plant manager. This finding suggests the existence of a well-established market for executives, although precise historic comparisons are difficult due to different definitions of careers and sample constructions (cf. Kruk 1972: 170–1).

The 'external-internal path' and the 'parachute path' may not exclude continuity in the sense of a 'branch career' (Hartmann 2006). Thus, we also asked for a response as to whether the last company change implied a change of branch. Approximately half of managers did not work in the same branch in their previous companies. Hence, the market for executives reaches beyond industry boundaries to a significant extent.[19]

As to *job durations* in the current company, our findings contradict the conjecture of generally falling tenures of business leaders in Germany, in spite of the significant change in career types. The durations differ across the three career types, but are generally rather long: on average, 27 years in the case of 'in-house', 16 years for 'external-internal', and the 'parachutists' work 14 years in one company. The time span varies with the size of the company, but even for the largest-size category the mean duration is not less than 13 years. In short, even 'parachuting' implies an appreciably long tenure. The drastically shorter tenures that Höpner and Freye observe are statistically not visible in our sample. This finding at least puts a question mark on the general assumption that the emergence of a market for executives implies a radical shortening of the time span that the leading management personnel actually spend in a company.

With respect to the referenced statements about processes of social closure in German economic elites, correlations between social origins and age are of special interest. Our data exhibit such a connection between the age group '45 and younger', the service classes I and II, and 'in-house careers'. Additionally, the group of business leaders older than 45 years at the time of the survey correlates with the Goldthorpe classes IV and VI. These differences in our German sample by career type and age might be interpreted in the light of the social closure thesis emphasized by Michael Hartmann (2007). This conjecture is studied in much more detail and in a comparative framework in Chapter 5 of this book on careers.

Correlations between attitudes and descriptive variables

In a third step of our analyses, we explore the attitudes of the German respondents regarding the 'German model' and bring them together with the descriptive variables we have already introduced (career pattern, education, social and regional origin, age and company size). In addition, we use the actual involvement of the company in vocational training, and in collective bargaining that we collected with the same questionnaire and by studying company reports.

In the questionnaire, a number of items are directly linked to institutions standing for three peculiar dimensions of the 'German model' as described in the first section. We asked the business leaders for a response of 'agreement' (scored 1) or 'disagreement' (scored 5) with a consensus approach in decision-making between stakeholders (Vitols 2005: 366); with the need for collective labour regulation and workers' participation; and with the offering of vocational training.[20]

The three items operationalize attitudes towards the method of corporate governance and the definition of company goals, separating the attitudes into a consensus-oriented stakeholder approach and a shareholder approach (Table 4.3,

Table 4.3 Items suitable for the operationalization of the 'German model'[a]

Items	E Germans	W Germans	Used in index building	Significance
1. Vocational training is a task of government but not of business.	3.96	4.00	Involvement in vocational training	0.335
2. Collective regulations between social partners are important for the functioning of the economy.	2.31	2.22	Labour relations	0.003
3. If German companies are to remain competitive, co-determination should be abolished in Germany.	3.61	3.77	Labour relations	0.114
4. Labour participation in company decisions only leads to higher costs.	3.78	4.01	Labour relations	0.020
5. Trade unions are superfluous.	2.78	3.47	Labour relations	0.000
6. In conflicts over company goals, owner interests should clearly be the first consideration.	2.57	2.70	Corporate governance	0.290
7. In conflicts over company goals, one should first and foremost attempt to reach a compromise.	1.90	1.97	Corporate governance	0.544
8. The goal of a company is only maximising profit.	2.60	3.00	Corporate governance	0.000

Note
a Means, number of cases: East Germans 135, West Germans 278.

items 6–8). Respondents are perceived as 'stakeholder oriented' if they disagree with the idea that owners' interests should clearly prevail in case of conflict and that a company's goal consists in maximizing profit only, and if they display a preference for compromises. If they have answered in the opposite direction, we regard them 'shareholder oriented'. Therefore 'stakeholder', as a traditional aspect of the 'German model', and 'shareholder' orientation are measured as opposite stances (Gergs and Schmidt 2002). The orientation is measured by an additive index of the three items.

Attitudes towards labour relations are operationalized with four items describing the use of workers' involvement in decision-making in general, the need for collective bargaining between social partners for the functioning of the economy, the agreement with the presence of trade unions in general, and with the German system of co-determination in particular (Table 4.3, items 2–6). The items are drawn together in an index of 'labour participation'. The dimension of vocational training we capture with just one item (Table 4.3, item 1).

All items that reflect the core institutions got high approval levels from the business leaders, challenging the idea of a general turning away from the 'German model'. The strongest approval we find is the rejection of vocational training as a task of government alone. Only 5 per cent of the German respondents agree with this statement and a tiny size effect for the smallest companies is visible, with 9.6 per cent agreement. Ninety-five per cent of the companies are involved in vocational training and this figure is almost the same as that regarding attitudes on whether it should be organized by companies.[21] The correlation between the attitudes and the actual behaviour tends to be zero (0.07). Hence we can say that the turn towards a restrictive cost-oriented perception of vocational training (cf. Baethge *et al.* 2007) did not lead towards a general questioning of the companies' involvement, and even among East German business leaders the vocational training system is highly valued. As the agreement with the responsibility of business in vocational training is overwhelming, we restrict our further attention to corporate governance and labour relations in order to explore variance in the attitudes towards the 'German model'.

A first overview of the data reveals striking East–West differences, especially regarding the agreement to union representation, differences which persist over the ten years of our panel analyses (cf. Martens 2008; Schmidt 2008). East Germans perceive the role of collective bargaining between social partners more positively than they do the need for unions, which 39.2 per cent of the East German business leaders deem superfluous, in contrast to only 20.9 per cent of the West Germans. In the negative perceptions of unions, East German business leaders are much closer to Polish business leaders (see Chapter 8). Otherwise, the agreement with collaboration with works councils and with labour participation comes closer to the West German responses indicating that there is not a rejection of *all* German institutions of organized labour (Table 4.3).[22]

This mixed outcome is reflected in the organizational practice of the surveyed companies, as the coverage with sector-wide agreements of unions and employers' association in East German medium-sized companies is still much lower (16 per cent) than in West German companies of similar size (40 per cent) in spite of an ongoing decline in the figure for the western sample.[23] The presence of works councils in East German companies is notably higher and the collaboration with them is more often accepted than are unions, although both are significantly lower than in the West (for more, see Chapter 8; Schmidt 2008).

Regarding corporate governance, contrasts between East and West Germans occur in respect of the question of profit as the exclusive aim of the company. West German business leaders are not so decisive on this question. Previous analyses have revealed that the East German preference for profit is at least partially explained by the lower incomes compared to West Germans (Martens 2007: 127).

As we are interested in two sets of variables (attitudes and descriptive variables), we proceed in determining 'set correlations' using canonical correlation analyses (Timm 2002; Cohen *et al.* 2003). In order to test the effect of descriptive variables on attitudes, we introduced them into a second set of variables together with age, regional origin (East or West) and company size as controlling variables.[24] Our main descriptive variables were qualifications, career paths, including international experiences (measured by studying and working abroad 6 months and more), education and social origin. The canonical correlation analysis searches for two factors (so-called canonical variates representing the original variables of the two data sets) that maximally correlate. In this case, only the first canonical variates explain a significant amount of variation (Table 4.4). The analyses essentially reveal that merely small amounts of the variance of orientations can be explained by the descriptive variables (only 5 per cent for the first canonical variates, Table 4.4) and additionally the canonical loadings do not provide a clear picture of the relationships between orientations and descriptive variables.[25] Therefore we followed an alternative approach of analysis, which does not look at functional linear relationships between orientations and descriptive variables, but tries to explain different patterns within the data (types of orientations).

For the purpose of pattern construction, the values of the two indices of 'labour participation' and 'corporate governance' are used to distinguish dichotomy perspectives: approval vs neutral or negative attitudes towards collective labour participation; a 'stakeholder' approach vs a pronounced 'shareholder' orientation. The difference between pursuing or rejecting one of these perspectives is operationalized by the agreement score in the indices. If this score is 2.4 or less, the respondent approves of labour participation and collective bargaining. The same applies for the stakeholder approach in corporate governance; in addition if the corporate governance score exceeds 3.6, he or she is assessed as 'shareholder' oriented. The six possible combinations of perceptions, called 'patterns' (outlined in Table 4.5) – reflect a varying attitude towards the 'German model'. The pattern that would be closest to the 'German model' according to theory would be D, with a high approval of labour participation *and* stakeholder values. We call this pattern 'strong support for the "German model"'. The cognitive pattern that would be the

Table 4.4 Characteristics of the canonical correlation analysis of orientations and actor variables[a]

Canonical variates and canonical correlations	Covariation of orientations and descriptive variables	% of variance of orientation that can be attributed to actor variables (redundancy)	Significance
1, 0.373	14%	5%	0.024
2, 0.311	10%	6%	0.134

Note
a Weighted sample of German business leaders (number of cases 266); the data are weighted in such way that the proportion of East German companies is equal to their percentage related to Germany as a whole.

Table 4.5 Configural frequency analysis of the six combinations of orientations[a]

Pattern	Shareholder	Stake-holder	Labour participation	% of the sample	Observed frequencies	Expected frequencies	Adjusted standardized residuals
A	no	no	no	26.7	115	112.1	0.553
B	no	no	yes	26.1	113	136.3	-4.291
C	no	yes	no	10.5	45	53.5	-1.752
D	no	yes	yes	21.9	94	65.1	5.799
E	yes	no	no	9.0	34	19.2	4.279
F	yes	no	yes	6.7	29	23.4	1.155

Note
a German sample of business leaders, residuals larger than 1.96 or smaller than −1.96 are significant.

most opposed to the 'German model' – a 'neoliberal model' – would be E, with a high approval of shareholder value and distance from or even rejection of labour participation, especially in its institutionalized form. Pattern A also displays no support for either of the two ideas but remains undecided in terms of corporate governance. All other patterns (B, C and F) share at least one core idea with the 'German model'.

By comparing the observed frequencies of the six orientations with the expected ones,[26] in this case there would be no correlations between the orientations at all (null hypothesis), three empirical patterns differ significantly from the hypothetical ones: pattern B, sole approval of labour participation is less frequent than expected (which is no real wonder for a sample of business leaders of a broad variety of company sizes). Pattern D, the strong support for the 'German model', is also more frequent than expected under the assumption of the null hypothesis, although only a minority of business leaders (21.9 per cent) clearly advocate a stakeholder approach as well as organized labour participation. The same holds true for – according to our operationalization – the opposing pattern, E: the actual frequency of this orientation is fairly small (7.9 per cent), although under the assumption of the null hypothesis it would even be significantly smaller. Therefore it can be deduced that both adherence to the 'German model' as well the opposing neoliberal pattern are special features of our sample of German business leaders. Both patterns are in need of explanation, because their frequencies do not go along with merely random impacts. For these explanations we will use the descriptive variables.

Supporters of the 'German model' are leaders of the largest companies (1,000 employees and more), who are more frequently in favour of the two core ideas (38.7 per cent of the business leaders of the large companies compared with 20.4 per cent of smaller companies). The companies of the supporters of the 'German model' also more often have works councils (79.1 per cent compared to 62.5 per cent, which correlates with the company size); leaders of these companies more often came through an external-internal career path and not an in-house career as predicted in the literature (29.3 per cent compared to 19.1 per cent for the two other career paths); and they are less often engineers (16.1 per cent of all respondents with technical qualifications compared to 30.1 per cent of the business leaders with non-technical qualifications).[27] Those of West German origin are more likely to be strong supporters of the 'German model' (27.2 per cent compared to 10.0 per cent of the East Germans).

For pattern E ('neoliberal model'), it is much more difficult to find clear relations between descriptive variable and attitudes, unless we split the German sample into East and West. The statistical relationships for the East and West Germans are quite different, as separated logistic regressions reveal. In the East German case, working experience in foreign countries has the effect of supporting a shareholder orientation and distance to institutions of collective labour participation: eight out of ten East German business leaders with working experience in foreign countries follow pattern E. The West German case reveals that no clear statistical connections are notable between attitudes and studying or working abroad.

Contrasting only the two patterns D and E, the support for the 'German model' among West Germans becomes rather overwhelming: 80 West Germans hold to pattern D in comparison with just 19 who are in favour of pattern E. The figures are quite different for the East German business leaders, with 14 followers of pattern D and 15 of pattern E. The expected frequencies under the null hypothesis for the two regional groups[28] indicate that the support for the 'German model' correlates with the regional origin. West German business leaders are very much in favour of the 'German model' while East German business leaders are not. However, it is not possible to break down this general assent of West Germans to find the influence of descriptive variables like qualification, career paths or international experience.

Neither strong support for the 'German model' nor the 'neoliberal model' is predominant among the business leaders, as they together cover just 29.8 per cent of the whole German sample (Table 4.5). Therefore we have also to take the other patterns into account that provide us with a more differentiated picture and allow the evaluation of the 'deviations' from the 'German model' in a strict sense.

Pattern F is particularly interesting from a theoretical point of view. Twenty-nine business leaders favour the combination of a shareholder approach in corporate governance *and* collective workers participation. Although this group is the smallest (6.7 per cent of the sample, Table 5) and permits no further reliable analyses, it indicates that advocating a shareholder approach does not automatically go along with an individualist approach to labour relations – a finding that is in accordance with company case studies, which show that the implementation of finance-driven management concepts did not question the – decentralized and weakened – organized labour participation in larger German companies (cf. Dörre 2002), or that organized labour may have even played 'a subtle role shaping the implementation of corporate strategies aimed at improving share price performance' (Jackson *et al.* 2005: 112).

The largest single group of business leaders share pattern A, which reflects an undecided position in terms of corporate governance combined with a neutral or negative perception of organized labour participation (Table 4.5). Pattern A is especially seen among leaders of smaller businesses (45–249 employees), and the relative frequency of this group amounts to 32.4 per cent (compared to only 8 per cent in the group of business leaders of the largest companies). As many of these companies are run by owners, these findings reflect two interesting variations which we would argue have always been present in German business: for managing owners for whom the risk of failure is more personal, it is more difficult to adopt a broader stakeholder approach or to embrace collective regulation, since both challenge their control. Yet, they do not believe that profit maximizing is companies' only goal (see more Bluhm and Martens 2008). Owners are also more sceptical than employed managers about the use of unions. In our sample, a gap between managing owners and employed managers is clearly visible, again with an 'East German effect'. Sixty per cent of the East German *owners* do not agree with any use of unions, in contrast to only 25 per cent of the *managers*, while in the West the ratio is 30 per cent to 15 per cent. In addition, there is an influence of age, as younger respondents fit more frequently into pattern A.

In spite of the described variations, one outcome, however, is obvious: the vast majority (85.3 per cent) of business leaders have not embraced a clear shareholder approach, either in the neoliberal version or combined with an agreement with collective labour participation. If we add together (see Table 4.4) those who are in favour of organized labour participation and do not support the shareholder approach but a stakeholder approach (pattern B) with those who show a clear preference for stakeholder participation, even if not in favour of organized labour participation (patterns C and D), then we have a majority of 58.6 per cent of the German respondents who support at least one of the two core ideas of the 'German model' and who are not in favour of the shareholder approach. For we consider support for the shareholder approach a crucial contrast to the traditional 'German model', as the shareholder-value thinking radically alters the idea of reconciliation of owners' and labour interests even if unions and works councils turn out to be useful in implementing new corporate strategies.

In the following, we set this group of (at least partial) supporters of the 'German model' against those who are in favour of a shareholder approach (patterns E and F, 14.7 per cent) and the ones who neither agree with one of the two core ideas nor believe in a clear dominance of owners' interest and profit maximization as the only goal for a company (pattern A, 26.7 per cent of the sample).

The variety of orientation patterns and the relatively weak support for a 'German model' in its strict sense illustrate why finding functional relationships between complex attitudes and independent characteristics by means of traditional regression methods is difficult. Nevertheless, we explore again whether any of the descriptive variables that we have used before may correlate with the re-grouped patterns. In addition, stock holding of the respondents is taken into account.

In a multivariate perspective, the statistical relationships are to some extent similar to the comparison to patterns D and E (Table 6).[29] The East Germans provide a clearer picture than do their western counterparts.[30] In the first case, belonging to the partial supporters of the 'German model' is positively influenced by increasing age, while working activities in foreign countries and a smaller company size have negative effects. The result for the West Germans is again not comparable to the East German analysis. Managing owners and smaller company size have negative effects on support for the 'German model' in the defined sense, but they also show less support for a 'shareholder' approach. It seems that in the West German case the combination of smaller company size and ownership on the part of the respondents is more frequently accompanied with being neither decided in terms of corporate governance nor in favour of labour relations (Table 4.6).

Partial supporters of the 'German model' (patterns B, C and D) are most often to be found among business leaders of the large and very large companies in West Germany. Working experience in foreign countries influences this support, as discussed in a previous section, but, as we have said, only among East Germans. As East German business leaders are in general more distant from core ideas of the 'German model', this is hard to interpret as a simple confirmation of the suggested conjuncture between foreign experiences and a growing estrangement from the model. All other independent variables, particularly the characteristics discussed

Table 4.6 Results of a multinominal logistic regression with the probability of three types of orientations (patterns B C D, E F, and A) as dependent variables and a subset of all descriptive variables which has at least one significant relation[a]

East German business leaders (number of cases 131, Nagelkerke's R² = 0.247)

Variables	Partial support for the 'German model'[b]		Shareholder orientation[b]	
	Odds ratio	Significance	Odds ratio	Significance
Working more than 5 months abroad	0.349	0.046	3.207	0.029
Respondent possesses company shares	0.662	0.331	0.444	0.137
45 years or older	5.805	0.014	1.556	0.531
Company size 45–249 employees[c]	0.200	0.075	0.334	0.254

West German business leaders (number of cases 241, Nagelkerke's R² = 0.114)

Variables	Partial support for the 'German model'[b]		Shareholder orientation[b]	
	Odds ratio	Significance	Odds ratio	Significance
Working more than 5 months abroad	1.042	0.902	1.111	0.821
Respondent possesses company shares	0.466	0.022	0.362	0.040
n>45 years	1.795	0.118	1.094	0.857
Company size 45–249 employees[d]	0.213	0.047	0.170	0.038
Company size 250–999 employees[d]	0.246	0.082	0.074	0.008

Notes
a Odds ratio (exp [b]) smaller than 1 (larger than 1) indicate negative (positive) effects, the significances refer to the null hypothesis; German sample of business leaders.
b The reference category is 'lack of orientation'.
c The reference category is 'company size larger than 249 employees'.
d The reference category is 'company size larger than 999 employees'.

in the literature – social origin, career paths, and qualifications (including academic education abroad) – do not have a noteworthy influence, although the relationship with age can be seen as an unspecified hint that younger East German business leaders show lower degrees of support for the traditional 'German model' than older East Germans. But this age effect (which is found in West as well as East German managers, as we have seen) cannot be further specified by the personal features already discussed, as, for instance, careers or qualifications. Additionally, the opposite categories of both independent dichotomized variables – being

45 or younger and East German origin – are connected with higher frequencies of pattern A, not, as one might perhaps assume, with 'shareholder' orientations. Thus it is not possible to conclude a decisive shift towards a shareholder approach in younger age cohorts as some scholars expected (Gergs and Schmidt 2002).

For the *Mittelstand* of the sample (companies with 45–999 employees), at least partially comparable previous data is also available from two succeeding panel waves conducted in 2002 and 2005. Therefore it can be estimated how stable single attitudes are.[31] In our context, the principal item of interest is the abandonment of the traditional German co-determination. If one restricts one's attention only to cases with valid data for all three panel waves (n = 286), some variation in the data will be visible – the agreement on the need to abandon co-determination for reasons of German competitiveness (item 3 in Table 4.3) was 17.6 per cent in 2002, 21.1 per cent in 2005, and 11.7 per cent in 2010 – and we do not see an ascending trend, as one might have expected. Item 8 (maximizing profit as goal of the company) reveals a declining trend (agreement 58.4 per cent, 52.1 per cent, and 43.5 per cent), while item 6 (owner's interests always have priority) is rather stable (43.5 per cent, 46.0 per cent, and 46.5 per cent).

To sum up, among business leaders of different company sizes we found an astonishingly high level of agreement with key institutions of the 'German model'. A closer look, however, reveals a significant variation of positions, with only a minority who strongly support the 'German model' in all three dimensions operationalized in this chapter: vocational training; a consensus-oriented stake-holder approach in corporate governance; and approval of labour participation within the traditional framework of the German dual system. Especially, top managers of very large companies present attitudes which we see as coherent with support for the 'German model'. Most of the respondents partially support the 'German model', being either less decided in terms of a stakeholder approach or less in favour of organized labour. In any case, only a minority display a clear shareholder orientation, and this is quite often combined with the acceptance of organized labour. While company size obviously matters, only regional origin, age, ownership of company shares, and working experience in foreign countries are actor-related features that cause significant effects on level of support for various features of the 'German model'. Only in the East German sample and only to a minor extent, however, do we find a correspondence between working experience abroad (as an actor-related feature discussed in the literature) and distancing oneself from key ideas of the 'German model'. Although careers have changed, as discussed in the literature, including the growing relevance of studying and working abroad, which is most common in large and very large companies (see Table 4.2), neither academic degrees nor social origin possess a generally significant explanatory power.

Conclusion

Germany underwent a double transformation after 1989. The exceptional experiment of an almost complete transfer of institutions from a highly developed and coordinated market economy onto an emerging market economy following unification has been combined with accelerated changes in those very same institutions. In the debate on the erosion of the 'German model' and its causes, there was an underlying assumption that the expectations, attitudes and values of central actors are crucial for stability and change in institutions, and that business has reassessed the advantages of the traditional model partly due to changing social characteristics of these actors, partly due merely to changing power relationships. Business leaders were thus perceived as a driving force of institutional change. While some scholars assumed a 'cultural turn' towards the 'Anglo-American model' owing to changing career and educational patterns, others stressed the new opportunity structure and the new hegemonic neoliberal discourse.

In this debate, neither East German business leaders nor the beliefs of the so-called German *Mittelstand* are reflected at all, which has to do with the elite focus of this school of research, meaning that only the ideas of top managers of very large companies are regarded as important for institutional change. This restriction not only neglects the contribution of East Germany to the institutional erosion but also underestimates the relevance of the *Mittelstand* for the German political economy (cf. Herrigel 1996; Berghoff 2006). We argue that both medium-sized industry and East German business are important in evaluating the thesis of a 'cultural turn' in German business (cf. Gergs and Schmidt 2002).

Our findings provide mixed and contradicting results with regard to the thesis of a radical break with core ideas of the 'German model' for whatever reasons. First of all, it is hard to see that top managers of very large companies decisively embrace the shareholder approach, casting at least some doubt on the idea that the institutional and strategic changes in the German political economy were in some way preceded by a radical cultural turn among business elites. The shareholder-value thinking appears not to be as widespread as the academic and public discourse in Germany has suggested. Moreover, it seems to be that collective labour participation is even more accepted among business elites than a strict stakeholder approach, if we reflect upon the distribution of all possible patterns. And this acceptance of collective labour participation is general, even though the top managers of very large companies in particular display characteristics which are predicted as actor-related causes for a growing detachment from the 'German model'. Hence, we conclude that the linkage between attitudes and educational and career patterns is much weaker than suggested in the literature.

The inclusion of the *Mittelstand* and East Germany broadens the variety of positions, which can hardly be subsumed under the thesis of a 'cultural turn'. In qualitative interviews, business leaders of medium-sized companies often distance themselves from a shareholder approach but also show greater distance from the dual system of labour relations (cf. Bluhm and Martens 2008; Schmidt 2008), while employed managers of large companies learned to live quite well with it, once the system was installed in the late 1970s (Artus 2001; Plumpe 2006: 411). Whether the distance between unions or works councils and the *Mittelstand* has widened since the hey-days of the 'German model' is hard to say. Our panel analyses over the last decade have revealed a relative stability in the attitudes of the West Germans, while actual participation in the sector-wide collective bargaining system has declined. Yet it would be going too far to claim that the industrial *Mittelstand* en masse is avoiding or even impeding the co-determination by works councils, as Berghoff (2006) suggests.

We have seen that the East German origin of managers and entrepreneurs has some explanatory power regarding variation of attitudes, indicating differences in beliefs, even after an immense institutional transfer and 20 years of unification. This holds especially true when it comes to the labour-relations system and the acceptance of unions in particular, and even if we only compare them with West German business leaders of medium-sized companies. Compared to their opposition to unions, East Germans are more ready to accept works councils and their responsibility in vocational training. The ambivalent and more distant perception of the 'German model' might be explained by socialization but also reflects the huge problems faced by East German companies in gaining competitiveness given the quickly rising wages after unification (cf. Artus 2001). To these experiences, actor attributes of qualification, social origin or even age contribute little variation, although having started the professional career under market conditions and foreign experience seem to widen the distance even more. However, it would be going too far to put East Germans in the vanguard of institutional change, as was occasionally argued especially during the 1990s; indeed, the persisting differences contribute to the increasing cultural heterogeneity within German business after 1990.

Besides this heterogeneity, how are we to interpret the lack of a radical reassessment of the 'German model', especially by the business elite of very large companies? Four strands of argument are possible. First, there may be a gap instead of a conjuncture between beliefs and institutionally relevant behaviour or even a kind of lip service. Managers are still aware of what the public want to hear and therefore give politically correct answers in surveys – especially when they run large companies which attract a lot of public attention. Yet, this argument provides that there is still a societal discourse with some normative power.

Second, our sample is biased due to the limited branch selection and therefore institutional and cultural changes are found to be more moderate than if we had included more companies from service sectors. However, most of the arguments outlined in the literature refer particularly to the core industrial and financial sectors of the 'German model'. Hence, we supposed a 'cultural turn' precisely here.

Third, the financial crisis of 2007–9, during which our survey took place, may have diminished the glamour of the neoliberal project. Therefore, our findings might reflect a return to the strengths of the 'German model', leading to different results than a study that might have taken place at the end of the 1990s or the beginning of the new century, when Germany was called the 'sick man' of Europe. Yet, based on earlier research over the last decade, we perceive attitudes to be relatively stable.

Fourth, the attitudes we found already reflect the ongoing institutional change and adjustment in which large companies in particular have used their growing power against unions to decentralize and flexibilize the system while smaller companies more often take the 'exit option'. Top managers of large companies do appreciate an already changed institutional system that has proven be flexible enough not to need to be challenged openly and still maintains its institutional advantages in global competition.[32] In our view, this explanation is the most plausible one, and suggests that the institutional change within traditional channels corresponds with slow cognitive changes rather than with a clear-cut ideological shift. In this sense one might speak of a 'long shadow' of the 'German model', a shadow that is weaker in East Germany but not absent.

Notes

1 We would like to express our heartfelt gratitude to the following people for their helpful and constructive comments on a previous version of this chapter: Michael Hartmann, Christoph Deutschmann, Jürgen Beyer and Barbara Dippelhofer-Stiem.
2 Compare, for example, Streeck (2009), Hassel (1999) and Rehder (2003) for industrial relations, Thelen (2004) for the skill-formation system, Höpner and Krempel (2004) and Beyer and Höpner (2003) for corporate governance.
3 During the 1990s, the official unemployment rate in East Germany increased continuously from approximately 10 per cent in 1991 to over 20 per cent in 2005 in spite of the intra-German labour migration. The decline after 2005 is mainly due to the demographic change following the dramatic drop in birth rates after 1989 but at 8 per cent in 2011 is still higher than in West Germany (6.7 per cent) (Bundesagentur für Arbeit 2012).
4 In 1998, Chancellor Schröder called for an 'Alliance for Jobs, Training and Competitiveness' (*Bündnis für Arbeit*) to solve the problem of high unemployment. However, the tripartite commission could not agree on any far-reaching tripartite decisions. As a consequence, Schröder formed a high-level group of experts to develop suggestions on how to deal with labour-market problems. Peter Hartz, personnel director at Volkswagen at the time, headed the commission and gave his name to the reform package. By the beginning of 2003, almost all of the commission's suggestions had found their way into the most far-reaching reforms in the regulation of the labour market since World War II. At the same time the reforms marked the end of the German 'century of corporatism' for many observers (Streeck 2003).
5 The Hartz Reform was part of a broader reform of the social security system (health care, compulsory long-term care, unemployment benefits and pensions), which was traditionally insurance-based and added to labour costs as non-wage costs. With these reforms, the so-called *Riester* pension, a privately-funded but state-subsidized pillar was established.
6 In 2008, around €72 million was made available through the Federal-Regional programme alone. At least the same amount was provided by the regions within the programme agreements. The training ratio (company trainees per 100 employees), adjusted for external training programmes, at 4.6 is far below that of West Germany, at 5.2. Other indicators also show clear differences between the East and the West. The share of training companies among all companies in the East is only 19.2 per cent, around 7 per cent less than the corresponding figure for the West, at 26.4 per cent (Troltsch *et al.* 2009: 2).
7 The reform process had already started in 1998, with the KonTraG bill (*Gesetz zur Kontrolle und Transparenz im Unternehmensbereich*) that abolished unequal voting rights and legalized share buybacks and stock options, and which was supported by all parties (Höpner and Krempel 2004). Busch (2005: 130) concludes: 'Joint criticism from the political left and the political right of the "power of the banks" meant that "Deutschland AG" no longer enjoyed any support in parliament.'

8 In addition, Sigurt Vitols points to the impacts of the lower growth environment of the 1990s, in which 'the demand from industrial companies for bank credit diminished, and interest rate margins were squeezed due to increasing competition' (Vitols 2005; Deeg 1999). He also stresses the Basel II-related regulatory changes within the EU that increased the capital costs of equity holdings.

9 According to a study by Kienbaum Consultants International (2007), the substantial increases in earnings in the last three decades are almost completely limited to the top management of the 100 largest German companies: 'The development of board-member salaries in the top 100 companies up until the mid-1990s moved only slightly faster than the income development in the other company classes and relatively parallel to the development of GNP. Only from the late 1990s did the salaries increase markedly. The [salary] relation between top-level executives to the board members (*Vorstände*) in the top 100 companies was for many years about 6:1, but this is today 15:1. Still starker is the relation between workers/office staff and the top 100 board members: from 1976 to 1996, top managers earned 15–20 times more; today the relation is about 43:1' (own translation).

10 The Corporate Code confirms the collective responsibility of the management board, of which the chairman coordinates the work (DCGK 2010, Foreword).

11 The Government Commission of the German Corporate Governance Code consists of bankers, advisors, scholars and a union member. The Code has a legal basis through the declaration of conformity pursuant to Article 161 of the Stock Corporation Act (AktG), as amended by the Transparency and Disclosure Law, which came into force on 26 July 2002.

12 The first German Corporate Governance Code in 2002 (DCGK 2002, 5.4.2) only suggested that not more than two former executive/management board members should move up to the supervisory board. According to the amendment of 18 June 2009, former management board members 'may not become members of the Supervisory board of the company within two years after the end of their appointment unless they are appointed upon a motion presented by shareholders holding more than 25 per cent of the voting rights in the company', which is called a 'cooling-off-period' in the literature. (DCGK 2009, 5.4.4). An identical formulation can be found in the *Gesetz zur Angemessenheit der Vorstandsvergütung* (VorstAG, § 107; Abs. 3), which came into effect on 5 August 2009.

The 'Amendments to the Corporate Governance Code' from 2009 is also of interest in other aspects. It suggests that executive board members should not have more than a total of three seats on the supervisory boards of non-group-listed companies, in order to have enough time for this task. At the same time, it establishes tougher regulations for top manager earnings and stresses much more explicitly than the first Code the idea of sustainability, the interests of employees and other stakeholders and the 'conformity with the principles of the social market economy' (DCGK 2009, Foreword/4.1.1).

13 According to Saskia Freye (2009a), who studied the biographies of board chairpersons in the 50 biggest industrial companies in Germany, tenures shortened from 11 to 8 years over the period 1960–2000.

14 A study by the personnel consultants Heidrick & Struggles departs from the narrow reference to industry but comes to a similar result. In mid-2007, the study analysed the CVs of 189 DAX board members in all sectors, showing that 85 of them had degrees in business administration or economics, followed by law (25 degrees), mechanical engineering (16), industrial engineering (9), chemistry (9), mathematics (8), physics (8), electrical engineering (8) and computer science (5).

15 Only a minority of business leaders are women (6.7 per cent). There are more women heading medium-sized companies (9.6 per cent) and companies in East Germany (12.4 per cent) than large companies (5.2 per cent), banks (3.4 per cent), and in the West in general (4.0 per cent). Yet their proportion is too small for detailed investigations.

16 The East or West German origin was operationalized by the question: 'Where did you live on the 30th of June 1990?' That was the day of the introduction of the German mark in the GDR.

17 By contrast, no statistically relevant correlation with the class membership of mothers exists, so this information is not considered here.

18 Scholars of managerial careers sometimes even use the still narrower concept of the 'chimney career'. Managers on a chimney track are promoted within the same functional or professional area, e.g. finance, production, sales, HRM. Sometimes they change companies but not functional area (Faust 2002). As our data provide an accurate picture of branch and sector changes, but did not pursue the career steps in the detail required for the precise reconstruction of 'chimney careers', we use the term 'sector career' here.

19 Our questionnaire did not allow us to differentiate between external and internal labour markets for executives, as we only asked for positions in other companies. Yet the percentage suggests the relevance of external recruitment.

20 A first analysis of the whole battery of 20 attitude items was given by Bluhm *et al.* 2011.

21 In comparison: 80.2 per cent of the Polish and 75.2 per cent of the Hungarian respondents state that their companies have a stake in vocational training. However, 33.5 per cent of Polish business leaders and even 56.0 per cent of their Hungarian counterparts agree with the statement that vocational training should be a task for government alone.

22 In our first article on findings based on the whole data set (Bluhm *et al.* 2011), we used a narrower index that only focuses on the acceptance of collective regulation and unions as the core of a corporatist approach to labour relations (items 2 and 5 of Table 4.3). Due to the broader approach we have chosen here, that includes co-determination by works councils and labour participation in order to capture the dual character of the German system of labour relations, East Germans come closer to the West Germans. The pronounced reluctance against trade unions on the part of East Germans is partly balanced by positive values on the other items, 3 and 4 (Table 4.3), regarding co-determination. The different operationalizations of 'corporatism' (ibid.) and 'labour participation' cannot be compared directly across countries, since items 3 and 4 are only asked in the German survey.

23 Compared to earlier waves of the German panel study since 2002, the survey 2009/10 revealed a further decline among the West German medium-sized panel companies, while the poor coverage in East Germany has been stable during this decade.

24 In contrast with the principal component analysis, two canonical factors are determined which explain the covariance of *both* variable sets. For two variable sets with p and q variables, there exist min (p, q) canonical correlations and accordingly min (p, q) canonical variates. Only those canonical factors are taken into consideration which significantly contribute to the explanation of covariance. In our case, this is only true for the first components (Table 4.4). Factor loadings and the canonical weights of the original variables on the canonical variates provide the opportunity to analyse the structure of correlations between the two sets of variables and give hints for interpretations.

25 Canonical correlation analyses as well as multiple regressions are computed with weighted data. The differences between the weighted and unweighted results are, in general, only minor; however, on the basis of Germany as a whole, the East German samples are weighted by their proportion in regard to the number of enterprises in Germany (21.5 per cent in 2008).

26 The method is a Configural Frequency Analysis (CFA, von Eye 1990).

27 In contrast to this result, the qualification of the business leaders does not correlate with the attitude towards vocational training.

28 The expected frequencies for the West German business leaders are 63 and 23, and 31 and 11 for East German.

29 The results refer to a multinomial logistic regression (Long 1997). The dependent variables are the probabilities of being a partial supporter of the 'German model' or a 'shareholder' orientation, always in reference to pattern A. The analyses are undertaken separately for the East and West German samples. The independent variables (Table 4.6) are those which show at least one significant relation.

30 This difference is clearly indicated by the different amount of explained variations. The small percentage in the West German case reveals, for example, that the large extent of partial support for the 'German model' can only be poorly explained by the independent variables.

31 Unfortunately, only a limited number of items are collected in all three panel waves. Therefore the orientations operationalized above cannot be analysed diachronically.

32 A functional perspective on co-determination is also confirmed by several empirical studies in Germany on the effects of workers' participation on the economic performance of companies: the majority of studies stresses that the impacts are at least neutral but in no case negative. Kotthoff (2009: 437–8) gives a recent synopsis of different studies about the economic effects of the German co-determination during recent decades.

5 From 'deputy revolution' to markets for executives?

Social origin, careers and generational change of business leaders twenty years after regime change

Katharina Bluhm and Bernd Martens

Introduction

The social origin, recruitment and careers of the new economic elite were an area of intensive research in the 1990s. The international comparative study on elites, 'Social Stratification in East Central Europe after 1989', contributed significantly to the understanding of continuity and change in post-socialist elites, focusing particularly on Hungary and Poland.[1] Using a reference period of 1993/1994, it studied the first generation of economic elite after the regime change. It was not just the classic question of elite circulation vs reproduction over the course of the regime change that was asked, but also questions on the formation of a new social class of 'grande bourgeoisie' and a new system of property ownership. Particular attention was paid to the continuing role of 'nomenklatura'. This means examining whether political capital is transformed on a large scale into economic capital. With the increasing influence of western multinational companies on the key sectors of the economies of Central Europe, interest in the indigenous economic elites dwindled, as they were now seen as relevant as a factor of power only insofar as they operated as a part of the 'comprador service sector' of foreign investors (Drahokoupil 2008). Thus we know little about the business leaders in the consolidated market economies of Poland and Hungary, termed 'foreign-led' or 'dependent market economies' (see Chapter 1).

Our contribution follows on the elite studies of the 1990s, and examines the changes in social origins, training and careers 20 years after the end of the soviet system. Three questions are to the fore: (1) How is the younger generation of business leaders, whose entire career has been in a market economy, different from the cohort that took up leadership positions in the economy immediately after 1989? (2) Are different patterns observed in companies with foreign and domestic ownership? (3) What are the national specificities and what influence do they have?

The chapter is laid out as follows. We begin with an analysis of a central issue in the discussion of the changing economic elites in the early years of the transformation, that of vertical reproduction. As a next step, we ask how East

Germany fits into these findings. Following the 'vertical reproduction' thesis, we argue that the recruitment of the new – regionalized – economic elite can, as in Poland and Hungary, be seen as promotion from the second tier. As a third step, we show that 20 years after 1989, the replacement of the 'deputy' generation in Poland, Hungary and East Germany took place in very different ways, and we ask whether the new elite varies from the business leaders of the transition period, examining the thesis of increasing social closure. The earlier elite studies were based on a 'before and after' analysis: from a starting point in 1988, the continuity in the old economic elite and the origin of the new is investigated, which means that they do not arrive at an analysis of the career patterns as such. This is something we can achieve with our data. Our analysis reveals a strong impact of the transition paths in Poland, Hungary and East Germany. We can show that foreign ownership in Poland and Hungary has above all an impact on the speed of the generational change as such, while the peculiarities of the East German transformation still hinders a takeover by the next generation. While in all three countries a market for executives has emerged over the last two decades, foreign capital in large companies in Poland and Hungary rather fosters the prevalence of 'in-house' careers, which we understand as a second important impact of the 'dependent capitalism' in East Central Europe.

The vertical reproduction thesis

In the 1990s, two theses formed the opposing poles of the debate: the thesis of *political capitalism,* with the 'nomenklatura' as a new 'grande bourgeoisie'; and the thesis of *managerial capitalism.* Elemer Hankiss (1990) first suggested that the transition to capitalism could most peacefully and most safely be carried out by the transformation of an old management elite into a propertied bourgeoisie. According to Erzsebet Szalai (1994), describing primarily Hungary, large-company management began to transform itself into a propertied bourgeoisie during the early stages of transition through a series of management buyouts. Jadwiga Staniszkis (1991: 129) first coined the concept, which can be traced to Max Weber, of political capitalism to describe the pattern of privatization of the state sector 'from above', which began in Poland as early as in 1987 (at least two years before the 'round table' and political reforms), and which would be labelled by her as 'the second wave of "primitive accumulation" in Eastern Europe (now at the expense of the state sector and not at that of agriculture)'. This privatization was 'not a result of the expansion of the traditional private sector, but was a peculiar linkage of political power and capital'.

Opposing this was the thesis of 'managerial capitalism', which was applied to the experiences of privatization at the end of the 1980s – often characterized as 'spontaneous'. Gil Eyal, Iván Szelényi and Eleanor Townsley defended this thesis in their well-known work from 1998.[2] Following the line of 'recombined property' by David Stark and Laszlo Bruszt (1998), they argued that in East Central Europe (unlike in Russia) an extensive conversion from political to economic capital by the old cadre elite, as proposed by Staniszkis, did not take place. Their central finding is that the post-socialist countries simultaneously bypass the creation of a 'grande bourgeoisie' and develop a system of corporate governance in which the managers take control, without becoming at the same time large-scale owners.

The proponents of both theses see reproduction of elites as decisive in the economy, rather than any turnover of elites. The political capitalism thesis includes the claim that there is a comprehensive reproduction of the old elites (including the old political elite as new property-owners), so that the focus is placed on 'reproduction by conversion' (cf. Wasilewski 1998). Eyal *et al.* (1998) suggest a reproduction by succession. Wasilewski and Wnuk-Lipiński (1995: 686) speak of an 'intergenerational vertical reproduction' (cf. also Hatschikjan 1998).

Both thesis where not quite right. The emergence of oligarchs and the conversion of political capital into ownership observed in Russia (cf. for example Krishtanovskia and White 1999) was combined with a widespread promotion of younger deputies to the leading managerial positions (Hanley *et al.* 1995: 657), while the phenomenon described as 'managerial capitalism' did not turn out to be a stable outcome of the privatization process in East Central Europe. Nevertheless, the Elite Study of 1993/94 shows that despite a considerable continuity of the old economic elite,[3] it was above all the 'deputies', that is, those who already, during state socialism, had had careers at various levels of management, who came to the fore in the 1989/90 collapse. As Szelényi *et al.* (1995: 715) put it: 'A sizeable proportion of new economic leaders were already in command positions in 1988, but an even larger percentage of them held lower managerial jobs'. From this it follows that the relatively high turnover rate of the economic elite, compared to other post-socialist transition paths (see Walder 2003), was 'thwarted to a considerable degree' by the succession of the 'deputy department heads', who took over the seats of their predecessors, reached the top by changing the company or founded their own business.

It was therefore not political capital but *cultural and positional capital* in East Central Europe that was the decisive resource in ensuring the new elite positions: 'Indeed, most of the economic command positions in the post-communist corporate sector are occupied by former communist technocrats who were younger and much better educated than senior cadres. Even this group, however, has not pursued political capitalism: former communist technocrats exercise managerial authority, but there is little evidence to suggest that they have acquired substantial private wealth' (Eyal *et al.* 1998: 13; Hanley 1999). 'The main winners in the transformation so far have been highly educated middle-aged men. Members of this group are the least likely to be unemployed and the most likely to be self-employed' (*ibid.*: 34).

What did the social composition of the new economic elite look like? The studies agree that the post-socialist economic elite had been rejuvenated. While in 1988, 42.2 per cent of the Polish economic elite who were questioned were between 50 and 59 years old and only 40 per cent between 40 and 49, the age profile had shifted in 1993 to a 40-something age cohort, which represented the largest group, with 45.5 per cent, followed by 50-somethings at 29 per cent and those under 40 having risen to 17.2 per cent (Wasilewski and Wnuk-Lipiński 1995: 684; Szelényi *et al*. 1995; for similar results, see Matějů and Hanley 1998). According to Lengyel and Bartha (2000: 168), the Hungarian economic elite had been substantially rejuvenated already in the second half of the 1980s. Nevertheless, the age structure of the Hungarian economic elite in 1993 greatly resembled that of Poland: the statistically dominant age cohort in Poland and Hungary were in their forties, followed by the age cohort in their fifties (cf. Szelényi *et al*. 1995; Wasilewski and Wnuk-Lipiński 1995; Matějů and Hanley 1998). The all in all moderate redistribution in terms of age, found between 1988 and 1993, highlights the high degree of continuity implied in the notion of a 'vertical reproduction' from lower managerial jobs to the top.

The social composition of the economic elite did not seem to have been changed all that much with the break-up of state socialism. In Hungary, as in Poland, the share of members of the economic elite with tertiary education in 1993 compared to 1988 actually *dropped* slightly (from 100 per cent to 94 per cent in Hungary and from 97.3 per cent to 86.4 per cent in Poland, cf. Szelényi *et al*. 1995; Wasilewski and Wnuk-Lipiński 1995). Hence, the new possibility of private business provided at least a small window of opportunity for people without a university degree, that is, with lower institutionalized cultural capital. A large part of the new economic elite was made up of engineers and scientists (52 per cent in Poland and c. 40 per cent in Hungary, from which around 56 per cent had at least a partially technical major degree-subject) (Szelényi *et al*. 1995).[4]

Reform-communist Hungary was one of the first state-socialist countries that abandoned the recruitment pattern of elite personnel based on party loyalty. This meant that non-Party members could also reach the highest economic elite positions; in most of the other state-socialist countries they were excluded. However, the pattern of 'party-specialists' or 'loyal experts' that prevailed in Poland and in other state-socialist countries until the breakdown of the soviet system did not completely ignore meritocratic principles in management selection (cf. Wasilewski and Wnuk-Lipiński 1995).[5] At the same time, party membership remained an informal selective mechanism to reach elite positions even in the Hungarian economy before 1989, as György Lengyel (2009: 259) showed.

The difference in recruitment patterns between Poland and Hungary is most clear in the percentage of fathers with tertiary education, a percentage which in Poland has risen less sharply since 1988 than in Hungary, but also in contrast to the Polish population in general. In Poland the share of fathers with tertiary education among business leaders went from 6.5 per cent in 1988 to c. 10 per cent in 1993; while the share of fathers with tertiary education among the working population was at 4.2 per cent. In Hungary, 29 per cent of fathers of the economic elite in 1993 held a third-level qualification, compared to around 17 per cent of fathers of the elite in 1988; the share of fathers with tertiary education among the working population was at 8.5 per cent in 1993 (cf. Szelényi *et al*. 1995; Wasilewski and Wnuk-Lipiński 1995).[6] The earlier introduction of meritocratic principles in the recruitment of the economic elite in Hungary compared to Poland appears, therefore, to manifest itself above all in the fathers of the deputies.

Yet, in 1988 the percentage of fathers with an occupation as skilled manual worker – according to the Elite Study of 1993/94 – was also slightly higher in Hungary than in Poland.

How does East Germany fit in?

The transformation in East Germany represents an extreme case of elite turnover (see also Walder 2003), since in fact in all sectors a professional 'counter-elite' was available due to the German re-unification. The far-reaching institutional transfer which was involved in the re-unification entailed at the same time the transfer of top personnel from West to East. In the middle of the 1990s, the East German elite were underrepresented at a national level in comparison to share of the overall population: Of the 2,341 elite positions in politics, economics, science and culture, only 11.6 per cent (272) were occupied by East Germans (cf. Bürklin 1996; Welzel 1996). The proportion of the East German population is about one fifth. Among the 180 largest companies listed in the DAX, just two chairpersons were born or socialized in the German Democratic Republic (GDR) (Mau 2012).

The privatization agency, the *Treuhandanstalt*, quickly brought about a high turnover of elites in the economy, because it put in place the takeover of firms by strategic (western) investors and systematically obstructed or outright prevented buyouts by East German management in favour of West German buyers (cf. Pohlmann and Gergs 1999). The *Treuhand* policy of very fast and direct sales of assets to strategic (western) investors lead to an even more extreme version of 'dependent capitalism' than in the other post-socialist countries of East Central Europe, with the important difference that the top positions of the larger privatized companies could much more easily be staffed with western, that is, West German, personnel only (Bluhm 2010; Windolf *et al.* 1999). Most of the large companies are subsidiaries of western or West German companies. Just one headquarter of a large manufacturing company is located in formerly highly industrialized East Germany, that is, in Jena, and only because there was particular political support for this company.

In addition, the *Treuhand* policy and the massive deindustrialization following the currency union in July 1990 led to a quick and dramatic structural change not only in branches but also in company size. The *Treuhandanstalt* already broke larger state-owned enterprises into smaller pieces in order to make selling them easier; in addition, departments and smaller production sites looked themselves for western investors, contributing to the dissolution of bigger units (cf. Bluhm 2000). However, the attractiveness of East Germany for West German and foreign investors remained too low to develop high foreign-led growth rates since the wage increases by far exceeded productivity growth and even surpassed West German levels in terms of labour unit costs (Busch 2006; Demary and Röhl 2009: 11).[7] The products consumed in East Germany could be easily produced with the capacities in the West, while the Visegrád states had to offer similar skills but with stark low-wage advantages for cost-cutting production shifts from West to East. Within three years (1988–92), the percentage of industrial companies with 1,000+ employees more than halved, from 75.7 per cent to 31 per cent of what was already below the West German percentage (34.4 per cent), and continued decline (Fritsch 2004: 532; Bluhm and Martens 2011).[8] East German companies mainly survived in market niches and as a supplier of West German companies, with relatively little prospects of growth contributing to a long period of macroeconomic stagnation and increasing unemployment that lasted until the mid of the next decade.[9] For the transformation of the economic elite, the downsizing of the East German industry contributed to their 'regionalization'.

Nevertheless, studies about the fate of former economic elites who had worked at the top levels of state conglomerates (*Kombinate*)[10] in the GDR found that the largest proportion of this group of former economic cadres (80 per cent) continued their careers in management positions. At least 40 per cent even found jobs at the very top level of company management during the 1990s (Schreiber *et al.* 2002: 141).[11] In comparison to general employment rates in different economic sectors, the personnel in the higher organizational strata had a better chance of keeping and finding adequate jobs after the historic upheaval than other workers (Lutz and Grünert 1996: 85).

In spite of a high elite turnover in the East German economy and the widespread decline of its indigenous elite to the level of a 'regional elite' due to the reduction in size of the companies and the takeover of the remaining large state enterprises by multinational companies, the thesis of 'vertical reproduction' is also applicable here (cf. Pohlmann and Gergs 1999). The thesis is even more applicable to the East German case if one takes into account the founding of new companies during the economic transformation, which were often based on the ruins of the former state enterprises even though the *Treuhandanstalt* did not support management buyouts by preferential prices done for West German investors.

In our panel study, vertical reproduction can be read directly from the results of the middle-sized manufacturing companies. So, in the first series of panels, in 2002, around two thirds of firms were managed by East Germans and one third by West Germans, a ratio that did not change substantially in the first decade of the 2000s. But the initial disadvantages faced by the former GDR management still continue 20 years after unification. Larger companies in East Germany are more likely to have West German or foreign capital holders and West German executives, and if East Germans do own shares, their holdings are smaller. Only one East German heads a company with 1,000+ employees, another is head of a small savings bank (see sample description in Chapter 1). Nonetheless, there has been a remarkable continuity in career paths across the period of state-socialist system collapse in the sense of vertical reproduction. Many 'deputies' moved to the top level. In 1989, those who made this move were approximately 40 years old, engineers or technicians with a university degree; around half of them made this step as shareholders, so either as spin-offs of former companies or founding their own new companies in order to become small but real entrepreneurs (cf. Martens 2008). Only a few ever worked outside the economic sector.

Generational change and the growing advantages of the highest social classes

Twenty years after the collapse of the soviet system, the 'deputy generation' has in its turn been replaced by a new generation of economic elite, who have had their entire careers under market conditions. This process is progressing at a markedly different pace in the different countries and is bound up with clear advantages for the highest social classes.

Different speed of generational change

Concerning the age distribution in our Polish, Hungarian and German samples, the business leaders of 2009/10 are a little bit older than the first post-socialist cohort: On average, at the time of the survey, the Hungarians were 51 years old, the Poles 49, the East Germans are the oldest at 55, older also in comparison with the West Germans, who were 52 at the time of our survey (Table 5.1). In our

Table 5.1 Characteristics of the business leaders

Variables	Poland	Hungary	E Germany	W Germany
Age (mean in years)	49.2	50.8	54.8	52.2
Age of the first managerial position (mean in years)	29.1	28.5	29.0	29.2
% of managers with the first managerial position after 1989	60.6	47.8	33.1	46.0
% of the younger generation, age ≤ 45	34.7	29.6	14.5	22.7
Duration of the recent position, younger generation (mean in years)	9.0	8.3	14.0	9.0
Duration of the recent position, older generation (mean in years)	16.1	18.7	23.5	18.3
% of owners, younger generation	20.0	35.0	50.0	31.9
% of owners, older generation	26.5	45.7	45.9	33.8
% of owners, younger generation, company size < 1,000 employees	18.2	41.9	50.0	35.8
% of owners, older generation, company size < 1,000 employees	31.2	53.9	46.3	40.6
% of companies with foreign capital, younger generation	46.4	66.7	14.3	28.4
% of companies with foreign capital, older generation	29.5	33.7	11.3	19.5
% of companies owned by other firms, younger generation	54.5	75.0	30.0	36.4
% of companies owned by other firms, older generation	39.2	46.8	29.5	39.6
Number of cases	160	136	145	298

sample, the age of approximately 45 years can be seen as a demarcation line between those who entered a first manager position before 1989/90 and those who had their entire managerial career in a market economy.[12]

Regarding the age distributions of the Polish, Hungarian and East German samples, the differences in terms of generational change are remarkable. While the majority of the Polish respondents (60.6 per cent) reached their first managerial position in 1989 or later, the generational change seems to be still on-going in Hungary. Here 47.8 per cent of the respondents got their first managerial job after the structural change. The percentage of 'new managers' with an East German origin is even smaller: just 33.1 per cent of the East German respondents started their managerial career after 1989.

The reason for these differences may be found in the *national peculiarities* of the transformation processes: the varying openness and the duration, during the early 1990s, of the window of opportunity to advance to the highest managerial positions; the varying presence of manager-entrepreneurs in the sample; the ownership of the companies; and the weight of foreign capital.

While in Poland the highest positions remained open to the next age cohorts due to relatively late mass privatization and slow direct privatization of large state enterprises and banks towards strategic investors, beginning in fact in the mid-1990s',[13] the Hungarian first post-socialist cast of leading positions succeeded much better in keeping them and narrowing the chances for its immediate successors, which might be explained partly by the early elite change and the faster privatization (cf. Chapter 3) but also by the high share of ownership among the Hungarians in our sample compared to the Polish sample which might reflect the more decentralized mode of privatization at the beginning of the transition (cf. Hanley 1999). The second explanations also fit for East Germany, where the window of opportunity in the early 1990s was extremely short-lived, and the generation of deputies could save their own jobs by mainly founding their own businesses (Martens 2005).

For Poland and Hungary, we observe a significant impact of foreign capital on the speed of generational change, that is, their business leaders belong more often to the younger generation.[14] Age effects are especially promoted by subsidiaries in all countries.[15] Therefore such companies totally owned by foreigners can be seen as a driving force of generational transition. The same holds true for the two countries regarding companies owned by other companies and – in the Polish case – by companies which are run by employed managers. In other words, companies belonging to a larger conglomerate have younger employed top managers, especially in the case of foreign ownership. While in Poland and Hungary around one-third of the 'deputy generation' hold top management positions in foreign-owned companies (29.5 per cent and 31.3 per cent, respectively), this holds true for 46.4 per cent of the new generation of business leaders in Poland and even 66.7 per cent in Hungary. The contrast is much weaker in Germany, while the percentage of East German business leaders in foreign-owned companies is particularly low in both of the generations (see Table 5.1).

For East German business leaders, the road to top positions of mainly medium-sized companies, as mentioned above, is linked to ownership, as is also the case for the younger generation. East German business leaders show the highest proportions of manager-entrepreneurs among the younger generation, but this evidently constrains the possibilities of the younger generation, due to the need for equity, in comparison to Poland and Hungary, where the percentages of employed executives are higher. The situation of the East German business leaders is characterized as 'lagged generational change' (Martens 2008).

Social background of the fathers

Regarding the social origin of our respondents, our study indicates an increase in social closure under post-socialist conditions – especially in Poland – with regard to the findings of earlier studies. More than one third of the fathers of the business leaders in Poland and Hungary have higher education, while among the remaining two thirds the greater proportion has at least secondary education (see Table 5.2). The percentage of Polish fathers with third-level or second-level education is significantly higher than in the Elite Study of 1993/94, and slightly higher for the Hungarian sample.[16] West Germans have the lowest share of fathers with tertiary education, with 20 per cent. However, the lower level of education does not translate into a lower position in society. Similar gaps between education and status of the fathers were also observed by the Elite Study of 1993/94 for Poland and Hungary. This opportunity seems to be more restricted today. The rising level of tertiary education among the fathers speaks for the cultural-capital thesis of Eyal *et al.* (1998).

In all three countries, a majority of fathers had positions as higher-grade officials and higher-grade professionals – in West Germany and Poland the percentage is highest (Table 5.2).[17] More than 50 per cent has a social origin in the service classes comprising the higher strata of society (classes I and II of Goldthorpe's scheme). In comparison, for example, with German society as a whole, the proportion of the service classes I and II are two to three times larger in our sample of German business leaders. This holds especially true for the highest social stratum, which characterizes 9.9 per cent of the fathers' social origin of the general German population,[18] but about one third of our sample of German business leaders (see Table 5.2).

Looking at fathers with managerial jobs only, we again see the strongest connection between fathers and sons[19] in Poland where almost 10 per cent of the fathers were top managers in very large companies. The percentages for Hungary, and East and West Germany are 8 per cent, 2 per cent and again 2 per cent, respectively. In the German cases (in East as well as in West), ownership has a larger relevance. The relative frequencies of business leaders with a proprietor as father amount to 19.5 per cent and 14.2 per cent respectively. The figures for the other two countries, at 8.4 per cent (Hungary) and 3.0 per cent (Poland), are significantly smaller. In Hungary, 22.2 per cent of fathers were managers; in

Table 5.2 Fathers' education and job position, percentages related to the total number of cases in the national sample; international data set

Goldthorpe categories	Categories used in survey	Poland	Hungary	E Germany	W Germany
Class I	Higher grade officials; top managers in large firms; large proprietors; higher grade professionals	38.0	24.8	30.7	34.0
Class II	Lower grade officials; top and lower managers in small firms; lower managers in large firms; lower grade professionals	26.8	29.3	22.1	30.5
Class I and II		64.8	54.1	52.8	64.5
Class III	Routine non-manual employees (sales, administration, commerce, services)				
Class IV	Small proprietors with and without employees; farmers and smallholders; other self-employed workers in primary production	12.0	6.8	15.7	16.8
Class V	Lower-grade technicians; lower-grade supervisors; office workers	4.9	7.5	10.0	6.0
Class VI	Skilled worker	15.5	25.6	20.7	11.9
Class VII	Unskilled, semi-skilled workers	2.8	6.0	0.7	0.7
	Number of cases	142	133	140	285
Highest educational degree	Tertiary	34.5	35.3	26.8	20.0
Highest educational degree	Primary/secondary school	28.9/34.5 = 0.84	16.5/45.9 = 0.36	48.0/6.7 = 7.16	53.4/11.8 = 4.53[a]
Education	PhD	2.1	2.3	2.9	3.0

Note
a Secondary education does not imply vocational training in the West German case, but only education at school.

Poland, 25.2 per cent of fathers were managers, whether in top or lower positions in large companies, medium-sized or even small companies (with less than 50 employees). In Germany (East and West), this kind of self-recruitment seems to be lower: only 9.2 per cent of the East German sample had fathers who were managers at any of these levels (the percentage of the West German sample amounts to 13.1 per cent).

We found the lowest percentage of respondents with skilled workers as fathers in Poland. Compared to the findings of Wasilewski and Wnuk-Lipiński (1995: 681), the percentage of skilled workers among the fathers has halved to just 15.7 per cent in 2009/10. This is even more remarkable as our study includes proportionally more medium-sized companies by employees than did the Elite Study of 1993/94, which focused on the biggest companies by turnover, and it could be argued that smaller companies are less socially selective due to entrepreneurship. In addition the percentage of routine non-manual workers has reduced from about 20 per cent in 1993 according to Wasilewski and Wnuk-Lipiński to 4.9 per cent in our sample of 2009/10, and also the share of farmers, the self-employed and employees in the primary sector has declined, while the share of higher skilled professionals, top and lower managers has significantly increased. In Hungary the decline of the workers among the fathers refers only to the routine non-manual workers, while the share of skilled workers, at a quarter, remains on a similar level as in the Elite Study of 1993/94 (cf. Szelényi *et al.* 1995).[20] Compared to the other sub-samples, the percentage of skilled workers as fathers is the highest in Hungary, followed by East Germany (see again Table 5.2).

The transition from one *generation of business leaders* to the next is in all countries connected with the improving chances of the upper classes, again underlining the significance of cultural and social capital. If we study the social origin of the business leaders, we find a high rate of social reproduction. This holds true for the socialist era (as the high percentages of service class origin for the older generation indicate) as well as for the transformation period. Nevertheless social upheaval has always augmented the chances of the children of the service classes, and especially the children of the highest social stratum, of reaching top positions in the new economies. According to our data, changes of this kind are largest in East Germany with 75 per cent of the new generation with fathers in the service classes I and II, compared to Poland and Hungary where they reach approximately 69 and 64 per cent. Especially in Hungary, the large influence of foreign capital additionally strengthens the privileges of higher social strata: 80 per cent of the managers of subsidiaries have a social origin in the service classes, but only 40 per cent of the Hungarian firms without foreign investment are directed by personnel with the same social background. The situation in West Germany, however, is characterized by stable advantages of the service classes, which do not vary to a significant extent between the generations of business leaders. The upper classes across all three countries apparently have better chances of getting higher positions in the enterprises and they realize faster careers. Consequently, the social origin of business leaders has changed in such a way that the term 'social closure' is appropriate.

Social status of mothers and marriage patterns as indicators of national characteristics

In order to strengthen the comparative perspective, we also take into account the social origin of the mothers. The analyses will in the end confirm that the social origin of the mothers and their marriage patterns shed light on nationally specific characteristics of the social origin of business leaders.

The countries can be positioned on three different scales regarding the socio-economic situation of the mothers of respondents (Table 5.3). Hungary and East Germany are similar in respect of mothers working outside the home. Only a small minority of the mothers, 5.0 per cent (East German sample) and 9.5 per cent (Hungarian sample), were economically inactive. The Polish situation, with 20.0 per cent of economically inactive mothers, resembles to some extent the West German position, where nearly one third of the mothers did not work.[21] These figures reflect the policy in the former socialist countries to foster the work of women outside the home, but these policies had varying degrees of rigour.

The special role of Poland in this respect is also visible in the very high percentage of mothers coming from higher social strata. More than the half of all Polish business leaders has a mother with a social origin in the service classes. The other extreme on this scale is given by West Germany where only 13.4 per cent of the mothers have such a social background. Hungary and East Germany are located between these two extremes. The same sequence of countries can be seen on a third scale: East and West German business leaders quite often have mothers with a non-service class origin, while in Hungary and especially in Poland the relative frequencies are much smaller.

In summary, each country/region is characterized by a specific profile of mothers' working activities. Poland is remarkable for the large percentage of mothers of a high social origin combined with a rather large minority of economically inactive women. In Hungary, the social origin is 'balanced' between higher and lower social classes in combination with a higher rate of working women. The mothers of East German business leaders show in this latter respect the highest frequencies; and they have a rather low social status, two thirds held jobs that are classified as non-service classes. In West Germany also, the relative amount of mothers having a lower social origin is rather high, but in this case this feature correlates with nearly one third economically inactive mothers. It seems that these different national patterns are a result (a 'mixture') of three processes: privileges

Table 5.3 Social background of the mothers; international data set (%)

Social background of the mothers	Poland	Hungary	E Germany	W Germany
Economically inactive	20.0	9.5	5.0	31.7
Service classes I or II	54.3	44.4	28.1	13.4
Non-service classes	25.7	46.0	66.9	54.8
Number of cases	140	126	139	290

of higher social strata; traditional ideology with regard to women's labour; and socialist policies. These national patterns are further described in terms of the marriage behaviour.

Although in all three countries the majority of the fathers had a social background in the higher social strata, the former socialist countries differ significantly in the marriage patterns. In Poland and Hungary a strong trend to marry within the service classes is visible: 44.2 per cent of Polish business leaders have both parents with a social origin in Goldthorpe's classes I and II; in Hungary the percentage is 36.5 per cent (Table 5.4). The comparable figure of 17.5 per cent for the East German business leaders shows that 'equal marriages' within the service classes had a lower weight in the GDR than in Poland and Hungary. Furthermore, the rather large frequency of 37.2 per cent of East German parents both stemming from lower strata also clarifies the relatively high

Table 5.4 Marriage patterns, parents of the business leaders according to countries, percentages related to the total number of cases in the national sample; international data set

Poland (number of cases 138)

Social background of the mother	Social background of the father	
	Service classes I or II	Non-service classes
Economically inactive	8.7	10.1
Service classes I or II	44.2	10.9
Non-service classes	8.7	17.4

Hungary (number of cases 126)

Social background of the mother	Social background of the father	
	Service classes I or II	Non-service classes
Economically inactive	3.2	6.3
Service classes I or II	36.5	7.9
Non-service classes	15.9	30.2

E Germany (number of cases 137)

Social background of the mother	Social background of the father	
	Service classes I or II	Non-service classes
Economically inactive	2.9	2.2
Service classes I or II	17.5	9.5
Non-service classes	30.7	37.2

W Germany (number of cases 285)

Social background of the mother	Social background of the father	
	Service classes I or II	Non-service classes
Economically inactive	18.2	13.0
Service classes I or II	10.5	2.8
Non-service classes	32.6	22.8

impact of non-service classes. In comparison to the other two former socialist countries, the social origin of the recent business leaders shows that East Germany has in some respect a more 'egalitarian heritage' than Hungary and especially Poland.

A seemingly (in this study at least) particularly German marital pattern is characterized by the social advancements of women by marriages with men of higher social strata (Table 5.4). This can be seen in the case of nearly one third of the West and East German business leaders. It is astonishing that this traditional German marriage pattern remained stable also during the GDR era, while the economic inactivity of women seems exclusively a historic legacy in the western part of Germany. In other words, a Polish and Hungarian peculiarity is the similarity of parents in terms of social origins, while in Germany, East as well as West, the social dissimilarity of parents and the advancement of women by marriage are marked characteristics.

In all countries – irrespective of whether it had a socialist or a capitalist history – the relationships between the social strata of the parents and the social position of the business leaders are primarily influenced by the fathers, since more than half of the respondents always have a father stemming from the service classes. In comparison to this, the social origin of the mother has only a small impact, the highest in Poland, the lowest in West Germany. This marginal influence of the mother in the West German case is furthermore emphasized by the large percentages of mothers who did not work at all, rather independently of the social origin of the fathers (Table 5.4).

Taking into account the changes between younger and older business leaders as already mentioned, two features of the new economic elites become clear for all former socialist countries, and also illustrate features of the West German society: (1) The already ascertained increase of social exclusiveness is also indicated by changes in marriage patterns. Among the parents of the younger generation of Polish, Hungarian, and East German business leaders, marriages remaining within higher social strata become more usual with percentages between 42.1 per cent (East Germans) and 69.4 per cent (Poland).[22] Again West Germany forms a special case, which is still characterized by the social advancement of women by marriages with men of higher social origin. The percentage of such marriages even rises from 30.5 per cent to 40.0 per cent. (2) The rate of working mothers increases in all countries within the younger generation. That holds true for Poland (the special former socialist case) as well as for the West German business leaders, although in the last case the percentage of economically inactive mothers remains comparatively high at 24.6 per cent (the corresponding portion for the older generation is 33.8 per cent). The East German mothers are the only exception with a stable high working rate.[23]

Additional analyses of the parents' educational background give evidence that in all countries fathers' academic degrees have gained importance over time. This holds especially true for Hungary, where the percentage of fathers with an academic degree has grown from 30.4 per cent for the older age group of business leaders to 50.0 per cent for the younger one. Among the East Germans, the corresponding increase of tertiary education is even larger (from 21.2 per cent to 60.0 per cent). Such processes of educational expansion with regard to fathers, visible for all countries, are more differentiated for the mothers. In Poland and Hungary the percentages of mothers with secondary or tertiary education rise from almost 60 per cent (the older cohort of business leaders) to nearly 90 per cent (younger age group). In contrast, East German and West German mothers show particular patterns, which do not exhibit such a degree of increase in educational level of mothers as are visible in the two East Central European countries. Also for the younger age group from East as well as West Germany, the proportion of mothers possessing secondary or tertiary education does not exceed a quarter. It seems that, as in the case of social origin, national peculiarities and the legacies of the socialist period are more clearly visible in educational characteristics of the mothers than of such of the fathers.

Career patterns

Career patterns for managers are influenced by the education systems, the strategies of the companies and existence of markets for executives. In analysing career patterns, three dimensions are usually regarded as decisive: (1) the career paths, that is, the way and steps to the top, and tenure; (2) the educational background (vocational training, secondary/tertiary education and field of study); and (3) internationalization of careers (studying and working abroad). Following these dimensions, we found that moderate company changes are quite common, indicating the existence of a market for executives in all three countries; we also observe the growing importance of economics degrees and studies abroad. However, there are significant differences between the three countries.

Career paths

On the basis of our sample, we can distinguish three different career paths. By the term 'in-house career' we refer to a career in which the working life took place entirely – with an exception of an early 'search period' of five years – in the very same company that the respondent is now running.[24] The opposite of the 'in-house' career is what we call the 'parachute career' where managers take over executive positions without having worked in that company before. Usually they hold a high position in another company before they change. A third career type is an 'external-internal path' that characterizes careers which began outside of the current company, but in which the person has worked within the current company before being promoted to his or her current position.

Table 5.5 shows that in all three countries the 'parachute career' represents the predominant path to reach the top of a company, with 46 per cent in Germany, 54 per cent in Poland, and even 64 per cent in Hungary. The 'parachute career' is followed by the 'external-internal paths', while the 'in-house career' appears to be much less prevalent. Thus, most of the respondents in the three countries have a significant number of company moves in their management careers.

Table 5.5 Distribution of the three career paths across the business leaders (%)

Career type	Poland	Hungary	E Germany	W Germany
In-house career	26.4	16.4	31.7	26.7
Parachute career	54.0	63.6	45.5	45.3
External-internal career	19.6	20.0	22.8	28.0
Number of cases	163	140	145	300

The overall picture, however, is misleading unless one considers size, ownership and sector effects. These characteristics reveal remarkable differences between the three countries. In particular, the difference between very large and medium-sized companies is often ignored, as the conceptualization of 'national career paths' only takes very large corporations into consideration. Medium-sized and even larger private companies are more vulnerable to market volatility compared to very large ones and therefore less stable. They are also more often run by a manager-entrepreneur or families who may give non-family members less room for advancement to the highest level. As founders of a company, they start as 'parachutists' anyway. Hence, we have assumed that the high rate of parachute careers in our sample can be explained by size effects, while 'in-house careers' due to higher stability and longer hierarchical ladders are more likely in very large companies. In addition, we checked the ownership structure, especially the existence of foreign capital and the influence of a manager-entrepreneur who owns company shares. The effects were evaluated by logistic regressions.

For all countries, 'in-house careers' are more common in larger companies. These size effects are larger in Hungary and Poland, with around 40 per cent of business leaders of companies with 1,000 and more employees showing 'in-house careers'. In Germany, the corresponding proportion of this career path amounts to one third of West German business leaders.

The Polish case is striking, because 'in-house careers' are more widespread among young business leaders (younger than 45 years): 46 per cent, compared with 16 per cent in the older group. This difference is larger than in the other two countries and had a significant influence on the prevalence of 'in-house careers' in Poland as well as the possibilities of the younger generation of Polish business leaders ascending in large corporations, particularly compared to the East German counterparts.

Depending on which career path is followed, independent of the company size, tenure in the current company varies: German 'in-house careers' last about 27 years (West Germans 25 years and East Germans 31 years, which indicates once more the lagged generational change in East Germany). In Hungary, the time span from starting working in the company until the year of the survey is approximately 28 years. In Poland, 'in-house careers' lasted 'only' 18 years, as a consequence of the younger mean age of the respondents. Of course, the other career paths shorten the affiliation with the current company significantly. The average across all three countries for tenures in the current company for the other career paths is as follows: 15 years for 'external-internal' and 13 years for 'parachute'. Thus, the careers we find in our sample are far from being 'short-term', just the contrary.

The 'external-internal path' and the 'parachute path' may not exclude continuity in the sense of a 'branch career' (Hartmann 2006). Thus, we also asked for a response as to whether the last company change implied an additional change of branch. In Poland and Germany, approximately half of the respondents did not work in the same branch in their previous companies. Only in Hungary a clear majority (64 per cent) of the respondents did not leave the branch. Comparing the company types, German and Polish bank managers have had the fewest branch changes, while almost half of the Hungarian bankers did change branch, much more than in all the other company types in that country.

Only minorities of managers in any of the three countries spent time working outside the business sector at all (mostly in science and education). They are more common in Poland (29 per cent) and in Hungary (31 per cent) than in Germany (16 per cent of the East German and 24 per cent of the West German business leaders). The Polish top managers of the banking sector who had a job outside the business sector had worked mainly in science and education and in the cultural sector. Switches from politics are negligible. They are even more rare in Hungary, Poland and East Germany than in West Germany, indicating that after the transition period the 'functional reproduction' of the economic elites from within the sector is even stronger than in a region that never experienced state socialism (Sattler and Boyer 2009: 61).

The salient points seem to be: 'in-house careers' are still widespread in Poland and particularly in Hungary in very large companies and in firms with foreign ownership; (West) German corporations with 1,000+ employees have in fact abandoned the 'in-house-career'; and even 'branch careers' are not the dominant pattern. In other words, while in Germany a market for executives is growing beyond the medium-size sector (cf. Chapter 4), in the other two countries the larger subsidiaries of foreign companies offer in-house-careers as a recruitment strategy, and this is more prevalent in the manufacturing industries than in the banking sector.

Educational background and internationalization of careers

Early studies on German managers in very large and medium-sized companies found that a distinct feature of German management was the high number of engineers, even at the top level (cf. Lawrence 1980; Lane 1989; Stewart *et al.* 1994; Byrkjeflot 2000; see Eberwein and Tholen 1993, and Hartmann 1995 for a more nuanced study). Recent studies have observed an accelerated decline in the relevance of an engineering background for elite positions, due to the on-going 'financialization' of business (cf. Fligstein 2001; Chapter 4). One might expect a similar picture of the business elites in the Polish and Hungarian sample, as we have seen that engineers and scientists were well presented among the 'deputy generation'.

In general, the percentage of respondents with tertiary education is at a similar level to that found in the Elite Study of 1993/94: 82 per cent of the Hungarian business leaders have tertiary education (everyone in very large companies and banks, with only one exception); in Poland 89 per cent of the respondents have completed third-level education (everybody in very large companies and banks); and 87 per cent in Germany (95 per cent of the East Germans and 82 per cent of their western counterparts).[25] PhD/doctoral degrees and MBAs play only a minor role in all countries, even in very large companies.

As concerns the fields of study, in all three countries the relevance of business/ economics has increased markedly, while technical or engineering studies still play the most significant role. It is, however, not easy to say which holds the upper hand, since there are remarkable variations across the countries and company sizes, which undermines the impression of homogeneity. Although in Germany, 54 per cent of all respondents have studied in a technical or engineering field, this is mainly due to its preponderance in medium-sized and large companies (60 per cent of the respondents); here again the proportion is still higher among the East Germans (67 per cent) than West Germans (45 per cent). While banks have no engineers in their top management, the percentage among very large corporations (39 per cent) is significantly lower than in Hungary and Poland (53 per cent and 48 per cent, respectively). Among West Germans, 53 per cent of the business leaders have studied economics/business, with the highest percentage in banks (91 per cent) and very large companies (52 per cent). The percentage for the East Germans is much lower (24 per cent). Only a minority of 8 per cent of the respondents has studied sciences and the percentage of jurists is below 5 per cent in every country, except Poland where one third of the bank managers studied law.

In Poland, significantly fewer respondents studied in technical and engineering fields (45 per cent); the percentage among the top managers in very large compa- nies, however, is higher (53 per cent) than in Germany. The same holds true for Hungary, where the percentage of engineers is 49 per cent, but in very large firms it is 53 per cent. This result confirms that, as in East Germany, an engineering qualification was useful for making a career among the business elite in the 1990s.

In the former state-socialist countries (including East Germany), the percentages of older respondents with an engineering education are higher than for the younger generation, indicating in fact a further decline of the importance of technical education for top ranks. In Poland and Hungary, only 34 per cent of the people younger than 45 years have such an engineering education, which points to a significant decline in both countries compared to the study in 1993. In contrast, among the younger East Germans the proportion of engineers is still relatively high, at 47 per cent, stressing again the specific transition path in Germany's East.

The general decline in percentage of engineers and the overall trend towards business degrees independent of the country, mark quite a difference in comparison to the situation regarding vocational training, where national peculiarities and dissimilarities are to a large extent stable (Table 5.6). Interestingly, the percentage of German respondents who completed vocational training is still very high (72 per cent), even higher in the banking sector taken separately (90 per cent), and in the East German sample (80 per cent). In Poland, the frequency is also high, with 88 per cent of respondents having vocational training. Here the focus lies on commercial fields (this resembles the situation of the West German business leaders), but the high percentages of this type of training as well as vocational training in industrial fields indicate that double training qualifications are quite frequent in Poland. Of the Hungarian respondents, however, only a small minority has vocational training (18 per cent), and most of those are heads of medium-sized companies, which reflects a significant deviation from the soviet type of enterprise-based vocational training in the wake of the Kádár's reforms.[26]

A rather large percentage, 28 per cent, of Hungarian managers studied abroad; the proportions for the Polish and the West German respondents are 19 per cent and 24 per cent, respectively. The percentage of the East Germans is much lower, at 6 per cent.

Age differences with regard to internationalization are most striking in West Germany, where we observe among the younger generation the largest growth in internationalization in terms of studying abroad. The percentages rise from 19 per cent of the older generation to 39 per cent of the younger generation (Table 5.6). In other words, while in Germany (and even only for West German business leaders) internationalization of education is a more recent development, it has a long tradition in Poland as well as in Hungary and is not a distinct feature of that age cohort who made their entire professional career under market conditions.

Table 5.6 Qualifications and characteristics of the business leaders

Variables	Poland	Hungary	E Germany	W Germany
% of business leaders with a vocational training degree	88.3	17.5	80.0	66.2
% of industrial vocational training	55.6	60.6	76.7	32.8
% of commercial vocational training	76.4	21.7	20.7	60.1
% of business leaders studied abroad	18.3	28.8	5.8	23.5
% of business leaders studied abroad, older generation	18.7	25.3	5.0	18.6
% of business leaders studied abroad, younger generation	18.4	35.3	11.1	39.3
% of business leaders working abroad, 6 months or longer	34.8	32.5	28.1	56.7
Median of working abroad (in months)	0	0	0	6
% of engineers	44.8	49.1	71.0	45.1
% of respondents with a degree in business	35.9	66.7	23.9	52.5
Number of cases	163	139	145	300

In addition, our study showed the relative influence of studying abroad (and that of foreign capital interest in the recent enterprise) on generational change.[27] Such a relationship with higher education abroad is only detectable for the West Germans (but in this case not for foreign capital), while in Poland and Hungary significantly more younger business leaders who studied abroad are employed by foreign companies.[28] East Germans are a special case, owing to the lagged generational change, with low frequencies of studying abroad, and few foreign companies in this part of Germany. The data reveal no significant correlations at all.

The US and the UK are the most frequent destinations for study abroad in all three countries. Yet this trend is less overwhelming than might be expected given the discourse on liberalization and 'Anglo-Saxonization' of business, and there are national peculiarities which indicate the continued importance of historic national patterns. In Poland, French universities are in a strong second place. Hungarian business leaders frequently study in Germany, and West Germans quite often acquire academic experiences in other continental European countries, with the lack of any particular focus indicating the widespread use of European student-exchange programmes.

The relatively high level of internationalization of West Germans is also indicated by the amount of working experience abroad. Looking only at business leaders with foreign working experience of six months and longer, more than half of the West German respondents meet this criterion. Poles, Hungarian, and East Germans are less active in foreign countries, but nevertheless between 28 and 35 per cent have worked for six months or longer outside their homeland. However, the distributions of the duration of working stay in foreign countries are rather uneven, since for the three post-socialist cases the median of this feature is 0, which means that at least 50 per cent of the Polish, Hungarian, and East German respondents have no work experience abroad at all. The median for the West German sample amounts to 6 months.

A further evaluation of this feature reveals that the time working abroad after finishing education depends significantly in all countries/regions on the export quota of the firm for which the manager now works, indicating that personal internationalization is linked to the internationalization of the firm.[29] On the other hand, the effects of foreign capital, company size, and academic experience in foreign countries differ between the national samples. In Poland and Germany, foreign capital has a significant influence on the time spent working abroad, while in Hungary no such significant influence is detectable (owing to the general high frequency of foreign investment, which apparently does not covariate with the explaining variables sufficiently, but provokes a heterogeneity of the data). Hence we can argue that multinational companies not only select for their subsidiaries highly qualified, younger managers who studied abroad, but also provide them with the possibility of experience in their transnational networks. Only in our West German sample, the business leaders of medium-sized companies have a surprisingly high level of international experience, even in comparison with the very large corporations, which might be an indicator of the high level of internationalization of the German manufacturing sector.

The educational background provides a twofold picture: on the one hand we see national institutional peculiarities (for example the lasting tradition of engineering education in East Germany or double qualifications in Hungary); on the other hand, an overarching trend towards business studies is visible. Despite the very uneven level of foreign activities in the three transformation cases (more than half of the Polish, Hungarian, and East German respondents had not spent any time in foreign countries on their job, although the percentages of business leaders working half a year or longer abroad range between 28 and 57 per cent), education in foreign countries and foreign ownership have, in general, effects on international activities on the job in all three countries.

Conclusion

In this chapter, we argued that the specific paths towards market economy and its outcome had a remarkable impact on the formation of the economic elite not only in the first generation, but also in second. They contribute to the persistence of nation-specific patterns in spite of the closeness of the three post-socialist cases regarding the high influence of external investors in key sectors and a relatively high elite exchange compared to other post-socialist cases (see Chapter 1). We consider both influences as important in the development of the new economic elites: the inflow of foreign capital in the economic core sectors and the 'window of opportunity' for the formation of domestic 'real capitalists' even though their chances to become a 'grande bourgeoisie' were more restricted than in Romania, Ukraine or Russia (cf. King and Szelényi 2005; Chapter 1). Domestic ownership is in East Central Europe rather small and medium-sized, while large companies are controlled by foreign capital. The accumulation of big private industrial capital by insiders was most restricted in East Germany, while at the same time the region did not manage to attract enough foreign investment to compensate for the huge deindustrialization of this formerly highly industrialized country. This distinguishes the East German version of a 'dependent capitalism' from other former state-socialist economies in East Central Europe. This development together with the elite transfer following the re-unification contributed to strikingly different features of the East German economic elite compared to similar groups in West Germany and their post-socialist neighbour countries: a radical 'regionalization' of the economic elite (more than in politics), a very short 'window of opportunity' in the early 1990s'; the acquisition of elite positions via the establishment of one's own company that is, becoming an owner (even with mostly minority stocks); and a lagged generational change together with a significantly older age distribution of the top managers, longer durations at the current position than in the two other transformation countries. This special situation in East Germany will probably lead to a 'family capitalism' (James 2006) in the future, because the transfer of ownership will frequently take place along traditional lines of kinship (Martens 2008; Bluhm and Martens 2011). In contrast to this, the Polish sample displays the most advanced generational change, which we explain by the influence of foreign capital and the national trajectory of economic transformation that framed a different window for opportunity to what was the case in East Germany and Hungary.

In all regions and countries, the numbers of 'parachute careers' are astonishingly large, a fact which confirms the existence of national markets for executives, although the sizes of those markets vary. What is different, though, are the patterns regarding very large companies. While in West Germany we observe a significant decline of the traditional in-house career in very large companies (see Chapter 4), large companies combined with foreign ownership foster this type of career in Poland and Hungary, indicating that transnational parent companies are more inclined to trust company-internal socialization and qualification for their subsidiaries than the mechanism of the manager market in these countries, while West German companies seem to rely increasingly on this manager market in their home country. Foreign capital is also supportive of generational change and transnational working experiences, and therefore influences a distinct pattern of careers which is absent among the East Germans in our sample, but also differs from those in the West.

In addition, an internationalization of careers is visible in all countries, while again at its weakest among the East Germans. In Poland and Hungary, the internalization concerns primarily the education of managers, although the strong weight of foreign capital interests had an influence on generational change in the past and accordingly on the recent composition of economic elites. Higher rates of studying abroad can especially be observed among the younger generation of the West German business leaders. However, any trend toward internationalization during the activities on the job seems only a limited phenomenon in Poland and Hungary. Contrary to that, West German business leaders rather often have experience in working abroad. This holds especially true for larger companies, but internalization can also be seen as a trend in smaller firms.

The economic transformation and the establishment of new economic elites in all former socialist cases went along with a growing exclusiveness of the social origin of business leaders. The processes can be described in terms of social closure, but the comparative perspective shows that national peculiarities are meaningful here as well, particularly when the mothers of the business leaders are taken into account. The different role of women in society (higher rates of women working outside the home) is a legacy of former socialist policy which has still an impact, while in regard to the social origin of the mother the relative stability of the West German situation indicates the lasting influence of old German traditions (female advancement by marriage, together with economic inactivity of women). While in Poland the share of economically inactive mothers is, for a former socialist country, relatively high, which may be explained by the relatively strong influence of Catholicism on society, the new economic elites in Poland also has the largest proportion (of the countries studied here) of mothers who earned a high social position through their own work, which distinguishes the Polish case strikingly from the West German one. In spite of the long tradition of meritocratic principles in career making that tends to prefer persons with high cultural capital, the Hungarian pattern appears to be less exclusive than the Polish one. However, there is a significant change in the younger generation. We observe a similar picture in East Germany, with the least exclusive features in terms of social origin, but a significant difference between the two age cohorts, indicating that the next generation is 'catching-up' with other countries in terms of exclusivity based on social origin.

In summary, the answers to the three questions posed at the beginning of this paper show a landscape of marked change: (1) The economic transformations in all cases have favoured the higher social classes. The social origin of the younger generation of business leaders in all three countries has become more exclusive. (2) At the same time, the analyses, especially of maternal social origin, also reveals 'long waves' of social change which have shaped recent economic elites in line with socialist legacies and much older traditions in German society. (3) However, the recent composition of the economic elites also depends on the ownership structure that developed during the 1990s. In this context, the effect of foreign capital on careers and generational change is detectable in Poland and Hungary, in contrast to West and East Germany (due, as we have seen, to peculiarities in the East German case) where foreign ownership produces little variation in these respects. While, in all three countries, markets for executives exists and a trend towards economic degrees can be detected, the market for executives plays a bigger role in West Germany than in Poland and Hungary where the integration in transnational value-chains and the foreign-led corporate governance led to a preference for in-house socialization and engineer-technical qualifications.

Notes

1 The 1993 study of other post-socialist countries, including in particular the systematic analysis of data on Russia. In 1994, a survey in the Czech Republic was added but is only partly included in Eyal *et al.* (1998). Newer contributions are to be found in Lane *et al.* (2007) and Sattler and Boyer (2009).

2 All the authors cited here belong to a research project in which the first large study of elites was carried out in 1993/94: 'Social Stratification in East-Central Europe after 1989' (cf. Eyal *et al.* 1998: 197ff.). The various interpretations arise from concentrations on different elements of the analysis.

3 This sample should ideally include the 3,000 large companies (by turnover), in order to ensure that not only the (formerly) state-run employment-heavy companies are taken into account, but also more profitable businesses which operated with relatively small numbers of employees. (Eyal *et al.* 1998: 204). The research includes a sample of very heterogeneous companies with regard to employment figures (unfortunately, these size effects were not investigated).

4 Unfortunately, the publications based on the Elite Study of 1993/94 do not reveal data for 1988 about the fields of study.

5 A similar development was observed in East Germany, i.e. the former GDR (cf. Solga 1994).

6 See Matějů and Hanley (1998: 168) for the data on the entire population which was used in the 1993/94 Elite Study.

7 At the same time, real wage gap is still existent. In our sample we also see a significant gap between the income of West German and East German business leaders even if we

only take the medium-sized companies. While the median of West German income lies between €150,000 and €200,000, the median of the East German counterparts lies between €75,000 and €100,000.

8 Compared in the wider EU context, however, the average size of West German manufacturing companies peaks out and East German companies are more closer to the European average (Bluhm and Martens 2011: 132).

9 The long period of stagnation is traced back to the small size of East German companies and the lack of central or regional headquarters (cf. Busch 2006; Demary and Röhl 2009).

10 The interviewees included 565 former members of executive boards ('Generaldirektoren' and 'Fachdirektoren') of 62 combines (Schreiber *et al.* 2002: 28).

11 Eighty-six per cent of the respondents see themselves as 'winners' in the economic transformation, only 36 per cent as 'losers'. The two percentages indicate that a small proportion of former economic elites stress positive as well as negative aspects of their careers after 1989 (Schreiber et al. 2002: 151).

12 This reference to age works because on average all managers in the three countries reached their first managerial job, defined as a position with supervisory responsibility, in their late twenties (Table 5.1). We consider the older group of business leaders as part of the 'deputy generation', since they were already on the career track when the planned economy collapsed. The younger group are a new generation of business leaders who were certainly too young to be pre-selected for a managerial career under the old system.

13 Initially one of the most important methods of privatization in Poland has been the 'worker propertization', a mutation of the worker self-management idea. At the end of 1995 there were about thousand employee-owned companies (specially medium and small) employing in total of about 300,000 persons. The transitional stage of the employee ownership that turned concentrated ownership either by further privatization or by selling of the employee shares to the executives. This Polish peculiarity contributed to the longer 'window of opportunity'. The delay, regarding foreign investment, compared to Hungary was also result of an only reluctant growing interest of western companies in Poland.

14 In most cases (94 per cent), the proportion of shares owned by foreign investors exceeds 25 per cent of all of a company's shares. In 71 per cent of the cases with foreign investment, it is a case of subsidiaries, with all shares in the hands of foreign owners. Owing to these distributions, companies are classified in the following as 'foreign owned' without further explanation, in the case of minority as well as majority ownership by foreign investors.

15 The percentages of managers from the younger generation roughly double if it is a subsidiary; and the strongest effects are visible in Poland and Hungary (30.4 per cent and 48.7 per cent of the younger generation are leading companies totally owned by foreign investors, the German percentage amounts to 21.7 per cent).

16 According to the study by Matějů and Hanley (1998: 167), even in 1993 only around 10 per cent of fathers in the Polish working population and around 16 per cent in the Hungarian had a third-level degree. See also Wasilewski and Lipiński (1995).

17 To analyse the class position in society, we have grouped our categories according to the Goldthorpe class scheme, dividing society into classes by the nature of the employment relationship. Goldthorpe uses occupational categories, whose members would compare in terms of their sources and levels of income, their degree of economic security and chances of economic advancement and, on the other hand, in their location within the systems of authority and control in governing the processes of production, including a degree of autonomy in performing their work-tasks and roles (Goldthorpe 1980).

18 The result refers to the German General Population Survey for the Social Sciences, Allbus 2008, variable v347.

19 They are mainly 'sons' as the percentage of female business leaders is negligible.

20 Other studies on Hungarian economic elites, however, observe a drastic decline of fathers with 'manual occupations' compared to 1988 and 1993 (Kristóf 2012: 114).
21 In a study about top managers of the 61 business leaders of the largest German companies the percentage of housewives were even higher (55 per cent), see Buß (2007: 22).
22 The equivalent relative frequencies for the older cohorts are: 13.6 per cent (East Germans) and 34.4 per cent (Poland).
23 The other percentages of economically inactive mothers for the older and younger generation are: Poland 26.4 per cent, 8.2 per cent; Hungary 12.9 per cent, 2.6 per cent; East Germans 5.0 per cent, 5.3 per cent.
24 Scholars on manager careers sometimes even use the still narrower concept of a so called 'chimney career'. Managers on a chimney track are promoted within the same functional or professional area, e.g. finance, production, sales, HRM. Sometimes they change companies but not functional area (Faust 2002). As our data provide an accurate picture on branch and sector changes, but did not pursue the career steps in the detail required for the precise reconstruction of 'chimney careers', we use the term 'branch career' here.
25 At first glance, it is surprising that while the percentage in very large firms, at 96 per cent, is slightly higher than in medium-sized companies, the top managers of the German banking sector lie below the average (76 per cent). This has to do with a particularity of the German system, the vocational training system in this sector.
26 Laki and Szalai (2006: 335) state that at the time of the Hungarian 'reform socialism' in the 1960s and 70s, the secondary school system was expanded very fast by technical and commercial secondary schools. Most important for elite recruitment were the technical and commercial third-level schools (usually three or four years of special higher education). In 1962, 45 per cent of the Hungarian economic elite received higher education, while in 1984 the number was 91 per cent (Lengyel 2007: 55).
27 The results refer to logistic regressions with probability of being a member in one of the two age cohorts (45 years or younger and older than 45 years, respectively) as dependent variable. Independent variables are foreign capital and studying abroad.
28 Other types of ownership (by the managing director itself or by the state) do not mark a distinction between the countries.
29 Due to the uneven distributions, logistic regressions were conducted for each country, with the time working abroad after finishing education as dependent variable (6 months or longer) and studying abroad, foreign capital in the current company, company size (more than 999 employees), and the export quota as independent variables.

6 Contractual trust

The long shadow of the shadow economy

Béla Janky and György Lengyel

Introduction

This chapter examines the impacts of varieties of state-socialist economy on the country-specific patterns of inter-firm relations. The point of departure of our analysis is Mari Sako's 1992 study of cultural influence on contractual relations, in which she describes diverging Japanese and British managerial strategies of dealing with inter-organizational transactions. We have a relatively narrow geographical focus, investigating differences between Poland, Hungary and Germany, but we will also study the impact on institutional developments of the state-socialist and welfare capitalist legacy. Country-specific varieties of the state-socialist system may add to the explanation of managerial strategies and the role of trust within them.

Much research has shown the low level of trust, solidarity and economic morale in the post-socialist Hungarian society compared to countries with a similar socio-economic background (cf. Skrabski *et al*. 2003; Kopp and Réthelyi 2004; Janky 2007; Keller 2009, 2010; Inglehart and Baker 2000). Those findings, at first sight, pose a puzzle for institutionalist analyses. Specifically, the Hungarian state-socialist regime left significantly more room for the proliferation of market coordination than did its counterparts in Central and Eastern Europe (CEE) societies (cf. Stark and Nee 1989; Szelényi 1989). Since theory and evidence alike suggest that the dominance of bureaucratic coordination undermined social capital in state-socialist economies (cf. Raiser 2002), one might expect that the relatively market-friendly design of the command economy should have fostered trust and moral discipline among economic actors – compared to more hard-line communist regimes (cf. Raiser 1997).

Our primary aim is to better understand the seemingly paradoxical legacy of the Hungarian regime by putting it in a comparative framework. We hypothesize that social cohesion deteriorated partly due to, rather than in spite of, the legacy of the Hungarian model of economic governance. We emphasize that all kinds of state-socialist regimes ruined trust among economic actors, but early market reforms had, paradoxically, a particularly detrimental effect on inter-organizational trust.

Our argument relies on two propositions. First, good experience fuels trust better than no experience, but no experience still entails more trust than bad experience. Second, market interactions in the context of a command economy are inevitably perverted by the lack of opportunities for proper competition, reputation building, accumulation of capital, and by the lack of effective norm enforcement. Learning to cooperate in such a context might require skills and attitudes strikingly different from those prevalent in advanced market economies.

We carry out factor and regression analyses to show, first, that the legacy of state-socialist corporate culture still has a significant influence on managerial strategies even twenty years after the transition. This effect can also be detected in East Germany. Second, in line with the findings of earlier comparative research on value systems, we reveal that the detrimental effect of the state-socialist past on contractual trust is strongest in Hungary. Third, we shed light on some of the mechanisms through which varieties of state-socialist legacies overshadow current business transactions. Our analysis shows that differences in contractual strategies among West German business leaders can, for the most part, be traced back to firm-level characteristics. On post-socialist economies, on the other hand, managers' socio-economic background, their values and beliefs also shape inter-organizational trust. Among post-socialist managers, the Hungarians are the most sensitive to and critical of the perceived lack of moral discipline in economic life.

Although, our analysis has been primarily motivated by puzzles posed by the Hungarian socio-economic development, the lessons we have learned are of more general interest for research on varieties of capitalism.

Contractual trust

Sako's (1992) analysis on the inter-firm relations of British and Japanese electronics companies and their suppliers laid the ground for empirically based research on contractual trust. In order to better understand divergent managerial strategies in the two societies, she distinguished two ideal-types of contractual relations: arm's length (ACR); and obligational (OCR) relationships. While the level of interdependence in the case of ACR is low and the time-span of the contract is relatively short, the OCR type can be characterized with high level of interdependence and long-term cooperation. Sako's analysis revealed that inter-firm relations in Japan, as opposed to in the UK, tend to be closer to the OCR type of contracts.

The term *contractual trust* encompasses the major managerial decisions which distinguish ACR and OCR types of strategies. For instance, the decision to start production before a binding contract is fixed, is a sign of high level of contractual trust on the side of the supplier. It also indicates an OCR-type link between the buyer and supplier. Another crucial indicator of trust is the written contract itself. A very detailed, comprehensive contract, ceteris paribus, stems from a low level of trust between the parties, and is most common in ACR-type inter-firm transactions.

Sako (1992) pointed out that societal level cultural differences may have an enduring impact on contractual strategies. One should note, however, that technology and market structure also play an important role in shaping contractual trust (cf. Whitley *et al.* 1996; Sako and Helper 1998; Sako 1998; Csabina *et al.*

2002; Lengyel and Janky 2005). No one of the two ideal-types of contractual relations is superior to the other. As Uzzi's (1997) seminal study showed, too much trust can be as harmful as the complete lack of it.

Contractual trust has a complex relationship with institutional and generalized trust. On the one hand, trust in institutions fosters the development of new trustful inter-organizational partnerships in a market with many players. On the other hand, the lack of enough trust in institutions forces business actors to rely on long-standing, even more trustful relationships (cf. Yamagishi *et al.* 1998; Lazzarini *et al.* 2008). This is the case where (generalized) inter-personal trust may step in to fuel inter-organizational trust. Our analysis highlights this interaction between institutional and inter-personal trust. Moreover, we emphasize that the legacy of state socialism has deprived economic actors of trusted institutions without giving them the opportunity to build trustful business networks. Further complexities related to contractual trust (cf. MacDuffie 2011), however, are outside of the scope of this chapter.

In our analysis, contractual trust is operationalized by the managerial decisions on delivering without contracts and designing contracts. In our context, institutional trust is interpreted in a special sense: namely, as a belief in the rule of formal laws and informal norms over economic behaviour. For the sake of conceptual clarity, we will often refer to it as 'normative trust'. The concept of (generalized) inter-personal trust, on the other hand, is operationalized in the standard way common in attitude surveys. Finally, in an explorative manner, we also try to detect how these concepts are related to managers' beliefs in their own employees' ability to make responsible decisions (cf. MacDuffie 2011).

Contractual trust in post-socialist economies

In this section, we present our hypotheses, which rely on the institutionalist tradition of socio-economic research. This line of research emphasizes the path-dependency of the evolution of business organization, corporate culture and market structure. We focus on the contractual strategies and investigate the legacy of the state-socialist past overshadowing current business organization. However, we take a leap forward by distinguishing the possible impacts of varieties of command economies. Specifically, our analysis is centred on the long-run consequences of the market reforms which distinguished Hungarian economic policy after 1968.

Sako (1992) investigated the impacts of company and societal culture on contractual relations. We argue that the state-socialist legacy is a relevant cultural factor with a significant impact on corporate behaviour. Sako's (1992) focus was primarily on the varieties of capitalist development. We address the issue of varieties of state socialism. We do so, however, in order to also help to explore current varieties of capitalist development.

In spite of advanced formal market institutions, contractual strategies in post-socialist economies might differ from those prevalent in culturally similar societies without the legacy of state socialism. In an advanced market economy, not only formal institutional settings, but also long-standing conventions, norms and informal institutions govern inter-organizational cooperation. Hence, business leaders in such societies can safely rely on those specific normative and institutional settings. The dominance of bureaucratic coordination in state-socialist regimes, on the other hand, inhibited the development of such a stable cognitive framework which could have smoothed the way to voluntary contracts between independent business organizations. As a result of weak conventions, managers in an emerging market economy are forced to make extensive use their own particular knowledge and expertise to shape contractual strategies. In an advanced market economy, on the other hand, consensual expectations on the optimal contractual patterns diminish the impact of managers' particular resources.

Nonetheless, legacies of state socialism may vary, as the politico-economic structures of those regimes differed significantly. Following Stark and Nee (1989) and Szelényi (1989), we characterize the economic regime of the German Democratic Republic (GDR) as an effort to develop a comprehensive and rational central planning system. On the other hand, to put it simply, the Polish system was characterized by voiced opposition but no real alternative to bureaucratic coordination. Finally, in Hungary, early market reforms were introduced and the 'second economy' became quite large after 1968.

Varieties of state-socialist economies differed in how much room they left for market or quasi-market transactions. Comparing the economic regimes of the three countries, comprehensive central planning, which characterized the economic policy of GDR, left the least room for discretional managerial decisions. Market reforms and the development of the 'second economy' in Hungary, on the other hand, gave the most opportunities for learning how to manage inter-firm relations.

Sometimes, however, no experience might be better than bad experience. That is, quasi-market experience in a state-socialist economy may have had detrimental effects on inter-organizational trust. Market interactions in such a command economy were too often connected to the shadow economy, where opportunities for effective contract enforcement were missing. Unreliability was the rule rather than the exception (cf. Gál 1997). This could lead to the proliferation of risk-averse and short-sighted managerial strategies, which survived the fall of the command economy (Gábor 1994a, b, 1997). One should note that a system based on such strategies can be self-sustaining due to self-reinforcing mutual expectations among corporate actors. Nonetheless, case studies of ten large Hungarian companies (Whitley *et al.* 1996) revealed that the level of interdependence and mutual risk sharing was very low in the early nineties, although in some respects these companies seemed to be closer to the OCR model (only one declared that it never started production before written purchase orders were received).

The hypotheses outline the arguments to be tested in the comparative survey. First, hypothesis on the legacy of state-socialist regimes:

H1. 'Good experience is better than no experience'. We suppose that the institutional framework of command economies has had an enduring and detrimental effect on inter-organizational relationships in the post-socialist transformation. The lack of long-standing norms and institutions has led to an elevated level of uncertainty in contractual relations in post-socialist economies.

H1.1. The level of contractual trust is higher among West German firms (managed by West German business leaders) than among East German, Polish and Hungarian – even after 20 years of transition.

H1.2. Lack of consensus (i.e. uncertainty) about the optimal contractual patterns might leave significant room for discretion based on the variety of individual beliefs and attitudes. We suppose, therefore, that business leaders' attitudes, and their personal and social resources affect contractual strategies more strongly in post-socialist economies than in West Germany.

Now, we turn to our hypothesis on the paradoxical legacy of the market reforms in state-socialist Hungary.

H2. 'No experience is better than bad experience'. The relatively market-friendly Hungarian model of state-socialist economic governance may have created more fertile ground for pessimistic beliefs on business cooperation than the stricter central planning policies followed by the Polish and East German regimes.

H2.1. We suppose that the fear of contractual fraud is strongest among the Hungarian business leaders; hence, the level of contractual trust is lower in Hungary than in the Polish and German economies.

H2.2. Without long-standing business conventions, pessimistic beliefs about generalized trust affect low-trust contractual strategies among East German and Polish business leaders. On the other hand, with memories of imperfect market coordination, distrust in economic morale fuels low-trust contractual strategies among Hungarian managers. With a background of long-standing business conventions, no such connections are expected to exist among the executives of West German firms.

Finally, our empirical investigation is also a re-test of the hypothesis on the impacts of technology and market structure on contractual trust (cf. Whitley *et al.* 1996; Sako and Helper 1998; Csabina *et al.* 2002; Lengyel and Janky 2005).

H3. Some aspects of manufacturing technology, organization and market position play key roles in shaping contractual trust in any market economy. That is, we expect that some firm-level characteristics (namely: size, sector, foreign embeddedness and ownership type) have significant effects on contractual trust in all of our four sub-samples.

The next section on data and methods presents the operationalization of our hypotheses.

Data and methods

Two items operationalize the concept of contractual trust in our questionnaire. The first indicates how often the firm starts production before a written contract. The second measures the management's efforts to avoid overly detailed contracts. Five-grade Likert scales measure frequency and intensity (as degrees of agreement with statements on production patterns and contractual efforts).

We use those variables independently when carrying out a factor analysis on various indicators of trust. We composed a simple *contractual trust index* as a proxy characterizing corporate strategies along the dimension of inter-organizational trust. The index is constructed as the sum of the Likert-scale values of those two items.

We adopted a linear-regression model – with the contractual trust index as dependent variable – to delineate the managerial and firm-level characteristics which may be responsible for shaping contractual strategies. The model takes into account managers' basic socio-demographic characteristics as well as indicators of the performance of the business organization they lead. We run distinct regression estimations for each sub-sample.

Explanatory or control variables are grouped into three categories. First, we control for some firm-level characteristics (H3). Second, we incorporate into the model a few of the respondent's basic socio-demographic characteristics, including indicators on educational and career patterns (H1.2, H2.2). Finally, two indicators on the manager's value orientations are also selected as regressors (H1.2).

As far as the organizational context is concerned (H3), size does matter. Large organizations may face different kinds and levels of uncertainties than do smaller firms. Large numbers of contractors may indicate a shift towards arm's-length relationships. On the other hand, large size provides a security that small companies never can enjoy when interacting with business partners. In our model, size of organization is indicated by the number of employees. Adjusting for non-linearities in its effect, we adopt the square root of this number in our regression estimates.

Size matters, but its dynamics may also shape managers' confidence in dealing with business to business relationships. Dissmisals of employees and the reduction of the organization's business activities may reflect market failures, which, in turn, may have accompanied some conflicts and negative experiences in inter-organizational settings. A successful business, on the other hand, may grow on the fertile ground of good partnerships with contractors, consumers and strategic partners. So the sign of a recent change in size is indicated by another variable (indicating the occurrence of negative, zero or positive change by values −1, 0 and 1, respectively).

Few would doubt that the level of the firm's international embeddedness may influence the characteristics of managers' business relationships. However, the sign of the impact of any kind of internationalization is far from evident. On the one hand, a high level of multinationality may be an indicator of solid professional and financial background. On the other hand, interacting with foreign actors calls for a higher level of cautiousness. International embeddedness is indicated by the share of exported products (expressed by per cent of turnout). A dummy variable indicates, on the other hand, whether the firm is, at least partly, foreign owned. Multinational, public, stock market corporations are at one end of a scale, the other end of which is occupied by small family firms. We have a dummy variable on family firms in our model to control for this specific intra-organizational setting.

Sector-specific characteristics may matter even more than size and other basic aspects. At this phase, we differentiate between manufacturing firms and financial institutions by a dummy variable. Rigorous protocols and large numbers of business partners, we suppose, push bankers towards maintaining arm's-length relationships and general cautiousness in business interactions.

Let us turn to the business leader's human resources and personality traits (H1.2, H2.2). We start with the family background concentrating on the 'first-level' managers in our sample, specifically his/her parents' cultural resources. Our regression models include a variable summing up the years the respondent's father and mother spent in education. In line with earlier research, we suppose that education makes people more tolerant, confident and trusting.

Due to the skewed distribution of the years spent in education by today's business leaders, the simple indicator of years in education does not reflect differences in managers' business-related cultural resources. Four dummy variables delineate important groups along the dimension of cultural resources. The first one distinguishes those without a college degree. The second one indicates those with additional education after their first degree (second degree, Ph.D., etc.). A third dummy variable distinguishes business school graduates. We suppose that manager's confidence in inter-organizational interactions increases not only with additional degrees but also by getting specific, business-oriented education. Foreign educational experience may contribute to a business leader's communication skills, and increases his/her confidence in other ways as well. So we also incorporated a dummy on this item. Age is present as a control variable in our models. Contrasting mechanisms behind the indicator, however, make it hard to form conjectures on age-trust profile.

The manager's social resources, ceteris paribus, might increase as his/her business-related social network expands. Occupying management positions at other organizations is very likely to contribute to such network expansion. On the other hand, opportunities to be involved in the management of multiple business organizations may be in themselves a sign of a high level of human resources. A dummy on multipositionality is also present among the regressors.

The survey we analyse allows us to look at the impact of some personality traits: namely, value orientations about managers' roles. A set of items investigates the importance of various groups and entities in their life. The items include family, company, the nation and the global business class. As the research on general value systems indicates, trust might be connected to an individual's cognitive frames about in-groups and out-groups. We carried out explorative factor analysis to extract latent values representing openness and familiarism. Two independent and easily interpretable factors emerged from the analysis. One of them indicates the business leader's affection towards the national community. The other one is a fairly clear measure of a latent scale on the degree of familiarism.[1]

We carry out explorative factor analysis to analyse the latent structure of trust-related beliefs and behaviours. Trust is a complex concept which can hardly be measured by any single questionnaire item. Trust in law enforcement, and societal norms on fair processes may be among the building blocks of inter-organizational trust just as much as trust in people in a given society. Besides two indicators of contractual trust, some other items on trust were included in the questionnaire: generalized trust; trust in the possibility of law abiding behaviour in the economy (belief in the possibility of success without rule-breaking); and, finally, an item indicating managers' trust in employees (belief in the usefulness of allowing employees not to follow supervisors' orders blindly).

We analysed the structure of trust in the four socio-economic contexts separately. The first dimension of the principal component analysis was singled out as a general indicator of trust which more or less filtered out particular, non-trust related concerns in responses to the individual items.

Results

Let us start with the most elementary data on trust among corporate actors. Table 6.1 summarizes the findings on the level of contractual trust in the four sub-samples we investigated. H1.1 states that the post-socialist legacy has a negative impact on the level of contractual trust. Empirical data only partly support this hypothesis. The Hungarian and Polish trust indices are significantly lower than the West German one. Germany clearly stands out, as it is characterized by significantly higher level of trust than the two post-socialist countries included in the analysis. However, patterns of contractual trust among East German managers are fairly similar to those found for West Germans (see for the German sample Chapter 1). Hypothesis 2.1 takes a leap forward, by stating that the Hungarian model of socialist economic governance has created the most fertile ground for pessimistic beliefs regarding business cooperation. In this case, our findings are clearly in line with our expectations: the lowest average level of trust is detected among Hungarian business leaders. As a matter of fact, it is not West Germany, but rather Hungary, which stands out, albeit in a negative sense. The impact of the Hungarian legacy seems to be stronger than the general regime effect.

We argued that we can capture the mechanisms shaping strategies related to contractual relationships by investigating links among various types of trusts. According to H2.2, contractual trust correlates with generalized trust more

Table 6.1 Elementary statistics of contractual trust

	W Germany[a]	E Germany[a]	Hungary	Poland
Starts production before contract (%)[b]	40	41	36	42
Avoids overly detailed contracts (%)[b]	26	24	12	4
Contractual trust index[c]	42.8	43.5	29.3	36.5
N	221	140	140	163

Notes
a Sample of East and West Germans.
b Sum of two 5-grade Likert scale, transformed to a 0–100 scale.
c % of those agreeing with the statement (denoting 4 or 5 on the scale).

strongly in post-socialist economies than in West Germany. Moreover, we supposed that the patterns of relationships among various kinds of trust might be different in the Polish, East German and Hungarian sub-samples.

Table 6.2 summarizes the results of the explorative factor analysis we ran on the trust items. One should be cautious with the interpretation of these results. What can be clearly seen, nonetheless, is that contractual trust (type 2, in particular) distinguishes managers from the three countries, and contractual trust is unrelated to other concepts of trust in West Germany. East German business leaders, on the other hand, are divided as regards generalized trust. 'Normative trust' is the major distinguishing dimension in Poland.[2] What one can also see is that contractual trust is somewhat more strongly linked to other types of trust among East German and Polish managers than of West Germans. As in the case of contractual trust, the factor analysis also implies that Hungarians seem to be the outlier, and the – otherwise significant – post-socialist vs West German difference is quite moderate in comparison with the degree of 'Hungarian exceptionalism'. Our results show that the two indicators of contractual trust and the belief in success without rule-breaking are strongly linked to one another in Hungary. Accordingly, the communality of the first factor is higher in the Hungarian sub-sample than in the other three. Matrices of bivariate correlations, not surprisingly, reinforce the above conclusions.

We also carried out regression analyses in the four sub-samples. As one can see in Table 6.3, there are significant cross-country differences in the results of the ordinary least squares (OLS) regression estimates of our models. Findings in the Polish sub-sample may cast doubt on arguments about a general effect of the socialist legacy. Nonetheless, one can get a more coherent picture comparing the models run in the other three sub-samples. Moreover, some of the findings in the Polish dataset are also in line with the results of the East and/or West German surveys.

Table 6.2 Results of exploring the factor analysis on trust indicators (principal component analysis, one factor solution)

	W Germany[a]	E Germany[a]	Hungary	Poland
Generalised trust	0.253	0.555	−0.162	−0.162
Contractual trust 1 (production before contract)	0.373	−0.056	0.584	0.429
Contractual trust 2 (no detailed contract)	0.717	0.368	0.598	0.251
Normative trust (belief in success without rule breaking)	−0.013	−0.329	0.612	0.806
Employee trust (trust in employees' own opinions)	0.209	0.207	−0.190	0.093
Communality	29%	28%	36%	30%

Note
a Sample of East and West Germans.

Table 6.3 Results of the OLS regression analyses. Non-standardized regression coefficients. Dependent variable: Contractual trust index

	W Germany[a]		E Germany[a]		Hungary		Poland	
	Model 1	Model 2	Model 1	Model 2	Model 1	Model 2	Model 1	Model 2
Firm								
Employment	-0.001	-0.002	-0.002	-0.038	-0.007	-0.003	-0.005	-0.006
Change of empl. (−,0,+)	0.518 ***	0.527 ***	-0.299	-0.292	0.039	-0.075	0.077	0.064
Export (%)	0.006	0.006	0.010	0.004	0.007	0.011 **	-0.001	0.000
Foreign	0.361	0.328	-0.239	-0.618	-0.827 *	-0.889 *	0.191	-0.015
Family firm	-0.187	-0.174	0.649 *	0.761 **	-0.229	-0.234	0.757 *	0.623
Bank	-0.446	-0.595			-1.291 **	-0.915	-0.471	-0.587
Manager: human resources								
Age (ys)		-0.015		-0.069 ***		-0.010		-0.001
Parents' edu (ys)		0.010		0.031		-0.093 **		0.058 **
No univ. degree		0.416		-1.518 *		-0.778		0.379
Post-grad degree		0.395		0.719		0.029		0.564
Business School		0.323		-0.698 *		-1.067 **		0.116
Studies abroad		0.057		0.098		1.084 **		-0.270
Multipositional		0.173		0.313		0.256		0.171
Manager: attitudes								
Identity: nation (score)		0.267		-0.144		0.299		0.023
Identity: company (sc.)		-0.267		0.616 **		-0.476 *		-0.049
Constant	5.292 ***	5.483 ***	5.196 ***	9.050 ***	4.835 ***	7.662 ***	4.967 ***	3.599 ***
N	220	220	139	139	139	139	162	162
R²	5%	9%	5%	18%	13%	25%	5%	10%

Notes
* p<0.1; ** p<0.05; *** p<0.01.
a Sample of East and West Germans.

Before outlining the general lessons we have learned, we move forward step by step, looking at each hypothesis separately. Let us look at Hypothesis 3, which deals with our conjectures on the effects of technology and market position. Namely, we hypothesized that some firm-level characteristics have significant effects on contractual trust in all four of our sub-samples. In Table 6.3, the coefficients belonging to Model 1 represent only the effects of firm-level characteristics. In the Polish sample and in both of the German sub-samples, Model 1 explains about 5 per cent of the total variance of the dependent variable. In the Hungarian data, the explanatory power of Model 1 stands out. However, strong predictors in this regression model, banking sector and foreign ownership in particular, may reflect not only firm-level but also managerial characteristics. In sum, in line with H3, the effects of technology and market situation seem, at least at first sight, similar in the four samples. A closer look at the coefficients, however, reveals that different variables play a key role in shaping contractual trust in the four countries and regions we investigate. Among West German business leaders, for instance, market trend play a key role in influencing contractual strategies. East German and Polish family firms build more trustful relationships than do other types of corporations. In Hungary, on the other hand, foreign ownership indicates a significantly lower level of contractual trust than average.

An additional note of caution on H3 is warranted. The small group of variables we could incorporate in the regression model covers only a minor part of the undoubtedly large set of potential characteristics belonging to technology and market position. Hence, it would be premature to argue, relying upon Model 1, for the irrelevance of companies' technical and business conditions in determining managers' contractual behavioural patterns.

In H1.2, we hypothesize that the manager's personal resources – cultural and network resources in particular – might affect his/her strategies of coping with inter-organizational relationships. However, the effect of a manager's cultural and network resources is stronger in post-socialist economies than in West Germany. One can see that the introduction of Model 2 results in only a moderate increase in the explanatory power of the regression analysis – compared to Model 1 – in the West German sub-sample (R^2 increases from 5 per cent to 9 per cent). Anyway, there is no significant coefficient in the extended part of the model in this Western sample. The impact of personal resources and attitudes, on the other hand, is much stronger among East German and Hungarian business leaders (R^2s increase from 5 per cent to 18 per cent and from 13 per cent to 25 per cent, respectively). In Hungary, the explanatory power of Model 1 is also higher than in the other sub-samples, but note that some of the firm-level variables in Model 1 might correlate with managers' personal resources. In contrast with the above results, the Polish data do not fit Hypothesis 1.2. Further inquiries would be needed to shed light on the possible reasons for the Polish evidence.

As far as the effects of individual variables are concerned, there are significant cross-country differences. Among East German managers, for instance, age has a strong effect: younger managers, ceteris paribus, tend to trust their partners more than do older managers. Moreover, East German business leaders without a university degree trust less than do their counterparts with higher level of education. Parents' cultural resources also have a positive but weak effect in the model run on this sub-sample. One might assume that a business school education would foster familiarity with the real risks of inter-organizational relationships and the market forces strengthening contractual discipline. Our findings among East German business leaders do not support this conjecture.

Schooling experience abroad increases the level of contractual trust among Hungarian managers. But the effect of a business school education, similarly to the East German sample, shifts the level of trust in the opposite direction from what one might expect. Moreover, coming from a family with high cultural resources entails low-trust contractual strategies in Hungary.

In H1.2 we drew a link between contractual trust and business leaders' attitudes. We supposed that this correlation is stronger among post-socialist managers than among business leaders in West Germany. Our data fit the hypothesis in the West German, East German and Hungarian sub-samples. Further estimations aiming to distinguish the explanatory power of attitudes (not shown) reinforce what one can see by looking at the coefficients of attitude-factor score variables. Namely, East German and Hungarian business leaders' attitudes towards managerial role models (on belonging to the nation and the firm) do have significant impacts on contractual strategies, while West Germans' do not. The effects of those attitudes are even weaker in the sample of Polish managers than among West German leaders. For East Germans and Hungarians alike, identification with the orthodox, company-centred managerial mission correlates strongly with contractual strategies.

However, this variable has the opposite effect in Hungary to that in the East German sample. We conjectured that in post-socialist economies, managers' stronger attachment to the shareholder-centred concept of managerial philosophy would entail a higher level of trust in market forces governing inter-corporate relationships. Indeed, among East German managers, stronger attachment to those orthodox values makes them likely to implement high-trust contractual strategies. This is not the case in Hungary, where those orthodox managers are more cautious about inter-corporate transactions than their less orthodox counterparts.

Looking at the big picture, our findings mostly support our argument on the impacts of the legacy of state-socialist regimes on inter-organizational cooperation. Nonetheless, some parts of the evidence do not fit our hypotheses, at least in parts of the international survey sample. In the concluding section, we sum up what we have learned from those unexpected results.

The comparison of strategies of East and West German business leaders provides the most straightforward evidence in favour of our theoretical model on institutional embeddedness and path-dependency. On average, East German managers adopt similar patterns of contractual strategies as their West German counterparts, who work more or less in the same cultural and institutional framework. East Germans, however, also use, indirectly at least, lessons learned in a state-socialist society when forming their contractual strategies. Moreover, cultural resources, it seems, help East German managers to cope with the risks of transactions in a local market context which is without long-standing normative and institutional traditions. The detrimental effect of business school education, however, is a notable exception to the rule. It may have to do with the fact that the vast majority of East German managers got a technical education. Contrary to expectations, in an environment where business education of leaders is an exception, it might lead those who have a business education to be closer to the prudential, contract-based ACR-type of behaviour pattern.

Our international survey also presents new evidence of a kind of 'Hungarian sickness' manifesting itself in weak social cohesion. The concept of entrepreneurship is strongly linked to moral weakness and unjust success in post-socialist countries. But the spectacular strength of those beliefs in a relatively advanced socio-economic context, we argued, is a paradoxical legacy of early market reforms in a fundamentally anti-capitalist institutional and ideological regime. However, Hungarian data on the determinants of trust also warns us that our general hypotheses could not fully grasp the particular mechanisms of how this special legacy influences managers' beliefs and behavioural patterns: the hypotheses too often contrast with findings.

Conclusion

In this chapter, we discussed the role of the legacy of state-socialist economy in shaping the country-specific patterns of inter-firm relationships in Central Europe. Our analysis relied upon Sako's (1992) seminal study into the cultural influence on contractual relations. The research was motivated by a puzzle set by the Hungarian pattern of socio-economic development, that is, the low level of social cohesion in Hungarian society compared to countries with a similar socio-economic background – a finding in sharp contrast with plausible expectations derived from comparisons of the socio-economic legacies of state-socialist regimes in East Central Europe (cf. Stark and Nee 1989; Szelényi 1989; Raiser 1997, 2002).

We carried out factor and regression analyses to single out the mechanisms through which the legacy of state-socialist corporate and societal culture influences managerial strategies even twenty years after the transition. Our point of departure was a simple, straightforward hypothesis about the detrimental effect of the legacy of the state-socialist era on contractual trust. Our conceptual leap was to hypothesize on the ways this legacy impacts on the development of post-socialist managers' contractual strategies. We found that the level of contractual trust, compared to West Germany, is lower in Hungary and Poland but not among East German managers who overwhelmingly work in East Germany. However, unlike West German managers, East German business leaders – like their Hungarian and Polish counterparts – rely extensively on idiosyncratic knowledge and social resources when building their strategies in inter-organizational transactions. This, we argued, stems from the lack of well established norms and institutions governing business relationships in post-socialist economies. That is, in the post-socialist context, there is no common knowledge among managers about the proper reactions to various forms of uncertainties in inter-organizational relationships. Hence, many other factors may influence managerial strategies, specifically their human capital, personal experience or simply impressions of the manager they interact with; or even their generalized trust in other people.

We added some complexity to our theoretical argument by forming conjectures on the paradox effects of early market reforms in the state-socialist era. The development of the so called 'second economy', in particular, may have contributed to the erosion of trust in business partners in Hungary.

One of our unexplored findings may deserve further investigation. Namely, cultural resources could be a liability rather than an asset in the 'post-second-economy' context, when it comes to contract-related transaction costs (see Hungarian data in Table 6.3). Szelényi (1978), Szelényi and Manchin (1987) and Nee (1991), among others, argued early on that market reforms may help some working class groups and could reduce inequalities. This could be the case because the 'second economy' provided new opportunities for actors who occupied low-status positions in state-controlled organizations. Building upon this thesis, one might hypothesize that the detrimental effect of market reform on business leaders' strategies does not stem simply from a kind of bad experience shared by everyone in the state-socialist era, but rather from the unfamiliarity of the white collar upper-middle-class managers in particular with the rules of the games in the special context which the working-class-dominated 'second economy' created, which then proliferated and has survived into the post-socialist era. Hence, the well-educated majority of managers behave as would if they were operating in a foreign culture: avoiding informal settings and tending to rely upon formal contracts to ensure technical and financial discipline. Wider comparative research may help to explore these tentative conclusions.

Notes

1 The above dimensions were extracted as the second and third factors. The first component of the factor model shows equally strong positive relationship with all kind of items, and, thus, is interpreted as a consequence of some respondents' ignorance as regards those attitude questions.
2 One should note, however, that these data in large part simply reflect the differences between the types of trust in various sub-samples.

7 Varying concepts of corporate social responsibility

Beliefs and practices in Central Europe

Katharina Bluhm and Vera Trappmann

Introduction

In continental Europe, corporate social responsibility (CSR) is once again a public issue. This is partly due to globalization and liberalization, partly due to the perceived weakening of public welfare (cf. Vogel 2005; Hiß 2006; Bluhm 2008; Hassel 2008). Many scholars see in the CSR movement since the mid-1990s a development that leads continental European companies away from their former 'implicit' mode of taking responsibility for society, towards an Anglo-American, demonstrative style of 'explicit' CSR (Matten and Moon 2008). Germany is often regarded as a leading case of this development. The perspective implies a tendency towards the substitution of binding, collective labour relations with broader, stakeholder-oriented, voluntary CSR (cf. Habisch 2006; Hiß 2009), supported by an ideological turn toward neoliberalism (Imbusch and Rucht 2007; Kinderman 2008). However, other research still stresses the persisting institutional and cultural peculiarities of continental European capitalism and how companies define their responsibility (Campbell 2007; Gjølberg 2009; Witt and Redding 2012).

Research on Central and Eastern Europe (CEE) has been a late-comer to this debate. The transition from planned to market economies dramatically changed the role of companies in those societies and led to an externalization of social functions previously held by enterprises under state socialism. This process has been most far-reaching in the new EU member states where privatization and liberalization policies went further than in other post-socialist countries. Under the increasing influence of western multinationals and the European Union, however, one can observe a diffusion of CSR into these countries. In Karl Polanyi's terms this diffusion would be a countermovement to deregulation, but it could equally well be considered part of a 'neoliberal' project of explicit CSR obstructing more powerful regulation.

The academic debate on the emergence of CSR as a new concept is to a large extent dominated by an institutionalist view on actors which does not take into account the perceptions of individuals. Yet, institutions not only constrain the strategies of corporate and individual actors, they also rely on a common understanding on the part of those actors. Although this is widely accepted, there has been astonishingly little research exploring how executives and entrepreneurs understand the responsibility of companies towards society. The few studies dealing with business leaders' perceptions suggest most business leaders follow a neoliberal approach (Eyal *et al.* 1998; Machonin *et al.* 2006), which the authors associate with a rather restrictive view of responsibility due to an anti-communist reflex.

In this chapter, we explore the *cognitive concepts of corporate responsibility* for the wider society on the part of senior executives and entrepreneurs in Germany, Hungary and Poland and how they see the role of the state and the social outcome of the market economy. In the first section, we develop a more elaborate theoretical design than offered in the literature so far, which allows us to identify a variety of concepts relevant to the institutionalist debate. In the next sections, we formulate assumptions on how these theoretically developed varieties are distributed in the sample and explore what makes respondents more likely to belong to one of the groups. We briefly examine whether the concepts correspond to actual practices of the companies. In the final section, we discuss the results in the light of our research hypothesis and enhance them with qualitative material.

Our findings show that there is little convergence towards a single 'neoliberal' or 'liberal' concept of corporate responsibility. The differences between West Germany, East Germany, Poland and Hungary are significant. While in West Germany the traditional understanding of corporate responsibility has remained more current than is suggested in the literature, the perceptions in East Germany and particularly in Hungary and Poland are more mixed. Advocates of the view that is mostly associated with 'explicit' CSR are particularly rare (Backhaus-Maul 2005; Habisch 2006; Matten and Moon 2008). This is true not only for West Germany but also for the post-socialist constellations of East Germany, Poland and Hungary, indicating that the institutional setting in all three countries is – still – not very supportive of this version of corporate responsibility.[1]

A framework for cognitive concepts of corporate responsibility to society

In a well-known work, Dirk Matten and Jeremy Moon (2008: 410) differentiate between 'explicit' and 'implicit' CSR on the axis of voluntary vs involuntary, where the latter refers to institutionalized CSR. While 'explicit' CSR is always voluntary, deliberative and often strategic, 'implicit' CSR is the result of well-established rules, norms, and values that form (mandatory and customary) requirements for companies and 'define proper obligations of corporate actors in collective rather than individual terms' (ibid.: 409). Culturally, implicit CSR is underpinned by collectivism, while national institutions that encourage explicit CSR also encourage individualism, liberalism and discretion (Matten and Moon 2008: 411). The coordinated market economies (CME) of continental Europe are perceived as traditionally having an implicit concept of corporate responsibility. State-owned companies in CEE, however, are also thought to demonstrate 'elements' of implicit CSR (ibid.: 417).

The conceptual framework of implicit and explicit CSR has some substantial weaknesses. The contrast between deliberative and voluntary (explicit) vs mandatory and customary (implicit) raises the question as to whether or not the latter should be called CSR at all. This has to do with the historic origin of CSR as a new label and management practice since the late 1980s, but also with the normative background of the CSR debate, in which Corporate Social Responsibility is by definition 'voluntary' and goes beyond what companies are legally required to do (cf. Carroll 1991; Matten and Crane 2004). In fact, applying the label 'CSR' to practices in which business leaders only react to or reflect an institutional environment existing independently of them is conceptually inconsistent (Matten and Moon 2008: 408 and 410; for this critique see Kinderman 2008). Moreover, the differentiation along the voluntary/involuntary axis overstates the voluntary quality of the CSR movement among companies, and underestimates the need for strategic agreement in neocorporatist arrangements. On the one hand, the relatively high standardization of explicit CSR communication and practices calls into question the freedom of choice and the degree of individual 'authorship' on the part of the companies. The diffusion of CSR among companies and from the transnational to the national space can only be explained by an increase of isomorphic pressure from the institutional environment which makes companies' investment in CSR worthwhile (cf. Hiß 2006; Bluhm 2008; Hassel 2008). On the other hand, collective regulation by unions and employer representatives does not have the same legal status as tax law or labour codes. Although contracts between social partners are legally binding, in most European labour-relations systems they rest on free membership in employers' associations. This implies agreeing to do more than what is 'required by law' but also provides companies with easier ways to opt out compared to labour codes. In addition, the boundaries between institutionalized arrangements and 'voluntary' activities are sometimes blurred. For example, the vocational training opportunities offered by German companies sometimes exceed their actual training needs, being motivated by societal responsibility for keeping youth unemployment low or to enjoy a reputation as a 'good employer'. Therefore care needs to be taken before placing neocorporatist traditions into the same category as the welfare functions that state enterprises took over from the former Soviet regimes, as in Matten and Moon's concept of implicit CSR.

For these reasons, the dichotomy between 'implicit' and 'explicit' is not suitable for cognitive concepts of responsibility (for an attempt of doing this and its limits, see Witt and Redding 2012). If explicit CSR is voluntary and implicit CSR is simply enforced by institutions, then only in the first case do the ideas and beliefs of people running the businesses actually matter. Consequently, our conceptualization abandons the 'explicit/implicit' dichotomy which, in our view, only distinguishes between the presence vs absence of a formal label for CSR activities, specialized management practices, and of internal and external communication and supervision.

To understand varying cognitive concepts of corporate responsibility, we need to incorporate all of the dimensions or 'levels' of the so-called 'pyramid of CSR' devised by Archie Carroll (1991) – although 'a pyramid' is arguably not the best metaphor. A successful business that generates profit and therefore generates employment, income and tax payments undisputedly represents the foundation of all other endeavours in a market economy. It is sometimes called 'economic responsibility' – in contrast to 'legal', 'ethical' and 'philanthropic' responsibility, which are nearer the top of the pyramid (cf. Matten and Crane 2004; Hiß 2006). While according to the CSR literature companies have to go beyond economic and legal responsibility, Milton Friedman's famous dictum that 'the responsibility of business is to increase its profits' (Friedman 1973) polemically rejects this broader view. According to Friedman, any deviation from this narrow concept of a company's responsibility is problematic, as it distracts from the primary task of business, which is to maximize economic welfare. Obeying the rules of the game, like paying taxes, is included here, as Friedman's neoliberalism provides for well-functioning law enforcement by the state. Yet this is not self-evident, as business leaders may feel their economic responsibility to be in conflict with legal demands.

We refer to a view with this restricted understanding of economic responsibility as *minimalist*, and devise an interview item close to Friedman's dictum: 'The social responsibility of companies consists only of increasing profit' (Table 7.1). Our respondents who clearly agreed with this item on a Likert scale from one to five belong to the minimalist group. In addition, we tested their answers in combination with a wider view of company responsibility which goes beyond mere legal obligations: we combined the Friedman item with *disagreement* with – or at least *neutrality* towards – the statement 'Companies have to do more than is required by law.' If the respondents felt uneasy with this item, we classified them as *strict minimalists*, in contrast to *soft minimalists* who do not clearly reject this notion.

Legal responsibility is not considered a distinct concept but is commonly regarded as intertwined with economic responsibility by both Friedman and the CSR literature. True Friedmanites should comply with the rules when they pursue their economic goals; just as voluntary CSR that is supposed to go beyond economic and legal responsibility implies a similar rule-obeying behaviour. In the real world of market economies, this is not necessarily the case, since economic and legal responsibilities follow different, sometimes contradicting logics, even more so if the rules of the game are inconsistent, badly implemented and weakly enforced. In the transition research on CEE, distance from and lack of trust in institutions has been a prominent issue from the beginning, even in the most successful regime-change countries, like Poland and Hungary, as illustrated by the country chapters elsewhere in this volume. Hence, we examine whether legal responsibilities are regarded as being in conflict with other dimensions of corporate responsibility operationalized with the agreement to the same statement that Béla Janky and György Lengyel use for 'normative trust' (Chapter 6): 'One has to break the rules in order to get ahead' (see Table 7.1).

In contrast with the low-commitment concept, we distinguished between two high-commitment concepts of responsibility: a *'liberal'* and a *'neocorporatist'* concept of corporate responsibility. We operationalize high commitment as

Table 7.1 Concepts used, range 1 = total agreement, 5 = total disagreement

Concepts	Operationalization	Expected correspondence
Low Commitment concepts, economic responsibility only		
Minimalist	(1) Social responsibility of companies consists only of increasing profits. (1, 2)	Might be etatists, in which case they are not true Friedmanites
Strict minimalist	(1) Social responsibility of companies consists only of increasing profits. (1, 2) (2) Companies have to do more for the community than what is required by law. (4, 5)	Should be more consequent Friedmanites
Legal responsibility		
Disagreement with or uncertainty about rule obedience	One has to break the rules if one wants to get ahead (1, 2, 3)	Most likely for soft minimalists, if they are not true Friedmanites
High-commitment concepts, beyond economic and legal responsibility		
Liberal	(1) Companies have to do more for the community than what is required by law. (1, 2) (2) Voluntary commitment to social and environmental issues is, even in time of a crisis, an indispensable part of a company's strategy. (1, 2) (3) Collective regulations between social partners are important for the functioning of the economy. (3, 4, 5) (4) Trade unions are superfluous. (1, 2, 3)	Should be anti-etatists but rule-followers; should exclude both versions of minimalists
Neocorporatist	(1) Companies have to do more for the community than what is required by law. (1, 2) (2) Voluntary commitment to social and environmental issues is, even in time of a crisis, an indispensable part of a company's strategy. (1, 2) (3) Collective regulations between social partners are important for the functioning of the economy. (1, 2) (4) Trade unions are superfluous. (4, 5)	In the German version more likely to be anti-etatists but rule-followers; should exclude both versions of minimalists
Position viz. state intervention		
Etatist	(1) The government should monitor and regulate the economy. (1, 2) (2) The socio-political responsibilities of the state can only be achieved through the redistribution of wealth. (1, 2)	Might be less likely to pursue high commitment

agreement with two items. The first is 'Companies must do more for the community than what is required by law', and the second is 'Voluntary commitment to social and environmental issues, even in a time of a crisis, is an indispensable part of a company's strategy' (see Table 7.1). If this is not only lip service, it should also translate into practice in the form of CSR activities and personal unpaid work.

Our basic assumption is that *both* concepts, 'liberal' and 'neocorporatist', display a high commitment to corporate responsibility, but in different ways. They are the only concepts that we construct complementary, that is, only 'liberals' cannot be 'neocorporatists' and vice versa at the same time. We argue that the readiness to accept formal collective bargaining with social partners constitutes the major difference between the two concepts and not the presence or absence of choice. The adherents of the neocorporatist concept share the view that collaboration with social partners, including unions, is important for the functioning of the economy and accept *collective self-binding* (see Table 7.1). This pattern, sometimes also identified as 'traditional continental European', lies in Carroll's pyramid between legal and ethical responsibility because although it creates legally binding rules it is (with a few exceptions) based on free association.

Respondents who, in our terms, tend toward a 'liberal' concept share the broader stakeholder view of corporate responsibility. We therefore distinguish high-commitment liberalism from minimalism and Friedmanites. In contrast to 'neocorporatists', so defined 'liberals' refute the usefulness of collective binding, or are at least undecided (Table 7.1). As they prefer an individualistic, firm-specific approach, their beliefs represent the cultural foundation of explicit CSR as understood by Matten and Moon (2008).

In addition to these three concepts of responsibility, we introduced a fourth concept, '*etatism*', that refers to the *role of the state* in the economy and for redistribution of economic wealth (see again Table 7.1). The reasons for including etatism in the analysis are twofold. First, we assume that the perception of state intervention sheds an important additional light on the three concepts of responsibility. Second, we consider etatism an *indirect* concept of corporate responsibility since state intervention might be perceived as allowing less corporate input in public well-being. If minimalists share the neoliberal ideology, they should be hesitant to endorse or may even despise state regulation of the economy and redistribution (see Table 7.1). However, a reductionist view on companies' role in society might, on the other hand, imply a delegation of the responsibility for public well-being onto a pro-interventionist state. In this regard, minimalist and etatists may share a similar view. Adherents of our definition of a high-commitment liberal concept, in contrast, should be equally reluctant to agree to government regulation and redistribution because this, too, restricts freedom of choice on the side of the companies. Neocorporatists might not, per se, be against state intervention, especially for redistributive purposes. However, again, the German tradition of neocorporatism stresses an idealized form of autonomous self-regulation that is supposed to replace the need for state intervention (especially for state regulation). Hence, we expect that of the neocorporatists in our sample, the Germans do not share the etatist position.

Hypothesis and assumptions

The theoretical framework outlined above enables us to make a few tentative assumptions about the distribution of the cognitive concepts in our sample.

First, we assume that we will find more minimalists in our sample of medium-sized companies than in the larger companies and banks, which are the more likely candidates for high-commitment concepts. Resource restrictions in medium-sized companies and less public attention on their behaviour might account for such a distribution. Tight resources may be an issue especially for medium-sized manufacturers in the post-socialist context because – compared to those in the West – they are usually newly-founded businesses and often still have to fight to increase their market share using low-cost and low-wage strategies. Smaller companies with restricted economic resources might also be more inclined to see economic and legal responsibility as conflicting. Hence, it is most likely that respondents who agree with the need for rule breaking are also minimalists. Yet this might be only half the story, as smaller companies are perhaps more bound to local communities and therefore obliged to show some degree of commitment to (local) society beyond what is legally mandated.

Second, we expect to find more minimalists in the post-socialist context than in West Germany when also controlling for company type and size. With privatization, companies were freed from all societal assignments beyond the pursuit of business. In East Germany, this crucial institutional change was based on the regulations of municipal constitutions (*Kommunalverfassung*) created during the process of unification, which stipulated the transfer of quasi-municipal structures from companies to local communities (for example, apartments, medical infrastructure or vocational training schools that had been provided by state-socialist enterprises). Other social functions like holiday camps or workplace cafeterias were abolished during the economic collapse and downsizing of the East German state enterprises after unification.

A very similar development could be observed in post-socialist countries following a more or less rapid process of liberalization and privatization. In Hungary, the abandonment of social functions had already started with the 'spontaneous privatization' of the late 1980s, in which top managers outsourced the more profitable parts of the state enterprises. Interestingly the Polish 'Law on Commercialization and Privatization of State Enterprises' (*Ustawa o komercjalizacji i prywatyzacji przedsiębiorstw państwowych*) of 1996 says that social and ecological obligations have to be considered only in fixing the price during privatizations. However, unlike the other two post-socialist cases we deal with here, privatization and communalization in Poland was accompanied with a 'Law on Workplace Social Funds' (*Zakladowego funduszu swiadczen socjalnych*) which stipulated that every private or state company independent of size needed to set up a social fund. Further, management had to agree with either unions or employees over the particular uses of the social fund, such as supporting employee recreation, culture, sport, childcare or further education. Thus Poland did not abandon all elements of the state-socialist or 'implicit'

CSR. However, the law did not hinder a drastic reduction of such collective goods, as vocational training schools and childcare facilities did usually not survive communalization in Poland because communities could simply not afford to keep them.[2]

The overburdening of companies with social functions in the state-socialist past and the companies being freed from this kind of responsibility in the transition process makes it plausible that a relatively restrictive concept of corporate responsibility towards society would now be widespread – independent of the available resources of companies (which we equate with their size).

Third, we expect more high-commitment liberals in very large companies and in the financial sector since they are the first to come under isomorphic pressure of the CSR movement and might also take on the corresponding beliefs. Also, given the weak system of collective bargaining and social partnership, we assume that liberalism should be more present in East Germany, Hungary and Poland compared to Western Germany. For Polish leaders of very large companies and financial institutions, in particular, we expect them to whole-heartedly embrace liberal ideas since collective bargaining is weakest in Poland (see Chapter 8). We also assume that foreign ownership would be significant in this respect.

Fourth, and contrary to the debate on the neoliberal turn among German business leaders in the last decade, we assume that the German neocorporatist tradition is still strong enough to distinguish German business leaders from the others despite the institutional change. In other words, we expect that West German business leaders are still used to neocorporatist labour relations and regard them positively (see Chapter 4).

Fifth, we expect a clear rejection of etatism by West German leaders deriving from the German tradition of collective self-regulation. For East Germany, Poland and Hungary, we may expect a similar effect arising from a lasting negative memory of state-controlled business and society. However, since collective organizations are generally weak in post-socialist societies, especially in Poland and Hungary, there is little experience of self-regulation without the state. As a result, it is difficult to formulate a more precise hypothesis in context.

Sixth, apart from effects of the country of origin and of the type of company, we assume that age and international experience (studying and working abroad, especially in Anglo-Saxon countries) support a high-commitment liberal viewpoint. In other words, we expect persons of a younger age and with more international experience to be more up-to-date with the international CSR movement. For age we used a dichotomized variable that counts 45-year-old and younger respondents as 'young' (for reasons see Chapter 5).

Data and methods

The analysis of the cognitive concepts of corporate responsibility is based on the same data set of 2009/10 as described earlier (see Chapter 1). For this chapter only the respondents occupying top-level positions in their business hierarchy were taken into consideration. We again differentiate between medium-sized

(45–249), large (250–999) and very large companies (≥1,000 employes), and banks. Of these respondents, approximately 37 per cent possess shares in the companies they head. While in Hungary and Poland location of company and origin of the respondents is identical, this is not the case for the German sample. For Germany, we use the distinction between East and West Germans based on the place they lived a day before the German–German Monetary Union in 1990. West Germans head about one-third of the companies in the East German sample and mostly larger companies, while only a few East Germans are in similar positions in West Germany. East German executives usually hold minority shares in their companies and run smaller businesses (see in more detail Chapter 1). As we assume that post-socialist legacies matter, we refer to the 'geographic origin' of the top-level respondents when we analyse 'country effects' in this chapter.

In addition to our concepts, we add statements about nationalization of companies, vocational training as a company's or state's task, social justice, shareholder value and other issues which we have not integrated in the theoretical constructs but which are related to them and can be used as validation variables to test the consistency of the cognitive concepts respondents share. All answers are recorded as binary responses (agree/disagree) (see Table 7.1 to view the variables integrated into the concepts and the Appendix, Table A7.1, for the validation variables). The adherents of each concept form a 'responsibility group'. Given that only the adherence to the high-commitment concepts excludes each other, these groups may overlap. We then estimate the impact of qualitative, explanatory variables on the probability of membership of the respondents to a particular group ('concept') with a logit model.[3] The explanatory variables are a) the additional statements to validate the concept use; b) socio-demographic characteristics of the respondents, such as age (younger vs older), educational and social background, personal unpaid work and studying and working abroad; c) objective characteristics of the companies: ownership, labour relations and CSR practices. Taken together, these variables allow us to explore the situation of those who share a particular concept in more detail, control for observed differences in the respondents, and test for a correspondence of cognitive concepts with company-related features beyond the country effects and company types.

Due to the limited amount of data, we first estimate the effect of each explanatory variable separately on each concept (see as an example Table 7.4), in order to account for differences in the concepts solely due to the 'geographic origin' of the business leaders and the company types. We then additionally introduce a set of dummy variables indicating differences in these characteristics into each regression model. In a second series of regressions, interaction terms between the explanatory variables and the 'geographic origin' of the respondents and the type of the company, respectively, are added to each model. The resulting coefficient estimates can be used to analyse country and company specific differences in the effect of a particular variable on a concept. The estimates of coefficients indicate the change in the log odds of the outcome for a one unit increase in the explanatory variable. In the case of binary explanatory variables, this is equivalent to comparing the odds of adhering to a particular concept if a certain feature is present with the odds that the feature is not present. In the final discussion, we add some quotations from business leaders in the three countries from the semi-structured interviews conducted between 2010 and 2011, and then relate these to our concepts.

Findings

The four theoretically distinct concepts we created – the minimalist, liberal, neo-corporatist and etatist concepts – cover slightly more than half of the respondents occupying the top hierarchy level (386 of 749 respondents). The other half of the sample disagreed with the Friedman item, but did not fit any of the other concepts either. Although this sample is considerably smaller than the original sample, it retains a similar distribution of respondents across countries and company types. Medium-sized companies are slightly underrepresented, while very large companies and financial institutions are somewhat overrepresented in the new subsample. Since the percentage of very large companies and banks is quite small in the original sample, a slight oversampling of the two company types in the new sample which our study examines is actually advantageous for further detailed analysis of the results. The fact that heads of larger companies as well as bankers are more likely to fit into our theoretical concepts may indicate that they reflect more upon their role in society than those in smaller businesses.

Minimalists

More than one-third (112 respondents) of the subsample belong to the minimalist group, which is the second-largest group with an identified concept after the neo-corporatists. Yet, when compared to the entire sample of top-level respondents, the percentage is 15 per cent – only a minority of business leaders openly agreed with the idea that the social responsibility of a company consists solely of increasing profit. A Fisher test indicates that minimalists are statistically less likely to be

Table 7.2 Percentage of respondents with a clear concept of corporate responsibility (compared to all respondents of each subgroup)

	Minimalist	Etatist	Neocorporatist	Liberal
W Germany	7.0	1.0	25.3	8.3
E Germany	12.4	2.8	11.3	10.4
Hungary	17.9	31.4	10.0	10.7
Poland	29.5	19.0	12.7	6.8
Medium-sized	14.0	9.7	9.7	10.0
Large	21.0	13.3	13.3	6.3
Very large	10.0	13.0	13.0	9.0
Banks	17.6	12.0	11.8	6.0
Total in absolute terms	112.0	82.0	126.0	66.0

present among West Germans than East Germans, Poles or Hungarians. Only 7 per cent of the West German business leaders are minimalists, whereas approximately 12 per cent of East Germans, 18 per cent of Hungarians and 30 per cent of the Poles share a minimalist concept (Table 7.2). The regression model that includes the geographic origin of the respondents and the company types reveals that minimalists are significantly more likely to be found among East Germans – and in *particular in Hungary and Poland* – than among West Germans; they are also more likely to run large companies with 250 to 999 employees (Table 7.3). Hence, we do observe a post-socialist effect, but we *cannot* confirm that minimalism is only a phenomenon of smaller businesses. Among Polish leaders, minimalists are particularly strongly represented, with 25 per cent in large companies and 40 per cent in very large companies, far above the average for the three countries.

Only half of the overall minimalist group (53 from 112 respondents) agree to the Friedman item but in addition reject the statement 'companies have to do more for the community than is required by law' and are therefore considered strict minimalists. Being from Poland doubles the likelihood of belonging to this subgroup of minimalists (Table 7.3). Given the number of strict minimalists, this group is often too small for producing significant results in the interaction analysis.

In terms of company ownership, partly foreign-owned companies (with foreigners owning between 25 and 99 per cent of the shares) are more likely to be in the minimalist group compared to 100 per cent subsidiaries, while the absence of foreign ownership shows no significant deviation from subsidiaries. When the

Table 7.3 Coefficient estimates of the impact of country and company type on adherence to CSR concepts

Regression	I	II	III	IV	
Dependent variable[a]	Liberal	Neocorporatist	Etatist	Minimalist	Strict minimalist
E Germany	0.142	−0.431	1.138	0.649*	0.725
Hungary	0.283	−1.149***	3.950***	1.172***	0.698
Poland	−0.202	−0.969***	3.202***	1.709***	1.451***
Large	−0.430	0.771***	0.517	0.455*	0.437
Very large	−0.053	1.457***	0.304	−0.370	0.005
Banks	−0.557	1.819***	−0.207	0.163	0.09
N	741	740	738	740	740
Pseudo R²	0.013	0.152	0.299	0.110	0.059

Notes
All estimates were obtained using a logistic regression model. They represent the change in the log odds of the outcome for a one unit increase in the explanatory variable. The intercept was omitted from the table. The asterisk denotes the following levels of statistical significance: * – $p < 0.10$, ** – $p < 0.05$, *** – $p < 0.01$. The Pseudo-R² was calculated following Nagelkerke (1991).
a Reference category: West German business leaders in medium-sized companies.

respondents head large joint stock companies or a publicly listed joint stock company they are also more likely to be minimalists (for latter: 1.569***), when controlling for country effects and company type. We also observe this effect for family-run companies (0.689*). Otherwise companies managed by owners (including founders) are not significantly more likely to belong to this responsibility group. In short, minimalists are not simply just owner-managers and heads of companies with tighter resources as measured by size, as expected. This is also supported by the fact that respondents who characterize themselves as belonging to the global business class are significantly more likely to be minimalists than those who do not share this self-characterization (Table 7.4). The effect of this additional variable on the odds of being a minimalist is significantly lower for East Germans.

In terms of labour relations, members in employers' associations with collective bargaining function are neither more nor less present in the minimalist group than companies without this feature when also controlling for country effects and company type. In Poland there is even a statistically higher probability of being run by a minimalist if the company is a member in such an association (1.887**), which may still be saying little in the face of the country's low level of collective bargaining and the predominant self-definition of employers' associations as lobby organizations (see Chapter 8). What is more striking is that companies with a plant-level employee representation (works/employee council or a company union) are significantly less likely to be headed by a minimalist, again while controlling for company type (−0.484**).

Table 7.4 Impact of belonging to the global business class on adherence to CSR concepts

Regression	I	II	III	IV	V
Dependent variable[a]	Liberal	Neocorporatist	Etatist	Minimalist	Strict minimalist
E Germany	−2.284	−1.973	1.144	0.838*	0.859*
Hungary	0.140	−0.339***	4.014***	1.589***	0.672
Poland	0.373	−0.908***	3.229***	1.800***	1.480***
Large	−0.186	−0.992***	0.430	0.345	0.323
Very large	−0.466	0.796***	0.163	−0.454	0.000
Banks	−0.190	1.508***	−0.236	0.230	0.214
Global business class	0.137	0.301	0.301	1.175***	0.803**
N	710	709	706	709	708
Pseudo R²	0.045	0.201	0.362	0.213	0.149

Notes
All estimates were obtained using a logistic regression model. They represent the change in the log odds of the outcome for a one unit increase in the explanatory variable. The intercept was omitted from the table. The asterisk denotes the following levels of statistical significance: * – $p < 0.10$, ** – $p < 0.05$, *** – $p < 0.01$. The Pseudo-R^2 was calculated following Nagelkerke (1991).
a Reference category: West German business leaders in medium-sized companies.

Regarding *socio-demographic characteristics,* one of the most unexpected results is that being 45 and younger (or older) at the time of the survey, does not matter much. Other results are harder to interpret. Contrary to our expectations, business leaders who had spent some time abroad are more likely to be minimalists, but not liberals. Minimalist business leaders are the only responsibility group for which studying abroad matters: individuals who *studied abroad* are almost twice as likely to be minimalists (0.634**), even more so when they had studied abroad for a period longer than six months (the destination where respondents study did not produce useful results). Yet these explanatory variables reveal no significance for the subgroup of strict minimalists. Bankers with upper-class fathers are significantly more likely to belong to the minimalist group.[4] Otherwise, social origin does not contribute to explaining concept differences, nor does gender or the educational background of the respondents.

Our minimalists are not a consistent group. As expected, there is some overlap with etatists in the sample. Of the 112 minimalists, 23 respondents also agreed with a strong role of the state in regulation and redistribution. Yet, 13 respondents also agreed with the liberal concept that combines a high level of commitment beyond economic and legal responsibility with the rejection of collective regulations. Ten respondents even fit the neocorporatist concept. The overlap is immediately reduced if we look at the 53 strict minimalists, of whom only six also agreed with state intervention.

Despite the overlap with other concepts, minimalists share a *unique set of ideas* that separates them from the others, but does not fit simply into a Friedmanite belief system.

Business leaders seeing a *conflict between economic and legal responsibility* are significantly more likely to be in the minimalist group than respondents who do not share this view, that is, who disagree with the rule-breaking statement. Although a larger number of business leaders can also be found in the liberal group, the probability that business leaders not being strict with the rules belong in the minimalists camp is outstanding (0.964***) after controlling for country effects and different company types. Interestingly, it is also twice as likely for the group of strict minimalists (0.883***), who were supposed to be even more Friedmanite. The effect of the legal-responsibility variable on the odds of being a minimalist is lower for West Germans. A similar country-specific effect reveals the regression analysis of this statement for the whole top-level sample (see Chapter 5). The effect of rule breaking on minimalism is particularly striking when we consider that, in simple percentages, a majority of business leaders reject the rule-breaking notion (58 per cent). Yet, we find the weakest disagreement to rule breaking in Poland (52 per cent) and in medium-sized and larger companies (*c.* 55 per cent of the respondents), while 70 per cent of the respondents of very large companies and 66 per cent of the bankers rejected the statement.

In line with our assumptions, the minimalists are the most *profit-oriented group.* Agreement to the statement 'the goal of a company has to be maximizing profit' doubles the probability of belonging to minimalist group (all: 0.714*** and strict: 0.665**), which fits a Friedmanite perspective (see Appendix, Table A7.1, item 3). Respondents who accept a weaker formulation of companies' responsibility, namely that companies are also responsible for public well-being, are half as likely to be minimalists (−0.774***), and even less likely to be strict ones (−1.467***), when also controlling for company type and size (see Appendix, Table A7.1, item 7). Hence, the additional item validates their narrow view on corporate responsibility. Only respondents of very large companies do not follow this line of thinking. The idea that voluntary commitment is indispensable in times of crisis (see Table 7.1) is also rejected by minimalists. The variable reduces the probability of belonging to the strict minimalists in particular (−1.108***). We observe a similar effect for the statement that the shareholder-value approach is unsustainable that significantly reduces the probability to be a strict minimalist as well (−1.052***; for the statement see Appendix, Table A7.1, item 11).

Business leaders who agree to the statement that nationalization is the wrong path, even in times of crisis are also statistically more likely to be in the soft minimalist group (see Appendix, Table A7.1, item 4). The effect of this statement on the odds is significantly higher for East Germans and Hungarians and for business leaders of very large companies. At the same time, respondents who agree with the first etatist statement that government should monitor and regulate the economy are significantly more often soft minimalists (0.815***), which distinguishes them from strict minimalists, neocorporatists and liberals. Regarding the role of state, the overlap between minimalists and etatists matters. The fact that business leaders who perceive vocational training as a governmental task and not a responsibility of business are also more likely to be in the broad minimalist camp (0.654*, see Appendix, Table A7.1, item 8) also supports this finding. Interestingly, the effect loses significance when we analyse the effect on strict minimalists only. Strict minimalists seem to be less 'etatist' with respect to regulation, but even more so regarding redistribution. Respondents who agree with the redistribution statement are significantly less likely to be strict minimalists than those who do not share this view (−0.9**).

In *views on employee relations*, respondents agreeing to or are at least undecided about the statement that employees should be dismissed when not performing at full capacity are more likely to be minimalists (i.e., they do not reject disagreeing with this item (see Appendix, Table A7.1, item 6), all: −1.269***; strict: −1.302***).[5] Adherents of etatist or liberal concepts tend in the same direction, but the effect of the statement on the odds is not significant here. Companies with employee representatives are less likely to be in the minimalist group, as we have seen earlier. We see a similar effect when respondents *dis*agree with the view that trade unions are superfluous. They are also less likely to be in the minimalist group (all: −0.962*** and strict: −1.387***). A similar effect is observed for the second neocorporatist item regarding the importance of collective regulation for functioning of the economy (all: −0.479** and strict: −1.22***). There is no country variation, but a variation in company type as respondents from very large companies deviate from this position positively. And if companies *have* an employee representation and regard them superfluous they are also more likely to be minimalists. Hence, the minimalist camp is more antagonistic to formalized labour representation than etatists, in spite of the overlap.

However, respondents who believe in *free entrepreneurship and social justice* as being mutually exclusive are also more likely to be minimalists (all: 1.696*** and strict: 1.669***). We find a similar effect for the statement that competition erodes social cohesion (yet only significant for all minimalists: 0.519**),[6] which again brings minimalists closer to the etatists position, as we will show in the next section.

In short, minimalists tend to reduce the role of a company in terms of responsibility and goals in society to economic responsibility, even if they think that a company has to do more for the community than is required by law (soft minimalists); they more often perceive general economic responsibility to be in conflict with legal requirements, and display a greater distance from institutionalized labour relations. Otherwise, their position towards the state's role is more mixed than what one would expect for Friedmanites, and they are very sceptical of the social outcomes of the market economy.

Their scepticism about social cohesion and justice (Appendix, Table A7.1, items 1, 2 and 9), however, has little impact on their own perceived role in society. In this respect, they are consistent in regard to their personal involvement in unpaid work, that is, business leaders with an official unpaid position are significantly less likely to be found among minimalists (all: −0.602** and strict: −0.718**, after controlling for country effects and company types). In all of the countries, companies run by minimalists do less in terms of CSR practices than do non-minimalists.[7] Yet, the deviation is significant only in the case of the strict minimalists, especially regarding internal CSR (−0.895*).[8] The reason for the weak outcome may lie in the fact that only a few of the minimalists are strict in their attitude. Isomorphic pressure from the societal environment might also play a role. Yet, the effect of the statement that the company invest in CSR activities 'in order to avoid risks' on the odds of being a minimalist is significantly higher in Poland and Hungary (Appendix, Table A7.1, item 13).

Etatists

There are 82 etatists who represent approximately 11 per cent of the entire business leader sample. The greatest overlap is with the minimalists (23 etatists represent themselves at the same time as minimalists), while only a few etatists share the assumptions of the two high-commitment concepts of responsibility. Disproportionately many Hungarian and Polish respondents are among the etatists (see Table 7.3), and the Fisher tests indicate that this difference is statistically significant. Germans are least etatist, especially West Germans (independent of where the business is based), but also East Germans differ strikingly from their Polish and Hungarian counterparts (see also Bluhm *et al.* 2011). Interestingly, the company type has no impact on this result.

Top managers of state enterprises are not more likely to be in this group than others – even in Poland. Yet, ownership matters in a different way. The odds ratio suggests that domestic companies without any foreign capital are twice as likely to be managed by an etatist as are companies financed through foreign capital (0.734**). We find a similar effect for companies in which managers own more than 25 per cent of the company's shares. In contrast, companies which are owned by other companies are half as likely to be led by etatists.

As for the other concepts, *socio-demographic characteristics* show only little effects. Age has no explanatory influence; the same holds true for whether they have had vocational training, and even a tertiary educational background provides little help in describing the inclination towards this or any other concept. Yet, those who identify with their company and with their local community, nationality and religion are statistically more likely to be also for state regulation and redistribution ('etatism') (see Appendix, Table A7.1, item 12).

Etatists also tend to combine their views in a specific way. A respondent who regards vocational training as a governmental task and not a responsibility of businesses is four times more likely to be in the etatist group (1.219***). Yet, the analysis reveals a significant deviation of business leaders from very large companies who disagree with the statement. As for minimalists, we find that respondents who view free entrepreneurship and social justice as mutually exclusive are more likely to be in this group (0.641**). A similar effect is shown by the results of the statement that today's focus on competition is eroding social cohesion (0.552**), controlling for company type and country. In the interaction analysis the effect of the two items on the odds of being an etatist is lower in West Germany, but due to the small number, not significantly. Hence, etatists seem to share a sceptical view of the social outcomes of a market economy with the minimalist – both are more present in Poland and Hungary (see Table 7.3). Given their positive inclination towards state regulation and redistribution, etatists seem to be the most *market-critical group.*

Respondents agreeing with the Friedmanite notion of corporate responsibility are not significantly more likely to be etatists, although there is a positive trend.[9] However, if they are of the opinion that companies should do more than is required by law (0.45*) and that companies are responsible for public well-being (1.412***), respondents are more likely to belong to this group. The latter statement sets them clearly apart from minimalists and brings them closer to neocorporatists. Hence, an interventionist view of the state's role in the economy does not necessarily imply a delegation of all of the responsibility for public goods to the state. Respondents agreeing that the financial crisis has shown that an orientation towards shareholder value alone is not suitable as a guiding principle for companies are also more likely to be etatists (0.474*). A similar effect can also be observed for the corporatists.

Rule compliance has no effect on the odds of being an etatist. In contrast to minimalists, etatists also show average trust in other people, yet this is mainly due to the East Germans etatists, who, compared with Hungarian and Polish business leaders, stand out in regard to their generalized trust (see Appendix, Table A7.1, item 15).[10] Hence, one cannot say that etatists have respondents with greater institutional trust in their ranks.

Regarding *labour relations*, etatists tend to be more moderate compared to minimalists. If the company is a member of an employers' association with bargaining functions, their leaders are slightly more likely to be etatists when they are Hungarians, but significantly less so when they are Poles. Respondents who consider collective regulations useful for the functioning of the economy are also more likely to be etatists (0.55**), which contrast them from minimalists and liberals. However, this statistical effect cannot be found for the rejection of the statement regarding trade unions being superfluous, which separates them from neocorporatists. Interestingly, business leaders of very large companies who agree to the need for collective regulation are less likely to be etatists (−1.897**), which may be driven by Polish and Hungarian respondents who in particular regard collective regulation negatively, but not significantly so (see Chapter 8). There are more etatists among respondents who perceive employee councils or company unions as superfluous if they have them, but, unlike in the case of the minimalists, this finding is not significant (Appendix, Table A7.1, item 14). At the same time, respondents agreeing to the statement that social concerns should be supported even at the cost of efficiency are significantly more likely to be etatists when controlling for country and company type (1.159***, Appendix, Table A7.1, item 5). The effect on the odds of being an etatist is significantly higher for East Germans. Etatists are the only group where this statement has a significant effect.

Compared with the entire sample and other cognitive concepts, etatists do not stand out positively or negatively in regards to their CSR activities. The same can be said for their personal unpaid work.

Neocorporatists

In contrast to all other concepts of corporate responsibility, respondents who adhere to what we call the neocorporatist concept lead companies with an outstanding performance record in CSR, including both internal and external CSR activities (see endnote 7). Internal CSR practices include health and safety at work, training and life-long learning and measures to maintain the work-life balance; companies with neocorporatists in the top management positions display significantly more activities in this area than do others (0.906***). External CSR activities include different kinds of sponsoring and anti-corruption efforts, and companies led by neocorporatists also stand out here (1.091***). Companies run by neocorporatists are twice as likely to belong to the subsample of companies with both more internal and external CSR, and which have a label for these activities like CSR, Corporate Citizenship or Sustainability.

The adherents to neocorporatism, with 126 respondents, represent the largest group – 17 per cent of the whole business-leader sample. As expected, they are significantly more often West Germans and East Germans, as opposed to being from Hungary or Poland (according to the Fisher test). The same ranking emerges with either method of sample construction in Germany when we consider the western or eastern origin of the respondents or the location of the companies in the East or West. Thus we can say that East Germans are clearly more inclined towards this high-commitment concept than their Hungarian and Polish counterparts. Even in West Germany, however, only one-quarter of the business leaders belong to this responsibility group as outlined above, with the highest proportion among the very large companies and banks (see also Chapter 4).

The odd ratio suggests that Hungarians and Poles are less than half as likely to be in this group as the reference group (see Table 7.3). The probability of being a neocorporatist doubles with company size in all countries. While leaders of large companies are twice as likely to share the neocorporatist concept of responsibility, top managers of very large companies are four times more likely to think this way, and bankers are even more likely to belong to this group (see gain Table 7.3). In Hungary, neocorporatists are significantly less likely to run companies not in foreign ownership, which may be due to a hidden German effect, as German multinationals have invested considerably in Hungary. Individual ownership, however, does matter here. Managers who own 25 per cent and more of the shares of their company are less likely to be neocorporatists (−0.636***) than those who do not, when controlled for country and company type. We observe a similar effect when a family owns the shares (−0.618**). The finding reflects the distance of entrepreneurs to collective labour (see Chapter 8).

While membership in an *employers' association* with collective bargaining function is a weak predictor for the concept, *works councils or trade-union committees at plant level* strongly increase the probability that the business leaders have a neocorporatist view (0.796***), with differences in terms of company type. If the business leaders have an employee council or a union in their company and regard them superfluous, they are less likely to share the neocorporatist concept when we control for country and company type (−1.788**, see additional item 14 in the Appendix, Table A7.1). Thus, we see a correspondence between the institutions of labour relations and a neocorporatist concept of corporate responsibility.

Regarding the *socio-demographic characteristics*, employed managers are more likely to be a neocorporatist compared to manager-owners, even if they only have some shares. The business leaders with fathers from the upper class are less likely to be in this group (−0.494**), controlling for company type and country. Business leaders who changed from politics into business during their career are also more likely to be in the neocorporatist group (2.63**). We observe a similar effect if the respondent has worked abroad (6 months and longer), which seems to be driven by West Germans who work abroad more often and for longer periods.

Sharing this concept of corporate responsibility means that the respondents are as strongly convinced as the etatists about the need to contribute to general public well-being (1.332***). Respondents agreeing to the statement 'financial crisis has proved that the sole orientation on shareholders' interest is not suitable' are also more likely to be neocorporatist (see again Appendix, Table A7.1, item 11). However, the idea that the government should monitor and regulate the economy does not increase (or decrease) the probability of belonging to the neocorporatist camp that separates them from etatists. Interestingly, only bankers with this view are more likely to be neocorporatists. In contrast to state regulation, being positive towards the *redistribution of public wealth* can be found more often among neocorporatists, but this difference is not significant. However, the effect differs significantly by company type. Business leaders of large and very large companies tend to *disagree* with redistribution if they share the neocorporatist concept. Thus, neocorporatists are less positive with regard to intervention in the economy than are etatists, although a few neocorporatists nominally overlap with the etatists (8), who agree with regulation *and* redistribution, or with the soft minimalists (10), who vote for state regulation of the economy. There are no significant differences among countries. Moreover, respondents agreeing with the idea that only the state is responsible for vocational training are significantly less likely to be corporatists (−1.052***, controlling for country and company type). This, too, distinguishes them from etatists, who clearly delegated this role onto the state.

At the same time, they have the more frequent law-abiding people in their ranks, that is, respondents who agree with or are at least undecided about the idea of breaking the law to get ahead are significantly less likely to be neocorporatists (−0.557**), when also controlling for country effects and company type. Bankers are the most decisive in this respect. Their strong commitment to playing according to the rules corresponds to a more frequent, generalized trust (0.766***, Appendix, Table A7.1, item 15.1),[11] although controlling for country differences and company type reveals a non-significant negative impact if the respondent is a Hungarian or a banker.

In contrast to liberals and etatists, Friedmanites are clearly less likely to be neocorporatists, that is, they are almost half as likely to have business leaders in their ranks who share the minimalist view that companies' social responsibility consists of increasing profits only (−0.668*). The effect is even stronger when we exclude the undecided answers and take the *dis*agreement with this notion only, that is, it more than doubles the probability of belonging to this responsibility group (0.953***).[12] West Germans and business leaders of very large companies in particular seem to reject the minimalist view but with no significant effects. This result corresponds to the finding that respondents who clearly agree with profit *maximization* as companies' goal are also less likely to be neocorporatists (−0.565***), especially when they are Germans. Both statements separate them from etatists and indicate that their broad view on corporate responsibility is robust. Sharing a neocorporatist concept corresponds not only with higher CSR activities mentioned above but also translates into the personal unpaid activities of these respondents. Business leaders who do unpaid work on non-business-related posts are twice as likely to have a neocorporatist concept of responsibility (0.615***) when controlling for country and company type.

Their more collaborative approach towards employee representation goes together with a general preference for a stakeholder approach. Regarding the question as to whether or not the owners' interests should come first in case of a conflict (Appendix, Table A7.1, item 10), respondents agreeing with this statement are significantly less likely to be neocorporatists (−0.374*). Yet there is heterogeneity among countries. While business leaders are less likely to put the owner's interest first in the more consensually-oriented industrial culture of Germany, neocorporatists from Hungary and Poland deviate positively from this result.

What is even more striking is their optimism regarding the social outcome of the market economy, which distinguishes neocorporatists from etatists and minimalists. Those who regard free entrepreneurship and social justice as mutually exclusive, are less likely to be neocorporatists when controlling for differences in company type ($-0.662*$). Yet, in the interaction analysis for country-specific effects, the Polish neocorporatists deviate from this finding with weak statistical significance. Respondents agreeing with the statement that today's competition is eroding social cohesion are also less likely to be neocorporatists although without significance (see Appendix, Table A7.1, item 6). They are more likely to be corporatists when they disagree with an easy employee dismissal policy in the case of weaker performance (ibid., item 7; $0.491**$), when controlling for country and company type. In sum, neocorporatists seem to share a set of ideas that approach the German idea of 'social market economy'.

High-commitment 'liberals'

We defined respondents as adherents to a liberal concept if they positively answered the question whether voluntary commitment to social and environmental issues should be an indispensable part of a company's strategy, even in times of crisis. According to our definition, they believe that companies should do more for the community than is required by law. At the same time they are negative regarding the importance of collective regulations between social partners for the functioning of the economy and consider trade unions superfluous (see Table 7.1).

We identify a total of 66 liberal business leaders. They comprise the second smallest responsibility group, representing only approximately 9 per cent of all business leaders. Among them are 13 respondents who agree with the Friedman dictum, and seven etatists, which partially contradicts the theoretical assumptions we made regarding the liberal concept of responsibility.

The Fisher test reveals that East Germans are significantly more often liberal in the above defined sense than their Polish or Hungarian counterparts (and West Germans more often than the Poles), while the West and East Germans do not display significant differences. The regression analysis did not show any significant variation according to country/geographic origin and company type. In simple percentages, the share of 'liberals' of East German and Hungarian origin is the highest, at approximately 10 per cent, and it is the lowest in banks (see again Table 7.2).

The odds ratios of the ownership variables suggest only that respondents who head a subsidiary of other companies are less likely to be in this responsibility group ($-0.851***$), controlling for country effects and different company types, and that West German managing owners and joint stock companies are more inclined to this position. Thus ownership by itself is not a sufficient predictor, nor is foreign ownership.

In contrast to our expectation, international experience in terms of having studied abroad did *not* foster this concept of responsibility, even when the studies were in an Anglo-Saxon country. The only exception are Polish liberals. Polish business leaders who have studied abroad are significantly more likely to belong to the liberal group than Germans and Hungarians who have studied abroad. Independently of this kind of international experience, respondents who identify themselves with Europe are significantly less likely to be liberals (-0.482^*, for the item see Appendix, Table A7.1, item 13). Yet the interaction analysis reveals strong country differences in this respect. East Germans (1.369^{**}), Hungarians (1.383^{**}) and Polish respondents in particular (2.168^{**}) are more likely to be in the liberal camp compared with the reference group. The self-characterization as part of a global business class only reveals an effect on the odds of being a liberal for Hungary. As we have seen in the earlier section, identifying themselves with a global business class increases significantly the probability of being a minimalist, rather than a liberal. In terms of social origin, no Goldthorpe social class is more prominent among our liberals; the positive correlation with the service class I is not significant. Similarly, other *socio-demographic characteristics* are not significant.

We also do not find a clear relationship between the existence of a *formal employee representation* and adherence to the liberal concept, in contrast to the neocorporatists, for whom we observe a significant positive correlation, and in comparison to minimalists for whom the correlation is negative. In Hungary, we found a weakly significant positive relation between the existence of a works council and the presence of a liberal concept. However, respondents who have formal employee representation in their company, but perceive it as superfluous, are significantly more often found to be liberals than those who do not regard it as superfluous (0.967^{**}). Hence, respondents who diminish the importance of trade unions also seem to be more critical of the existing plant-level employee representatives in their own companies.

In spite of some overlap with minimalists and etatists, who perceive social cohesion to be jeopardized by competition, the adherents to the liberal concept do not stand out in any particular way. However, there are significant country variations. Hungarians, in particular, seem to be far more sceptical about the social outcomes of the market economy when they share the liberal view. We observe a similar variation in the interaction analysis for the respondents who agree with profit maximization as prime company goal. Yet, the result, again controlled for country and company size, is not significant. East Germans, Poles and Hungarians agree to profit maximization, but only in the Hungarian case is the effect of the statement of statistical significance (1.679^*).

Among adherents to the liberal concept of responsibility, business leaders with unpaid posts that are not business-related are statistically less likely to be present, when controlling for country and company differences (-0.57^*); business leaders of very large companies do so even less (-1.975^*). They are closer to minimalists in this respect than to highly committed neocorporatists. We do not find an effect of the liberal concept on CSR activities, neither internal nor external.

The same holds for motivations to engage in CSR, aside from the fact that Polish respondents and very large companies are less likely to be in the group of liberal leaders, when their CSR is driven by the motivation to make a 'contribution to society' (Appendix, Table A7.1, item 13). In short, the assumed high commitment to corporate responsibility for those following a liberal concept fails to translate into practice.

Further development, discussion and conclusion

In this paper, we tried to underpin the institutional debate on variants of CSR with cognitive concepts of corporate responsibility. We abandoned the established dichotomy of 'explicit' and 'implicit' CSR in favour of a differentiation between three basic types: the neocorporatist, the liberal and the minimalist concepts of responsibility. We also introduced etatism as an indirect concept of corporate responsibility and the perception of legal responsibility in the analysis. We found that the four distinct concepts coherently cover only a bit more than half of the complete sample of business leaders, indicating that leaders' views on the social responsibility of companies are more diffuse than we had expected theoretically (for a more inductive analysis of the items, see Bluhm *et al.* 2011). This is especially the case in smaller companies. In the final part of this chapter, we review the most important findings and develop them further using passages from semi-structured interviews with top managers and entrepreneurs. The interviews were conducted respecting the sampling scheme of the original data, that is, the interviewees come from the same three countries and were selected from different company sizes and sectors.

As expected, a particularly robust result is that the neocorporatist concept is most widespread in Germany (especially West Germany) among employed managers and in larger companies. The concept is also consistent with other related views, such as an aversion to a strict shareholder-value approach and an acceptance of social concerns in business. It is not only the most internally consistent concept but also reflected in actual personal activities, that is, unpaid work beyond business. This consistency may speak for a lasting influence of the German institutional system and business culture of a 'social market economy', although even among West Germans, the combination of high commitment and self-binding to collective rules represents only a quarter of the entire business-leader sample. In particular, business leaders of medium-sized companies and companies owned by the respondents and his or her family are less likely to agree with a neocorporatist approach (see Chapter 4 and 8). As predicted, neocorporatists are reluctant toward state intervention, and government regulation of the economy in particular.

For neocorporatists, a strong commitment to companies' responsibility together with an acceptance of social partnership co-exists with a high level of internal and external CSR practices according to the EU definition. This finding contradicts the expectation expressed in the institutionalist CSR debate, because a high level of voluntary commitment to CSR and institutionalized labour relations are generally considered substitutes rather than complements, both in terms of practices and underlying ideas.

Liberals, as we defined them, are a rare species in our sample. Contrary to our expectation, foreign ownership of the company, international experience (except in Poland), or age do not increase the probability of belonging to this group. Very large company size and banks do not have a significant influence on the likelihood of belonging to this group either. In total numbers, just a few liberals manage very large companies and banks. Otherwise, managing owners and families are not more but also not less likely to be in the liberal group, as was the case for neocorporatists. It seems that if entrepreneurs share a high-commitment concept it is one without collective self-binding. Sometimes, this reluctance to engage in collective binding bears paternalistic features as our qualitative interviews reveal (see also Chapter 8). One shareholding CEO of a medium-sized East German IT company which sponsors various internal and external CSR activities put it this way:

INTERVIEWEE: I understand under [corporate responsibility (-auth. note)] that a company is like a living thing that lives in an environment and from it. And the success it achieves, it ought to give back to this environment. Therefore we support sports and everything we possibly can, and naturally our shareholders are a bit nervous about it. But that we support the football club, I see as a duty and not a luxury. [. . .] We support breakfasts for disadvantaged kids. Anywhere we can help, we do something. [. . .] That's the one thing; the other is the social responsibility, the entrepreneurial responsibility towards employees: that they have secure jobs and a good job environment. But everything is on condition that we can afford it. As long as everybody works like they do now, it's possible. If something changes with that, then we've got a problem. [. . .] [The] beautiful thing is that an organization has an inherent notion of who is useful and who isn't. If we employ people and it comes out that they're some of those parasite freeloading types, then I get them here in a jiffy at my desk and throw them out, you can be sure of that. People like that are of no help to us.

INTERVIEWER: So you have no works council here in the company – why not, actually?

INTERVIEWEE: I told the employees they were causing me trouble with the works council. And they knew what I meant. I [. . .] worked before for a large department store company. And it was always the works council that caused the difficulties. The worst thing was the corrupt people in it, who would say, 'you'll get permission for a dismissal only when you do such and such'. [. . .] Your actions in the firm are undermined by a works council. Those people have power, but don't have to answer for the responsibilities they have. [. . .] No, they're quite happy, because they know they've got it good [laughs]. What more could they want? What's a works council supposed to do, anyway? Sit themselves down and say right off, 'we want a change in the wage agreement', but the firm can't afford it, and that's all.

In contrast to our theoretical assumptions, liberals do not distinguish themselves clearly from etatist views regarding regulation and redistribution, which makes it hard to call them highly committed 'liberals' according to our definition. What is truly astonishing, however, is that they do not engage more frequently in CSR activities (with and without labelling them as such), nor do they take up unpaid work more frequently. In this regard, the claim of higher commitment to a wider range of corporate responsibility does not translate into a correspondingly higher degree of action than for the average manager. There is no correlation between explicit, that is, formalized and labelled CSR activities, and the liberal view on corporate responsibility. Internally as well as externally-oriented CSR seems not typically linked to the liberal concept as one would expect if this concept culturally underpinned 'explicit' CSR.

Compared to the adherents of an individualist high-commitment approach, minimalists are more widespread in general, and, as expected, particularly in the post-socialist environments, ranging from East Germans to Polish business leaders, with the Hungarians in the middle and most likely to share a minimalist view. Yet, we have also seen that minimalism is not as tightly linked to company size or individual ownership as expected. Moreover, particularly in Poland, minimalists also operate large and very large companies, that is, they are well represented in all company sizes, while in the other countries they more often lead medium-sized and large companies. From the total of 24 very large Polish companies in which we conducted top-level interviews, ten respondents belonged to the minimalist group (four of them strict minimalists). This finding is especially interesting because very large companies are under more intense public scrutiny and the new CSR movement is addressed precisely to companies of this size. One of our interviewees in a Polish bank confirms that CSR as a communicated management strategy has been established very quickly in recent years:

INTERVIEWEE: For the big firms, it's really true that CSR spread in Poland very fast, and there's also a kind of imitation effect – whatever the competition does, we want to do, too. Companies notice what other firms in the field are doing. Smaller and middle-sized companies though still have a big problem with this; they still have a kind of entrepreneurial egoism and are fixed on their own everyday business.

The observation of this Polish banker cannot so easily be confirmed by our statistical analysis of attitudes, although in terms of CSR practices, size effects are clearly visible. What the qualitative interviews reveal, however, more than the standardized questionnaire, is that a lack of resources and volatility of markets matter for respondents of medium-sized companies. Two executive managers of medium-sized companies rationalize their minimalist approach with the everyday fight for survival:

INTERVIEWEE: The responsibility is entrepreneurial responsibility, which means [ensuring] the company is going to still be there tomorrow, and bring in sufficient money to pay personnel with. [Long pause] And [...] for that I need customers. (Executive manager, medium-sized East German IT company)

INTERVIEWEE: [...] my responsibility as chief is to ensure for these people at least a secure short-term future. Usually we know seven weeks in advance whether a dismissal needs to be considered or not. (Executive manager, medium-sized Hungarian metal-sector company)

Yet the narrative of a reductionist view of companies' responsibilities can be quite different when the state is taken to be in charge of providing. A Hungarian executive manager states:

INTERVIEWEE: [...] a company's duty is not to provide social functions but to produce [something] in economic life, and to pay the employees from it. Social responsibilities are the state's task [...] since we pay them quite a lot of taxes for that. (Executive manager, medium-sized metal-sector company)

In contradiction to the transition literature that perceives the new business elite in East Central Europe as rather anti-etatist (Eyal *et al.* 1998; Machonin *et al.* 2006; for an institutionalist view see King and Szelényi 2005), agreement with state intervention is significantly more frequent in Hungary and Poland than in West and East Germany. The Polish case is especially astonishing, as the post-communist political elites strongly advocated the neoliberal reform agenda (see Chapter 2). The need for regulative and redistributive power on the part of the state is even more interesting since the etatists, along with the minimalists, are less convinced of self-regulating markets than liberals and neocorporatists. Minimalists seem to feel that their own scope of action to improve the social balance is limited or already met by their economic responsibility. Etatists, in contrast, do not underperform in terms of CSR and personal unpaid work. Otherwise, the call for state regulation and redistribution cannot simply be identified with institutional trust as we have seen and with high confidence in state capacities. One of our Polish interview partners expressed a striking combination of acceptance of regulation and scepticism about state performance:

INTERVIEWEE: Unfortunately in Poland many regulations are put through without much economic understanding. Often the politicians have the power but not the competence to put through sensible regulations in many areas. [...] I don't believe in wild-west capitalism without regulation. I think that people with a great deal of property and thereby in control of resources and power shouldn't be able to simply decide everything for everybody just as they please. (Executive manager/shareholder, IT sector, medium-sized company)

In sum, our analysis confirms that socialist legacies but also the institutional weakness of the newly emerged market economies in East Central Europe are influential in business leaders' perception of corporate responsibility. While the institutional setting and business culture in West Germany still seems to be more supportive for a consistent neocorporatist concept, this is already less so in the medium-sized sector of East Germany and Hungary, and again less in Poland. The remarkable inconsistencies in the concepts of corporate responsibility, especially in Hungary and Poland, can be interpreted as an indication that the institutional environment and business culture in those new market economies exert little normative power for shaping beliefs and enforcing action in one of the high-commitment directions, that is, they are just as far removed from the continental European neocorporatism as from the highly individualistic commitment to companies' responsibility towards society that is usually associated with the 'Anglo-American' business culture (Matten and Moon 2008). For both high-commitment concepts, the driving social forces of a Polanyian 'counter-movement' are too weak: for the first, above all, organized labour that enforces collective binding and for the second, a powerful civil society.

Facing the debate on the influence of foreign capital, our findings reveal that foreign ownership as such contributes little to explain the cognitive concepts. Business leaders of partly foreign-owned companies seem to be more inclined to minimalism than fully owned companies and domestic business. The finding indicates the limits of such a 'foreign-led' cultural change in post-socialist environments as sometimes the growing CSR literature in most advanced East Central European countries hopes for.

One of our Polish interview partners reflected upon what this may imply for the advancement of CSR as follows:

INTERVIEWEE: [We're] introducing [...] CSR into an environment where it hasn't existed in such a systematic form until now, and comprehension of it at first will be very much for appearance's sake. Later it will become an integral part of our entrepreneurial culture, after a few years, [...] but at first, our handling of CSR is going to be rather superficial. (Executive manager, IT sector, medium-sized company)

Notes

1 We would like to express our heartfelt gratitude to Richard Bluhm and Hans Christian Heinemeyer for their helpful and constructive comments on an earlier version of this chapter.
2 The decline was even more drastic than in East Germany and Hungary. In the public care of children below three years of age, Poland comes second last among 27 European countries, between the Czech Republic and Slovakia. But also Hungary is in the fifth last place, while Germany lies more in the middle (ISI 2012). Recently, the Polish state has been trying to bring companies back into the obligation to supply such goods. In the 'Amendment to the Law on Workplace Social Funds' that came into effect in 2009, the state explicitly cites the foundation of infant day-care, kindergartens and other forms of pre-school education as an option in companies' use of social funds, reflecting the radical cuts in childcare facilities in the 1990s.
3 All regressions were performed using the *GNU R package 2.13.1*. We thank Hans Christian Heinemeyer for his help in the analysis.

4 To analyse the class position in society, we have grouped our categories according to the Goldthorpe class scheme, dividing society into classes by employment relationship. To class 1 belong higher-grade officials, top managers of large companies, large-business owners and higher-grade professionals. For more detail, see Bluhm, Martens and Trappmann (2011).

5 For this additional item, we took disagreement as a positive answer (see Appendix, Table A7.1, item 6).

6 For the precise formulation, see Appendix, Table A7.1, items 1, 2 and 9.

7 For this analysis we use the concepts as explanatory variable.

8 In the differentiation between internal and external CSR activities, we followed a definition by the EU Commission. Internal CSR refers to environment and social issues linked to the value chain and to employment conditions. External CSR includes different sorts of sponsoring, as well as environmental issues, regional development and anti-corruption efforts. We measured internal and external CSR based on the number of positive answers to several items for both types of CSR (cf. European Commission 2001).

9 In addition to the agreement (1, 2) on the Likert scale that we used for constructing the minimalists, we analyse the results for disagreement (4, 5) in order to exclude the undecided once. When we analyse the effect of disagreement only, the respondents who reject the dictum are significantly *less* likely to be etatists ($-0.68**$).

10 If we look at simple percentages of the entire sample of business leaders, the national differences are quite striking: approximately 40 per cent of the Hungarians and 32 per cent of all Polish respondents agreed with the statement that in general most people can be trusted, in contrast to approximately 50 per cent of the rather anti-etatist Germans (including East Germans); almost 60 per cent of the Poles agreed with the sentence that 'one can't be too careful' in contrast to 37 per cent of the Hungarians and 14 per cent of the Germans (see a more detailed analysis in Chapter 6).

11 Neocorporatists are also less likely to agree with the statement that 'one cannot be too careful' ($-0.501*$), see Appendix, Table A7.1, item 15.2.

12 For the different operationalization see endnote 8.

Appendix

Table A 7.1 List of additional items

Items (Likert scaled, 1 = total agreement, 5 = total disagreement)	Use in the analysis
1. Free entrepreneurship and social justice are mutually exclusive.	1, 2
2. Today's focus on competition is eroding social cohesion.	1, 2
3. The goal of a company has to be maximizing profit.	1, 2
4. Nationalization, even in times of crisis, is always the false path.	1, 2
5. Social concerns should be supported even at the cost of efficiency.	1, 2
6. Those who do not perform at full capacity should be dismissed.	4, 5
7. In principle, companies are also responsible for the public well-being	1, 2
8. Vocational training is a task of government but not of business.	1, 2
9. Competition is the best way to social justice.	1, 2
10. In conflicts over company goals, owner interests should clearly be the first consideration.	1, 2
11. The financial crisis has proved that the sole orientation on shareholders' interest is not suitable for running companies.	1, 2

Items (Likert scaled, 1 = total agreement, 5 = total disagreement)	Use in the analysis
12. How important are the following items for your self-characterization: Company, religion, family, profession, Europe, the global business class, my nationality, my local community.	1, 2
13. I will give you a list of goals which companies connected with social activities. Please tell me how important are the following objectives for your company? (image, competitive advantage, contribution to society, employee relation, risk avoidance)	1, 2
Non-Likert scaled items	
14. Are the following statements true for your company's representation: The works council/union committee is superfluous.	1 (yes)
15. Generally speaking, would you say that most people can be trusted or that you can't be too careful with people? 15.1. Most people can be trusted. 15.2. Can't be too careful.	1

8 Institutions or attitudes?

The role of formal worker representation in labour relations

Vera Trappmann, Krzysztof Jasiecki and Dariusz Przybysz

Introduction

For the evaluation of the types of capitalism that emerge in East Central Europe, the role of labour relations is crucial. With Kathleen Thelen (2001), we assume that the micro company-level strategies pursued in response to global competition by employers explain the different outcomes of labour relations at macro level. Business leaders in liberal market economies (LME) search for the greatest flexibility and managerial freedom at company level, while in coordinated market economies (CME) employers oriented towards high-quality value-added production still think they have to seek a stable relationship with labour at plant level as well on wider levels. Micro-level strategies in East Central Europe are rarely analysed, there are only a few studies that try to explain industrial relations on the basis of company-level experience (for an overview see Sznajder-Lee and Trappmann 2010). While we cannot compensate for the lack of case studies here, we can provide analysis of what managers say about industrial relations in general and at micro-level, how business leaders perceive their leadership role at company level, clarifying what might influence such positions, like post-socialist legacies, organizational factors such as the sector in question, or more personal characteristics like age, education or income, and how the concrete institutions at company level influence the labour-relations system. While this is a very complex relation, it is quite easy to test whether the existence of labour representation at company level, such as works councils, influence both the attitudes of business leaders and the practices at company level.

The cases examined here differ in the way the collective institutions of labour relations were rebuilt after socialism. We find three different distinct variants, varying in the level of post-socialist transfer of industrial-relations infrastructure. East Germany represents an attempt at a complete institutional transfer through integration into the existing structures of West Germany. Hungary has been characterized by the attempt to implement the central elements of the German–Austrian system of industrial relations. Finally, Poland rejected institutional transfer and tried to apply the idea of self-organization prevalent during the 1980s. We look at West Germany as a contrasting example to the experiences in the three post-socialist cases of East Germany, Hungary and Poland. Germany as a whole represents an interesting test case here because we can test whether the very same institutions are appreciated as much by business leaders with a post-socialist background as they are by West German counterparts. We further assume that the difference in institutions will impact in the leadership style also.

In the following, we will give a more detailed picture of the evolution of labour relations in each country, and describe our sample which allows us to detect more precisely what kind of companies have what kind of labour representation. Then we will evaluate the perceptions of industrial relations in each country, describing what business leaders think about trade unions and works councils as well as about general socio-economic issues. Following this, we analyse the relationship between industrial relations and leadership styles, to then examine the influence of works councils or trade union committees on companies' policies. We conclude by looking at what our findings on this issue add to our understanding of post-socialist industrial development and on the real prospects for any role for labour-relations organizations within the countries' economic and social development.

Background: a comparative view of industrial relations in post-communist (East Central) Europe

Industrial relations in the three post-socialist cases we study here share many features. First, there is a lack of working-class political mobilization (King 2007; Krzywdzinski 2005). Second, actors had to reinvent themselves or establish themselves from scratch post-1989, which often meant a period of role (re-)invention (Sznajder-Lee and Trappmann forthcoming). Third, trade unions have lost members, which has resulted in a low union density, beneath the EU-27 average of 23 per cent, with East Germany at 18.6 per cent, Hungary at just under 16.8 per cent, and Poland at 15 per cent (ETUI 2012a); moreover, the organization of employers into associations is weak, about 20 per cent in Poland, 40 per cent in Hungary, and 21 per cent in East Germany, compared to 60 per cent in West Germany.[1] Fourth, as a consequence, coordination at national level is weak; the coverage of collective bargaining is low in general and is concentrated at company level, at 35 per cent in Hungary, 40 per cent in Poland, and 51 per cent in East Germany, compared to 65 in West Germany (ibid.). Fifth, the scale of deindustrialization was huge in all three countries and this entailed a huge decline in employment. Millions of workers have been pacified during the course of economic transition with the help of generous early retirement and disability schemes. Sixth, in all post-communist countries, labour relations were the subject of deep transformations, with foreign capital transforming corporate culture.

Despite these similarities, it is worthwhile highlighting the differences in the countries under study. First, there is a gradual difference in the real level of organization. Second, there are varying path dependencies related to what institutions are most accepted, in its turn related to the way capitalism was introduced.

East German capitalism has been characterized as an extreme case of the 'dependent market economy' and 'capitalism without (East German) capitalists'

(Bluhm 2010) in the case of large companies. Most of the businesses, however, are small and medium-sized and run by local owners (Bluhm and Martens 2009). Despite the complete transfer of labour-relations institutions, the new East German states deviate from the German post-war model in important areas, concerning corporate governance structure, the system of collective wage bargaining and vocational training (see Chapter 4). The fear that the lower level of labour relations would also entail an erosion of industrial relations in West Germany has proven true. Union membership, coverage with collective bargaining, and wages have also all declined in West Germany. The bargaining coverage rate has fallen from the late 1990s to 2009 from 72 per cent to 65 per cent in West and 51 per cent in East Germany. If we only refer to sectoral agreements, the percentage is even lower with 56 per cent in West Germany and 38 per cent in the East (Bispinck *et al.* 2010: 3) (for further details see Chapter 4).

The biggest difference manifests itself at company level. In Germany, co-determination between management and elected works councils is quite widespread. Thus, no trade union committees exist; the only union represen-tation at company level is a structure of union workplace representatives just informing about union policies without any workforce representational rights. According to German law, only works councils have co-determination rights that ensure that key decisions at the workplace are not taken by the employer alone but involve representatives of the workforce. The law provides the works council with two main types of right: participation rights, where the works council must be informed and consulted about specific issues and can also make proposals to the employer; and so-called co-determination rights, where decisions cannot be taken against the wishes of the works council. Most works councils are established in large companies, so that, as a result of the economic structure of East Germany, the total number of works councils is lower there. In total, 38 per cent of employees are working in companies with works council in East Germany, and slightly more (45 per cent) in West Germany. Along with this, works councils in East Germany are considered less powerful, more cooperative with management and consensus-oriented. They are more often thought to build a coalition with employers, a so-called *Notgemeinschaft* (which one might translate as an emergency organization or a community of survivors) to prevent job loss. Created in times of structural industrial decline, the foremost objective of works councils was to safeguard the company's very existence, often engaging in concession bargaining (Schmidt 2008).

Hungary is best understood as a foreign-led dependent market economy with a huge share of foreign direct investment and has adopted Western models of labour relations (see Chapter 3). Both employer associations and unions are highly fragmented. Labour organizations are weak due to segmentation and fragmentation, verbally radical but unable to mobilize, and dependent on state financial support, thus courting parties and governments for favours (Neumann 2005). At the macro level, in Hungary the first tripartite body of the regions was established already in 1988,[2] as a pre-emptive institution to guarantee peace during the reforms, functioning (as in Poland) as a wage-setting body. As in

Poland and Eastern Germany, the welfare system was generously extended to smooth the transition (Vanhuysse 2006), but was cut back by the so-called Bokoros package, the first severe austerity program in the 1990s, and by the Gyurcsany austerity package in the 2000s. On top of this, many of the responsibilities of unions were removed during the Orbán government from 1998–2002 (Mailand and Due 2004). Not only have workers and citizens suffered from deteriorating living conditions due to austerity, but also organized labour has become toothless in the face of governments that ally themselves more closely to representatives of transnational corporations than to unions (Bohle 2010). The latest setback in Hungarian labour relations is the approval of a new Labour Code that allows employers the absolute right of contract termination, under the right-wing Orbán government (Girndt 2012).

At company level, Hungary, drawing heavily on the experience of Germany, introduced works councils as early as 1992; though the works councils had fewer powers than those in Germany, Hungary had one of the most far-reaching co-determination systems in East Central Europe.[3] However, trade union committee rights were cut back and fierce competition arose between unions and works councils. The right-wing government elected in 1998 swung the balance further away from the unions towards the works councils. Later, the socialist government elected in 2002 changed the situation again, removing the right of works councils to negotiate and increasing the consultation rights of local trade unions. The main problem regarding workers' representation in Hungary today is the division of competences, and information and consultation rights between works council and trade union committees. While union committees have less participation rights than do works councils, the works councils do not have the strike rights that the union committees have. The most difficult situation however is that trade union representation at company level is very pluralistic leading to a strong competition over representation of workers' interest among unions. This pluralism makes the coordination between company level representation of works councils and trade union committees so difficult, and can lead to union-averse works councils. However, works councils seem more widespread in companies with trade unions (Kohl and Platzer 2003: 120). Nonetheless, a 2004 labour force survey showed that only one-third of workplaces with more than 50 employees have works councils, and they are more common at larger workplaces. It was found that representation through works councils went hand in hand with a union presence. Only 9 per cent of works councils were at workplaces without a union and 70 per cent of works councils were either entirely made up of trade unionists or overwhelmingly made up of them (ETUI 2012b).

While in Chapter 2 Poland was classified as foreign-led but not clearly liberal – rather more a hybrid of etatism, liberalism and corporatism – if we focus on industrial relations, the liberal components predominate in terms of the flexibilization of labour law and labour contracts. Compared with the 'German model', Polish industrial relations have often been called illusory when one looks at the weakness of the social partners, in particular trade unions (Ost 2005), and the strength of the state. Labour unions and employers' associations are highly fragmented and have difficulties in mobilizing their clientele. One exception has been the recent mobilization against the increase in the retirement age, against the privatization of health care service and in favour of an increase in the minimum wage. At the national level, collective bargaining has a tripartite character,[4] some authors go so far as to consider Poland etatist, given the strong stakeholder position of the state in tripartite agreements (Gardawski 2011; Sroka 2006; Meardi 2000); others stress the permissive character of labour relations, and the high level of regulation but the state's inability to control its implementation (Bluhm 2009). During transition, liberalization led to a unilateral strengthening of employers. In the private sector, industrial relations were fragmented and almost no collective bargaining occurred above company-level. However, Poland's EU accession negotiations, the economic slowdown of 2001–3, as well as the transposition of EU directives and the need to counteract the international economic crisis, have contributed to improving social dialogue, in particular the autonomous dialogue between employer organizations and trade unions. Still, the predominant view is that social dialogue in the Tripartite Commission falls short of expectations and has come to a standstill, which is primarily due to the stance of the government, which prefers technocratic and managerial approaches to state governance (Trappmann 2012).

At company level, works councils are quite a new phenomenon in Poland. Since the late 1970s workers had been asking for autonomous employee councils (workers' councils, *rada pracownicza*) with exclusive governance rights in state enterprises, motivated by the desire to establish economic and industrial democracy as cornerstones of civil society, and this was granted in 1981 (cf. Weinstein 2000). While the imposition of martial law hindered the employee councils' activity, their legal status however was not impinged upon (Federowicz 2004: 149). Employees' councils were dissolved following commercialization or privatization of the companies. In most cases, trade unions took over their position. Under the 1991 Trade Union Act, only unions were permitted to represent the legal and collective interest of all employees, regardless of their trade union membership. It is only with new legislation implementing the EU directive on information and consultation that the creation of works councils has been promoted. A law passed in 2006 and amended in 2009 aimed to establish works councils in all companies with more than 50 employees. By the end of June 2011 there were 3,218 works councils in Poland.[5] Works councils, however, only have limited power to receive information on economic issues and consultation on employment and work-organization issues (without any co-determination rights as exist in Germany). In practice, at company level, union committees and works councils often exist side by side, or as in many cases the often already-existing trade union committees act as the new works councils. Only 28 per cent of works councils are in workplaces which do not have representative unions. Almost two-thirds (65 per cent) of existing works councils are in medium-sized companies with between 50 and 250 employees, and 14 per cent in companies with more than 500 employees (ETUI 2012a).

To conclude: if we compare the three cases, we find important differences in the way labour-relations institutions were built, transferred, adopted or reinvented.

And these institutional differences have infused the post-socialist varieties of capitalism (see Chapter 1). However, in all we find one similarity: the dominance of company-level institutions and bargaining. This represents a legacy of transition and has been reinforced during privatization as membership in employers' association is rather weak. Nonetheless, from any point of view, worker representation in the three post-socialist cases under study is well below the EU average.

The sample: in what types of companies do we find employee representation?

Our sample is quite representative with regard to the overall figure for membership in business associations and the existence of worker representation. What we wish to add with our sample is a clearer view on what membership in business association and the existence of a worker representation body depend on. We must emphasize that we used company level data in most of the analyses, while in case of business leaders' attitudes we limited our analyses to respondents from the highest managerial level and we treated the East/West Germany comparison in a specific way. In contrast to other chapters, we chose only respondents who lived in East (or West, respectively) Germany before July 1990 *and* now work in a company located in East Germany (or West, respectively). In our analyses we will use standard statistical methods: comparison of percentages, linear and logistic regression, and measures of association between nominal variables.

In our sample, membership in business associations is most widespread in large and very large companies across all countries. However, the numbers for members of employers' association with a bargaining function are quite small even for these types of very large companies: only 38 per cent in Poland, 33 per cent in Hungary and 60 per cent in West Germany, in East Germany we have too few companies in this class to make valuable statements (see Table A 8.1 in Appendix).

Another variable is the ownership structure. In Hungary, state ownership and in Poland joint-stock company form has an influence on membership in an employers' association. Logistic regression shows that membership in an employers' association is most common in very large companies – controlling other variables – and this is true for all countries. It is more common in joint-stock companies in all countries although this association is significant only in Poland and Hungary. It is more common in foreign companies, especially in Poland (see Table A 8.2 in Appendix).

Comparing the cases, we see a clear post-socialist transformation effect as collective bargaining is most widespread in West Germany, lowest in Poland and Hungary. If we look at large companies, we see the transformation effect more clearly: the percentage for East Germany is little higher than in Poland and Hungary. In medium-sized companies, we have only a very few cases of supra-company collective bargaining at all (between 2 and 4 per cent for Poland and Hungary and 15 per cent in East Germany). These data are confirmed by the latest survey by the European Trade Union Institute, 65 per cent of all employees are directly covered by collective agreements in West Germany, while this is one-quarter lower in East Germany, at only 51 per cent. In Hungary the rate is only half as large as in West Germany, at 33 per cent. For Poland, depending on the estimates, bargaining coverage was somewhere between 14 and 30 per cent in 2009 and is decreasing (ETUI 2012c). The relatively small membership in employers' organizations conducting negotiations is an indirect indicator of the low level of businesses' engagement in higher-level negotiations, especially at the sectoral level, in those countries.

If we look at the existence of worker representation bodies at company level, our sample again is quite representative. Worker representation at company level, be it a works council or a trade union committee, is more widespread than is membership in an employers' association. This is due to the fact that in transition countries collective bargaining is most widespread at company level (see Table A 8.3 in Appendix).

What is quite remarkable is that there is a strong relation between those companies that have employee representational bodies and the likelihood that they are members of an employers' association. In Poland, 50 per cent of all companies that have an employee representational body are also members of an employers' association (20 per cent of them even with a bargaining function). For companies without a works council or trade union the percentage of employers' association membership is only about 12 per cent. This relationship is similar in other countries, but the strength of the relationship varies.

The interest-representation rate (measured by the percentage of companies where interests are represented in an organized manner) is similar in all four countries. There is a strong link between employees-interests organizations and size as well as ownership structure in all countries. Companies with more than 100 employees are most likely to have a works council or a trade union committee. In all countries, at least 80 per cent of companies in our sample with more than 249 employees have an association representing workers' interests (see Table A 8.3 in Appendix). There is a strong positive relationship between joint-stock companies and worker representation in Poland (see Table A 8.4 in Appendix).

Differences in interest representation consist in the form of representation, that is, whether the interests are represented by works councils, trade union committees or both (see Table A 8.5 and Table A 8.6 in Appendix). We can distinguish a clear pattern: works councils are most frequently found in West German companies, Hungarian and East German companies in the middle of the range, and least frequently in Polish companies, which clearly mirrors earlier studies with aggregated data. In each country, we find the similar size effect: works councils are most frequently found in large and very large companies, quite frequently in banks, and least frequently in medium-sized industrial companies.

While in Hungary trade unions are usually present in companies where there is also a works council, this is not the case in Poland (compare counts from Table 8.5). If we were to look for a relationship between these variables in Poland, it would be negative (although not very strong), that is, there is a trend for one of the two types of employee organization to be present, rather than both at the same time.

When companies do not have a works council, there are some slight differences in how this is explained by management across the countries. In West Germany, it is most often claimed that the employees lack initiative, while in East Germany the answer most often given is that the management opposes any workers-representation body. In Poland, the management answered that there already exists a trade union committee at the company level, or that the management simply does not know why there is no works council. They also often simply say there is no need for such a body. Finally, in Hungary, managers as often say that it is due to lack of employees' initiative as that there is no need for it.

To conclude, membership in business associations is dependent on companies' size, it is more common in foreign and joint-stock companies, and it is more widespread in large and very large companies, and we find a transformation effect across the different countries (controlling for the organization size). The existence of a worker representation body also depends on the size of the company, which is logical as this is linked to the regulation of works councils. Worker representation bodies are still more widespread than the voluntary membership in an employers' association. Works councils are more widespread in East Germany and Hungary, while in Poland trade union committees are predominant, reflecting the legacy of transformation and path dependencies.

Attitudes of business leaders

We will now turn to the important question of what business leaders think about worker representation, be it trade unions in general or union committees and works councils at company level.

Concerning the general question of whether trade unions are superfluous, we find Poland to have the most union-averse management (see first column of Table 8.1). About half of business leaders of medium-sized companies find unions superfluous. East German business leaders are very similar in their rejection of unions, while Hungarians and West Germans are more union-friendly. In all countries there is the general effect that antipathy to unions is more dominant among leaders of smaller companies; the bigger the companies, the more union-friendly they are. Rejection of trade unions is least widespread in West Germany and in Hungary, where only 5 to 10 per cent of leaders of very large companies would say that unions are superfluous.

There is no hint what characteristics share the respondents or the companies they come from that would explain the union averseness. In Poland and East Germany, agreement with the statement that 'Trade unions are superfluous' is expressed relatively more frequently by company owners as opposed to employed managers (with other features controlled).

Possibly as owners they want to have more control over their companies and in this sense they perceive trade unions as an unnecessary 'ballast' (in Poland it may be connected with the 'paternalist' management style often present in smaller companies; see next section). In West Germany, the view that trade unions are unnecessary is more often expressed by younger managers (parameter for linear

Table 8.1 Statements on works councils, trade unions and agreements between social partners – percentage of respondents who agree with the following opinion

Type of company	Trade unions are superfluous	Collective regulations between social partners are important for the functioning of the economy	Cooperation with the works council generally runs without difficulties[a]	The works council is superfluous[a]	The works council relieves the management from important tasks[a]	Cooperation with the union committee runs without difficulties[b]	The union committee is superfluous[b]	The union committee relieves the management from important tasks[b]
E Germany								
industrial 45–99 (m1)	52.3	49.2	91.7	16.7	25.0	---	---	---
industrial 100–249 (m2)	32.8	62.3	96.7	6.7	33.3	---	---	---
industrial 250–999 (l)	15.4[d]	76.9[d]	84.6[d]	7.7[d]	23.1[d]	---	---	---
W Germany								
industrial 45–99 (m1)	26.1	65.2	100.0	8.3	33.3	---	---	---
industrial 100–249 (m2)	25.0	67.9	90.0	5.0	30.0	---	---	---
industrial 250–999 (l)	10.5	60.5	96.6	6.9	37.9	---	---	---
industrial ≥ 1000 (xl)	11.3	83.0	89.8	4.1	24.5	---	---	---
financial	21.4	78.6	95.0	5.0	15.0	---	---	---
Hungary								
industrial 45–99 (m1)	34.0	38.3	88.9[d]	22.2[d]	0.0[d]	75.0[d]	37.5[d]	0.0[d]
industrial 100–249 (m2)	22.0	31.7	100.0[d]	0.0[d]	0.0[d]	100.0[d]	0.0[d]	0.0[d]
industrial 250–999 (l)	0.0[d]	16.7[d]	100.0[d]	20.0[d]	30.0[d]	90.0[d]	10.0[d]	30.0[d]
industrial ≥ 1000 (xl)	5.0	45.0	82.4	5.9	23.5	81.3	0.0	0.0
financial	20.0	75.0	71.4[d]	0.0[d]	21.4[d]	71.4[d]	0.0[d]	14.3[d]
Poland								
industrial 45–99 (m1)	55.3	63.2	100.0[d]	50.0[d]	50.0[d]	91.7[d]	33.3[d]	25.0[d]
industrial 100–249 (m2)	38.1	61.9	87.5	35.7[d]	40.0	76.2	38.1	50.0
industrial 250–999 (l)	46.2	61.5	91.3	5.3	40.0	83.3	11.1	58.3[d]
industrial ≥ 1000 (xl)	20.0	60.0	81.3	13.3	46.7	81.3	0.0[d]	75.0[d]
financial	26.3	57.9	100.0[d]	0.0[d]	20.0[d]	100.0[d]	0.0[d]	33.3[d]

Notes

a Percentage established based only on companies with works councils.

b Percentage established based only on companies with trade unions.

c Percentage established based on all respondents; in their answers respondents used a five-point scale; persons who answered '1 fully agree' and '1 agree' were classified as those who agreed with the opinion.

regression is –0.61 for 46–55 age category and 0.67 for 56+ category, if the reference category are respondents younger than 46-years-old). In Hungary, on the other hand, there is no clear indication of factors responsible for the diversity of answers.

In all countries, business leaders found consultations between social partners important. For business leaders of very large companies, more than 80 per cent of West Germans and about 60 per cent of Polish managers (but only 45 per cent of Hungarian) share this view (see second column of Table 8.1).There is however one interesting distinguishing fact: multivariate analyses for Poland and West Germany indicate that respondents from a company partly owned by foreign capital (with other factors controlled listed in footnote under Table A 8.8 in Appendix) recognize relatively less often the importance for the economy of consultations with social partners at national level (–0.43 for Poland and –0.31 for West Germany). In Hungary the relation would have the same direction; however it is statistically insignificant. This is very interesting as it nurtures the assumption that international business is less dependent on national laws or regulations or even less interested in it, as they are less concerned about national economies than about companies' individual profit.

In general, it seems that the state of labour relations is reflected in the evaluation of business leaders. Where the institutions of industrial relations are most robust they are most praised by the managers, as in West Germany. Where the institutions are more liquid, business leaders are not overwhelmingly convinced about their usefulness. It is thus very hard to judge in what way we can explain this relation. Are institutions not robust because actors are sceptical about them, or do actors not believe in these institutions because they do not work well? A form of test to begin to resolve this undecided problem is the differentiated analysis of those businessmen who lead a company with a worker representation body and those managers that lead companies without worker representation.

We find a clear correlation: those leading a company with worker representation agree much more seldom that trade unions are superfluous. Out of Hungarian companies with worker representation, only 7 per cent say that trade unions are superfluous and the corresponding percentage for companies without worker representation is 35. Similarly, we see differences in the percentages for companies that are a member of an employers' association and for other companies (13.3 and 22.4 per cent respectively, see Table 8.2).

We can see a similar trend in Poland and in Germany: respondents from companies with worker representation and companies that are a member of an employers' association relatively less often agree that trade unions are superfluous. Nonetheless, it should be emphasized that general approval to this statement is different in considered countries. In the Polish case – where approval is generally highest – anti-union views of business leaders can be seen as a manifestation of neoliberal social preferences in labour policy. They are also an indicator of a conflictual relationship between employers and trade unions.

Confirmation of this result can be found in linear regression analysis: from that model we can predict that business leaders from a company with a works

Table 8.2 Agreement[a] of business leaders with statement 'Trade unions are superfluous' by existence of employee association and membership in employer association

	E Germany		W Germany		Hungary		Poland	
	%	N	%	N	%	N	%	N
Existence of Employees Association								
no	51.4	72	29.3	58	35.2	71	56.1	41
yes	27.9	68	15.3	163	7.2	69	34.4	122
Membership in Employer Association								
no	42.1	121	26.0	127	22.4	125	39.6	139
yes	26.3	19	9.6	94	13.3	15	41.7	24

Note
a Percentage of respondents who agree or strongly agree with this statement.

council/trade union committee differ up to one point on a Likert scale (from −0.54 in West Germany to −0.94 in Hungary) in their judgement about the superfluity of unions.[6] And this holds true even when we control for company and individual variables (Table A 8.7 in Appendix), although the strength of association is weaker. Furthermore, the socio-demographic variables do not go far to explain the difference in attitudes/beliefs, but rather it seems more that factors like ownership, size and sector have an influence in explaining the variance. This means the type of company business leaders work in explains whether they agree or disagree with the statement that trade unions are superfluous. As mentioned above, the variable related to the individual which is relatively most important is age in the case of West German managers (older respondents less often support this statement) and the fact that the respondent is an owner of the company for Poland and East Germany.

A somewhat different picture emerges if we look at agreement with the statement 'Collective regulations between social partners are important for the functioning of the economy'. Here 'company' variables are of less importance than in the case of statements about trade unions, and a little less than variables related to the individual (Poland is an exception). In the case of East and West Germany, the membership of an employers' association has a stronger effect on a positive evaluation of the statement than does existence of a workers' association (see Table A 8.8 in Appendix), but generally this influence is small.

To conclude on this point, we see that there is a relation between the existence of a works council/trade union committee or the membership in an employers' association and the appraisal of trade unions in general and a rather weak but still existent relation between the existence of a works council/trade union committee or the membership in an employers' association and statements about collective regulations between social partners.

Interestingly enough, also very important is the influence of a European Works Council (EWC), although they are not widespread in Poland or Hungary. Business leaders of companies with an EWC more often completely disagree with the statement that unions are superfluous. However they do not necessarily consider collective regulations so important. This makes some sense, as transnational companies with an EWC do often negotiate company-specific issues, so if they have had some positive experience with EWCs, they might be more open to works councils than to national-framework regulations. This is supported by the next item to some extent.

If we look at the evaluation of cooperation between works councils and management at company level, we find overwhelmingly that the majority of those business leaders of companies where workers' organizations are present claim that cooperation with the organizations, both works councils and trade union committees, is problem-free (Table 8.1). In general, the percentage of such answers is above 80–90 per cent with few exceptions, for example, in the financial sector in Hungary the percentage is lower; one must stipulate, however, that this question was answered by only a few people, therefore very definite conclusions cannot be drawn from these numbers. There are no obvious patterns in the dissimilarities between companies of different sizes, mainly because percentages are in general similar. Of course it is difficult to say whether cooperation is as successful as declared by respondents.[7] Their answers may have been to a certain extent motivated by attempts to present their company in a good light. Respondents may also be expressing similar opinions about different realities, or about different legal and institutional solutions, which must inflect any interpretation of their attitudes – a common problem in international comparisons.

We may further suppose that the positive appraisal of cooperation with employee representatives in Poland and Hungary is mainly declarative. Furthermore, if one considers that such attitudes were expressed only by representatives of companies with functioning representations, the attitudes are therefore limited to a relatively small number of companies, primarily the largest ones, following different corporate standards. This interpretation is suggested by answers to subsequent questions. It turns out that, in general, much fewer than half of the respondents agree with the statement that management is supported in important issues by works councils. The positive appraisal is highest among respondents from Poland, with 40–50 per cent. In Germany, the question was asked in slightly different way due to translation inconsistencies, so here the question was not asking about support but about relief from important tasks, ('Der Betriebsrat nimmt der Geschäftführung wichtige Aufgaben ab') which is a bit more than just support in the Polish version ('Rada pracownicza pomaga kierownictwu w wielu ważnych zadaniach'). As a result only about 20–35 per cent of business leaders would say they feel that the works councils offer relief from important tasks.

The same is true for trade union committees. In Poland, much more frequently than in Hungary, business leaders agree that company management is supported in important issues by trade union committees (the question was the same as for works councils). This result concerns all categories of companies, even though it is most evident for large and the largest industrial companies where a majority of managers express appreciation for the useful role of trade union committees.

This may be a sign that in Polish companies of this size a new relationship pattern between managers and trade unions is emerging which may evolve towards an institutionalized coactivity model. (Empirical proofs in favour of this hypothesis are weakened by the small percentage of respondents answering this question). This observed phenomenon at micro-level is juxtaposed by the recent development at national level where, because of the economic crisis, autonomous dialogue has been put in force among the employer organizations and trade unions and bipartite national agreements created as the basis for government's anti-crisis programme.[8]

Hungarian executives, however, are less positive about the help of works councils and trade union committees alike. Their usefulness is completely rejected in medium-sized companies with between 45 and 249 employees, and among leaders of very large companies. Perhaps in this case it is the fragmentation and politicization of trade unions that is carrying across negatively into the dialogue with employers at micro-level (see also ETUI 2012b).

To summarize this point, a company's experience with a works council or a trade union committee has a positive effect on the manager's appraisal of social partnership, in particular unions, and when a works council exists the cooperation is widely evaluated as being problem-free, though the judgement can differ as the level of support offered by a works council to management.

Interestingly enough, we do not find that the presence of worker representation within the company has a huge influence on general attitudes of business leaders about the role of business in society, though the level of influence does vary across countries. In Poland for example, business leaders of companies with works councils are less likely to think that everybody is the architect of one's one future. In Hungary, business leaders of companies with works councils are less likely to think that one has to break the rules to get ahead, and in both East and West Germany business leaders of companies with works councils think that companies should do more for communities than what is required by law. In that line, East German business leaders and Hungarian business leaders of companies with works councils are less likely to think that regional development is the task of politics and not of business.

What we learn from this analysis is that the organizations present within a company influence the perception of business leaders. In each country it works slightly differently, making the biggest difference in areas that are very 'sensitive' topics. In individualistic Poland, where the belief in entrepreneurship and individualism is strong (Trappmann 2013), the collective institution of a works council diminishes the belief in pure individual merit. In Hungary, where corruption and trust relations are very sensitive for the functioning of the economy (Chapter 6), the presence of a worker representation organization leads to slightly more trustful attitudes among the business leaders. And in Germany, where there is a strong tradition of responsibility of business for the community, in particular in regional development and sponsoring, business leaders of companies with worker representation collective institutions are even more in favour of this perception of the duty of business. We will now test the effect of the presence of such organizations on leadership style.

Labour relations and leadership style

We distinguish two types of leadership styles: a participatory-delegative management style; versus a patriarchal authoritarian style (cf. Schmidt 2008). We make the assumption that in countries with weaker formalized workers' participation, which makes itself manifest in weaker labour relations, the latter style is more widespread, while in countries with strong formalized participation of workers, as also in countries with far-reaching co-determination rights, the management style will be more participatory. The effect which worker representation organizations may have on individual attitudes and more precisely on the leadership style of business leaders is particularly highlighted by an analysis such as ours that differentiates not only between countries but also between business leaders of companies with and without formal worker representation.

In general, we see explicit differences between the four cases. Managers in West Germany are clearly the most participatory-oriented while the managers in post-transition countries are less participatory-oriented, with Poland having the largest share of managers with a patriarchal leadership style. In all four countries we see a size effect, the larger companies being more frequently led by delegative managers and the medium-sized companies more often led by patriarchal managers.

To measure the managerial style, we asked questions about selected aspects of the superior-subordinate relationship such as the distance kept from employees, employee subordination or autonomy, meritocratic legitimacy of power, assertiveness, or personal relations between superiors and subordinates (see Table A 8.9 in Appendix). We did not build an index but compared item by item, as statistical analyses showed that the items are relatively poorly related with each other.

In general, only a minority of the business leaders think that, in the interest of an effective work input, managers should maintain a distant relationship with their employees. The idea of maintaining a distant relationship holds information about certain standards of behaviour regarded as appropriate in the culture of an organization. Regardless of the country of origin, adherents of maintaining distance less frequently lead very large industrial companies and financial institutions, but rather medium-sized companies. Particularly the Polish business leaders agree that distance is necessary to maintain effectiveness at the workplace, as in Poland friendly behaviour in relations between managers and their subordinates is often thought by the latter to give them freedom to blur the division of roles in the organizational structure, establish informal contacts with superiors, relax discipline, etc. (Gardawski *et al.* 2010) In relation to this, it is interesting to analyse to what extent managers think that employees could expect support from management with personal problems. In all countries and in all types of companies, more than 50 per cent of respondents agree with this statement. It is most frequently rejected by West Germans, but gets a high level of approval from post-transition leaders in East Germany, Hungary, and Poland. So a distance has to be kept but this includes the idea that business leaders care for their subordinates, which suggests the more paternalistic character of the relationship. This paternalistic view has the lowest percentage of advocates in the largest companies and financial institutions, as in such companies, relationships between manage-ment and employees are usually more anonymous (Hungary is an exception). An extensive organizational structure usually strengthens the hierarchy and the distance between employees at different managerial levels. Therefore large companies are often considered more anonymous and depersonalized; in various concepts the corporate man is described as 'a small cog in the company machine'.

The other important complex of issues is the question of employees' autonomy. Here we asked three different questions about participation, rule following and independent decision-making. In general, percentages of respondents who agree with the statement that 'For daily business it should be enough for employees that the supervisor knows what's going on in the company' are not very high. Positive attitudes are most frequent in Poland among small and medium-sized and large industrial companies where business leaders are apparently least in favour of a participatory leadership style; in the largest firms this percentage is much lower. The lowest level of agreement with the statement was expressed by East and West German executives, which seems to be in line with the participatory leadership style where exchange of information and consultation with employees is dominant. Additional analyses demonstrate (with other variables controlled) that in Germany and Hungary paternalism is supported less frequently by people with higher education. In Poland the statement given above is supported most frequently by older managers; it may be due to their life experiences that they see a relatively low level of information as a useful instrument in maintaining paternalistic relations.

Further, business leaders differ in their estimation of whether employees should be able to act on their own decisions even if these go against the opinion of supervisors. Generally, with some exceptions, less than 50 per cent of respondents agree with this statement. Here, as is to be expected, most agreement is found among respondents from West Germany where we suppose a more delegative leadership style. Percentages for Poland are similar to those in East Germany, and approval for this opinion is significantly lower in Hungary.

Autonomy and the need for independent decision-making is also reflected in a rather high level of disapproval among West Germans about the need to fulfil orders under all circumstances, and a high approval among East German, Hungarian and Polish business leaders. Generally we can also see that respondents from the largest industrial firms more often disagree with this position.

The third aspect we considered was the legitimization of leadership. Generally, more than half of the respondents think that the most important criterion for recognition of a supervisor by employees should be the supervisor's superior professional knowledge. Here we find the same trend as in the other items: West German business leaders least frequently see superior knowledge as a legiti-mization for hierarchy, in contrast to the East Germans, Poles and especially Hungarian business leaders, who consider professional knowledge the most important. Interesting is that this need for superior professional knowledge on the part of organizational superiors is least frequently supported by executives from the largest companies and the financial sector (Hungarian respondents are the exception); this relationship is the most evident in Germany. This seems quite logical as in large companies the requirement for management is much more leadership competences than professional knowledge (see Chapter 5). Additional analyses demonstrate that in each country the support of this statement is given relatively more often by older people with more professional and life experience.

While the findings reported up to now represent an understanding of leadership and management in daily business life, we were also interested in how business leaders relate to employees in extreme cases. In recent years, in all countries, we have witnessed an increase in global competition and pressure, which is transmitted onto employees as a need for higher productivity and flexibility. Interestingly, the business leaders in the transition countries are more willing to 'dismiss employees if they do not perform at full capacity'. More than half of Hungarian business leaders, in particular those in the financial sector (70 per cent agreement, and 50 per cent agreement among leaders of very large companies), are in favour of dismissal if efficiency decreases. In Poland, percentages of managers accepting this view are also significant, however not higher than 50 per cent. The percentages in Germany are, interestingly, the lowest in financial institutions and in the largest industrial companies (22–24 per cent). We might see this underlining of efficiency as a rejection of the socialist economy where full employment was predominant and workers were almost never dismissed due to poor work performance, with the exception of serious alcohol abuse. Thus, we could also recognize here the strong influence of a more liberal capitalism in Poland and Hungary compared to Germany where an 'easy hire-and-fire' regime is not yet as widespread.

The clear sign of a transformation legacy is also found if we ask about other conflicts in the company. The view that in conflicts over company objectives priority should be given to owners' interests is most often shared by business leaders in small and large industrial companies in Poland and in East Germany (52 per cent and 56 per cent respectively). Especially large and untypical differences between types of companies became apparent in Hungary, with the strongest support for owner rights expressed by managers in the financial sector and large industrial companies (for banks 60 per cent, for L 50 per cent, for XL 35 per cent.) Smaller companies and medium-sized companies in Hungary demonstrated a rather limited acceptance (23–29 per cent) for this point of view. In contrast, in West Germany, priority was given to owners' rights by a stable and relatively low number of respondents across all company-sizes (from 34 to 37 per cent in small, medium and large companies).

To summarize the above, regarding leadership styles we see a clear cut distinction between the more delegative, cooperative, leadership style and the more paternalistic, order-giving, leadership style. While West Germany is at the one end, East Germany is always in-between, and Poland and Hungary are at the other end of the line. The most coherent pictures of leadership are therefore offered by West Germany and Poland. In Poland we find a consistent picture of answers concerning professional knowledge of managers, unconditional following of instructions of supervisors, as well as support for employees in solving their private problems. Slightly weaker, but still significant are the positive correlations with maintaining distance and the statement that 'often it is enough if the supervisor knows what is going on in the company'. Since scores on those answers are relatively high for Poland, there is good reason to claim that these results describe a very paternalist pattern of company and employee management, and that Polish business leaders have a tendency to be more bureaucratic, authoritarian and paternalistic.

Given these national trends influenced by path dependency of transition and the formation of industrial relations in general, it is interesting to see that the existence of a labour organization at company level makes a difference to leadership style. This is again particularly true for Poland, where business leaders of companies with works councils or trade union committees consider a distant relationship less necessary for an effective work outcome than do those business leaders who lead companies without such a body. This is also true for Hungary, but there the difference is not as great. The same is true for following orders under all circumstances: while 78 per cent of all Polish business leaders of non-unionized companies say that this should be the case, only 57 per cent of business leaders say so in unionized companies. The same is also true for the question of whether it is enough for employees that the supervisor knows what is going on in the company. Managers of a company with a works council more often deny this (compare Table A 8.10 in Appendix). We clearly see here a relation between labour-relations institutions and management style. If there is a works council or trade union committee, an organ representing workers' interests, the management style is less autocratic and paternalistic. This is a clear sign of the positive effect of institutionalization of labour relations, a freeing from personal dependence on superiors. This is reflected in a greater aversion of business leaders of companies with works councils/trade union committees to the idea that management should support employees in their private problems.

Given the influence of labour-relations organization on personal characteristics like attitudes and leadership style, it seems almost natural that it also has an effect on company policy, where the institutions have more possibilities to directly influence the outcome. This will be analysed in the next section.

The impact of employee representation on company policies

The relation between the existence of a works council/ trade union committee and company policies in the area of employment and corporate social responsibility is quite obvious. Companies with a works council or a trade union committee offer more training for their workers, but are also more frequently involved in work-life balance measures. They employ fewer workers on a fixed-term contractual basis or agency workers. They also more likely carry out socially responsible restructuring.

Companies with worker representation are more likely to support community social activities and regional development, as well as more likely to be involved

Table 8.3 Various company characteristics depending on existence of employee association. Parameters of logistic regression (without and with the control of other company characteristics)

Parameter beta for variable describing existence of employee association	E Germany	W Germany	Hungary	Poland
	Work-life balance as a target of company			
Without control of other variables	0.92**	1.07**	0.22	−0.06
With control of company[a] variables	0.70*	0.72*	0.18	0.13
	Supporting community social activities			
Without control of other variables	1.12**	−0.11	0.55	0.56
With control of company[a] variables	1.13**	−0.65	0.22	0.47
	Involvement in environmental issues			
Without control of other variables	0.33	0.52*	1.21**	1.73**
With control of company[a] variables	0.03	0.14	0.67	1.36*
	Involvement in regional development			
Without control of other variables	0.35	−0.37	0.89*	1.35*
With control of company[a] variables	0.25	−0.57	0.09	1.12
	Fixed budget for social spending			
Without control of other variables	0.92**	0.47*	1.06**	1.13**
With control of company[a] variables	0.80**	0.34	0.39	0.87*

Notes
*significant at 0.05; **significant at 0.01.
a Company variables: size, type (bank), foreign (yes or no), joint-stock (yes or no), existence of employees association, membership in employer association.

in environment issues, and they are more likely to have a fixed budget for social spending. And this is true even if we control for other variables (see Table 8.3).

In short, effects of works councils and trade union committees are found in all countries. What is very interesting in the case of Poland, however, is that we detect a clear difference between the size of the effect of works councils and trade union committees.

It seems that workers' protection is higher in the case of trade union committees: they have on average 9 per cent fewer employees with limited contracts; they have 6 per cent fewer agency workers and the total number of companies that have agency workers at all is two times smaller (only 24 per cent of companies with trade union committees have agency workers, while 54 per cent of companies with works councils have agency workers, see again Table 8.4). Interestingly there is no positive relation between trade union committees and membership in an employers' association.

Companies with trade union committees in Poland more often invest in health and safety at work, lifelong learning, and work-life balance. What is a bit alarming is the difference is particularly large in the core area of health and safety: only

Table 8.4 Frequency of limited contracts and agency employees depending on type of employee representation

Country	Works council or unions	Mean of % of employees with limited contracts	% of companies which have employees with limited contracts	N	Mean of % of agency employees	% of companies which have agency employees	N
Poland	None	39.2	86.0	43	2.9	20.9	43
	Only wc	22.1	88.4	43	8.1	53.5	43
	Only unions	13.8	90.7	43	2.3	23.8	42
	Both	15.4	87.9	33	1.2	19.4	31
Hungary	None	18.8	63.6	66	2.8	29.1	55
	Only wc	8.8	72.7	22	4.8	27.3	22
	Only unions[a]	4.7	20.0	5	2.0	20.0	5
	Both	14.9	86.4	44	4.7	59.0	39

Note
a Less than 10 cases.

Table 8.5 Protection and development of employees depending on type of employee representation

Report		% of companies which promote				
Country	Works councils or unions	Health and safety at work	Training and lifelong learning	Social responsible restructuring	Work-life balance	N
Poland	None	77.3	65.9	13.6	22.7	44
	Only wc	47.7	50.0	15.9	18.2	44
	Only unions	74.4	69.8	20.9	30.2	43
	Both	76.5	76.5	23.5	23.5	34
Hungary	None	70.1	53.2	29.9	26.0	77
	Only wc	69.0	58.6	41.4	31.0	29
	Only unions[a]	57.1	42.9	28.6	14.3	7
	Both	83.7	79.6	61.2	32.7	49

Note
a Less than 10 cases.

48 per cent of companies with works councils invest in health and safety, while 74 per cent of companies with trade union committees do so (Table 8.5).

In Hungary the effect is quite interesting: regarding working contracts, companies with trade union committees have better conditions for employees, fewer workers with fixed-term contracts and fewer agency workers, but companies with works councils are much better at safeguarding health and safety, training programs, work-life balance and socially responsible restructuring.

Conclusion

In this chapter, we have found the interesting effect that labour-relations institutions at company level, in the form of works councils or trade union committees, have an impact on business leaders' attitudes, on leadership styles and on company policies. We detected intriguing differences between works councils and trade union committees in Poland and Hungary, and overall in all three countries we have found the same size effect, the influence of socialist legacies and the lack of explanatory power of socio-demographic characteristics of business leaders. In explaining variance in attitudes and leadership style, it is organizational characteristics and institutions that matter and not personal or socio-demographic attributes such as age, education or income. This is a quite strong result with regard to our overall question concerning the role of business leaders in post-communist Europe as a way to explain the varieties of capitalism, but the result corresponds with the findings in other chapters where the company size and sector is the most decisive difference. We find that institutions, such as labour representation at company level, influence both attitudes and leadership style. This is a quite strong result giving some hope that with the implementation of labour organizations at company level, the acceptance of labour representation does increase.

In all three countries, works councils were introduced as an important element of labour-interest representation. Their introduction was not carried out in the same manner in the different countries, however. In East Germany, works councils were introduced directly with reunification, and had an ambivalent role, defending more the survival of the company than workers' individual rights or interests, often to the disapproval of trade unions. In Hungary, where works councils were introduced early, existing side by side with trade union committees, the number of companies with only trade union committees is quite small. Works councils have managed to effectively take over responsibility in important areas of work organization, such as health and safety. However, in cases where both institutions exist at one company, which is in about 30 per cent of the cases, the protective effect is smaller than works councils or trade union committees operating alone.

Polish unions were afraid that works councils would undermine the influence of trade unions, thus they opposed the introduction of works councils the longest of any of the three countries. Works councils are therefore not so widespread and are less effective in protecting workers than are trade union committees.

In all three countries, the relationship between unions and works councils has been tense; even in West Germany trade unions have been sceptical about the introduction of works councils. Positive experiences with co-determination however, have led all the actors involved, unions as well as employers, to appreciate this workplace institution. There might be some hope that with positive experiences increasing, the recognition of workplace labour organizations might also increase in East Central Europe. The positive relation between the existence and positive appraisal of labour organizations found in our data might indicate that there is something of a learning curve in the relationship.

With regard to our assumptions about dependent market economies (Chapter 1) it is remarkable that the influence of foreign ownership is less visible than we would have expected. In Hungary, despite being a dependent market economy par excellence, the influence of foreign ownership is not easy to detect: companies with foreign ownership neither have more labour organizations at company level, nor are they more often members in an employers' association, nor do leadership style and company policies differ in foreign-owned companies. Controlling other variables, including size, our data do not confirm that there is a significant influence of foreign ownership in East Central Europe. In Poland, there does exist a positive relation between membership in an employers' association and foreign ownership, although it is not statistically significant, and the existence of employee representation is more widespread in foreign-owned companies. If we control for other variables, however, the influence becomes insignificant, so that we might assume that the effect of foreign ownership is an effect of size and organization features, such as being a joint-stock company.

As well as this, business leaders in foreign-owned companies more often regard trade unions as superfluous and consider collective regulation and consultation between social partners less useful. This could imply that although they bring with them or adopt the institutions of the homeland economy, they consider them less important than do the leaders of Polish companies.

If we take these two results together, the difference between foreign-owned and Polish companies is much greater than the difference between foreign-owned and Hungarian companies, but even in Poland the difference is not as great as might be theoretically plausible. This has some far-reaching impacts on theory building. While our sample is small and would need some replication, it does raise a doubt that the macro-level dependence of Central Eastern economies on foreign direct investment has a positive influence on industrial relations at company level. Our findings contradict earlier studies, where foreign ownership was perceived as accommodating labours interest better due to the need for skilled workers in high-cost production systems (Bohle and Greskovits 2006), especially the expectation that German owners were exporting core features of the German model, like the rather good employer–employee relations, or at least being more responsive to pressure from German works councils to implement good labour relations (Bluhm 2007). This assumption that foreign employers in dependent market economies in search of and in competition for skilled workers are readily offering better industrial conditions is not proven in our empirical analysis. At least, it seems that the effect is much more differentiated than previously thought and cannot be easily generalized.

Having put labour organizations to the fore in this chapter, we see that they account for some stark differences in the shape of post-communist economies; however, their coverage in post-socialist countries is so low that it is difficult to see in them a strong mover for the re-embedding of society into the economy (for an overview of exceptions, see Sznajder-Lee and Trappmann forthcoming,). They do not seem to have the power to be a countermovement in the Polanyian sense, and at this stage in East Central Europe they are at best a fly in the ointment. It is only with time that the existing positive influences will have a spillover effect.

Notes

1 See Industrial Relations in Europe (2010) for Poland and Hungary; Bispinck *et al.* (2010) for West Germany; for East Germany the numbers are only an estimation, as no clear data are available – cf. Schnabel (2005).
2 The main forum for consultation and tripartitism in Hungary is the National Interest Reconciliation Council (Orszagos Erdekegyezteto Tanacs, OET). There are also other important bodies in industrial relations, such as the Sectoral Social Dialogue Committees. The OET was set up in parallel with the Economic Council, which consisted of representatives of foreign investors, banks, professional associations and stock exchanges. The government elected in 2002 dissolved the Economic Council, strengthened the competence of the OET and limited its members to nine employer organizations and six trade unions (ETUI 2012c).
3 Employers/management had to consult works councils before reorganization, privatization or modernization of the company. And they had co-determination rights in the area of health and safety as well as the use of operating funds.
4 In Poland the 'Tripartite Commission for Socio-Economic Matters' (TK) was called only in 1994 after the unsuccessful proposition of a so-called pact on state companies in transformation that envisaged the inclusion of trade unions in settling conflicts in exchange for co-decisions in certain matters (e.g., selection of the method of privatization). The concept was being partly implemented when the TK was established as a forum for consultation between government, business organizations and trade unions. A law was passed on a negotiated system of wages in companies, making possible a consensus in the matter of the amount of the minimum wage and wage rises. However in the years 1997–2000 and 2005–07 the process of social dialogue was interrupted. In 2001 parliament accepted legislation restoring the Tripartite Commission and defining principles of worker representation and organization, but also in the area of negotiation and the institutional structure of social dialogue, including at the regional level (the voivodship commission for social dialogue). However the level of social dialogue remains low, and relations between the government and the social partners have remained fluid, which means that, depending on political and economic changes, they could evolve towards liberalism or neocorporatist solutions (Gardawski *et al.* 2012).
5 Dialog Społczny. Online. Available <http://www.dialog.gov.pl/radypracownikow> (accessed 12 April 2012).
6 The variable was measured on a scale from 1 (completely disagree) to 5 (completely agree). The results must be interpreted with caution because this is an ordinal variable and linear regression needs a dependent variable measured on an interval scale.
7 In order to confirm such impressions, one would have to conduct parallel interviews with employee organizations.
8 In March 2009, the Polish social partners agreed a package of measures, including major changes to working-time flexibility, the minimum wage, social security and taxes. The global economic crisis has led to attempts at closer links between trade unions and employers. As these are very recent developments, their effects on Polish industrial relations and the trade union movement remain to be seen (cf. Gardawski *et al.* 2012).

Appendix

Table A 8.1 Percentage of companies which are members of an employers' association, by size

Size and type	E Germany		W Germany		Hungary		Poland	
	%	N	%	N	%	N	%	N
Industrial 45–99 (m1)	10.3	97	34.0	50	5.7	53	2.6	38
Industrial 100–249 (m2)	20.4	103	37.5	64	1.9	52	2.3	43
Industrial 250–999 (l)	28.9	38	54.2	48	25.0	20	23.1	39
Industrial ≥ 1,000 (xl)			59.5	74	33.3	24	38.5	26
Financial			34.9	43	10.0	20	15.8	19

Notes
The classes we looked at were m = 45–249 employees, l = 249–999 employees; xl = 1,000 and more employees and banks. The companies with size m were split in two groups (m1 = 45–99; and l2 = 100–249) when doing the calculations as it represents a very large portion of the sample. In the text we however added m1 and m2.

For East Germany categories 'industrial companies with more than 1,000 employees' and 'financial institutions' are very rare, so we decided to exclude them from analysis.

Table A 8.2 Logistic analysis. Dependent variable: membership in an employers' association, independent variables: size and type of company

Size and type[a]	E Germany	W Germany	Hungary	Poland
	beta	beta	beta	beta
Industrial 100–249 (m)	0.81*	0.08	−1.02	−0.23
Industrial 250–999 (l)	1.30*	0.64	1.88*	1.72
Industrial ≥ 1,000 (xl)		1.61**	2.62**	2.52*
Financial		0.23	0.30	0.31
Foreign	0.76	0.57	−0.99	0.90
Joint-stock	0.50	0.60	1.08*	0.92*

Notes
*significant at 0.05; **significant at 0.01.

For East Germany categories 'industrial companies with more than 1,000 employees' and 'financial institutions' are very rare, so we decided to exclude them from analysis.

Table A 8.3 Percentages of companies with employee association (trade union or works council)

Size and type	E Germany		W Germany		Hungary		Poland	
	%	N	%	N	%	N	%	N
Industrial 45–99 (m1)	37.1	97	54.0	50	26.4	53	55.3	38
Industrial 100–249 (m2)	55.3	103	70.3	64	32.7	52	69.8	43
Industrial 250–999 (l)	89.5	38	79.2	48	90.0	20	87.2	39
Industrial ≥ 1,000 (xl)			94.6	74	91.7	24	96.2	26
Financial			74.4	43	70.0	20	73.7	19

Note
For East Germany categories 'industrial companies with more than 1,000 employees' and 'financial institutions' are very rare, so we decided to exclude them from analysis.

Table A 8.4 Logistic analysis. Dependent variable: existence of employee association, independent variables: size and type of company

Size and type[a]	E Germany	W Germany	Hungary	Poland
	beta	beta	beta	beta
Industrial 100–249 (m2)	0.76*	0.7	0.23	0.56
Industrial 250–999 (l)	2.73**	1.14*	2.9**	1.1
Industrial ≥ 1,000 (xl)		2.91**	3.04**	2.18*
Financial		0.91	1.29*	−0.65
Foreign	0.8	0.04	0.38	−0.02
Joint stock	0.73	0.49	0.39	2.4**

Notes
*significant at 0.05; **significant at 0.001.
a For East Germany categories 'industrial companies with more than 1,000 employees' and 'financial institutions' are very rare, so we decided to exclude them from analysis. Industrial companies 45–99 is reference category.

Table A 8.5 Percentages of companies with employee trade union

Size and type[a]	Hungary		Poland	
	%	N	%	N
Industrial 45–99 (m1)	16.7	48	31.6	38
Industrial 100–249 (m2)	20.0	50	51.2	43
Industrial 250–999 (l)	55.0	20	51.3	39
Industrial ≥ 1,000 (xl)	83.3	24	65.4	26
Financial	35.0	20	31.6	19

Table A 8.6 Percentages of companies with works council

Size and type[a]	E Germany		W Germany		Hungary		Poland	
	%	N	%	N	%	N	%	N
Industrial 45–99 (m1)	37.5	96	54.0	50	20.8	48	28.9	38
Industrial 100–249 (m2)	55.9	102	70.3	64	32.0	50	44.2	43
Industrial 250–999 (l)	89.5	38	80.9	47	85.0	20	59.0	39
Industrial ≥ 1,000 (xl)			94.5	73	87.5	24	65.4	26
Financial			86.1	36	70.0	20	42.1	19

Note
For East Germany categories 'industrial companies with more than 1,000 employees' and 'financial institutions' are very rare, so we decided to exclude them from analysis.

Table A 8.7 Agreement of business leaders with statement 'Trade unions are superfluous'[c] – linear regression analyses

Trade unions are superfluous	E Germany	W Germany	Hungary	Poland
Parameter b without control of other variables				
Existence of employee association	−0.82**	−0.54**	−0.94**	−0.86**
Membership in employer association	−0.55	−0.54*	−0.39	−0.02
Parameter b with control of other company[a] and individual[b] variables				
Existence of employee association	−0.49*	−0.29	−0.52*	−0.83*
Membership in employer association	−0.07	−0.41*	−0.05	0.32
Overall R^2	27.0%	16.6%	22.6%	15.2%
Partial R^2 'company'[a] variables controlling 'individual'[b] variables	21.4%	12.1%	13.1%	13.6%
Partial R^2 'individual'[b] variables controlling 'company'[a] variables	7.3%	5.7%	4.4%	3.9%

Notes
*significant at 0.05; **significant at 0.01.
a Company variables: size, type (bank), foreign (yes or no), joint stock (yes or no), existence of employees association, membership in employer association.
b Individual variables: years at managerial position, level of education of respondent (higher or not) education of parents, age (45 or less, 46–55, 56 or more), type of education (engineer, business), ownership of the company (more than 50% of company's shares).
c The variable was measured on a scale from 1 (completely disagree) to 5 (completely agree); The results must be interpreted with caution because this is an ordinal variable and linear regression needs an interval dependent variable.

Table A 8.8 Agreement of business leaders with statement 'Collective regulations between social partners are important for the functioning of the economy' – linear regression analyses

Collective regulations between social partners are important for the functioning of the economy	E Germany	W Germany	Hungary	Poland
Parameter b without control of other variables				
Existence of employee association	0.48**	0.06	–0.02	0.05
Membership in employer association	0.45	0.14*	–0.01**	–0.10
Parameter b with control other company[a] and individual[b] variables				
Existence of employee association	0.38*	0.06	–0.26	0.06
Membership in employer association	0.15	0.25	–0.02	0.14
Overall R^2	16.2%	17.0%	16.4%	10.5%
Partial R^2 'company'[a] variables controlling 'individual[b]' variables	7.0%	9.6%	6.6%	5.5%
Partial R^2 'individual'[b] variables controlling 'company'[a] variables	7.8%	10.1%	8.0%	4.2%

Notes
*significant at 0.05; **significant at 0.01.
a Company variables: size, type (bank), foreign (yes or no), joint stock (yes or no), existence of employee association, membership in employer association.
b Individual variables: years at managerial position, level education of respondent (higher or not) education of parents, age (45 or less, 46–55, 56 or more), type of education (engineer, business).

Table A 8.9 Managers' attitudes on superior–subordinate relations

Type of company	Percentage of respondents, who agree with the statements[a]							
	In the interest of an effective work input, managers should maintain a distanced relationship to their employees	For daily business it should be enough for employees that the supervisor knows what's going on in the company	Employees should be able to act on their own decisions even if these go against the opinion of supervisors	Employees with private problems should be able to expect support from management	The most important criterion for recognition of a supervisor by employees should be the supervisor's superior professional knowledge	Employees should view it as their duty to strictly follow orders under all circumstances	Those who do not perform at full capacity should be dismissed	In conflicts over company goals, owner interests should clearly be the first consideration
E Germany								
industrial 45–99 (m1)	33.8	6.2	40.0	70.8	70.8	78.5	46.2	52.3
industrial 100–249 (m2)	26.2	13.1	32.8	67.2	67.2	67.2	41.0	52.5
industrial 250–999 (l)	38.5	7.7	7.7	76.9	53.8	69.2	46.2	53.8
W Germany								
industrial 45–99 (m1)	28.3	8.7	41.3	78.3	56.5	39.1	32.6	37.0
industrial 100–249 (m2)	35.7	17.9	39.3	57.1	51.8	60.7	23.2	35.7
industrial 250–999 (l)	13.2	13.2	39.5	65.8	39.5	34.2	26.3	34.2
industrial ≥ 1,000 (xl)	20.8	11.3	50.9	52.8	13.2	18.9	28.3	52.8
financial	21.4	7.1	53.6	60.7	17.9	42.9	25.0	50.0

Hungary								
industrial 45–99 (m1)	29.8	29.8	8.5	72.3	89.4	80.9	61.7	23.4
industrial 100–249 (m2)	22.0	31.7	100.0ᵈ	0.0ᵈ	0.0ᵈ	100.0ᵈ	0.0ᵈ	0.0ᵈ
industrial 250–999 (l)	41.7	16.7	16.7	58.3	83.3	75.0	50.0	50.0
industrial ≥ 1,000 (x1)	10.0	20.0	25.0	75.0	75.0	45.0	50.0	35.0
financial	0.0	5.0	20.0	80.0	80.0	45.0	70.0	60.0
Poland								
industrial 45–99	44.7	52.6	26.3	86.8	76.3	76.3	44.7	52.6
industrial 100–249	26.2	38.1	31.0	83.3	73.8	81.0	33.3	59.5
industrial 250–999	38.5	41.0	35.9	71.8	53.8	51.3	41.0	56.4
industrial ≥ 1,000	16.0	20.0	44.0	60.0	40.0	40.0	36.0	44.0
financial	31.6	31.6	57.9	63.2	57.9	47.4	47.4	47.4

Note

a Percentages of respondents who chose answer '1 fully agree' and '1 agree' (except for the last question).

Table A 8.10 Managers' attitudes on superior–subordinate relations depending on existence of institutionalized employee representation in the company

Percentage of respondents, who agree with the statements[a]

Has a company association representing employees' interests?	In the interest of an effective work input, managers should maintain a distanced relationship to their employees	For daily business it should be enough for employees that the supervisor knows what's going on in the company	Employees should be able to act on their own decisions even if these go against the opinion of supervisors	Employees with private problems should be able to expect support from management	The most important criterion for recognition of a supervisor by employees should be the supervisor's superior professional knowledge	Employees should view it as their duty to strictly follow orders under all circumstances	Those who do not perform at full capacity should be dismissed	In conflicts over company goals, owner interests should clearly be the first consideration
E Germany								
no	27.8	13.9	36.1	75.0	72.2	75.0	51.4	55.6
yes	35.3	4.4	32.4	64.7	63.2	70.6	35.3	48.5
W Germany								
no	27.6	12.1	48.3	77.6	44.8	48.3	20.7	31.0
yes	23.9	12.3	42.9	57.1	34.4	36.2	29.4	45.4
Hungary								
no	26.8	23.9	11.3	74.6	83.1	71.8	53.5	28.2
yes	13.0	15.9	15.9	71.0	82.6	60.9	63.8	40.6
Poland								
no	43.9	46.3	31.7	85.4	65.9	78.0	34.1	56.1
yes	28.7	36.1	37.7	72.1	61.5	57.4	41.8	52.5

Note

a Percentages of respondents who chose answer 'I fully agree' and 'I agree' (except for the last question).

9 Income and influence

Hungarian, Polish and German business leaders compared

György Lengyel, Nikolett Geszler and Zita Ördög

Introduction

In this chapter we investigate how the income and influence of business leaders are related to organizational settings and personal conditions – among others, to occupation, multipositionality and education. The income and influence of business leaders are frequently interpreted in social science within the conceptual framework of agency, power and prestige. The explosive growth of performance-based executive compensation was a notable characteristic of late twentieth century economic scene, and was considered a way to align the incentives of managers with the interests of shareholders, and therefore was a solution to the underlying agency problem: that the shareholder cannot observe and contract upon actions taken by managers that affect profitability, that is, the shareholders' returns. The issue in contract design is to provide the agent with the incentive to take the privately costly action. The optimal contract reflects a trade-off between the incentive benefit of conditioning the agent's compensation on the observed level of profit, and the cost of inefficiently allocating the risk to the risk-averse party. As shown by Crocker and Slemrod (2007), it is also important in the optimal contract to minimize the agent's incentive to falsify earnings reports. One of the solutions is to offer equity incentives for managers. Those firms whose CEOs have relatively high amounts of equity incentives in the form of unrestricted stock and immediately exercisable options are more likely to engage in earnings management by reporting small earnings increases. Performance-based executive compensation (Jensen and Zimmerman 1985) is a closely related concept. It suggests that compensation packages of top-level executives help align manager and shareholder interests. Executive compensation and executive turnover are positively related to stock-price performance, and the adoption of short- and long-run compensation plans is associated with increases in shareholder wealth.

Another, different view on how the agency problem and executive compensation might be linked is the 'managerial power approach' (Bebchuk and Fried 2003). Here executive compensation is viewed not only as a potential instrument for addressing agency problems, but also as *part* of the agency problem itself. According to this approach, compensation arrangements might be shaped both by market forces that push toward value-maximizing solutions, and by the influence of managerial power, leading to departures from these arrangements in directions favourable to managers. This view claims that these departures from value-maximizing arrangements are substantial and that compensation practices thus cannot be adequately explained by optimal contracting alone, suggesting that executives have substantial influence over their own pay. If this reasoning is right, then the more power managers have, the greater their ability to extract rents.

The second key variable of this paper, *influence*, is interpreted as being in a close relationship with agency, power (Bruin 1999), occupational prestige (Davies 1953; Goldthorpe and Hope 1972), income and education. Lajos Leopold (1913) was among the first who devoted attention to the problem of prestige and specifically the prestige of occupations. His distinction between prestige and authority has been frequently applied in studies of occupational prestige. The distinction between prestige and authority however is more relevant in a wider social context of the division of labour than within the group of business leaders where prestige and authority are supposed to be interwoven. A refined study in the wider context found that occupational prestige has a stronger connection with education than with wages (Hauser and Warren 1996).

A clarifying conceptual distinction worth recalling here is the distinction between social and personal influence (Katz and Lazarsfeld [1955] 2006). We intend to deal with *social influence*, that is, with the problem of the effect different business leader groups can exert on important social issues. We do not address such characteristics of channels of influence as personal/public, formal/informal, or legal/illegal. These are relevant scientific and social issues, but are out of the scope of the present study. They would lead us too far from the question we are primarily interested in: to what extent can income and attributed social influence be explained by the specificities of organizational fields and the individual characteristics of business leaders?

The social influence of elite and other groups can be measured in several ways. *Process tracing* of case studies, or the investigation of *preference attainment* can be applied if there are clear cases, alternatives and preferences at the actors' disposal (Dürr and DeBievre 2007; Versucheren and Arts 2004). The relative weight of different elite groups, on the other hand, can be approached indirectly as well, by interviews or surveys addressing the subjective sense, or by *attributed influence* as suggested by James March (1955). This third approach is applied here, based on the comparative survey of business leaders working in Hungary, Poland, West and East Germany in 2009–10. For the sake of comparability and simplicity, equal weights are given to the leaders of the four territories. Three types of leaders are distinguished within them: *managers* (paid leaders of industrial companies), *entrepreneurs* (active owners of industrial companies under 1,000 employees) and *bankers*.

Concerning the different personal and organizational attributes that might affect the income and attributed influence of economic leaders, we refer to the theory of isomorphism outlined by DiMaggio and Powell (1983). Bureaucratization and other forms of homogenization emerge out of the restructuring of organizational fields. Structured organizational fields provide a context in which individual efforts to deal with uncertainty often lead to homogeneity in structure, culture and output. Isomorphism is the process of homogenization that forces one unit to resemble other units that face the same set of conditions. DiMaggio and Powell identify three mechanisms of institutional isomorphic change: coercive mechanisms of isomorphism that stem from political influence and the problem of legal frameworks; mimetic isomorphism resulting from standard responses to uncertainty, and finally the normative isomorphism that stems mainly from professionalization. Managerial and professional occupations are comprehensive, professional networks that have developed formal educational regulations which result in a pool of almost interchangeable individuals who occupy similar positions and possess similar orientations and dispositions. As a consequence all of these organizations become similar to each other in terms of personnel composition as well as attitudes. This may mean, of course, that the individual characteristics of leaders have come to constitute less the basis of income differences, because most leaders have similar attributes, qualification, experiences, career path etc. On the other hand, organizational field determinants continue to play a great part in income differences because they still have greater variability – despite their becoming isomorphic in many aspects affected by the organizational condition – for what concerns the company's operation and the payment of its business leaders dependent on company size, sector and many other factors. Therefore we may presume that income and influence become similar in order of magnitude within the same sector, company size, country etc., and that these organizational field attributes play a bigger role in the conformation of income and influence than individual characteristics do.

Among the explanatory variables one can take into account, there are organizational characteristics like branch, size and ownership structure of the company on the one hand, and individual-level characteristics such as the cultural and social resources of leaders on the other. Among the latter, study trips and work experiences abroad as well as multipositionality deserve special attention. Foreign experiences may have to do with the ownership structure of the company and therefore we should try to separate these effects. Multipositionality of leaders means their accumulation of simultaneous positions in business (and civic) organizations. From an organizational point of view this is the equivalent of the interlocking of companies through personal ties and it contributes to the explanation of behavioural codes of elites in many respects (Useem 1984; Mintz and Schwartz 1985; Mizruchi 1992, 1996; Lengyel 1993, 2007; Stark and Vedres 2012).

In the following we investigate first the variations in the income and attributed influence of business leaders within and between countries and sectors. Second, with regression models it is investigated to what extent organizational settings on the one hand, and individual characteristics of the leaders on the other, explain the variance in income. Finally, we build regression models in which the dependent variable is the subjective evaluation of influence and the explanatory variables are contextual and individual characteristics (among others: country, sector, size of the company, foreign ownership, career pattern, income, education, etc.). With this step-by-step approach, this chapter may shed light on country-specificities of business leaders' subjective and objective occupational status and the relation of this to organizational and personal characteristics.

Variability of income and influence

The respondents were asked about their annual gross income for 2008 – including bonuses – with the help of given income categories. A continuous variable was created from the centre of the interval in question. The highest category was ascribed a value of €350,000. Owing to the creation process, the variable is an approximate estimation of incomes. Table 9.1 presents its means and standard deviations according to countries.

The results of the first table show that among the four investigated territories, the business leaders of West Germany had the highest average income in 2008.

Table 9.1 Annual income of business leaders in Poland, Hungary, East and West Germany (€) in 2008[a]

		Poland	Hungary	E Germany	W Germany	Total sample
		N=68	N=39	N=70	N=53	N=230
Manager	Mean	92,677	41,744	134,091	176,029	115,776
	St. deviation	122,484	39,734	79,507	97,569	103,661
		N=21	N=35	N=50	N=36	N=142
Entrepreneur	Mean	69,521	37,743	119,304	204,871	113,617
	St. deviation	105,303	67,468	69,871	112,730	106,564
		N=9	N=20	N=0	N=6	N=35
Banker	Mean	280,682	138,125	-	237,500	192,400
	St. deviation	89,366	91,977	-	102,023	111,068
		N=98	N=94	N=120	N=95	N=407
Together	Mean	105,943	60,761	127,910	190,674	121,627
	St. deviation	129,117	75,338	75,679	104,329	107,297

Notes
a The question was the following: In what range is your yearly income in 2008? (Gross income including premium)
( ) up to €10,000
( ) up to €20,000
( ) up to €30,000
( ) up to €40,000
( ) up to €50,000
( ) up to €75,000
( ) up to €100,000
( ) up to €150,000
( ) up to €200,000
( ) up to €250,000
( ) more than €250,000
( ) don't know
( ) NA

They are followed by the East German business people, who had significantly lower income. Comparing the investigated countries, East Germany and Hungary had the lowest standard deviation of income data and consequently the incomes of business leaders here were closest to each other. In comparison to their German counterparts, the Polish leaders had lower average incomes. However, the Polish sample included a relatively large group of business leaders whose income fell into the highest category; therefore here the standard deviation is the highest. Leaders in Hungary had the lowest average annual income among the participant countries.

For the investigation of Hungarian incomes, an alternative database was also at our disposal containing income data on the business leaders of 53 state-owned enterprises in 2009. The compulsorily publicized annual gross income includes the annual gross basic wage, the other annual financial payments and the annual bonus of these Hungarian managers. We converted these data into euros and compared them with the findings of the current Hungarian research, focusing mainly on the competitive sector.[1] The leaders of state-owned Hungarian companies earned €51,700 on average in 2009, while the standard deviation was €45,500. The lowest annual income was €6,800, while the highest was €307,700 (Ördög 2010). In spite of the data referring to different years, it seems that the Hungarian results of the two databases indicate great similarities, in contradiction to preliminary suppositions that the incomes would be much higher in the competitive sector. According to these two databases there is consequently a difference in managerial incomes of private and public companies – with leaders of private companies earning more – but this difference is not considerable on average.

Survey respondents also had to assess on a scale of 0–100 how much influence people in various positions have on the country's important issues. The interviewees gave their opinion of how much influence on the current situation average citizens, top managers of big companies and banks, entrepreneurs of medium-sized firms and persons in similar positions as theirs, actually have. Several technical solutions are possible for measuring the subjective social influence that business leaders attribute to themselves. We have observed, however, that the leaders usually underestimate their personal influence,[2] and therefore their relative influence compared to that of average citizens is also biased. To get a distribution of attributed influence which most resembles normal distribution, we created a variable which measures the scale points given on the question of the influence of big companies' managers when the respondent is such a manager, of bank leaders in the case that the respondent is a banker, and finally the estimate of the entrepreneurs' influence when the respondent is the owner of a medium-sized company. That is, it does not measure the attributed influence of one's personal position, but the attributed *influence of one's own profession*. The distribution of this newly created variable is shown in Table 9.2. In terms of countries, Polish and Hungarian business leaders have a worse opinion of the influence of their own profession than do the leaders of East and West German companies.

Results indicate that in all four investigated territories, entrepreneurs have the lowest self-confidence concerning the influence their own profession. This

Table 9.2 Attributed influence of one's own profession on a 0–100 point scale[a]

		Poland	Hungary	E Germany	W Germany	Total sample
		N=95	*N=65*	*N=80*	*N=81*	*N=321*
Manager	Mean	36.65	44.91	57.79	50.81	47.16
	St. deviation	22.63	27.14	25.98	23.17	25.77
		N=28	*N=49*	*N=57*	*N=37*	*N=171*
Entrepreneur	Mean	21.45	13.49	22.93	21.72	19.73
	St. deviation	17.93	13.11	17.38	18.56	16.98
		N=16	*N=20*	*N=0*	*N=18*	*N=54*
Banker	Mean	49.00	60.50	–	53.00	54.56
	St. deviation	24.66	25.95	–	25.20	25.31
		N=139	*N=134*	*N=137*	*N=136*	*N=546*
Together	Mean	35.01	35.75	43.26	43.16	39.29
	St. deviation	23.24	28.78	28.52	25.77	26.86

Notes
a The question was the following: People may differ according to their influence on important issues of the country. Please mark on a scale from 0 to 100 how much influence do the following persons have on important issues of [country]. (Here 0 means no influence at all, and 100 means absolutely great influence.) [We are interested in how do you evaluate the present conditions, not an ideal one.]
1. An average citizen
2. A member of the national Parliament, who has experience in government or in key committees of Parliament
3. A top manager of one of the greatest companies in [country]
4. A top manager of one of the greatest banks in [country]
5. A leader of one of the greatest employers' organizations in [country]
6. An entrepreneur with a medium-sized company
7. A leader of one of the greatest trade unions in [country]
8. A man in a position like yours

is true for the Hungarian entrepreneurs first of all, whose average opinion was that they could only play a very insignificant role in the important issues of the country. The subjective estimations of Polish, West and East German leaders were fairly similar and slightly more positive than that of their Hungarian colleagues; however they also believe that they have only little influence in important nationwide issues. Half of the Hungarian entrepreneurs give themselves just slightly more than 10 points as an evaluation of their own situation, while this is 20 points for the Polish, West and East German leaders. The standard deviation of entrepreneurs is the lowest among all three professions. Consequently the opinions of entrepreneurs fall closest to each other, especially in the case of Hungarian respondents, while among West German entrepreneurs they are the least similar.

Leaders occupying managerial posts consider their own profession more positively than the entrepreneurs of the investigated countries. Among the managers the East Germans hold their profession in the highest esteem, while the Polish managers ascribe the least value to their professional situation. Half of the managers of West Germany and Hungary believe that they have more than 50 scale points of influence regarding the main issues of their country. Half of the Polish managers award their own situation more, the other half less than 30 scale points, while the median value of East German managers is 65. With respect to the attributed influence of bankers, the database includes information only about the Hungarian, Polish and West German business leaders. This means that bankers value their own influence the most among the investigated position types in the three territories. Hungarian bankers esteem relatively highly their own profession on average, while Polish and West German bankers consider it medium-high estimable.

Models explaining the variance in income

In studies dealing with the subject of income it often occurs that incomes do not follow a normal distribution. That is why using a transformed version of income for various estimation procedures counts as an accepted method. As expected, the distribution of income in our study is not normal either. In order to solve this problem we used a logarithmic normal distribution model which is the most common transforming method in the income research literature. Therefore the logarithm of income was used in the regression models as the dependent variable. This transformation also has the positive effect of reducing the influence of large values and outliers.

The findings are shown in Table 9.3.a and Table 9.3.b. According to the organization model – with the other explanatory variables controlled for – the company size has a significant positive effect on the income of business leaders. The income of business leaders occupying positions in big companies is higher on average than that of leaders working in medium-sized companies.

Another relation can be observed between the incomes of bankers and other company leaders. The data indicate that the average income of bankers was significantly higher than that of the other company leaders. In the same way a positive connection can be revealed between the average annual income of leaders and foreign ownership. Controlling for the other explanatory variables, it is seen that leaders working in companies partly or fully in foreign ownership earn significantly more than the leaders of domestic firms.

We can see in the case of the organization model that the geographical location of the company is decisive for the manager income. German, especially West German business leaders, earned significantly more, and Polish leaders slightly more than their Hungarian colleagues. However, the country variable can be rather considered a contextual variable and its effect should be taken into account in the case of the other model as well, and thus it cannot with certainty be reckoned to be among the organizational characteristics.

As a conclusion regarding the organization model it can be stated that the average annual income of business leaders is truly influenced by the company's *sector* (bank or other company), *size and ownership*. However, the development

Table 9.3.a Organization model

Model	Unstandardized coefficients		Standardized coefficients		
	B	Std. error	Beta	t	Sig.
(Constant)	10.010	0.116		86.427	0.000
Size	0.577	0.087	0.253	6.638	0.000
Bank	0.970	0.146	0.257	6.664	0.000
Polish[a]	0.411	0.112	0.163	3.674	0.000
W German[a]	1.756	0.114	0.698	15.454	0.000
E German[a]	1.525	0.110	0.656	13.812	0.000
100 % foreign ownership[b]	0.352	0.106	0.125	3.332	0.001
Partly foreign ownership[b]	0.447	0.140	0.119	3.182	0.002
Number of employees increased[c]	−0.058	0.098	−0.026	−0.592	0.554
Number of employees decreased[c]	−0.214	0.105	−0.091	−2.038	0.042
Number of employees fluctuated[c]	−0.076	0.138	−0.022	−0.550	0.583

Notes
Dependent Variable: Logarithm of income in Euro.
a Reference category: Hungarian sample.
b Reference category: no foreign ownership.
c Reference category: number of employees did not change.
N = 400
Adjusted R^2 = 0.514
F = 43.230; Sig. = 0.000

of employment dynamics of the past three years has had an effect only in the case of employment decline. Compared to companies where no changes in employment occurred, the leaders of firms where employment previously decreased had less income.

According to the individual characteristics model, two personal attributes especially have an effect on business leaders' income. One of those is *multipositionality* (interlocking). Controlling for the other explanatory variables, it can be clearly seen that those leaders who occupied other business posts along with non-business posts in addition to their current position, had higher incomes than those not having any further business or non-business positions. Also those leaders who occupied more than one business post – in addition to their actual position – earned more annual income than those colleagues who did not have any further business position or position outside of business. However, it seems that in reality the extra business position causes the increase in the income, because a further non-business position alone has only a slightly significant influence on the development of income.

The other individual characteristic which has an important impact on a leader's earnings is *foreign experience*. This is true not only for education but for work experience as well. The income of those business leaders who have worked abroad is significantly higher than those who have not had any foreign work experience.

Table 9.3.b Individual characteristics model

Model	Unstandardized coefficients		Standardized coefficients		
	B	Std. error	Beta	t	Sig.
(Constant)	10.207	0.349		29.269	0.000
BA/MA	0.238	0.264	0.050	0.903	0.368
Engineer/business	−0.015	0.113	−0.008	−0.130	0.896
Have learnt abroad	0.596	0.133	0.255	4.464	0.000
Have worked abroad	0.253	0.108	0.133	2.343	0.020
Starting year of the career	−0.065	0.055	−0.065	−1.178	0.240
Number of companies	0.005	0.075	0.003	0.062	0.951
Entrepreneur	−0.100	0.112	−0.050	−0.896	0.371
Multipositionality: only business[a]	0.390	0.142	0.160	2.750	0.006
Multipositionality: only outside business[a]	0.216	0.128	0.102	1.685	0.093
Multipositionality: business and outside business[a]	0.571	0.160	0.216	3.576	0.000
Polish[b]	0.031	0.180	0.013	0.171	0.864
W German[b]	1.223	0.166	0.565	7.364	0.000
E German[b]	0.907	0.172	0.455	5.261	0.000

Notes
Dependent Variable: Logarithm of income in euro.
a Reference category: no other position.
b Reference category: Hungarian sample.
N = 226
Adjusted R^2 = 0.391
F = 12.119; Sig. = 0.000

Similarly, business leaders with educational experiences abroad earned more than those who never studied in a foreign country.

As expected, the impact of the country variable remains in the case of this model – except for the significant relation between Poland and Hungary, which has vanished. These facts fortify that argument, whereas the country where the company is located and where the business leader is working can rather be considered a contextual variable, which includes numerous latent variables. Thus strictly, it can be reckoned among neither model's variables; however, its effect has to be taken into account independently of the models. Summarizing the findings of the individual characteristics model it can be stated that, in the income of business leaders, *the interlocking* and *the foreign educational and work experiences* play a significant role.

In considering both models it seems that the organizational characteristics exert a greater influence on incomes compared to the individual attributes. To verify this argument we put all the significant variables of both models into one multiple regression. Table 9.3.c presents the results. First of all, although most of the

Table 9.3.c Impact of organizational and individual characteristics on income

Model	Unstandardized coefficients		Standardized coefficients		
	B	Std. error	Beta	t	Sig.
(Constant)	9.917	0.135		73.532	0.000
Size	0.423	0.092	0.208	4.611	0.000
Bank	0.676	0.154	0.217	4.386	0.000
Polish[a]	0.241	0.140	0.107	1.717	0.087
W German[a]	1.623	0.143	0.727	11.379	0.000
E German[a]	1.373	0.141	0.677	9.745	0.000
100 % foreign ownership[b]	0.343	0.113	0.139	3.033	0.003
Partly foreign ownership[b]	0.562	0.153	0.163	3.673	0.000
Have studied abroad	0.385	0.110	0.159	3.513	0.001
Have worked abroad	0.045	0.087	0.023	0.513	0.608
Multipositionality: only business[c]	0.299	0.111	0.120	2.680	0.008
Only outside business[c]	0.047	0.101	0.021	0.469	0.639
Business and outside business[c]	0.377	0.125	0.141	3.014	0.003

Notes
Dependent Variable: Logarithm of income in euro.
a Reference category: Hungarian sample.
b Reference category: no foreign ownership.
c Reference category: no other position.
N = 302
Adjusted R^2 = 0.502
F = 26.291; Sig. = 0.000

variables have lost in their independent explanatory power, their effects have still remained significant except for the foreign work experience. Consequently, it seems that the models label variables influencing the income of business leaders. On the other hand, according to the standardized coefficients, the organizational characteristics count more.

Models explaining the variance in attributed influence

In this part we investigate how the judgement of social influence is affected by the organizational and personal explanatory variables mentioned above. We use linear regression analysis – within countries and for the total sample – to examine how corporate attributes on the one hand, and individual characteristics on the other have an impact on the business leaders' opinions on the influence of their own profession on important social issues.

For Poland, it is the sector, or more exactly, the banking sector, that has the biggest effect among the organizational characteristics affecting attributed influence. As in Table 9.4.a, bankers judge their own profession's chances to influence social issues as significantly better on average than do the leaders of

Table 9.4.a Organization model

	Poland (N=154)	Hungary (N=132)	E Germans (N=213)	W Germans (N=186)	Total sample (N=517)
Constant	33.9	23.9	41.9	38.2	29.0
Bank	17.3	21.3	ns	ns	18.1
Size	−7.6	ns	ns	10.6	ns
Foreign ownership[a]	ns	19.6	16.9	ns	11.9
Employment increased[b]				−9.5	ns
Polish[c]	−	−	−	−	ns
W German[c]	−	−	−	−	9.4
E German[c]	−	−	−	−	12.8
Adjusted R^2	0.14***	0.2****	0.05	0.13****	0.09****
F	3.9	6.6	2.1	5.5	6.7

Notes
Dependent variable: attributed influence of one's own profession on a 0–100 scale. B values.
Significance: **** = 0.000; *** = 0.00.
a Reference category: no foreign ownership.
b Reference category: did not change.
c Reference category: Hungarian sample.

other companies. Company size also has a significant impact on attributed influence among the Polish leaders. Leaders of big companies estimate their profession's influence less highly than their counterparts from medium-sized companies. Due to the fact that banks are overrepresented among big companies, there is an overlap between sector and size which may lead to a cross effect between the variables. If leaders of smaller banks assess their profession's influence highly, in a regression model it may lead to the result of a positive 'bank' and negative 'size' effect.

The banking sector, as well as foreign ownership, among organizational attributes, play a significant role in the case of Hungarian leaders. Hungarian bankers, ceteris paribus, assess the social influence of their profession higher than leaders of other types of companies. Furthermore, respondents working at foreign firms see their power on the country's important issues much more positively than do their counterparts from domestic companies.

For the East German sample, the model is not significant and we found only the effect of foreign ownership as a significant factor among organizational character-istics – respondents from foreign owned companies think more positively about the influence of their profession than the leaders of domestic firms. The reason for this is probably that this sub-sample does not contain banks, and therefore the impact of the bank/company distinction could not appear.

For West Germany, a significant positive effect can be pointed out for company size, and a negative one for growth. Leaders from companies where employment had increased in the last three years estimated their attributed influence lower than managers of those firms where the number of employees remained unchanged. In this case, organizational change has a negative connection with the leaders' subjective sense of occupational prestige. Here again, the effect of the organizational field could reverse the impact of employment dynamics: banks increased their employee numbers less than industrial firms, on average.

Analysing the countries together, the *banking sector* and the form of ownership, to put it properly, *foreign ownership*, plays an important role in the evaluation of influence. The analysis shows that, with all the other variables controlled for, bankers assessed the attributed influence of their profession more positively than the business leaders of other companies. Furthermore, leaders of foreign companies valued their influence on the country's important questions higher than did the respondents of domestic firms. We argue that, referring to the role that countries – as contextual explanatory variables – played in the explanation of attributed influence, a significant difference can be pointed out between the German and other respondents' opinions. Both West and East German business leaders considered their profession's influence to be significantly greater than the Hungarian and Polish respondents did theirs.

As to the analysis of personal characteristics, the time spent in a leading position affects the evaluation of influence – however, not in a relation of 'the longer the higher', but the later the starting point of the career of Polish business leaders, the higher is their self-attributed influence. Every extra year of delay in starting a leader's career means an increase of 0.8 scale points in attributed influence on average. It seems that respondents having a long career path become more and more disappointed with their attributed influence over time. We did not find any sector effect behind this coincidence: both bankers and industrial leaders started their careers around 1985 on average. Studies abroad had a negative effect as well. However, the whole model, in the case of Poland, could not explain much and was not significant.

In Hungary there is a significant negative effect on the subjective judgement if the respondent is an *entrepreneur*. The results in Table 9.4.b indicate that entrepreneurs see much more negatively their own profession's influence than their manager and banker colleagues in all the investigated countries. Multipositionality on the other hand had no significant effect on the attributed influence of business leaders in Hungary.

As in the Hungarian results, the entrepreneurial position also has a significant negative effect on attributed influence among the personal characteristics in the case of West and East German leaders. In this respect the findings for the two German territories are very similar. It can be said that in both parts of Germany, owner-managers judge their own influence regarding the important issues of the country by 32 scale points less on average than managers do. The model fits leaders of East German companies better.

In the total sample, the entrepreneurial position has a significant negative impact on the attributed influence, if all the other explanatory variables are controlled for. The results indicate that entrepreneurs esteem their own profession's influence worse than the leaders in managerial positions. As to the effect of

Table 9.4.b Individual characteristics model

	Poland (N=50)	Hungary (N=42)	E Germany (N=77)	W Germany (N=57)	Total sample (N=226)
Constant	−1567.6	−550.2	−271.5	−160.3	586.9
Entrepreneur	ns	−30.9	−31.6	−32.1	−29.1
Studied abroad	−20.1	ns	ns	ns	ns
Starting year of the career	0.8	ns	ns	ns	0.3
Polish[a]	−	−	−	−	−11.5
W German[a]	−	−	−	−	ns
E German[a]	−	−	−	−	ns
Adjusted R^2	0.1	0.4***	0.2***	0.2**	0.3****
F	1.8	3.9	3.5	2.6	7.9

Notes
Dependent variable: attributed influence of one's own profession on a 0–100 scale. Variables not significant in any of the above models: level and type of education; work experiences abroad; multipositionality, income; B values. Significance: **** = 0.000; *** = 0.00; ** = 0.01.
a Reference category: Hungarian sample.

countries there is a statistically significant difference between the Polish and the Hungarian business leaders' opinions. Polish respondents attributed to their profession less influence than Hungarian leaders did to theirs.

There was no connection between income and influence in any of the investigated business communities when other personal characteristics were controlled for. Without controlling for the other personal variables, a weak, not significant, negative correlation is seen between the variables of income and influence in most of the investigated countries, while in Hungary the correlation is modest, significant and positive. Even by taking into consideration the managerial, banking and entrepreneurial positions separately, no significant connection between attributed influence and income can be observed. This does not mean that in a wider social context there is no connection between income and occupational prestige. Indeed, according to most research evidence, there is. But within the relatively homogenous group of business leaders, because of isomorphic processes, these connections are relatively weak and negligible.

In investigating the impact of organizational and individual conditions on perceived influence together, neither country, foreign ownership nor multipositionality effects could be detected. Among the three remaining explanatory variables, the most important is entrepreneurship (Table 9.4.c). There is a size effect behind this, because entrepreneurs are usally active owners of smaller companies and they tend to systematically estimate as lower the effect of their profession's influence than managers do theirs.

The economic sector – if the company is a bank – has a positive effect on perceived influence. Here again, the effects of size, sector and profession are interlinked, with sector the most important. Finally, a slight negative impact of

Table 9.4.c Impact of organizational and individual characteristics on influence

Model	Unstandardized coefficients		Standardized coefficients		
	B	*Std. error*	*Beta*	*t*	*Sig.*
(Constant)	−645.9	331.2		−1.9	0.05
Bank	12.4	6.4	0.15	1.9	0.05
Entrepreneur	−27.9	3.8	0.48	7.4	0.000
Starting year of the career	0.33	0.17	0.12	1.9	0.05

Notes
Dependent variable: attributed influence of one's own profession on a 0–100 scale. Further non-significant variables: size, country, change of employees' number, foreign property, foreign educational and work experiences, level and type of education, income, multipositionality.
N = 227.
Adjusted R^2 = 0.29.
F = 5.9; Sig. = 0.000.

the length of career could be observed: the shorter the respondents' career, the higher they valued their profession's social influence. In this respect there are no differences between banks and other corporations – bankers do not differ significantly in terms of career length from the rest of the leaders – however other effects of organizational field and profession could be detected. Leaders of foreign companies and especially those of very large companies have shorter careers than the average; furthermore managers have shorter careers than owners: all these may add to the slight negative connection between length of career and perceived influence.

Conclusion

Relying upon these findings we may conclude that, for the explanation of business leaders' income, organizational attributes are more important than individual characteristics. This result coincides with the hypothesis of DiMaggio and Powell (1983), and the assumptions we made based on it.

Income could be better explained by the investigated organizational and individual characteristics than by attributed influence. As for attributed influence, among organizational characteristics, primarily the sector, namely, the bank/industry distinction and the foreign ownership have an impact on the attributed influence of business leaders. Company size possess a significant effect only in the case of Poland: while employment dynamics, only in West Germany.

Concerning personal characteristics affecting attributed influence we can establish that the entrepreneurial position – compared to the managerial one – is a negative factor in most of the participating countries. In Poland, the length of managerial experience also plays a negative role in the respondents' opinions about their influence, while multipositionality at the same time has no impact on attributed influence.

While in the case of income, the organizational characteristics proved to be more important, the attributed influence of one's own profession could be explained better in most of the cases by some of the individual characteristics of the business leaders. However, in most of the countries we could not find a significant connection between attributed influence and the type of degree or diploma, foreign work experience, multipositionality or income.

Earnings did depend more on organizational conditions, while influence had more to do with individual characteristics of leaders. That might be one of the reasons why there is no substantial connection between income and attributed influence in the business leaders' world.

According to our analysis, there are significant differences between economic sectors that affect business leaders' income and influence. However, processes of homogenization, coercion, mimesis and professionalization make these differences less significant and more casual within countries and within organizational fields.

Notes

1. One euro was the equivalent of HUF280.58 according to the average exchange rate in 2009. See MNB (Hungarian National Bank) statistics on foreign exchange rates (http://www.mnb.hu/Statisztika/statisztikai-adatok-informaciok/adatok-idosorok/vi-arfolyam, last accessed 27 March 2011).
2. There could be several reasons for that, and we mention just the two most plausible here. First there is a 'shyness factor', which suggests that one should be modest concerning his or her own position. The other explanation is a purely technical one: The instructions for the interviewers were straightforward and limited the interview to top personnel. In spite of that, in some cases we could not always get the most influential among these persons at a given company, especially in the case of computer-assisted telephone interviewing, in which the possibility of controlling the reliability of data is limited.

References

Chapter 1

Albert, M. (1993) *Capitalism against Capitalism*, London: Whurr.

Amable, B. (2003) *Diversity of Modern Capitalism*, Oxford: Oxford University Press.

Åslund, A. (2005) 'Comparative oligarchy: Russia, Ukraine and the United States', *Center for Social and Economic Research*, no. 296: Warsaw. Online. Available: <http://www.case.com.pl/upload/publikacja_plik/4931074_SA%20296last.pdf> (accessed 15 June 2012).

—— (2007) *Russia's Capitalist Revolution. Why Market Reforms Succeeded and Democracy Failed*, Washington, D.C.: Peterson Institute for International Economics.

Beyer, J. (2007) 'Primat der Finanzmarktorientierung. Zur Logik der Auflösung der Deutschland AG', *Berliner Debatte Initial*, 18 (4): 1–10.

Bluhm, K. (2007) *Experimentierfeld Ostmitteleuropa? Deutsche Unternehmen in Polen und der Tschechischen Republik*, Wiesbaden: VS Verlag.

—— (2010) 'Theories of capitalism put to the test: Introduction to a debate on Central and Eastern Europe', *Historical Social Research*, 35 (2): 197–217.

Bluhm, K. and Schmidt, R. (2008) 'Why should the varieties literature grant smaller firms more attention? An introduction', in K. Bluhm and R. Schmidt (eds): *Change in SMEs: Towards a New European Capitalism?*, Houndmills: Palgrave Macmillan: 1–14.

Bluhm, K. and Trappmann, V. (2010) 'Varianten des Kapitalismus in Ostmitteleuropa. Varianten und externe Einflüsse. Eine Literaturkritik', *Osteuropa*, 60 (6): 61–74.

Bohle, D. (2002) *Europas neue Peripherie: Polens Transformation und transnationale Integration, Münster*: Westfälisches Dampfboot.

Bohle, D. and Greskovits, B. (2007a) 'Neoliberalism, embedded neoliberalism and neocorporatism: Towards transnational capitalism in Central and Eastern Europe', *West European Politics*, 30 (3): 433–66.

—— (2007b) 'The state, internationalization, and capitalist diversity in Eastern Europe', *Competition & Change*, 11 (2): 89–115.

—— (2009) 'Varieties of capitalism *and Capitalism* "tout court"', *European Journal of Sociology*, 50 (3): 355–86.

—— (2012) *Capitalist Diversity on Europe's Periphery*, Cornell: Cornell University Press.

Bohner, G. (2001) 'Attitudes', in M. Hewstone and W. Stroebe (eds) *Introduction to Social Psychology*, Oxford: Blackwell: 239–84.

Buchen, C. (2007) 'Estonia and Slovenia as antipodes', in D. Lane and M. Myant (eds) *Varieties of Capitalism in Post-Communist Countries*, Houndmills: Palgrave Macmillan: 65–89.

Burawoy, M. (2001) 'Neoclassical sociology: From the end of communism to the end of classes', *American Journal of Sociology*, 106 (4): 1099–1120.

Byrkjeflot, H. (2001) *Management Education and Selection of Top Managers in Europe and the United States*, Bergen: LOS-senteret rapport.

Cernat, L. (2006) *Europeanization, Varieties of Capitalism and Economic Performance in Central and Eastern Europe*, Houndmills: Palgrave Macmillan.

Crouch, C. and Farrell, H. (2004) 'Breaking the path of institutional development: Alternatives to the new determinism in political economy', *Rationality and Society*, 16 (1): 5–43.

Denzau, A. T. and North, D. (1994) 'Shared mental models: Ideology and institutions', *Kyklos,* 47 (1): 3–31.

DiMaggio, P. and W. Powell (eds) (1991) *The New Institutionalism in Organizational Analysis*, Chicago: University of Chicago Press.

Dogan, M. and J. Higley (1998) 'Elites, crisis, and regimes in comparative analysis', in M. Dogan and J. Higley (eds) *Elite Crisis and the Origins of Regimes*, Lanham: Rowman & Littlefield Publishers: 3–27.

Drahokoupil, J. (2008a) *Globalization and The State in Central and Eastern Europe. The Politics of Foreign Direct Investment*, London: Routledge.

—— (2008b) 'The investment promotion machines. The politics of foreign direct investment promotion in Central and Eastern Europe', *Europe-Asia Studies*, 60 (2): 197–225.

Ebbinghaus, B. and P. Manow (eds) (2001) *Comparing Welfare Capitalism. Social Policy and Political Economy in Europe, Japan and the USA*, London: Routledge.

Elster, J., Offe, C. and Preuß, U. K. (1998) *Institutional Design in Post-Communist Societies: Rebuilding the Ship at Sea*, Cambridge: Cambridge University Press.

Eyal, G., Szelenyi, I. and Townsley, E. (1998) *Making Capitalism Withouth Capitalists: The New Class Formation and Elite Struggles in Post-Communist Central Europe*, London: Verso.

Faust, M. (2002) 'Karrieremuster von Führungskräften der Wirtschaft im Wandel – Der Fall Deutschland in vergleichender Perspektive', *SOFI-Mitteilungen*, 30: 69–90.

Feldmann, M. (2006) 'Emerging Varieties of Capitalism in Transition Countries. Industrial Relations and Wage Bargaining in Estonia and Slovenia', *Comparative Political Studies*, 39 (7): 829–54.

Frane, A. and Tomšič, M. (2002) 'Elite (re)configuration and politico-economic performance in post-socialist countries', *Europe-Asia Studies*, 54 (3): 435–454.

—— (2012) 'The dynamic of elites and the type of capitalism: Slovenian Exeptionalism?', *Historical Social Research*, 37 (2): 53–70.

Ganev, V. I. (2005) 'The "Triumph of Neoliberalism" reconsidered: Critical remarks on ideas centred analysis of political and economic change in post-communism', *East European Politics and Societies*, 19 (3): 343–78.

—— (2007) *Preying on the State. The Transformation of Bulgaria after 1989*, Ithaca: Cornell University Press.

—— (2009) 'Postcommunist political capitalism: a Weberian Interpretation', *Comparative Studies in Society and History*, 51 (3): 648–74.

Grabbe, H. (2006) *The EU's Transformative Power. Europeanization through Conditionality in Central and Eastern Europe*, Houndmills: Palgrave Macmillan.

Granovetter, M. (1985) 'Economic action and social structure: the problem of embeddedness', *American Journal of Sociology*, 91 (3): 481–510.

Hall, P.A. and Soskice, D. (2001) 'Introduction to varieties of capitalism', in P. A. Hall and D. Soskice (eds) *Varieties of Capitalism: The Institutional Foundations of Comparative Advantage*, Oxford: Oxford University Press: 1–68.

Hancké, B., Rhodes, M., and Thatcher, M. (2007) 'Introduction: Beyond Varieties of Capitalism', in B. Hancké, M. Rhodes and M. Thatcher (eds) *Beyond Varieties of Capitalism: Conflict, Contradictions, and Complementarities in the European Economy*, Oxford: Oxford University Press: 3–38.

Hanley, E. (1999) 'Cadre capitalism in Hungary and Poland: Property accumulation among communist-era elites', *East European Politics & Societies*, 14 (1): 143–78.

Hartmann, M. (2006) 'Vermarktlichung der Elitenrekrutierung? Das Beispiel der Topmanager', in H. Münkler, G. Straßenberger and M. Bohlender (eds) *Deutschlands Eliten im Wandel*, Frankfurt am Main: Campus.

Hellman, J. S. (1998) 'Winners take all: The politics of partial reforms in postcommunist transitions', *World Politics*, 51 (2): 203–34.

Higley, J. and Lengyel, G. (2000) 'Introduction: Elite configuration after state socialism', in J. Higley and G. Lengyel (eds) *Elites After State Socialism. Theories and Analysis*, Lanham: Rowan & Littlefield: 1–21.

Höpner, M. (2003) 'Der organisierte Kapitalismus in Deutschland und sein Niedergang', *Politische Vierteljahresschrift*, Sonderheft 34: 300–324.

—— (2004) 'Was bewegt die Führungskräfte? Von der Agency-Theorie zur Soziologie des Managements', *Soziale Welt*, 55 (3): 263–282.

Imbusch, P. and Rucht, D. (eds) (2007) *Profit oder Gemeinwohl? Fallstudien zur gesellschaftlichen Verantwortung von Wirtschaftseliten*, Wiesbaden: VS Verlag.

King, L. P. and Szelényi, I. (2005) 'Post-Communist Economic Systems', in N. Smelser and R. Swedberg (eds) *The Handbook of Economic Sociology*, Princeton; Princeton University Press: 205–29.

King, L. P. (2002) 'Post-Communist divergence: A comparative analysis of transitions to capitalism in Poland and Russia', *Studies in Comparative International Development*, 37 (3): 3–44.

—— (2007) 'Central European capitalism in comparative perspective', in R. Hanké, M. Thatcher and M. Rhodes (eds) *Beyond Varieties of Capitalism*, Oxford: Oxford University Press: 307–27.

Knell, M. and Srholec, M. (2007) 'Emerging varieties of capitalism in Central and Eastern Europe', in D. Lane and M. Myant (eds) *Varieties of Capitalism in Post-Communist Countries*, Houndmills: Palgrave Macmillan: 40–63.

Kogan, I. (2008) 'Education systems in Central and Eastern European countries', in I. Kogan, M. Gebel and C. Nölke (eds) *Europe Enlarged. Handbook of Education, Labour and Welfare Regimes in Central and Eastern Europe*, Bristol: Policy Press: 7–37.

Kornai, J. (1990) *The Road to a Free Economy. Shifting from a Socialist System: The Example of Hungary*, London: W. W. Norton.

Krishtanovskaia, O. and White, S. (1999) 'From *Nomenklatura* to New Elite', in V. Shlapentokh, C. Vanderpool and B. Doktorov (eds) *The New Elite in Post-Communist Eastern Europe*, Texas: Texas A&M University Press.

Kutter, A. and Trappmann, V. (eds) (2006) *Das Erbe des Beitritts. Europäisierung in Mittel- und Osteuropa*, Baden-Baden: Nomos.

Lane, C. (1989) *Management and Labour in Europe. The Industrial Enterprise in Germany, Britain and France*, Aldershot: Edward Elgar.

Lane, D. (2007) 'Post-state socialism: A diversity of capitalism?', in D. Lane and M. Myant (eds) *Varieties of Capitalism in Post-Communist Countries*, Houndmills: Palgrave Macmillan: 65–89.

—— (2011) *Elite and Classes in the Transformation of State Socialism*, New Brunswick: Transaction Publications.

Lepsius, M. R. (1990a) 'Institutionenanalyse und Institutionenpolitik', *Kölner Zeitschrift für Soziologie und Sozialpsychologie* Sonderheft, 35: 392–403.

—— (1990b) *Interessen, Ideen und Institutionen.* Opladen: Westdeutscher Verlag.

Machonin, P., Tuček, M. and Nekola, M. (2006) 'The Czech economic elite after fifteen years of post-socialist transformation', *Czech Sociological Review*, 42 (3): 537–556.

Myant, M. (2003) *The Rise and Fall of Czech Capitalism: Economic Development in the Czech Republic since 1989*, Cheltenham: Edward Elgar Publishing Limited.

Myant, M. and Drahokoupil, J. (2011) *Transition Economies: Political Economy in Russia, Eastern Europe and Central Asia*, Hoboken: Wiley & Sons.

Nölke, A. and Vliegenthart, A. (2009) 'Enlarging the varieties of capitalism. The emergence of dependent market economies in East Central Europe', *World Politics*, 61 (4): 670–702.

Orenstein, M. A. (2001) *Out of the Red. Building Capitalism and Democracy in Post-Communist Europe*, Ann Arbor: University of Michigan Press

Ost, D. (2005) *The Defeat of Solidarity: Anger and Politics in Postcommunist Europe*, Ithaca: Cornell University Press.

Polanyi, K. ([1944] 1957) *The Great transformation: the Political and Economic Origins of Our Time*, Beacon Hill: Beacon Press.

Powell, W. W. (1990) 'Neither market nor hierarchy: Network forms of organization', in B.W. Staw and L.L. Cummings (eds) *Research in Organizational Behavior*, 12: 295–336.

Rae, G. (2008) *Poland's Return to Capitalism: From the Socialist Bloc to the European Union*, London: Tauris Academic Studies.

Rehberg, K. S. (2002) 'Institutionen, Kognitionen, Symbole-Institutionen als symbolische Verkörperungen, in A. Maurer and J. Schmidt (eds) *Neuer Institutionalismus*, Frankfurt am Main: Campus: 39–56.

Shield, S. (2012) *The International Political Economy of Transition*, London: Routledge.

Schmidt, R. and Gergs, H.J. (2002) 'Generationswechsel im Management ost- und westdeutscher Unternehmen. Kommt es zu einer Amerikanisierung des deutschen Managementmodells?', *Kölner Zeitschrift für Soziologie und Sozialpsychologie*, 54 (3): 553–78.

Schmidt, V. A. (2003) 'French capitalism transformed yet still a third variety of capitalism', *Economy and Society*, 32 (4): 526–54.

Scott, R. W. (2008) *Institutions and Organizations. Ideas and Interests*, London: Sage.

Sorge, A. and Warner, M. (1980) 'Manpower training, manufacturing organisation and workplace relations in Great Britain and West Germany', *British Journal of Industrial Relations*, 18 (3): 318–33.

Staniszkis, J. (1991) *The Dynamics of the Breakthrough in Eastern Europe: The Polish Experience*, Berkeley: University of California Press.

Stark, D. and Bruszt, L. (1998) *Postsocialist Pathways. Transforming Politics and Property in East Central Europe*, Cambridge: Cambridge University Press.

Stewart, R., Barsoux, J. L., Kieser, A., Ganter, H. D. and Walgenbach, P. (1994) *Managing in Britain and Germany*, New York: St. Martin's Press.

Streeck, W. (1997) 'German capitalism. Does it exist? Can it survive?', in C. Crouch (ed.) *Political Economy of Modern Capitalism. Mapping Convergence and Diversity*, London: Sage: 33–54.

—— (2009) *Re-Forming Capitalism: Institutional Change in the German Political Economy*, Oxford and New York: Oxford University Press.

—— (2012) 'How to study contemporary capitalism?', *European Journal of Sociology*, 53 (1): 1–28.

Streeck, W. and Yamuara, K. (eds) (2001) *The Origins of Nonliberal Capitalism: Germany and Japan*, Ithaca: Cornell University Press.

Trappmann, V. (2013) *Fallen Heroes in Global Capitalism. Workers and the Restructuring of the Polish Steel Industry*, Houndsmill: Palgrave Macmillan.

Volkov, V. (2000) 'Patrimonialism versus rational bureaucracy: on the historical relativity of corruption', in S. Lovell, A. Ledeneva, and A. Rogachevskii (eds) *Bribery and Blat in Russia*, London: MacMillan Press: 35–47.

Walder, A.G. (2003) 'Elite opportunity in transitional economies', *American Sociological Review*, 68 (6): 899–916.

Williamson, O. E. (1996) *Mechanism of Governance*, Oxford: Oxford University Press.

Chapter 2

Amable, B. (2003) *The Diversity of Modern Capitalism*, Oxford: Oxford University Press.

Amsden, A. H., Kochanowicz, J. and Taylor, L. (1994) *The Market Meets Its Match. Restructuring the Economies of Eastern Europe*, Cambridge: Harvard University Press.

Balcerowicz, L. (1995) *Wolność i Rozwój. Ekonomia Wolnego Rynku*, Kraków: Znak.

Barlik, E. (1998) 'Polscy Menedżerowie: zarządzanie w czasach zmian', Warszawa: Coopers & Lybrand.

Berend, I. T. (1996) *Central and Eastern Europe 1944–1993. Detour from the Periphery to the Periphery*, Cambridge: Cambridge University Press.

Błaszczak, A. (2010) 'Polskie szkoły szefów dużych firm', *Rzeczpospolita*: B4.

Bohle, D. and Greskovits, B. (2012) *Capitalist Diversity on Europe's Periphery*, Cornell: Cornell University Press.

Boni, M. (2009) *Polska 2030. Wyzwania rozwojowe*, Warszawa.

Borragán, N. P. S. and de Waele, J. M. (eds) (2006) 'Special issue: Interest politics in Central and Eastern Europe', *Perspective on European Politics and Society*, 7 (2).

Bratkowski, S. and Bratkowski, A. (2011) *Gra o Jutro. Co Warto Zrobić Teraz z Myślą o Wnukach*, Warszawa: Studio Emka.

Castells, M. (2004) *The Power of Identity. The Information Age: Economy, Society and Culture*, Volume 2, Oxford: Wiley-Blakwell.

Chojna, J. (2010) 'Miejsce podmiotów z kapitałem zagranicznym w gospodarce narodowej Polski', in J. Chojna (ed.) *Inwestycje zagraniczne w Polsce*, Warszawa Instytut Badań Rynku, Konsumpcji i Koniunktur: 184–216.

Cześnik, M. (2009) *Partycypacja wyborcza Polaków*, Warszawa: Instytut Spraw Publicznych.

Deeg, R. (2010) 'Institutional Change in Financial Systems', in G. Morgan, J. L. Campbell, C. Crouch and O. K. Pedersen (eds) *The Oxford Handbook of Comparative Institutional Analysis*, Oxford: Oxford University Press: 309–34.

Domański, H. (2002) *Polska Klasa Średnia*, Wrocław: Fundacja na rzecz nauki polskiej.

—— (2009) *Społeczeństwa Europejskie. Stratyfikacja i Systemy Wartości*, Warszawa: Scholar.

Drahokoupil, J. (2008) *Globalization and The State in Central and Eastern Europe. The Politics of Foreign Direct Investment*, London: Routledge.

Drahokoupil, J. and Myant, M. (2010) 'Varieties of capitalism, varieties of vulnerabilities: Financial crises and its impact on welfare states in Eastern Europe and the Commonwealth of Independent States', *Historical Social Research*, 35 (2): 266–95.

European Commission (EC) (2006) *Industrial relations in Europe 2006*, Brussels: European Commission. Directorate-General for Employment, Social Affairs and Equal Opportunities.

European Industrial Relations Observatory (EIRO) (2010) *Industrial relations developments in Europe 2009*, Luxembourg: Office for Official Publications of the European Communities.

Federowicz, M. (2004) *Różnorodność Kapitalizmu. Instytucjonalizm i Doświadczenie Zmiany Ustrojowej po Komunizmie*, Warszawa: IFiS PAN.

Galbraith, J. K. (2004) *The Economics of Innocent Fraud. Truth for Our Time*, New York: Houghton Milfin Company.

Gardawski, J. (2001) *Powracająca Klasa: Sektor Prywatny w III Rzeczypospolitej*, Warszawa: Wydawn. Instytutu Filozofii i Socjologii PAN.

—— (2009) *Polacy Pracujący a Kryzys Fordyzmu*, Warszawa: Wydawn. Naukowe Scholar.

Górniak, J. (2010) 'Relacje między przedsiębiorstwami, urzędami a państwem: obszary problemowe', in *Państwo-Urzędy-Przedsiębiorstwa: Bariery Rozwoju Biznesu a Rynek Pracy*. Warszawa.

Greskovits, B. (2000) 'Rival views of postcommunist market society. The path dependence of transitology', in M. Dobry (ed.) *Democratic and Capitalist Transitions in Eastern Europe. Lessons for the Social Sciences*, Dordrecht: Kluwer Academic Publishers: 19–24.

Grzymała-Busse, A. (2007) *Rebuilding Leviathan. Party Competition and State Exploitation in Post-Communist Democracies*, Cambridge: Cambridge University Press.

Hall, P. A. and Soskice, D. (2001) *Varieties of Capitalism. The Institutional Foundations of Comparative Advantage*, Oxford: Oxford University Press.

Hampden-Turner, C. and Trompenaars, A. (1993) *The Seven Cultures of Capitalism*, London: Piatkus.

Hausner, J. (2007) *Pętle Rozwoju. O Polityce Gospodarczej Lat 2001–2005*, Warszawa: Scholar.

Hausner, J., Kwiecińska, D. and Pacut, A. (2007) 'Modele polityki społecznej-doświadczenia europejskie', in D. K. Rosati (ed.) *Europejski Model Społeczny-Doświadczenia i Kierunki Zmian*. Warszawa.

Hofstede, G. and Hofstede, G. J. (2005) *Cultures and Organizations. Software of the Mind*, New York: McGraw-Hill.

Huntington, S. P. (2005) *Who Are We? America's Great Debate*, London: Simon & Schuster.

Jackson, G. (2010) 'Actors and Institutions', in G. Morgan, J. L. Campbell, C. Crouch, and O. K. Pedersen (eds) *The Oxford Handbook of Comparative Institutional Analysis*, Oxford: Oxford University Press: 63–115.

Jałowiecki, B. (2010) *Społeczne Wytwarzanie Przestrzeni*, Warszawa: Scholar.

Jasiecki, K. (2002) *Elita Biznesu w Polsce: Drugie Narodziny Kapitalizmu*, Warszawa: Wydawn. IFiS PAN.

—— (2004) *Postrzeganie Polskiej Marki w Krajach Unii Europejskiej*, Warszawa: Polska Agencja Rozwoju Przedsiębiorczości.

—— (2007) 'Korzyści i koszty działania hipermarketów', *Prakseologia*, 147: 115–146.

—— (2008a) 'The changing roles of the post-transnational economic elite in Poland', *Journal for East European Management Studies*, 13 (4): 327–59.

—— (2008b) 'The Europeanization of Polish Democracy', *Polish Sociological Review*, 4 (164): 359–382.

Jasiecki, K., Molęda-Zdziech, M. and Kurczewska, U. (2006) *Lobbing. Sztuka Skutecznego Wywierania Wpływu*, Kraków: Oficyna Ekonomiczna.

Jaworski, W. L. (2009) 'Kredyty banków komercyjnych warunkiem ograniczenia kryzysu', in S. Jan (ed.) *Globalny Kryzys Finansowy i Jego Konsekwencje w Opiniach Ekonomistów Polskich*, Warszawa: Związek Banków Polskich: 71–4.

Kamiński, A. Z. and Kurczewska, J. (1994) 'Institutional transformations in Poland: The rise of nomadic political elites', in M. Alestalo, E. Allard, A. Rychard, and W. Wesołowski (eds) *The Transformation of Europe. Social Conditions and Consequences*, Warsaw: IFiS Publisher: 132–53.

Kaufman, D., Krasy, A. and Massimo, M. (2009) 'Governance matters VIII: Aggregate and individual governance indicators for 1996–2008', World Bank Policy Research Working Paper No. 4978. Online. Available from: <http://papers.ssrn.com/sol3/papers.cfm?abstract_id=1424591> (accessed 24 April 2012).

Kłosiewicz-Górecka, U. (2010) 'Wielkość i struktura oraz skutki BIZ w sferze handlu wewnętrznego w Polsce', in *Inwestycje Zagraniczne w Polsce*, Warszawa: Instytut Badań Rynku, Konsumpcji i Koniunktur: 265–92.

Komisja Nadzoru Finansowego (2012) 'Raport o sytuacji banków w 2011 r.', Urząd Komisja Nadzoru Finansowego, Warszawa. Online. Available from: <http://www.knf.gov.pl/Images/RAPORT_2011_tcm75–31319.pdf> (accessed 24 April 2012).

Kowalik, T. (2000) *Współczesne Systemy Ekonomiczne*, Warszawa: Akademia im. Leona Koźmińskiego.

Koźmiński, A. K. (2011) 'Czy polscy menedżerowie są przygotowani do konkurencji na rynkach europejskich?', in W. Kieżun (ed.) *Krytycznie i Twórczo o Zarządzaniu. Wybrane Zagadnienia*, Warszawa: Wolters Kluwers: 224–37.

Kułakowski, J. and Jesień, L. (2004) *Spotkania na Bagateli. Polska, Europa, Świat*. Warszawa: Rhetos.

Kuokstis, V. (2011) 'What type of capitalism do the Baltic countries belong to?', *EMECON: Employment and Economy in Central and Eastern Europe*, 1(2011). Online: Available from: <http://www.emecon.eu/current-issue/second/vytautas-kuokstis/>.

Kuźniar, R. (2005): *Polityka I siła. Studia strategiczne—zarys problematyki*, Warszawa: Scholar

Laki, M. (2007) 'Attitudes and actions of the members of the hungarian business elites towards foreign owned companies', in D. Lane, G. Lengyel, and T. Jochen (eds) *Restructuring of the Economic Elites after State Socialism. Recruitment, Institutions and Attitudes,* Stuttgart: ibidem-Verlag: 199–209.

Lane, D. (2010) 'Post-socialist states and the world economy: The impact of global economic crisis', *Historical Social Research*, 35 (2): 218–41.

Lane, D., Lengyel, G. and Tholen, J. (eds) (2007) *Restructuring of the Economic Elites after State Socialism. Recruitment, Institutions and Attitudes*, Stuttgart: ibidem-Verlag.

Lane, D. and Myant, M. (2007) *Varieties of Capitalism in Post-Communist Countries*, Houndmills: Plagrave Macmillan.

Lepsius, M. R. (2007) 'Wpływ ładów instytucjonalnych na kulturę polityczną Republiki Federalnej Niemiec', in M. R. Lepsius (ed.) *O Kulturze Politycznej w Niemczech*, Poznań: Wydawnictwo Poznańskie: 207–33.

Lis, K. A. and Sterniczuk, H. (2005) *Nadzór Korporacyjny*. Kraków: Oficyna Ekonomiczna.

Mach, B. and Wesołowski, W. (2000) *Poland: The Political Elite's Transformational Correctness*, Landham New York Oxford: Rowman & Littlefield Publishers, INC.

Martens, B. (2008) 'East German economic elites and their companies two decades after the transformation ("Wende"): Still following the patterns of the 1990s', *Journal for East European Management Studies*, 13 (4): 305–26.

Mayhew, A. (1998) *Recreating Europe. The European Union's Policy towards Central and Eastern Europe*, Cambridge: Cambridge University Press.

Miklaszewska, E. (ed.) (1998) *Rozwój Polskiego Rynku Bankowego*, Kraków: Międzynarodowe Centrum Rozwoju Demokracji.

Misala, J. (2010) 'Rozwój handlu zagranicznego i imiędzynarodowej konkurencyjności gospodarki narodowej Polski', in M. A. Weresa (ed.) *Polska. Raport o Konkurencyjności. Klastry Przemysłowe a Przewagi Konkurencyjne*, Warszawa: Instytut Gospodarki Światowej. Szkoła Główna Handlowa: 71–88.

Myrdal, G. (1970) *The Challenge of World Poverty: The World Anti-Poverty Program in Outline*, New York: Random Hause.

Nölke, A. and Vliegenthart, A. (2009) 'Enlarging The varieties of capitalism: The emergence of dependent market economies in East Central Europe', *World Politics*, 4: 670–702.

Offe, C. (1996) *Varieties of Transition: The East European and East German Experience*, Cambridge: Polity.

Osborn, E. and Slomczynski, K.M. (2005) *Open for Business. The Persistent Entrepreneurial Class in Poland*, Warsaw: IFiS Publishers.

Ost, D. (2005) *The Defeat of Solidarity. Anger and Politics in Postcommunist Europe*, Ithaca: Cornell University.

Pieronkiewicz, H. (1998) 'Nierówny start', in E. Miklaszewska (ed.) *Rozwój Polskiego Rynku Bankowego*, Kraków: Międzynarodowe Centrum Rozwoju Demokracji: 13–20.

Radomski, B. (2010) 'Konkurencyjność Polski według raportów Międzynarodowego Instytutu Rozwoju Zarządzania (IMD) i Światowego Forum Ekonomicznego (WEF) w 2009', in M. A. Weresea (ed.) *Polska. Raport o Konkurencyjności 2010*, Warszawa: Instytut Gospodarki Światowej, Szkoła Główna Handlowa: 239–48.

Sapir, A. (2003) An Agenda for A Growing Europe. Making the EU Economic System Deliver, Brussels. Online. Available from: <http://serviziweb.unimol.it/unimol/allegati/docenti/2545/materiale/sapir%20report.pdf> (accessed 26 April 2012).

Schmidt, V. A. (2002) *The Futures of European Capitalism*, Oxford: Oxford University Press.

Sedelmeier, U. (2005) *Constructing the Path to Eastern Enlargement*, Manchester: Manchester University Press.

Shabad, G. and Słomczyński, K. (2010) 'National and/or European identity: Political elites and the mass public', in W. Wesołowski, K. M. Słomczyński and J. K. Dubrow (eds) *National and European? Polish Political Elite in Comparative Perspective*, Warsaw: IFiS Warsaw: 29–53.

Smelser, N. J. and Swedberg, R. (1994) *The Handbook of Economic Sociology*, Princeton: Princeton University Press.

Stark, D. and Bruszt, L. (1998) *Postsocialist Pathways. Transforming Politics and Property in East Central Europe*, Cambridge: Cambridge University Press.

Stiglitz, J. E. (2003) *The Roaring Nineties. A New History of the World's Most Prosperous Decade*, New York: W.W. Norton.

Sztanderska, U. (2010) 'Qualifications for Employers' Needs', Warsaw: Polish Confederation of Private Employers Lewiatan.

The World Bank (2004) 'Tertiary education in Poland', Warsaw: Warsaw Office.

—— (2012) 'The Doing Business 2012', *The World Bank*.

United Nations Development Programme (2009) *Human Development Report 2009. Overcoming Barriers: Human Mobility and Development*, Houndmills: Palgrave Macmillan.

228   *References*

Wedel, J. R. (2001) *Collision and Collusion. The Strange Case of Western Aid to Eastern Europe*, Houndmills: Palgrave Macmillan.
Zagoździńska, I. (2010) 'Podmioty z kapitałem zagranicznym w Polsce według danych Głównego Urzędu Statystycznego', in J. Chojna (ed.) *Inwestycje Zagraniczne w Polsce*, Warszawa: Instytut Badań Rynku, Konsumpcji i Koniunktur: 151–83.
Zarycki, T. (2009) *Peryferie. Nowe Ujęcia Zależności Centro-Peryferyjnych*, Warszawa: Scholar.
ZBP (Związek Banków Polskich) (2010) 'Wnioski z Forum Bankowego 2010', in ZBP (ed.) *XVI Forum Bankowe*, Warszawa.
Zerka, P. (2010) *Turning Gaps into Niches. For a New Innovation Paradigm in Central Europe*, Warsaw: Center for European Strategy.
Zieliński, R. (2012) 'E-afera', *Tygodnik Powszechny*: 10–11.
Zielonka, J. (2006) *Europe as Empire. The Nature of Enlarged European Union*, Oxford: Oxford University Press.

Chapter 3

Antalóczy, K. and Éltető, A. (2002) 'Magyar vállalatok nemzetköziesedése – indítékok, hatások és problémák', *Közgazdasági Szemle*, 49 (2): 158–72.
Antalóczy, K. and Sass, M. (2005) 'A külföldi működőtőke-befektetések regionális elhelyezkedése és gazdasági hatásai Magyarországon', *Közgazdasági Szemle*, 52 (4): 494–520.
Báger, G. and Kovács, Á. (2004) 'A magyarországi privatizáció néhány tanulsága' *Fejlesztés és Finanszírozás*, 4: 27–37.
Bank D., Bíró P., Tompa, T. and Udvardi, A. (2009) *A társadalmi felelősségvállalás szerepe és szintje a hazai vállalkozások körében*, GKI Zrt. (GKI Economic Research Co.): 3–10.
Bauer, T. (1978) 'Investment cycles in planned economies', *Acta Oeconomica*, 21 (3): 243–60.
Berend, T. I. (2003) 'A jóléti állam: válság és kiutak', *Magyar Tudomány*, 10: 1273.
Bohle, D. and Greskovits, B. (2009) 'Varieties of capitalism and capitalism "tout court"', *European Journal of Sociology*, 50 (3): 355–86.
—— (2012) *Capitalist Diversity on Europe's Periphery*, Cornell: Cornell University Press.
Brinton, M. C. and Nee, V. (eds) (1998) *The New Institutionalism in Sociology*, York: Russel Sage Foundation.
Czakó, Á., Lengyel, G., Kuczi, T. and Vajda, Á. (1994) *Vállalkozások és vállalkozók 1993*, Budapest: KSH.
Dervis, K. and Condon, T. (1994) 'Hungary – partial successes and remaining challenges: The emergence of a "dradualist" success story?', in O. J. Blanchard, K. A. Froot and J. D. Sachs (eds) *The Transition in Eastern Europe*, Vol. 1, Chicago: Chicago University Press: 123–54.
Drahokoupil, J. (2009) *Globalization and the State in Central and Eastern Europe. The Politics of Foreign Direct Investment*, London: Routledge.
EBRD (2011) *Transition Report 2010*, Online. Available from: <http://www.ebrd.com/pages/research/publications/flagships/transition.shtml> (accessed on 15 September 2012).
EBRD (2005) *Transition Report 2004*, Online. Available from: <http://www.ebrd.com/downloads/research/transition/TR04.pdf > (accessed on 14 September 2012).

Gazsó, F. (1990) 'A káderbürokrácia és az értelmiség', *Társadalmi Szemle*, 45 (11): 3–12.
—— (1993) 'Elitváltás Magyarországon', *Társadalmi Szemle*, 48 (5): 16–26.
Gábor, R. I. and Galasi, P. (1985) 'Second economy, state and labour Market', in P. Galasi, and G. Sziráczki (eds) *Labour Market and Second Economy in Hungary*, Frankfurt am Main: Campus: 122–32.
Giczi, J. and Sik, E. (2009) 'Trust and social capital in contemporary Europe', in I. Gy. Tóth (ed.) *European Social Report 2009*, Budapest: Tárki: 63–82.
Grabbe, H. (2006) *The EU's Transformative Power. Europeanization Through Conditionality in Central and Eastern Europe*, Houndmills: Palgrave Macmillan.
Hall, P. A. and Soskice, D. (eds) (2001) *Varieties of Capitalism. The Institutional Foundations of Comparative Advantage*, Oxford: Oxford University Press.
Hankiss, E. (1989) *Kelet-európai alternatívák*. Budapest: KJK.
Hanley, E., King, L., and Tóth, I. J. (2002) 'The state, international agencies, and property transformation in postcommunist Hungary', *American Journal of Sociology*, 108: 129–67.
HCSO (2007) *Hungarian Central Statistical Office Yearbook 2006*, Budapest: HCSO.
Higley, J. and Lengyel, G. (eds) (2000) *Elites after State Socialism. Theories and Analysis*, Lanham: Rowman & Littlefield.
Holusha, J. (1989) 'Venture Planned by G. E. in Hungary', *The New York Times*, 16. November 1989. Online. Available from: <http://www.nytimes.com/1989/11/16/business/venture-planned-by-ge-in- hungary.html> (accessed 17 October 2012).
Hunya, G. and Schwarzhappel, M. (2008) *Decline to Follow Uneven FDI Inflow Growth, WIIW Database on Foreign Direct Investment in Central, East and Southeast Europe*, Vienna: WIIW.
Jánossy, F. (1970) 'The origins of contradictions in our economy and the path to their Solution', *Eastern European Economics*, 3 (4): 357–90.
Juhász, P. (2006) *Emberek és intézmények. Két zsákutca az agráriumban*, Budapest: Új Mandátum Kiadó.
King, L. P. and Szelényi, I. (2005) 'Post-communist economic systems', in N. Smelser and R. Swedberg (eds) *The Handbook of Economic Sociology*, Princeton: Princeton University Press: 205–29.
King, L. P. and Sznajder, A. (2006) 'The state-led transition to liberal capitalism: Neoliberal, organizational, world systems, and social structural explanations of Poland's economic success', *American Journal of Sociology*, 112 (3): 751–801.
Kolosi, T. (2000) *A terhes babapiskóta. A rendszerváltás társadalomszerkezete*, Budapest: Osiris.
Kornai, J. (1990) *The Road to a Free Economy. Shifting from a Socialist System: The Example of Hungary*, London: W.W. Norton.
—— (1992) 'Posztszocialista átmenet és az állam. Gondolatok fiskális problémákról', *Közgazdasági Szemle*, 39 (6): 489–512.
—— (1996) 'Paying the bill for Goulash Communism: Hungarian development and macro stabilization in a political-economy perspective', *Social Research*, 63 (4): 943–1040.
Kovách, I. (ed.) (2011) *Elitek a válságkorában. Magyarországi elitek, kisebbségi magyar elitek*, Budapest: MTA Politikai Tudományok Intézete.
Kovács, Á. (2000) 'The effect of privatisation on state property', *Privatization in Hungary*: 55–63. Online. Available from: <http://www.nao.org.uk/nao/intosai/wgap/8thmeeting/hungary2chpt4.pdf> (accessed on 15 September 2012).
Köllő, J. (2009) *A pálya szélén – Iskolázatlan munkanélküliek a posztszocialista gazdaságban*, Budapest: Osiris.

Kuczi, T. (2000) *Kisvállalkozás és társadalmi környezet*, Budapest: Replika K.

Laki, M. (2002) 'A nagyvállalkozók tulajdonszerezési esélyeiről a szocializmus után', *Közgazdasági Szemle*, XLIX (1): 45–58.

Laki, M. and Szalai, J. (2004) *Vállalkozók, vagy polgárok?* Budapest: Osiris.

Lane, D. (2006) 'Post-state socialism: A diversity of capitalism?', in D. Lane and M. Myant (eds) *Varieties of Capitalism in Post-Communist Countries*, Houndmills: Palgrave Macmillan: 13–39.

Lengyel, G. (1992) *The Small Transformation: Changing Patterns of Recruitment of Managers and Entrepreneurs in Hungary*, Cornell Working Papers on Transitions from State Socialism, 92–7, Ithaca: Cornell University, Mario Einaudi Center for International Studies.

—— (2002) 'Social capital and entrepreneurial success. Hungarian small enterprises between 1993 and 1996', in V. E. Bonell and T .B. Gold (eds) *The New Entrepreneurs of Europe and Asia. Patterns of Business Development in Russia, Eastern Europe and China*, Armonk: M.E. Sharpe: 256–77.

—— (2007) *A magyar gazdasági elit társadalmi összetétele a 20. század végén*, Budapest: Akadémiai K.

—— (2012) *Potential Entrepreneurs. The Entrepreneurial Inclination in Hungary, 1988–2011*, Budapest: Corvinus University of Budapest.

Lengyel, G. and Rostoványi, Zs. (eds) (2001) *The Small Transformation. Society, Economy and Politics Hungary and the New European Architecture*, Budapest: Akadémiai K.

Lengyel, G. and Neumann, L. (2002) 'Hungary', in D. B. Cornfield and R. Hodson (eds) *Worlds of Work. Building an International Sociology of Work*, New York: Kluwer Academic/Plenum Publ.: 275–96.

Lengyel, G. and Róbert, P. (2003) 'Middle Classes in the Making in Central and Eastern Europe,' in V. Mikhalev (ed.) *Inequality and Social Structure during the Transition*, Houndmills: Palgrave Macmillan: 99–132.

Lengyel, G. and Ilonszki, G. (2012) 'Simulated democracy and pseudo-transformational leadership in Hungary', *Historical Social Research*, 37 (1): 107–26.

McMenamin, I. (2004) 'Varieties of capitalist democracy: What difference does East-Central Europe make?', *Journal of Public Policy*, 24 (3): 59–74.

Mihályi, P. (2010) *A magyar privatizáció enciklopédiája*, Budapest: Pannon Egyetemi Kiadó and MTA KTI.

NBH (National Bank of Hungary) (2007) *A közvetlen külföldi tőkebefektetés statisztikája Magyarországon, 1999–2005*, National Bank of Hungary: Budapest. Available from <http://www.mnb.hu/Statisztika/statisztikai-adatok-informaciok/adatok-idosorok/vii-kulkereskedelem/mnbhu_kozetlen_tokebef> (accessed on 15 September 2012).

Nölke, A. (2011) *Transnational Economic Order and National Economic Institutions. Comparative Capitalism Meets International Political Economy*, MPifG Working Paper 11/8, Max-Planck-Institut: Köln.

Nölke, A. and Vliegenhart, A. (2009) 'Enlarging the varieties of capitalism', *World Politics*, 61 (4): 670–702.

Polanyi, K. ([1944] 1957) *The Great Transformation: the Political and Economic Origins of Our Time*, Boston: Beacon Press.

Portes, A. (2010) *Economic Sociology. A Systematic Inquiry*, Princeton: Princeton University Press.

Rezler, J. (1973) 'An evaluation of the Hungarian economic reform of 1968', *Jahrbuch der Wirtschaft Osteuropas*: 369–95.

Róna-Tas, Á. (1997) *The Great Surprise of the Small Transformation: The Demise of Communism and the Rise of the Private Sector in Hungary*, Michigan: University of Michigan Press.

—— (2002) 'The Worm and the Caterpillar: The Small Private Sector in the Czech Republic, Hungary and Slovakia', in V. E. Bonell and T. B. Gold (eds) *The New Entrepreneurs of Europe and Asia*, Armonk: M. E. Sharpe: 39–65.

Rupp, K. (1983) *Entrepreneurs in Red. Structure and Organizational Innovation in the Centrally Planned Economy*, New York: State University of New York Press.

Soós, K. A. (2009) *Rendszerváltás és privatizáció – Elsődleges és másodlagos privatizáció Közép-Európában és a volt Szovjetunióban*, Budapest: Corvina.

—— (2010) 'Recension on Mihályi Péter: A magyar privatizáció enciklopédiája', *Közgazdasági Szemle*, 57 (9): 815–20.

Stark, D. and Vedres, B. (2006) 'Social times of network spaces: Network sequences and foreign investment in Hungary', *American Journal of Sociology*, 111 (5): 1367–412.

Szántó, Z., Tóth, I. J. and Szabolcs, V. (2011) *The Social and Institutional Structure of Corruption. Some Typical Network Configurations of Corruption Transactions in Hungary*, Budapest: Corvinus University of Budapest.

Szelényi, I. (1988) *Socialist Entrepreneurs. Embourgeoisement in Rural Hungary.* Madison, WI: The University of Wisconsin Press.

Szelényi, I. and Glass, C. (2003) 'Winners of the reforms: The new economic and political elite', in V. Mikhalev (ed.) *Inequality and Social Structure during the Transition*, Houndmills: Palgrave Macmillan: 75–98.

Tardos, M. (1998) 'Sikeres-e a privatizáció?', *Közgazdasági Szemle*, 45 (4): 317–32.

Tóth, I. G. (2009) *Bizalomhiány, normazavarok, igazságtalanságérzet és paternalizmus a magyar társadalom értékszerkezetében*, Budapest: Tárki.

UNCTAD (2002) *World Investment Report 2002: Transnational Corporations and Export Competitiveness*, New York/ Geneva: United Nations.

—— (2008) World Investment Report 2008: *Transnational Corporations and the Infrastructure Challenge, Transnationality Index for Host Economies*, United Nations, New York/Geneva: 12.

—— (2011) Table viewer, Online. Available from: <http://unctadstat.unctad.org/TableViewer/dimView.aspx> (accessed on 13 April 2012).

UNDP (2007) *Baseline Study on CSR Practices in the New EU Member States and Candidate Countries*, UNDP, Public Policy and Management Institute, EU: 18.

Várhegyi, É. (2001) 'Külföldi tulajdon a magyar bankrendszerben', *Közgazdasági Szemle*, 48 (7): 581–98.

Visa Europe (2011) *Hidden Economy*, Online. Available from: <http://index.hu/gazdasag/magyar/2011/09/07> (accessed 18 June 2012).

Voszka, É. (2005) 'Állami tulajdonlás – elméleti indokok és gyakorlati dilemmák', *Közgazdasági Szemle*, 52 (1): 1–23.

Whitley, R. (1992) *European Business Systems*, London: Sage.

Whitley, R., Czabán, L., Henderson, J. and Lengyel, G. (1996) 'Trust and contractual relations in an emerging capitalist economy: The changing trading relationship of ten large Hungarian enterprises', *Organization Studies*, 17 (3): 397–420.

Chapter 4

Allbus (2008) *Die Allgemeine Bevölkerungsumfrage der Sozialwissenschaften. Datenhandbuch 2008*, Köln: Gesis.

Allen, C.S (2010) 'Ideas, institutions and organized capitalism: The German model of political economy 20 years after unification', *German Politics and Society*, 28 (2): 130–50.

Artus, I. (2001) *Die Krise des deutschen Tarifsystems. Die Erosion des Flächentarifvertrags in Ost und West*, Wiesbaden: Westdeutscher Verlag.

Baethge, M., Solga, H., and Wieck, M. (2007) *Berufsbildung im Umbruch – Signale eines überfälligen Aufbruchs*, Berlin: Friedrich-Ebert-Stiftung. Online. Available from: <http://library.fes.de/pdf-files/stabsabteilung/04258/studie.pdf> (accessed 24 March 2011).

Becker, I. (2006) *Armut in Deutschland: Bevölkerungsgruppen unterhalb der Alg II-Grenze*. Arbeitspapier 3 (Oktober) des Projekts "Soziale Gerechtigkeit", Frankfurt am Main: Universität Frankfurt am Main. Online. Available from: <http://www.boeckler.de/pdf_fof/S-2006–863–4–3.pdf> (accessed 27 April 2012).

Behrens, M., Fichter, M. and Frege, C. M. (2001) Unions in Germany: Searching to Regain the Initiative, WSI-Discussion paper No 97, Düsseldorf.

Berghoff, H. (2006) 'The end of family business? The mittelstand and German capitalism in transition, 1949–2000', *Business History Review*, 80 (2): 263–95.

Beyer, J. (2003) 'Deutschland AG a.D.: Deutsche Bank, Allianz und das Verflechtungszentrum des deutschen Kapitalismus', in W. Streeck and M. Höpner (eds) *Alle Macht dem Markt? Fallstudien zur Abwicklung der Deutschland AG*, Frankfurt am Main: Campus: 118–46.

—— (2007) 'Primat der Finanzmarktorientierung. Zur Logik der Auflösung der Deutschland AG', *Berliner Debatte Initial*, 18 (4–5): 1–10.

Beyer, J. and Höpner, M. (2003) 'The disintegration of organized capitalism: German corporate governance in the 1990s', *West European Politics*, 26 (4): 179–98.

Bispinck, R. (2007) 'Löhne, Tarifverhandlungen und Tarifsystem in Deutschland 1995–2005', *WSI Discussion Paper*, 171. Online. Available from: <http://www.boeckler.de/wsi_5351.htm?produkt=HBS-003781&chunk=4&jahr=> (accessed 27 April 2012).

Bispinck, R., Dribbusch, H. and Schulten, T. (2010): 'German collective bargaining in a European perspective. Continuous erosion or re-stabilization of multi-employer agreements?', *WSI Discussion Paper*, 171. Available [from: <http://www.boeckler.de/wsi_5351.htm?produkt=HBS-004762&chunk=1&jahr=> (accessed 27 April 2012).

Bleicher, K. (1983) 'Organisationskulturen und Führungsphilosophien im Wettbewerb', *Zeitschrift für betriebswirtschaftliche Forschung*, 35 (1): 135–46.

Bluhm, K. and Martens, B. (2008) 'Change within traditional channels: German SMEs, the restructuring of the banking sector, and the growing shareholder-value orientation', in K. Bluhm and R. Schmidt (eds) *Change in SMEs: Towards a New European Capitalism?*, Houndmills: Palgrave Macmillan: 39–57.

—— (2009) 'Recomposed institutions. Smaller firms strategies, shareholder-value orientation and bank relationships in Germany', *Socio-Economic Review*, 7 (4): 1–20.

—— (2011) 'The restoration of a family capitalism in East Germany and some possible consequences', in I. Stamm, P. Breitschmid and M. Kohli (eds) *Doing Succession in Europe. Generational Transfers in Family Business in Comparative Perspective*, Zurich: Schulthess: 129–52.

Bluhm, K., Martens, B., and Trappmann, V. (2011) 'Business elites and the role of companies in society. A comparative study in Poland, Hungary and Germany', *Europe Asia Studies*, 63 (6): 1011–32.

Bosch, G. and Kalina, T. (2005) 'Entwicklung und Struktur der Niedriglohnbeschäftigung in Deutschland.', in Institut Arbeit und Technik (ed.) *Jahrbuch 2005*, Gelsenkirchen: Institut Arbeit und Technik. Online. Available from: <http://www.iaq.uni-due. de/aktuell/veroeff/jahrbuch/jahrb05/05-esch-stoebe.pdf> (accessed 27 April 2012).

BundesagenturfürArbeit (2012) <http://statistik.arbeitsagentur.de/Navigation/Statistik/ Statistik-nach-Themen/Arbeitslose-und-gemeldetes-Stellenangebot/Arbeislose-und-gemeldetes-Stellenangebot-Nav.html> (accessed 15 April 2013).

Bürklin, W., Kaina, V., Machatzke, J., Rebenstorf, H., Sauer, M. and Welzel, C. (1997) *Eliten in Deutschland. Zirkulation und Integration* , Opladen: Leske & Budrich.

Busch, A. (2005) 'Globalization and national varieties of capitalism: The contested viability of the German model', *German Politics*, 14 (2): 125–39.

Byrkjeflot, H. (2001) *Management Education and Selection of Top Managers in Europe and the United States*, LOS Report R0103, Bergen: LOS-senteret Universitetet i Bergen.

Cohen, J., Cohen, P., West, S. G. and Aiken, L. S. (2003) *Applied Multiple Regression/ Correlation. Analysis for the Behavioral Science*, London: Lawrence Erlbaum Association.

Crouch, C. (1995) 'Reconstructing Corporatism? Organized Decentralization and Other Paradoxes' in C. Crouch and F. Traxler (eds) *Organized industrial relations in Europe*, Aldershot: Ashgate, 311–331.

DCGK (2002) *Deutscher Corporate Governance Kodex*. Online. Available from: <http:// www.corporate-governance-code.de/ger/download/DCG_K_D20021107.pdf> (accessed 31 March 2011).

—— (2009) *Deutscher Corporate Governance Kodex*. Online. Available from: <http:// www.corporate-governance-code.de/ger/download/kodex_2009/D_CorGov_ Endfassung_Juni_2009.pdf> (accessed 31 March 2011).

—— (2010) Online. *Deutscher Corporate Governance Kodex*. Online. Available from: <http://www.corporate-governance-code.de/eng/kodex/1.html> (accessed 31 March 2011).

Deeg, R. (1999) *Finance Capitalism Unveiled: Banks and the German Political Economy*, Ann Arbor: University of Michigan Press.

Dörre, K. (2002) *Kampf um Beteiligung. Arbeit, Partizipation und industrielle Beziehungen im flexiblen Kapitalismus*, Wiesbaden: VS-Verlag.

—— (2010) 'Die neue Landnahme: Prekarisierung im Finanzmarktkapitalismus', *Neue Praxis. Zeitschrift für Sozialarbeit, Sozialpädagogik und Sozialpolitik*, 1 (10): 5–24.

Dörre, K. and Brinkmann, U. (2005) 'Finanzmarkt-Kapitalismus: Triebkraft eines flexiblen Produktionsmodells?', in P. Windolf (ed.) *Finanzmarkt-Kapitalismus. Analysen zum Wandel von Produktionsregimen*, Kölner Zeitschrift für Soziologie und Sozialpsychologie, Special Issue 45, Wiesbaden: VS-Verlag: 85–116.

ECB (2007) European Central Bank, *Monthly Bulletin*, 02/2007, Frankfurt am Main: ECB.

Erikson, R. and Goldthorpe, J. H. (1992) *The Constant Flux. A Study of Class Mobility in Industrial Societies*, Oxford: Clarendon Press.

Eye, A. von (1990) *Introduction to Configural Frequency Analysis: The Search for Types and Antitypes in Cross-Classifications*, Cambridge: Cambridge University Press.

Faust, M. (2002) 'Karrieremuster von Führungskräften der Wirtschaft im Wandel–Der Fall Deutschland in vergleichender Perspektive', *SOFI-Mitteilungen*, 30: 69–90.

Faust, M., Bahnmüller, R. and Fisecker, C. (2011) *Das kapitalmarktorientierte Unternehmen. Externe Erwartungen, Unternehmenspolitik, Personalwesen und Mitbestimmung* Berlin: Edition Sigma.

Freye, S. (2009a) *Führungswechsel. Die Wirtschaftselite und das Ende der Deutschland AG*, Frankfurt am Main: Campus.

—— (2009b) 'Entsteht ein Markt für Unternehmensleiter? Karriereverläufe deutscher Manager im Wandel', *Arbeits- und Industriesoziologische Studien*, 2 (2): 17–31. Online. Available from: <http://www.ais-studien.de/home/veroeffentlichungen-09/dezember.html> (accessed 27 April 2012).

Gergs, H. and Schmidt, R. (2002) 'Generationswechsel im Management Ost- und Westdeutscher Unternehmen – Kommt es zu einer Amerikanisierung des deutschen Managementmodells?', *Kölner Zeitschrift für Soziologie und Sozialpsychologie*, 54 (3): 553–78.

Gilbert, N. (2004) *Transformation of the Welfare State*, Oxford: Oxford University Press.

Hall, P. A. and Soskice, D. (2001) *Varieties of Capitalism: The Institutional Foundations of Comparative Advantage*, Oxford: Oxford University Press.

Hassel, A. (1999) 'The erosion of the German system of industrial relations', *British Journal of Industrial Relations*, 37 (3): 483–505.

—— (2010) 'Twenty years after German unification: The restructuring of the German welfare and employment regime', *German Politics and Society*, 28 (2): 102–15.

Hartmann, M. (1995) 'Deutsche Topmanager: Klassenspezifischer Habitus als Karrierebasis', *Soziale Welt*, 46 (4): 440–68.

—— (2000) 'Class-Specific habitus and the social reproduction of the business elite in Germany and France', *The Sociological Review*, 48 (2): 241–61.

—— (2006) 'Vermarktlichung der Elitenrekrutierung? Das Beispiel der Topmanager', in H. Münkler, G. Straßenberger and M. Bohlender, (eds) *Deutschlands Eliten im Wandel*, Frankfurt am Main: Campus: 431–54.

—— (2007) *Eliten und Macht in Europa. Ein internationaler Vergleich*. Frankfurt am Main: Campus.

—— (2009) 'Die transnationale Klasse – Mythos oder Realität?', *Soziale Welt*, 60 (3): 285–303.

Hartmann, M. and Kopp, J. (2001) 'Elitenselektion durch Bildung oder durch Herkunft? Promotion, soziale Herkunft und der Zugang zu Führungspositionen in der deutschen Wirtschaft', *Kölner Zeitschrift für Soziologie und Sozialpsychologie*, 53 (3): 436–66.

Herrigel, G. (1996) *Industrial Constructions: The Sources of German Industrial Power*, Cambridge: Cambridge University Press.

Höpner, M. (2003) *Wer beherrscht die Unternehmen? Shareholder Value, Managerherrschaft und Mitbestimmung in Deutschland*, Frankfurt am Main: Campus.

—— (2004) 'Was bewegt die Führungskräfte? Von der Agency-Theorie zur Soziologie des Managements', *Soziale Welt*, 55 (3): 263–82.

Höpner, M. and Krempel, L. (2004) 'The politics of the German company network', *Competition and Change*, 8 (4): 339–56.

Höpner, M. and Streeck, W. (2003) *Alle Macht dem Markt? Fallstudien zur Abwicklung der Deutschland AG*, Frankfurt am Main: Campus.

Jackson, G., Höpner, M. and Kurdelbusch, A. (2005) 'Corporate governance and employees in Germany: Changing linkages, complementarities, and tensions', in G. Howard and A. Pendleton (eds) *Corporate Governance and Labour Management*, Oxford: Oxford University Press: 84–121.

Kädtler, J. (2010) 'Finanzmärkte und Finanzialisierung', in F. Böhle, G. Voß and G. Wachtler (eds) *Handbuch Arbeitssoziologie*, Wiesbaden: VS-Verlag: 619–42.

Kädtler, J., and Faust, M. (2008) 'The Power of financial markets – what does that mean and how does it work for different categories of companies?', in K. Bluhm and

R. Schmidt (eds) *Change in SMEs. Towards a New European Capitalism?*, Houndmills: Palgrave Macmillan: 17–38.

Kienbaum Consultants International (2007*) 30 Jahre Vorstands- und Aufsichtsratsvergütung in Deutschland. 30 Jahre Vorstandsvergütung: Die Zwei-Klassen-Gesellschaft.* Kienbaum: Gumersbach.

Kitschelt, H. and Streeck, W. (2004) *Germany: Beyond the Stable State*, London: Routledge.

Kotthoff, H. (2009) '"Betriebliche Sozialordnung" als Basis ökonomischer Leistungsfähigkeit', in J. Beckert and C. Deutschmann (eds) *Wirtschaftssoziologie, Kölner Zeitschrift für Soziologie und Sozialpsychologie*, Special Issue 49, Wiesbaden: VS-Verlag: 428–46.

Kotthoff, H. and Wagner, A. (2008) *Die Leistungsträger. Führungskräfte im Wandel der Firmenkultur – eine Follow-up-Studie*, Berlin: Edition Sigma.

Kruk, M. (1972) *Die großen Unternehmer. Woher sie kommen, wer sie sind und wie sie auf-steigen*, Frankfurt am Main: Societäts-Verlag.

Lane, C. (1989) *Management and Labour in Europe: The Industrial Enterprise in Germany, Britain and Europe*, Aldershot: Edward Elgar.

—— (2000) 'Globalization and the German model of capitalism–erosion or survival?', *British Journal of Sociology*, 51 (2): 207–34.

Long, J. S. (1997) *Regression Models for Categorical and Limited Dependent Variables*, London: Sage.

Martens, B. (2007) 'Orthodoxie der Proselyten – Einstellungsmuster ökonomischer Funktionseliten im Ost/West-Vergleich', *Zeitschrift für Soziologie*, 36 (2): 118–30.

—— (2008) 'East German economic elites and their companies two decades after the transformation ("Wende"): Still following the patterns of the 1990s', *Journal for East European Management Studies*, 13 (4): 305–26.

Maurice, M., Sellier, F. and Silvestre, J.-J. (1979) 'Die Entwicklung der Hierarchie im Industrieunternehmen: Untersuchung eines gesellschaftlichen Effekts', *Soziale Welt*, 30 (3): 295–327.

Palier, B. and Thelen, K. (2010) 'Institutionalizing dualism: Complementarities and change in France and Germany', *Politics & Society*, 38 (1): 119–48.

Plumpe, W. (2006), Industrielle Beziehungen', in G. Ambrosius, D. Petzina and W. Plumpe (eds) *Moderne Wirtschaftsgeschichte. Eine Einführung für Historiker und Ökonomen*, Munich: R. Oldenbourg Verlag: 391–426.

Pohlmann, M. (2009) 'Globale ökonomische Eliten–Eine Globalisierungsthese auf dem Prüfstand der Empirie', *Kölner Zeitschrift für Soziologie und Sozialpsychologie*, 61 (4): 513–34.

Pross, H. and Boetticher, K.W. (1971) *Manager des Kapitalismus. Untersuchung über leitende Angestellte in Großunternehmen*, Frankfurt am Main: Suhrkamp.

Rang, R. (2004) *Ehemalige Vorstände als Kontrolleure. Untersuchung der Zusammensetzung von Aufsichtsräten mitbestimmter und börsennotierter Unternehmen im Auftrag der Hans-Böckler-Stiftung*, Düsseldorf: Hans-Böckler-Stiftung.

Rehder, B. (2003) 'Konversion durch Überlagerung. Der Beitrag betrieblicher Bündnisse zum Wandel der Arbeitsbeziehungen in Deutschland', in J. Beyer (ed.) *Vom Zukunfts-zum Auslaufmodell? Die deutsche Wirtschaftsordnung im Wandel*, Wiesbaden: Westdeutscher Verlag: 61–77.

Schmidt, R. (2008) 'Social relationships in German SMEs: An east-west comparison', in K. Bluhm and R. Schmidt (eds) *Change in SMEs: Towards a New European Capitalism?*, Houndmills: Palgrave Macmillan: 274–90.

Seifert, H. and Massa-Wirth, H. (2005) 'Pacts for employment and competitiveness in Germany', *Industrial Relations Journal*, 36 (3): 217–40.

Sorge, A. and Streeck, W. (1988) 'Industrial relations and technical change: The case for an extended perspective', in R. Hyman and W. Streeck (eds) *New Technology and Industrial Relations*, Oxford: Basil Blackwell: 19–44.

Streeck, W. (1997) 'German capitalism: Does it exist? Can it survive?', in C. Crouch and W. Streeck (eds) *Political Economy of Modern Capitalism: Mapping Convergence and Diversity*, London: Sage: 33–54.

—— (2003) '*No Longer the Century of Corporatism. Das Ende des „Bündnisses für Arbeit"*'. Max-Planck-Institut für Gesellschaftsforschung Working Paper 3/4 (Mai). Online. Available from: <http://www.mpifg.de/pu/workpap/wp03–4/wp03–4.html> (accessed 27 April 2012).

—— (2009) *Re-Forming Capitalism. Institutional Change in the German Political Economy*, Oxford: Oxford University Press.

—— (2011) '*Skills and Politics: General and Specific*'. Max-Planck-Institut für Gesellschaftsforschung Discussion Paper 11 (February). Online. Available from: <http://www.mpifg.de/pu/mpifg_dp/dp11–1.pdf> (accessed 27 April 2012).

Streeck, W. and Hassel, A. (2003) 'The Crumbling Pillars of Social Partnership', *West European Politics*, 26 (1): 101–24.

Thelen K. (2004) *How Institutions Evolve: The Political Economy of Skills in Germany, Britain, the United States and Japan*, Cambridge: Cambridge University Press.

Timm, N. H. (2002) *Applied Multivariate Analysis*, Berlin: Springer.

Troltsch, K., Walden, G. and Zopf, S. (2009) 'Im Osten nichts Neues?' BiBB Report 12/09. Online. Available from <http://www.bibb.de/de/52551.htm> (accessed 24 March 2011).

Vitols, S. (2005) 'German corporate governance in transition: Implications of bank exit from monitoring and control', *International Journal of Disclosure and Governance*, 2 (4): 357–67.

Walgenbach, P. and Kieser, A. (1995) 'Mittlere Manager in Deutschland und Großbritannien', in *Managementforschung*, 5: 259–309.

Wiesenthal, H. (2003) 'German unification and "Model Germany": An adventure in institutional conservatism', in *West European Politics*, 26 (4): 37–58.

Zapf, W. (1965) 'Die deutschen Manager. Sozialprofil und Karriereweg', in W. Zapf (ed.) *Beiträge zur Analyse der deutschen Oberschichten*, München: Piper.

Chapter 5

Bluhm, K. (2000) 'Reemerged small-business capitalism: The East German transition reviewed', *German Politics and Society*, 18 (3): 49–118.

—— (2010) 'Theories of capitalism put to the test. Introduction to a debate on Central and Eastern Europe', *Historical Social Research*, 35 (2): 197–217.

Bluhm, K. and Martens, B. (2011) 'The restoration of a family capitalism in East Germany and some possible consequences', in I. Stamm, P. Breitschmid and M. Kohli (eds) *Doing Succession in Europe*, Zürich: Schulthess: 129–52.

Bürklin, W. (1996) *Kontinuität und Wandel der deutschen Führungsschicht: Ergebnisse der Potsdamer Elitestudie 1995*, Potsdam: Universität Potsdam.

Busch, U. (2006) 'Gesamtgesellschaftliche Stagnation und zunehmender Transferbedarf', *Berliner Debatte Initial* 17 (5): 17–26.

Buß, E. (2007) *Die deutschen Spitzenmanager. Wie sie wurden, was sie sind. Herkunft, Wertvorstellungen, Erfolgsregeln*. Munich: Oldenbour.

Byrkjeflot, H. (2000) *Management Education and Selection of Top Managers in Europe and the United States*, Bergen: Los-senteret.

Demary, M. and Röhl, K. H. (2009) 'Twenty years after the fall of the Berlin Wall. Structural convergence in a slow-growth environment', in C. Wey and K. F. Zimmermann (eds) *Twenty Years of Economic Reconstruction in East Germany*, Berlin: Duncker & Humblot: 9–33.

Drahokoupil, J. 2008. *Globalization and The State in Central and Eastern Europe. The Politics of Foreign Direct Investment*, London: Routledge.

Eberwein, W. and Tholen, J. (1993) *Euro-Manager or Splendid Isolation? International Management. An Anglo-German Comparison*, Berlin: de Gruyter.

Eyal, G., Szelényi, I. and Townsley, E. (1998) *Making Capitalism Without Capitalists: Class Formation and Elite Struggles in Post-Communist Central Europe,* London: Verso.

Faust, M. (2002) 'Karrieremuster von Führungskräften der Wirtschaft im Wandel–Der Fall Deutschland in vergleichender Perspektive', *SOFI-Mitteilungen*, 30: 69–90.

Fligstein, N. (2001) *The Architecture of Markets: An Economic Sociology of Twenty-First-Century Capitalist Societies*, Princeton: Princeton University Press.

Fritsch, M. (2004) 'Entrepreneurship, entry and performance of new business compared in two growth regimes: East and West Germany', *Journal of Evolutionary Economics*, 14: 525–42.

Goldthorpe, J.H. (1980): *Social Mobility and Class Structure in Modern Britain*. Oxford: Claredon Press.

Hanley, E. (1999) 'Cadre capitalism in Hungary and Poland: Property accumulation among communist-era elites', *East European Politics & Societies* 14 (1): 143–78.

Hanley, E., Yershova, N. and R. Anderson (1995) 'Russia – Old wine in a new bottle? The circulation and reproduction of Russian elites, 1983–1993', *Theory and Society* 24: 639–668.

Hankiss, E. (1990) *East European Alternatives*, Oxford: Clarendon Press.

Hartmann, M. (1995), Deutsche Topmanager: Klassenspezifischer Habitus als Karrierebasis', *Soziale Welt*, 46 (4): 440–68.

Hartmann, M. (2006) *The Sociology of Elites*, London: Routledge.

Hatschikjan, M. A. (1998): 'Zeitenwende und Elitenwandel in Osteuropa', in M. A. Hatschikjan and F. L. Altmann (eds) *Eliten im Wandel. Politische Führung, wirtschaftliche Macht und Meinungsbildung im neuen Osteuropa*, Paderborn: Schöningh: 251–70.

James, H. (2006) *Family Capitalism: Wendels, Haniels, Falcks and the Continental European Model*, Harvard: Harvard University Press.

King, L. P. and Szelényi I. (2005) 'Post-communist economic systems', in N. J. Smelser and R. Swedberg (eds) *The Handbook of Economic Sociology*, 2nd edition, Princeton: Princeton University Press: 205–29.

Krishtanovskaia, O. and White, S. (1999): 'From Soviet Nomenklatura to Russian Elite', in V. Shlapentokh, C. Vanderpool and B. Doktorov (eds.) *The New Elite in Post-Communist Eastern Europe*. Texas: Texas A&M University Press, 27–52.

Kristóf, L. (2012) 'What happened afterwards? Change and continuity in the Hungarian elite between 1988 and 2009', *Historical Social Research*, 37 (2): 108–22.

Laki, M. and Szalai, J. (2006) 'The puzzle of success: Hungarian grand entrepreneurs at the turn of the millennium', *Europe-Asia Studies*, 58 (3): 317–45.

Lane, C. (1989) *Management and Labour in Europe. The Industrial Enterprise in Germany, Britain and France*, Aldershot: Edward Elgar.

Lane, D., Lengyel, G. and Tholen, J. (eds) (2007) *Restructuring of the Economic Elites after State Socialism. Recruitment, Institutions and Attitudes*, Stuttgart: ibidem-Verlag.

Lawrence, P. (1980) *Managers and Management in West Germany*, London: Croom Helm.

Lengyel, G. (2007) *A magyar gazdasági elit társadalmi összetétele a huszadik század végén*, Budapest: Akadémiai Kiadó.

—— (2009) 'Social factors conditioning the recruitment of the Hungarian economic elite at the end of the 1990s', in F. Sattler and C. Boyer (eds) *European Economic Elites*, Berlin: Duncker & Humblot: 251–64.

Lengyel, G. and Bartha, A. (2000) 'Hungary: Bankers and managers after state socialism', in J. Higley and G. Lengyel (eds) *Elites after State Socialism. Theories and Analysis.* Oxford: Rowman & Littlefield: 163–77.

Lutz, B. and Grünert, H. (1996) 'Der Zerfall der Beschäftigungsstrukturen der DDR 1989–1993', in B. Lutz, H. Nickel, R. Schmidt and A. Sorge (eds) *Arbeit, Arbeitsmarkt und Betriebe*, Opladen: Leske & Budrich: 69–120.

Martens, B. (2005) 'Der lange Schatten der Wende. Karrieren ostdeutscher Wirtschaftseliten', *Historical Social Research*, 30 (2): 206–30.

—— (2008) 'East German economic elites and their companies two decades after the transformation ('Wende'): Still following the patterns of the 1990s', *Journal for East European Management Studies*, 13 (4): 305–26.

Matějů, P. and Hanley, E. (1998) *The Making of Post-Communist Elites in Eastern Europe*, Praha: Sociologicky ustav AV ČR.

Mau, S. (2012) 'Ossifreie Zone', *Die Zeit*. Online. Available from: <http://www.zeit. de/2012/16/P-Ostdeutsche-Elite> (accessed 21 April 2012).

Pohlmann, M. and Gergs, H. (1999) 'Ökonomische Eliten vor und nach der Wiedervereinigung: Die Selektivität des Transformationsprozesses', in S. Hornbostel (ed.) *Sozialistische Eliten. Horizontale und vertikale Differenzierungsmuster in der DDR*, Opladen: Leske & Budrich: 223–52.

Sattler, F. and Boyer, C. (2009) 'European economic elites between a new spirit of capitalism and the erosion of state socialism', in F. Sattler and C. Boyer (eds) *European Economic Elites Between a New Spirit of Capitalism and the Erosion of State Socialism*, Berlin: Ducker & Humblot: 19–70.

Schreiber, E., Meyer, M., Steger, T. and Lang, R. (2002*) Eliten in „ Wechseljahren“: Verbands- und Kombinatsführungskräfte im ostdeutschen Transformationsprozess*, München: Hampp.

Solga, H. (1994) '"Systemloyalität" als Bedingung sozialer Mobilität im Staatssozialismus, am Beispiel der DDR', *Berliner Journal für Soziologie*, 94 (4): 523–42.

Staniszkis, J. (1991) *The Dynamics of the Breakthrough in Eastern Europe: The Polish Experience*, Berkeley: University of California Press.

Stark, D. and Bruszt, L. (1998) *Postsocialist Pathways: Transforming Politics and Property in East Central Europe*, Cambridge: Cambridge University Press.

Stewart, S., Kieser, A. and Barsoux, J.L. (1994) *Managing in Britain and Germany*, New York: St. Martin's Press.

Szalai, E. (1994) 'The power structure in Hungary after the political transition', in C. G. A. Bryant and E. Mokrzycki (eds) *The New Great Transformation*, London: Routledge: 120–43.

Szelényi, S., Szelényi, I. and Kovách, I. (1995) 'The making of the Hungarian postcommunist elite: Circulation in politics, reproduction in the economy', *Theory and Society*, 24 (5): 697–722.

Walder, A. G. (2003): 'Elite opportunity in transitional economies', *Amercian Sociological Review*, 68 (6): 899–916.

Wasilewski, J. (1998) 'Hungary, Poland, and Russia: The fate of nomenklatura elites', in M. Dogan and J. Higley (eds) *Elites, Crises, and the Origins of Regimes*, Lanham: Rowman & Littlefield: 147–68.

Wasilewski, J. and Wnuk-Lipiński, E. (1995) 'Poland: A winding road from the communist to post-solidarity elite', *Theory and Society*, 24: 669–96.

Welzel, C. (1996) *Eliten und Intelligenz im Postsozialismus: Herkunft, Demokratieverständnis und politische Integration am Beispiel der ostdeutschen Nach-Wende-Elite*, dissertation, Potsdam: Universität Potsdam.

Windolf, P., Brinkmann, U. and Kulke D. (1999) *Warum blüht der Osten nicht? Zur Transformation der ostdeutschen Betriebe*, Berlin: Edition Sigma.

Chapter 6

Csabina, Z., Kopasz, M. and Leveleki, M. (2002) 'Contractual trust in the trading relationships of Hungarian manufacturing firms', *Review of Sociology of the Hungarian Sociological Association*, 8 (1): 79–97.

Gábor, R. I. (1994a) 'Small entrepreneurship in Hungary – ailing or prospering?', *Acta Oeconomica*, 44 (3–4): 333–46.

—— (1994b) 'Modernity or a new kind of duality? Second thoughts about the second economy', in K. J. Mátyás (ed.) *Transition to Capitalism? The Communist Legacy in Eastern Europe*, New Brunswick: Transaction Publishers: 3–20.

—— (1997) 'Too many, too small: Small entrepreneurship in Hungary – ailing of prospering?', in G. Grabher and D. Stark (eds) *Restructuring Networks: Legacies, Linkages and Localities in Postsocialism*, London and New York: Oxford University Press: 58–75.

Gál, R. I. (1997) *Unreliability: Contractual Discipline and Contract Governance*, Amsterdam: Thesis Publishers.

Inglehart, R. and Baker, W. (2000) 'Modernization, cultural change and the persistence of traditional values', *American Sociological Review*, 65 (1): 19–51.

Janky, B. (2007) 'Social structure, transition and public attitudes towards tax evasion in Hungary', in N. Hayoz and S. Hug (eds) *Tax Evasion, Trust, and State Capacities*, Bern: Peter Lang: 269–87.

Keller, T. (2009) 'On the social norms regulating economic morality – norms obeyed and norms defied', in T. I. György (ed.) *Tárki European Social Report 2009*, Budapest: Tárki: 151–61.

—— (2010) 'The position of Hungary on worldwide map of human values', *Review of Sociology*, 20 (1): 27–51.

Kopp, M. S. and Réthelyi. J. (2004) 'Where psychology meets physiology: Chronic stress and premature mortality – the Central-Eastern European health paradox', *Brain Research Bulletin*, 62 (5): 351–67.

Lazzarini, S. G., Miller, G. J. and Zenger, T. R. (2008) 'Dealing with the paradox of embeddedness: 'The role of contracts and trust in facilitating movement out of committed relationships', *Organization Science*, 19 (5): 709–28.

Lengyel, G. and Janky, B. (2005) 'Security, trust and cultural resources: Manufacturing rnterprises in the post-socialist transformation', in S. M. Koniordos (ed.) *Networks, Trust and Social Capital. Theoretical and Empirical Investigations from Europe*, Aldershot: Ashgate Publisher Ltd.: 205–24.

MacDuffie, J. P. (2011) 'Inter-organizational trust and the dynamics of distrust', *Journal of International Business Studies*, 42 (1): 35–47.

Nee, V. (1991) 'Social inequalities in reforming state socialism: between redistribution and markets in China', *American Sociological Review*, 56 (3): 267–82.

Raiser, M. (1997) *Informal Institutions, Social Capital and Economic transition: Reflections on a Neglected Dimension*, EBRD Working Paper 25.

—— (2002) 'Trust in transition', in F. Bönker, K. Müller and A. Pickel (eds) *Postcommunist Transformation and the Social Sciences: Cross-Disciplinary Approaches*, Lanham: Rowmann and Littlefield: 77–96.

Sako, M. (1992) *Prices, Quality and Trust: Inter-Firm Relations in Britain and Japan*, Cambridge: Cambridge University Press.

—— (1998) 'Does trust improve business performance?', in C. Lane and R. Bachmann (eds) *Trust Within and Between Organizations*, Oxford: Oxford University Press: 88–117.

Sako, M. and Helper, S. (1998) 'Determinants of trust in supplier relations: Evidence from the automotive industry in Japan and the United States', *Journal of Economic Behavior & Organization*, 34 (3): 387–417.

Skrabski, Á., Kopp, M. S. and Kawachi, I. (2003) 'Human resources in a changing society: Cross sectional associations with middle aged female and male mortality rates', *Journal of Epidemiology & Community Health*, 57 (2): 114–19.

Stark, D. and Nee, V. (1989) 'Toward an institutional analysis of state socialism', in V. Nee and D. Stark (eds) *Remaking the Economic Institutions of Socialism: China and Eastern Europe*, Stanford: Stanford University Press: 1–32.

Szelényi, I. (1978) 'Social inequalities in state socialist redistributive economies', *International Journal of Comparative Sociology*, 19 (1–2): 63–87.

—— (1989), 'Eastern Europe in an epoch of transition: Toward a socialist mixed economy?', in V. Nee and D. Stark (eds) *Remaking the Economic Institutions of Socialism: China and Eastern Europe*, Stanford: Stanford University Press: 208–33.

Szelényi, I. and Manchin, R. (1987) 'Social policy under state socialism', in G. Esping-Andersen, L. Rainwater and M. Rein (eds) *Stagnation and Renewal in Social Policy*, White Plains: M. E. Sharp: 102–39.

Uzzi, B. (1997) 'Social structure and competition in interfirm networks: The paradox of embeddedness', *Administrative Science Quarterly*, 42 (1): 35–67.

Whitley, R., Czabán, L., Henderson, J. and Lengyel, G. (1996) 'Trust and contractual relations in an emerging capitalist economy: the changing trading relationship of ten large Hungarian enterprises', *Organization Studies*, 17 (3): 397–420.

Yamagishi, T., Cook, K. S. and Watabe, M. (1998) 'Uncertainty, trust, and commitment formation in the United States and Japan', *American Journal of Sociology*, 104 (1): 165–94.

Chapter 7

Backhaus-Maul, H. (2005): 'Corporate citizenship – Liberale Gesellschaftspolitik als Unternehmensstrategie in den USA', in F. Adloff, U. Birsl and P. Schwertmann (eds) *Wirtschaft und Zivilgesellschaft. Theoretische und empirische Perspektiven*, Wiesbaden: VS Verlag: 225–44.

Bluhm, K. (2008): 'Corporate social responsibility. Zur Moralisierung der Unternehmen aus soziologischer Perspektive', in A. Maurer and U. Schimank (eds) *Die Gesellschaft der Unternehmen – die Unternehmen der Gesellschaft*, Wiesbaden: VS Verlag: 144–63.

Bluhm, K., Martens, B. and V. Trappmann (2011): 'Business elites and the role of companies in society. A comparative study in Poland, Hungary and Germany', *European-Asia Studies*, 63 (6): 1011–32.

Campbell, J. L. (2007): 'Why would corporations behave in socially responsible ways? An institutional theory of corporate social responsibility', *Academy of Management Review*, 32 (3): 946–67.

Carroll, A. (1991): 'The pyramid of corporate social responsibility: Toward the moral management of organizational stakeholders', *Business Horizons*, 34 (4): 39–48.

European Commission (2001): *Promoting a Framework for European Corporate Social Responsibility*. Green Paper. Luxembourg: Office of Official Publication of the European Communities.

Eyal, G., Szelényi, I. and Townsley, E. (1998): *Making Capitalism without Capitalists: Class Formation and Elite Struggles in Post-Communist Central Europe*, London: Verso.

Friedman, M. (1973): 'The social responsibility of business is to increase its profits', in: M. Snoeyenbos, R. Almeder and J. Humber (eds): *Business Ethics. Corporate Values and Society*, New York: Prometheus Books: 73–83.

Gjølberg, M. (2009): 'The origin of corporate social responsibility: Global forces or national legacies?', *Socio-Economic Review*, 7 (4): 605–38.

Habisch, A. (2006): 'Die Corporate-Citizenship-Herausforderung: Gesellschaftliches Engagement als Managementaufgabe', in: K. Gazdar, A. Habisch, K. R. Kirchhoff and S. Vaseghi (eds) *Erfolgsfaktor Verantwortung. Corporate Social Responsibility professionell managen*, Berlin: Springer: 35–50.

Hassel, A. (2008): 'The Evolution of a Global Labour Governance Regime', in: *Governance: An International Journal of Policy, Administration and Institutions*, 21 (2): 231–51.

Hiß, S. (2009): 'From implicit to explicit corporate social responsibility–Institutional change as a fight for myths', in: *Business Ethics Quarterly*, Special Issue on 'The Changing Role of Business in a Global Society: New Challenges and Responsibilities', 19 (3): 433–51.

—— (2006): *Warum übernehmen Unternehmen gesellschaftliche Verantwortung? Ein soziologischer Erklärungsversuch*, Frankfurt am Main: Campus.

Imbusch, P. and Rucht, D. (eds) (2007): *Profit oder Gemeinwohl? Fallstudien zur gesellschaftlichen Verantwortung von Wirtschaftseliten*, Wiesbaden: VS Verlag.

Informationsdienst Soziale Indikatoren (ISI) (2012): *Form der Kinderbetreuung stark sozial selektiv*, ISU 48, July, Mannheim: GESIS.

Kinderman, D. (2008): *The Political Economy of Corporate Responsibility in Germany, 1995–2008*, New York: Cornell University, Mario Einaudi Center for International Studies, 5–08.

King, L. P. and Szelényi, I. (2005): 'Post-communist economic systems', in N. J. Smelser and R. Swedberg (eds) *The Handbook of Economic Sociology*, Princeton: Princeton University Press: 205–29.

Machonin, P., Tuček, M. and Nekola, M. (2006): 'The Czech economic elite after fifteen years of post-socialist transformation', *Czech Sociological Review*, 42 (3): 537–56.

Matten, D. and Crane, A. (2004): *Business Ethics: A European Perspective*, Oxford: Oxford University Press.

Matten, D. and Moon, J. (2008): '"Implicit" and "explicit" CSR: A conceptual framework for a comparative understanding of corporate social responsibility', *Academy of Management Review*, 33 (2): 404–24.

Nagelkerke, N. J. D. (1991) 'A note on a general definition of the coefficient of determination', *Biometrika*, 78: 691–2.

Vogel, D. (2005): *The Market of Virtue. The Potential and Limits of Corporate Social Responsibility*, Washington: Brookings Institution Press.

Witt, A. M. and Redding, G. (2012): 'The spirit of corporate social responsibility: Senior executive perceptions of the role of the firm in society in Germany, Hong Kong, Japan, South Korea and the USA', *Socio-Economic Review*, 10 (1): 109–34.

Chapter 8

Bispinck, R., Dribbusch, H. and Schulten, T. (2010) 'German collective bargaining in a European perspective. Continuous erosion or re-stabilization of multi-employer agreements?', *WSI Discussion Paper*, 171. Online. Available from: <http://www.boeckler.de/wsi_5351.htm?produkt=HBS-004762&chunk=1&jahr=> (accessed 27 April 2012).

Bluhm, K. (2007): *Experimentierfeld Ostmitteleuropa? Deutsche Unternehmen in Polen und der Tschechischen Republik*. Wiesbaden: VS Verlag.

—— (2009) 'The dilemma of labour-relations liberalisation in East-Central Europe before and after EU enlargement', in M. A. Moreau and M. E. Blas López (eds) *Restructuring in the New EU Member States. Social Dialogue, Companies Relocation and Social Treatment of Restructuring*, Bern: Peter Lang: 59–79.

—— (2010) 'Theories of capitalism put to the test. Introduction to a debate on Central and Eastern Europe', *Historical Social Research*, 35 (2): 197–217.

Bluhm, K. and Martens, B. (2009) 'Recomposed institutions. Smaller firms' strategies, shareholder-value orientation and bank relationships in Germany', *Socio-Economic Review*, 7 (4): 585–604.

Bohle, D. (2010) 'Countries in distress: Transformation, transnationalization, and crisis in Hungary and Latvia', *EMECON: Employment and Economy in Central and Eastern Europe*, 1/2010. Online. Available from: <http://www.emecon.eu/archive/info/?tx_damfrontend_pi1[showUid]=6&tx_damfrontend_pi1[backPid]=42&tx_damfrontend_pi1[pointer]=1> (accessed 28 June 2012).

Bohle, D. and Greskovits, B. (2006) 'Capitalism without compromise: Strong business and weak labour in Eastern Europe's new transitional industries', *Studies in Comparative International Development*, 41 (1): 3–25

ETUI (The European Trade Union Institute) (2012a) National Industrial Relations/ Countries/Trade Unions. Online. Available from: <http://www.worker-participation.eu> (accessed 25 May 2012).

—— (2012b): National Industrial Relations/Countries/Workplace Representation/ Hungary. Online. Available from: <http://www.worker-participation.eu> (accessed 26 May 2012).

—— (2012c): National Industrial Relations/Countries/Collective Bargaining/Germany/ Poland/Hungary. Online. Available from <http://www.worker- participation.eu> (accessed 26 May 2012).

—— (2012d): National Industrial Relations/Countries/Trade Unions/Hungary. Online. Available from: <http://www.worker-participation.eu> (accessed 1 June 2012).

Federowicz, M. (2004) 'Poland: Worker-driven transformation to capitalism?', in M. Federowicz and R. Aquilera (eds) *Corporate Governance in a Changing Economic Environment*, Houndmills: Palgrave Macmillan: 144–69.

Gardawski, J., Mrozowicki, A. and Czarzasty, J. (2012) *Trade Unions in Poland*, Brussels: European Trade Union Institute.

Gardawski, J. (2011) 'Partnerstwo społeczne oraz dialog w Europie i w Polsce', in K. Jasiecki (ed.) *Grupy interesu i lobbing. Polskie doświadczenia w unijnym kontekście*, Warszawa: IFiS PAN: 108–44.

Gardawski, J., Bartkowski, J., Męcina, J. and Czarzasty, J. (2010) *Working Poles and the Crisis of Fordism*, Warsaw: Polish Confederation of Private Employers Lewiatan.

Girndt, R. (2012) *Gelenkter sozialer Dialog: Ungarische Gewerkschaften zur Halbzeit der Orban-Regierung.* Friedrich-Ebert Stiftung Büro Budapest, Mai 2012. Online. Available from: <http://www.fesbp.hu/common/pdf/Nachrichten_aus_Ungarn_mai_2012.pdf> (accessed 1 June 2012).

Krzywdzinski, M. (2005) 'Die Entwicklung der Klassengesellschaft in Polen: Wie viel zählt Klasse in der Transformation?', *Kölner Zeitschrift für Soziologie und Sozialpsychologie*, 57 (1): 62–85.

King, L. (2007) 'Central European capitalism in comparative perspective', in B. Hancké, M. Rhodes and M. Thatcher (eds) *Beyond Varieties of Capitalism: Conflict, Contradications, and Complementarities in the European Economy*, Oxford: Oxford University Press: 307–27.

Kohl, H. and Platzer, W. (2003) *Arbeitsbeziehungen in Mittelosteuropa. Transformation und Integration. Die acht EU-Beitrittsländer im Vergleich*, Baden-Baden: Nomos.

Mailand, M. and Due, J. (2004) 'Social dialogue in Central and Eastern Europe: Present state and future development', *European Journal of Industrial Relations*, 10 (2): 179–97.

Meardi, G. (2000) *Trade Union Activists, East and West: Comparisons in Multinational Companies*, London: Ashgate

Neumann, L. (2005) 'Trade unions in Hungary. Between social partnership, political action and organizing drive', in D. Dimitrova and J. Vilrokx (eds) *Trade Union Strategies in Central and Eastern Europe: Towards Decent Work*, Budapest: International Labour Office: 63–110.

Ost, D. (2005) *The Defeat of Solidarity: Anger and Politics in Postcommunist Europe*, Ithaca: Cornell University Press.

Schmidt, R. (2008) 'Social Relationships in SMEs: An East-West Comparison', in K. Bluhm and R. Schmidt (eds) *Change in SMEs. The New European Capitalism*, Houndmills: Palgrave: 274–90.

Schnabel, C. (2005) 'Gewerkschaften und Arbeitgeberverbände: Organisationsgrade, Tarifbindung, und Einflüsse auf Löhne und Beschäftigung', *Zeitschrift für Arbeitsmarktforschung*, 38 (2–3): 181–96.

Sroka, J. (2006) 'Dialog społeczny i stosunki przemysłowe w krajach Europy Środkowej i Wschodniej', in A. Antoszewski (ed.) *Systemy polityczne Europy Środkowej i Wschodniej. Perspektywa porównawcza*, Wrocław: Uniwersytet Wrocławski: 167–92.

Sznajder-Lee, A. and Trappmann, V. (2010) 'Von der Avantgarde zu den Verlierern des Postkommunismus: Gewerkschaften im Prozess der Restruktutierung der Stahlindustrie in Mittel- und Osteuropa', *Industrielle Beziehungen*, 17 (2): 192–213.

——(forthcoming) 'Labour union regeneration in Central and Eastern Europe: Overcoming postcommunist weakness through external pressures?', *European Journal of Industrial Relations*.

Thelen, K. (2001) 'Varieties of Labor Politics in the Developed Democracies', in P. A. Hall and D. Soskice (eds) *Varieties of Capitalism: The Institutional Foundations of Comparative Advantage*, Oxford: Oxford University Press: 71–103.

Trappmann, V. (2012): *Związki zawodowe w Polsce–aktualna sytuacja, organizacja, wyzwania*, Warszawa: Friedrich-Ebert Stiftung, Przedstawicielstwo w Polsce.

—— (2013) *Fallen Heroes in Global Capitalism. Workers and the Restructuring of the Polish Steel Industry*, Houndsmill: Palgrave MaVanhuysse, P. (2006) *Divide and Pacify: Strategic Social Policies and Political Protests in Post-Communist Democracies*, Budapest: Central European University Press.

Weinstein, M. (2000) 'Solidarity's abandonment of worker councils: Redefining employee stakeholder rights in post-socialist Poland', *British Journal of Industrial Relations*, 38 (1): 49–73.

Chapter 9

Bebchuk, L.A. and Fried, J. M. (2003) 'Executive compensation as an agency problem', *Journal of Economic Perspectives*, 17 (3): 71–92.

Bruin, J. (1999) 'Social power and influence tactics: A theoretical introduction', *Journal of Social Issues*, 55 (1): 7–14.

Crocker, K. J. and Slemrod, J. (2007) 'The economics of earnings manipulation and managerial compensation', *RAND Journal of Economics*, 38 (3): 698–713.

Davies, A. R. (1953) 'Prestige of Occupations', *The British Journal of Sociology*, 3 (2): 134–47.

DiMaggio, P. J. and Powell, W. W. (1983) 'The iron cage revisited: Institutional isomorphism and collective rationality in organizational fields', *American Sociological Review*, 48 (2): 147–60.

Dürr, A. and DeBievre, D. (2007) 'The question of interest group influence', *Journal of Public Policy*, 27 (1): 1–12.

Goldthorpe, J. H. and Hope, K. (1972) 'Occupational grading and occupational prestige', *Social Science Information*, 11 (5): 11–73.

Hauser, R. M. and Warren, J. R. (1996) *Socioeconomic Indices for Occupations: A Review, Update and Critique*, CDE Working Paper No. 96–01. Online. Available from: <http://www.ssc.wisc.edu/cde/cdewp/96–01.pdf> (accessed 18 August 2012).

Jensen, M. C. and Zimmerman, J. L. (1985) 'Management compensation and the managerial labor market', *Journal of Accounting and Ecnonomics*, 7 (3): 3–9.

Katz, E. and Lazarsfeld, P. F. ([1955] 2006), *Personal Influence. The Part Played by People in the Flow of Mass Communications*, New Brunswick: Transaction Publishers.

Lengyel, G. (1993) *A multipozicionális gazdasági elit a két világháború között*, Budapest: ELTE.

—— (2007) *A magyar gazdasági elit társadalmi összetétele a huszadik század végén*, Budapest: Akadémiai Kiadó.

Leopold, L. (1913) *Prestige. A Psychological Study of Social Estimates*, London: T.F. Unwin.

March, J. G. (1955) 'An introduction to the theory and measurement of influence', *American Political Science Review*, 49 (2): 431–51.

Mintz, B. and Schwartz, M. (1985) *The Power Structure of American Business*, Chicago: Chicago University Press.

Mizruchi, M. S. (1992) *The Structure of Corporate Political Action, Interfirm Relations and Their Consequences*, Cambridge: Harvard University Press.

—— (1996) 'What do interlocks do? An analysis, critique, and assessment of research on interlocking directorates', *Annual Review of Sociology*, 22 (2): 271–98.

Ördög, Z. (2010) *Állami cégek, vezetői bérek*, unpublished thesis, Corvinus University of Budapest.

Stark, D. and Vedres, B. (2012) 'Political Holes in the Economy: Business Camps and Partisanship', unpublished thesis.

Useem, M. (1984) *The Inner Circle. Large Corporations and the Rise of Business Political Activity in the U.S. and U.K.,* Oxford: Oxford University Press.

Verschuren, P. and B. Arts (2004) 'Quantifying Influence in Complex Decision Making by Means of Paired Comparisons' *Quality & Quantity,* vol. 38, pp. 495–516.

Index

For Product Safety Concerns and Information please contact our EU
representative GPSR@taylorandfrancis.com
Taylor & Francis Verlag GmbH, Kaufingerstraße 24, 80331 München, Germany